OBADIAH

VOLUME 24D

THE ANCHOR BIBLE is a fresh approach to the world's greatest classic. Its object is to make the Bible accessible to the modern reader; its method is to arrive at the meaning of biblical literature through exact translation and extended exposition, and to reconstruct the ancient setting of the biblical story, as well as the circumstances of its transcription and the characteristics of its transcribers.

THE ANCHOR BIBLE is a project of international and interfaith scope: Protestant, Catholic, and Jewish scholars from many countries contribute individual volumes. The project is not sponsored by any ecclesiastical organization and is not intended to reflect any particular theological doctrine. Prepared under our joint supervision, THE ANCHOR BIBLE is an effort to make available all the significant historical and linguistic knowledge which bears on the interpretation of the biblical record.

THE ANCHOR BIBLE is aimed at the general reader with no special formal training in biblical studies; yet it is written with the most exacting standards of scholarship, reflecting the highest technical accomplishment.

This project marks the beginning of a new era of cooperation among scholars in biblical research, thus forming a common body of knowledge to be shared by all.

William Foxwell Albright
David Noel Freedman
GENERAL EDITORS

THE ANCHOR BIBLE

OBADIAH

A New Translation
with Introduction and Commentary

PAUL R. RAABE

THE ANCHOR BIBLE
Doubleday
New York   London   Toronto   Sydney   Auckland

THE ANCHOR BIBLE
PUBLISHED BY DOUBLEDAY
a division of Bantam Doubleday Dell Publishing Group, Inc.
1540 Broadway, New York, New York 10036

THE ANCHOR BIBLE, DOUBLEDAY, and the portrayal of an
anchor with the letters A and B are trademarks of
Doubleday, a division of Bantam Doubleday Dell
Publishing Group, Inc.

Library of Congress Cataloging-in-Publication Data

Bible. O.T. Obadiah. English. Raabe. 1996.
    Obadiah : a new translation with introduction and commentary /
Paul R. Raabe. — 1st ed.
        p.   cm. — (The Anchor Bible : 24D)
    Includes bibliographical references and index.
    1. Bible. O.T. Obadiah—Commentaries.   I. Raabe, Paul B., 1953–   .
    II. Title.   III. Series: Bible. English. Anchor Bible. 1964; v. 24D.
BS1593.R33   1996
224'.9106—dc20   95-36913
                                                                         CIP

ISBN 0-385-41268-1
Copyright © 1996 by Doubleday, a division of Bantam Doubleday Dell
Publishing Group, Inc.

All Rights Reserved
Printed in the United States of America
October 1996
First Edition

10 9 8 7 6 5 4 3 2 1

For Tom,
Mary and John,
and Becky
(psalm 133)

CONTENTS

◆

Contents

PREFACE

◆

It is a daunting task to write a biblical commentary, even for a short book like Obadiah. In many ways, the brevity of this prophet's legacy only masks the breadth that is needed to interpret it adequately. The ideal commentator would have command of a vast and expanding array of disciplines, each of which requires technical expertise in its own right, in addition to having the ability to think and write clearly. Therefore I am grateful to many others whose assistance has contributed to any strengths the present volume might have. Naturally, its shortcomings are solely my own.

First of all, I wish to thank David Noel Freedman. His gracious invitation to write a commentary on Obadiah has given me the opportunity to engage in further research of a biblical book that I have long enjoyed studying. As his students and the authors in the Anchor series can also attest, his prompt, insightful, and in-depth critiques consistently prove to be of great benefit.

I owe a debt of gratitude to members of the Society of Biblical Literature for their helpful feedback to presentations made at the Central States regional meetings and at the national meetings, and to Beth Glazier-McDonald, David Graf, Gary Herion, Claire Mathews, and Keith Schoville for generously sharing materials with me.

I am also grateful to Concordia Seminary for granting a sabbatical leave, and to Aid Association for Lutherans and Lutheran Brotherhood for grant money that enabled me to do research abroad. The staff of Concordia's fine research library has been most cooperative in providing the necessary resources. I have appreciated the support of all of my colleagues here and particularly the insightful suggestions of Andrew Bartelt, Jeffrey Gibbs, Horace Hummel, Christopher Mitchell, Paul Schrieber, and James Voelz. It is said that teachers learn just as much from their students as the reverse, and such has been my experience as well. I am thankful to my students for their interest and challenging responses in classes and seminars, and especially to Joel Elowsky, David Lewis, Alan Ludwig, Hal Toenjes, Paul Wenz, and Donald White for editorial and bibliographical assistance.

Finally, I am happy to express my deep appreciation to my parents and family for their loving encouragement and patience while hearing and learning much more about Obadiah than they had ever desired to know.

PAUL R. RAABE
June 1995

A Note to the Reader

◆

When the chapter and verse numbers of the Hebrew Bible differ from those of the English Bibles, the latter are enclosed in square brackets. Unless otherwise noted, all translations are by the author. Admittedly, at times they provide rather wooden word-for-word renditions, but, in my opinion, such literalness can better convey the shape of the text's grammar and vocabulary to readers who lack knowledge of the original. Thus they are intended not for public reading but solely for study purposes.

ABBREVIATIONS

◆

AASOR	Annual of the American Schools of Oriental Research
AB	Anchor Bible
ABD	*Anchor Bible Dictionary*
AnBib	Analecta biblica
AnOr	Analecta orientalia
ANVAO	Avhandlinger utgitt av det Norske Videnskaps-Akademi i Oslo
AOAT	Alter Orient und Altes Testament
ARM	Archives royales de Mari
ArOr	*Archiv orientální*
ATANT	Abhandlungen zur Theologie des Alten und Neuen Testaments
ATAT	Arbeiten zu Text und Sprache im Alten Testament
ATD	Das Alte Testament Deutsch
BA	*Biblical Archaeologist*
BARev	*Biblical Archaeology Review*
BASOR	*Bulletin of the American Schools of Oriental Research*
BASORSup	BASOR Supplement
BAT	Die Botschaft des Alten Testaments
BDB	F. Brown, S. R. Driver, and C. A. Briggs. A *Hebrew and English Lexicon of the Old Testament*
BETL	Bibliotheca ephemeridum theologicarum lovaniensium
BHS	*Biblia hebraica stuttgartensia*
Bib	*Biblica*
BibOr	Biblica et orientalia
BJS	Brown Judaic Studies
BKAT	Biblischer Kommentar: Altes Testament
BN	*Biblische Notizen*
BR	*Biblical Research*

BRev	*Bible Review*
BZAW	Beihefte zur ZAW
CAD	*The Assyrian Dictionary of the Oriental Institute of the University of Chicago*
CBQ	*Catholic Biblical Quarterly*
CHAL	*A Concise Hebrew and Aramaic Lexicon of the Old Testament*
CJ	*Concordia Journal*
ConBOT	Coniectanea biblica, Old Testament
COut	Commentaar op het Oude Testament
CTJ	*Calvin Theological Journal*
CTM	*Concordia Theological Monthly*
CurTM	*Currents in Theology and Mission*
DBSup	*Dictionnaire de la Bible, Supplément*
Did	*Didaskalia*
DISO	C.-F. Jean and J. Hoftijzer. *Dictionnaire des inscriptions sémitiques de l'ouest*
EA	Tell el-Amarna tablets. Cited from J. A. Knudtzon, *Die El-Amarna-Tafeln*
Ebib	Études bibliques
EI	*Eretz Israel*
EncMiqr	*Entsiqlopedia Miqra'it-Encyclopaedia Biblica*
FOTL	Forms of Old Testament Literature
FRLANT	Forschungen zur Religion und Literatur des Alten und Neuen Testaments
GKC	*Gesenius' Hebrew Grammar*, 28th ed.
HALAT	*Hebräisches und aramäisches Lexikon zum Alten Testament*
HAT	Handbuch zum Alten Testament
HBT	*Horizons in Biblical Theology*
HKAT	Handkommentar zum Alten Testament
HS	*Hebrew Studies*
HSM	Harvard Semitic Monographs
HTR	*Harvard Theological Review*
IBC	Interpretation: A Bible Commentary for Teaching and Preaching
ICC	International Critical Commentary
IDBSup	*Interpreter's Dictionary of the Bible Supplementary Volume*
IEJ	*Israel Exploration Journal*
Int	*Interpretation*
ISBE	*International Standard Bible Encyclopedia*, 2d ed.
JB	Jerusalem Bible
JBL	*Journal of Biblical Literature*
JJS	*Journal of Jewish Studies*
JNES	*Journal of Near Eastern Studies*

JQR	*Jewish Quarterly Review*
JSOT	*Journal for the Study of the Old Testament*
JSOTSup	Journal for the Study of the Old Testament Supplement Series
JTS	*Journal of Theological Studies*
KAI	H. Donner and W. Röllig. *Kanaanäische und aramäische Inschriften*
KAT	Kommentar zum Alten Testament
KB	L. Koehler and W. Baumgartner. *Lexicon in Veteris Testamenti Libros*
KEHAT	Kurzgefasstes exegetisches Handbuch zum Alten Testament
KHC	Kurzer Handcommentar zum Alten Testament
KJV	King James Version
KTU	M. Dietrich, O. Loretz, and J. Sanmartín. *Die keilalphabetischen Texte aus Ugarit*
LXX	Septuagint
MSU	Mitteilungen des Septuaginta-Unternehmens
MT	Masoretic Text
NASB	New American Standard Bible
NEB	New English Bible
NedTTs	*Nederlands Theologisch Tijdschrift*
NICOT	New International Commentary on the Old Testament
NIV	New International Version
NJPSV	New Jewish Publication Society Version
NRSV	New Revised Standard Version
NTT	*Nieuw Theologisch Tijdschrift*
OBO	Orbis biblicus et orientalis
OBT	Overtures to Biblical Theology
OLA	Orientalia lovaniensia analecta
OTG	Old Testament Guides
OTL	Old Testament Library
OTM	Old Testament Message
OTS	*Oudtestamentische Studiën*
PEQ	*Palestine Exploration Quarterly*
RB	*Revue biblique*
RevSém	*Revue sémitique*
RivB	*Rivista biblica*
RSV	Revised Standard Version
SANT	Studien zum Alten und Neuen Testament
SBLBMI	Society of Biblical Literature: The Bible and Its Modern Interpreters
SBLDS	Society of Biblical Literature Dissertation Series
SBLMasS	Society of Biblical Literature Masoretic Studies

SBLMS	Society of Biblical Literature Monograph Series
SBLWAW	Society of Biblical Literature: Writings from the Ancient World
SBS	Stuttgarter Bibelstudien
SEÅ	*Svensk Exegetisk Årsbok*
SOTSMS	Society for Old Testament Study Monograph Series
TA	*Tel Aviv*
TDOT	*Theological Dictionary of the Old Testament*
TEV	Today's English Version
THAT	*Theologisches Handwörterbuch zum Alten Testament*
ThStud	Theologische Studien
TOTC	Tyndale Old Testament Commentary
TSK	*Theologische Studien und Kritiken*
TWAT	*Theologisches Wörterbuch zum Alten Testament*
UF	*Ugarit-Forschungen*
UT	C. H. Gordon. *Ugaritic Textbook*
VT	*Vetus Testamentum*
VTSup	Vetus Testamentum Supplements
WMANT	Wissenschaftliche Monographien zum Alten und Neuen Testament
WZKM	*Wiener Zeitschrift für die Kunde des Morgenlandes*
YNER	Yale Near Eastern Researches
ZAW	*Zeitschrift für die alttestamentliche Wissenschaft*
ZTK	*Zeitschrift für Theologie und Kirche*

MAPS

◆

THE GEOGRAPHY OF OBADIAH

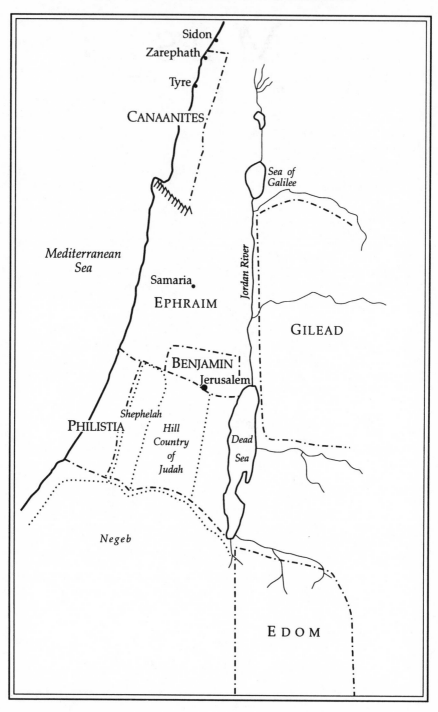

Sidon
Zarephath
Tyre
CANAANITES

Sea of
Galilee

Mediterranean
Sea

Jordan River

Samaria
EPHRAIM

GILEAD

BENJAMIN
Jerusalem

Shephelah
PHILISTIA   Hill
Country
of
Judah

Dead
Sea

Negeb

EDOM

THE LAND OF EDOM

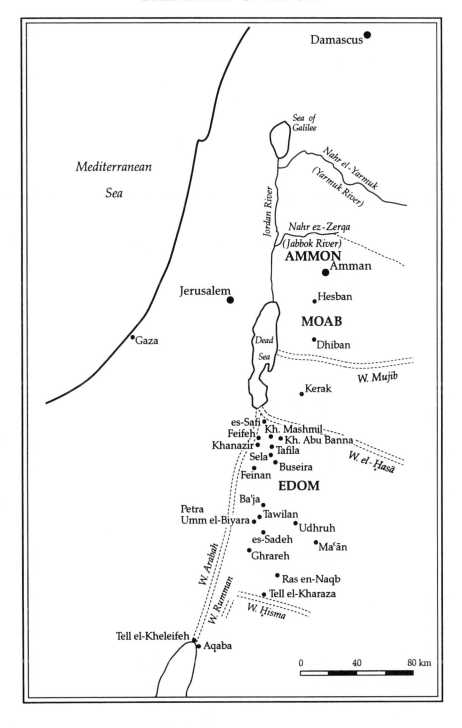

Damascus

Sea of
Galilee

Mediterranean
Sea

Nahr el-Yarmuk
(Yarmuk River)

Jordan River

Nahr ez-Zerqa
(Jabbok River)

AMMON

Amman

Jerusalem

Hesban

MOAB

Gaza

Dead
Sea

Dhiban

W. Mujib

Kerak

es-Safi
Kh. Mashmil
Feifeh
Kh. Abu Banna
Khanazir
Tafila
Sela
W. el-Ḥasā
Buseira
Feinan

EDOM

Ba'ja

Petra
Tawilan
Umm el-Biyara
Udhruh
es-Sadeh
Ma'ān
Ghrareh

Ras en-Naqb
Tell el-Kharaza
W. Hisma

W. Arabah

W. Rumman

Tell el-Kheleifeh
Aqaba

0   40   80 km

THE BOOK OF OBADIAH: A TRANSLATION

◆

Superscription (v 1a)

1a Obadiah's Vision.

I. Yahweh's First Utterance: Announcement of Doom Addressed to Edom (vv 1b–4)

1b Thus spoke the Lord Yahweh to Edom —
     A report we have heard from Yahweh:
          "A messenger has been sent among the nations (to say):
          'Arise so that we may rise against her for battle.'"
2   — Look! Insignificant I have made you among the nations.
          You are utterly despised.
3   The presumption of your heart has deceived you,
          you who dwell in the clefts of the crags,
                    in the height of your seat,
     you who say in your heart:
          "Who will bring me down to the earth?"
4   Even if you could exalt (your nest) like the eagle,
          and even if among stars you could set your nest,
                    from there I will bring you down —
                    utterance of Yahweh.

II. Yahweh's Second Utterance: Announcement of Doom Addressed to Edom (vv 5–7)

5 If thieves come to you,
  if plunderers of the night—
     How you have been similar/destroyed!
      —will they not steal what suffices them?
  If vintagers come to you,
      will they not leave gleanings?
6   How Esau has been thoroughly searched out,
       his hidden things thoroughly sought after!
7 To the very border they have expelled you,
    all those of your covenant.
  They have deceived you, prevailed over you,
     those of your peace.
    [Those who eat] your bread
  will establish a place of foreigners in your stead,
       in which there is no understanding.

III. Yahweh's Third Utterance (vv 8–18) A. Announcement of Doom, Accusation and Warning Addressed to Edom (vv 8–15)

8 Will it not indeed happen in that day—
      utterance of Yahweh
  —that I will destroy the wise from Edom,
        and understanding from Mount Esau,
9 and your warriors will be panic-stricken, O Teman,
  with the result that everyone will be cut off from Mount Esau by slaughter?
10 Because of the violence you did to your brother Jacob
    shame will cover you,
    and you will be cut off forever.
11 On the day when you stood opposite,
  on the day when strangers took captive his power,
     while foreigners entered his gates
     and cast lots for Jerusalem,
       also you were like one of them.

12 But do not gaze upon the day of your brother,
   on the day of his adversity.
 And do not rejoice over the Judahites,
   on the day of their ruin.
 And do not open your mouth wide,
   on the day of distress.
13 Do not enter through the gate of my people,
   on the day of their ordeal.
 Do not gaze, also you, upon its misfortune,
   on the day of its ordeal.
 And do not reach out (your hands) for its wealth,
   on the day of its ordeal.
14 And do not stand at the fork in the road
   in order to eliminate its escapees.
 And do not hand over its survivors,
   on the day of distress.
15 For the day of Yahweh is near
   against all the nations.
 Just as you have done, it will be done to you;
   your deeds will return upon your own head.

B. PROMISE OF RESTORATION AND VICTORY ADDRESSED TO JUDAH (vv 16–18)

16 For just as you have drunk on my holy mountain,
 (so) all the nations will drink continually;
   they will drink and slurp,
   and they will be as if they had never been.
17 But on Mount Zion will be escape,
 and (on Mount Zion) will be a holy place.
  The house of Jacob will possess their own possessions.
18 The house of Jacob will become fire,
 and the house of Joseph, flame,
 and the house of Esau, stubble;
   and they will set them on fire and consume them,
   and there will be no survivor for the house of Esau.
   For Yahweh has spoken.

IV. THE PROPHET'S EXPANSION: PROMISE OF ISRAEL'S RESTORATION AND YAHWEH'S KINGSHIP (vv 19–21)

19 The Negeb will possess Mount Esau,
   and the Shephelah (will dispossess) the Philistines;
   they will possess the territory of Ephraim and the territory of Samaria,
   and Benjamin (will possess) Gilead.
20 The exiles of this company, those belonging to the Israelites, who are [in . . .
         will dispossess] the Canaanites up to Zarephath;
   and the exiles of Jerusalem who are in Sepharad
         will possess the cities of the Negeb.
21 Deliverers will go up onto Mount Zion to judge Mount Esau,
   and the kingship will belong to Yahweh.

INTRODUCTION

◆

Preliminary Observations

The book of Obadiah is the smallest book in the Hebrew Bible, or the Old Testament. With only one chapter of 21 verses it can easily be overlooked by readers of the Bible. After all, what are 21 verses compared to, say, the 1,364 verses (MT) of Jeremiah? Yet close study of Obadiah is worth the effort. For one thing, its small size proves to be advantageous. Readers can hold in the mind and memorize the whole book without too much difficulty. This enables them to see the entire forest without getting lost among the trees, something that cannot be done so easily with a large book. Furthermore, Obadiah flows in the mainstream of the Israelite prophetic tradition, a characteristic that has not always been recognized. This short book elegantly summarizes many of the great prophetic themes, such as divine judgment against Israel's enemies, the day of Yahweh, the *lex talionis* as the standard of judgment, the cup-of-wrath metaphor, Zion theology, Israel's possession of the land, and the kingship of Yahweh. Thereby the book serves as a concise epitome for much of the message of the prophets. It also illustrates the nature of prophetic discourse: its poetry and prose; its types of speech, such as judgment, accusation, warning, and promise; and its rhetorical style. It especially exemplifies oracles against the foreign nations, a category that occupies much of the corpus of the Latter Prophets. Therefore attention to the little book of Obadiah should prove to be a rewarding experience for serious students of the Bible.

Although the book's small size offers advantages, it also has disadvantages. As Jerome noted, the book's difficulties are in inverse proportion to its size. In fact, the book's small size is the chief factor that causes the difficulties. An individual text becomes comprehensible only when readers can place it into some kind of larger framework or context, whether that be historical, literary, or theological.

Otherwise it appears as just so many meaningless sentences. Yet such a background is not self-evident for Obadiah. For example, unlike other books of the Latter Prophets this one has a superscription that lacks any historical data; all it gives us is the name "Obadiah." Any historical information must be inferred from the book's contents when interpreted in light of the history of ancient Israel, and even then our knowledge of the relevant parts of Israel's history has certain lacunae. Again, the book's adumbration of many of the Bible's larger themes necessitates that readers study these themes in other parts of the Bible in order to put "flesh" on Obadiah's "bones." In short, the book's small size requires its readers to put perhaps more effort than usual into developing an interpretive framework into which to set Obadiah.

The current postmodern environment is witnessing a veritable smorgasbord of interpretive methods and reading strategies being practiced by biblical scholars. No one approach generally enjoys the dominant or privileged position. Therefore it behooves commentators to state up front their approach to the text and to make some kind of argument for it. With respect to the small and somewhat cryptic book of Obadiah, the greatest danger, in my opinion, is that of imposing upon this ancient text an anachronistic or alien framework. Therefore the present commentary has adopted the strategy of following the leads and directions suggested by the text itself (cf. R. B. Robinson 1988).

The book of Obadiah is first of all a written text and therefore requires investigation of the grammar and semantics of its words, phrases, and clauses. With only 21 verses the book offers a commentator the unique opportunity to pay considerable attention to this basic grammatical and lexical level. Second, because vv 1–18 exhibit a poetic form, we will concentrate on the lines and their interrelationships, their parallelism and length, and the imagery that they use. Although a poem can give information, including historical information, it does not merely inform. Its poetic style also invites the readers to slow down and appreciate the aesthetic dimension, its skillful and artistic use of language. Furthermore, we should attend to the book's art of persuasion, its rhetorical strategies and goals. Third, Obadiah deals at considerable length with Edom, which suggests that we should relate it to other Edom oracles and especially to the close parallel of Jeremiah 49. This also means that the book constitutes part of the larger category of prophetic oracles against the foreign nations. Fourth, the text's references to known places, such as Edom, the Negeb, and Jerusalem, send us to Palestinian geography. Moreover, the realistic language used in vv 11–14 invites us to interpret the book within a historical framework as referring to the political relationship between Edom and Judah. In other words, the prophetic discourse does not operate within the realm of platonic ideas but within the down-to-earth world of space and time; the language is referential although not only that. Fifth, by mentioning "Jacob" and "Esau" Obadiah leads us back to the Jacob-Esau narratives of Genesis. Thus the prophet would have us interpret the relationship between Judah and Edom not only within the context of political history but also within the familial context of these two patriarchs. Finally, the references to Yahweh and his actions toward the nations and Israel bring to the fore the theological dimension. The statements about Yahweh's future actions need to be seen in light of the more general prophetic hopes for the future, what is often termed "prophetic eschatology." To sum up: the nature of the book promotes a reading strategy that operates on different levels — referential, literary, rhetorical, and theological.

To a great extent exegesis is the continual process of examining the text through two types of lens as it were: a close-up look at the details through a magnifying lens and a panoramic view of the whole through a wide-angle lens. Although the commentary focuses on the details in the Translation Notes and discusses the larger units in the Comment sections, the small and the large levels cannot be separated in the actual interpretive process. Rather, the specific details inform the interpretation of the whole, and the shape of the whole influences the understanding of the details.

Because exegesis is an interactive process between text and reader, there is no such thing as a purely objective, disinterested interpretation; exegesis is an art as well as a science. Readers inevitably bring to the text their own background, presuppositions, and beliefs. They direct questions to the text, questions that differ depending on individual interests and concerns. Our historical and chronological distance from the prophet of over two and one-half millennia can never totally be overcome. Furthermore, some readers might be inclined to criticize Obadiah for his harsh language and his pro-Israelite zeal or to dismiss his theological perspective as simply political propaganda. Nevertheless, in this commentary I strive to avoid an anachronistic reading of an ancient book in light of contemporary western views and sentiments. My goal, rather, is to read the text sympathetically, to ask the text questions that remain in continuity with the prophet's own concerns, to operate within the prophet's own worldview and belief system as much as possible. Hopefully, the present commentary provides an interpretation that accurately reflects or at least approximates the book's meaning for its original 6th-century-B.C. audience.

THE CONDITION OF THE TEXT

Although some biblical books exhibit a fluid text and pluriform editions in the early stages of transmission, Obadiah does not. The Hebrew text has been well preserved. The ancient versions witness to texts that are in general agreement with the text of the Leningrad Codex (1008 A.D.). The places where they differ are usually due to translational efforts — where their primary value lies — rather than to a different Hebrew *Vorlage*. The oldest Hebrew text of Obadiah that we have appears in the Minor Prophets scroll from Wadi Murabbaʿat dated to the Second Jewish Revolt (132–135 A.D.). It is a proto-Masoretic text that differs from the Leningrad Codex only in a few places. Some scholars emend Obadiah or attempt to reconstruct an earlier form of Obadiah on the basis of the parallel in Jeremiah 49. However, the ancient versions for both Obadiah and Jeremiah 49 generally indicate that the differences between the two are original and not the result of later scribal activity. Thus they need to be explained on other than text-critical grounds.

All of this is not to say that the MT of Obadiah lacks any scribal corruption. The text seems to be corrupt in some places, especially in v 7 and v 20 and possibly in v 6 and v 17. The Notes discuss the text-critical questions as they arise.

THE STYLE OF OBADIAH

A. POETRY AND PROSE

BHS rightly sets up vv 1–18 as poetry and vv 19–21 as prose. The distinction between the two sections is supported by the frequency of the so-called prose particles. It has long been recognized that the direct object marker *ʾet*, the relative pronoun *ʾăšer*, and the definite article written with *h* occur infrequently in texts generally considered to be poetic (cf. GKC § 2s). This observation has been confirmed by recent statistical analysis (Andersen and Freedman 1980: 60–66; Andersen and Forbes 1983; Freedman 1985). In standard prose the particle frequency is 15 percent or more, whereas in poetry the frequency is 5 percent or less. That is to say, for a text generally recognized to be poetic on other grounds (i.e., the dominance of parallelism and terse lines), if it has one hundred words, then *ʾet*, *ʾăšer* and words having the definite article written with *h* will comprise five or fewer of the words. For practical purposes, a "word" can be identified as the ink marks written between the white spaces.

Of the 245 words in Obadiah 1–18 (including the superscription) only nine are prose particles (3.67 percent), well within the range of poetry. For vv 19–21, of the 46 words sixteen are prose particles (34.8 percent), which indicates that these three verses are prose. The difference between the two sections is striking and confirms that the book of Obadiah consists of a poetic composition with a prose conclusion.

One can also recognize variations within the poetic section of vv 1–18. For vv 1–4 there are no prose particles and for vv 5–7 only one definite article *h* in v 7; one particle out of 92 words in vv 1–7 scores a frequency of 1.09 percent, at the low end of the poetry range. For vv 8–15 the particle frequency increases to the upper end of the poetry range: one *ʾăšer* in v 15 (actually *kaʾăšer*); one *ʾet* in v 14; and the article *h* once in v 8, v 14, and v 15; thus five particles out of 106 words score a frequency of 4.72 percent. In vv 16–18 we find one *ʾăšer* (again, *kaʾăšer*) in v 16, one '*et* in v 17, and one article *h* in v 16: three particles out of 47 words score a frequency of 6.38 percent. This last figure is a little higher, but it still remains very close to poetry.

Although the sample is admittedly small, one can reasonably conclude from the above evidence that the book of Obadiah moves gradually from pure poetry through v 15 to slightly more prosaic poetry in vv 16–18, followed by pure prose at the end. Freedman (private communication) notes that such a dramatic contrast between poetic and prosaic sections finds a parallel in Ezekiel, which places dense prose and pure poetry in contiguous chapters. Obadiah fits well in that chronological context (see below under "Date").

B. IMAGERY

Of the many features of Hebrew poetry the three that seem to be the most prominent are its frequent use of imagery, the dominance of parallelism, and the terseness of lines. (For introductory discussions, see Berlin 1985; Petersen and Richards 1992.) Verses 1–18 exhibit imagery in several places. Verse 4 compares Edom's lofty abode in the mountain heights with that of an eagle's nest. However, Obadiah intensifies the normal picture by entertaining the possibility of Edom locating its "nest" even among the stars. In vv 5–6 he refers to the ordinary activity of thieves and grape gatherers in order to set up a contrast with the complete plundering that Edom will experience. Verse 10 equates shame with a garment that will cover Edom. In v 11 he depicts the profanation of Jerusalem at the hand of its enemies by picturing them as casting lots for the city. Verse 16 employs the cup-of-wrath metaphor, which likens the experience of being punished by God's wrath to that of becoming drunk with wine. Finally, in v 18 the prophet compares Israel to fire that consumes Edom like stubble. In all of these instances he draws from a common stock of imagery, and the parallels have been noted in the commentary. The prophet does not develop any one image through a stretch of text beyond one verse. Rather, he projects onto the screen, as it were, separate and unrelated images one after another in a staccato fashion. In addition to the imagery, he uses realistic and nonfigurative language especially in vv 11–14, where he depicts Edom's anti-Judahite hostilities.

C. PARALLELISM

Another common feature of Hebrew poetry is its use of parallelism. This does not mean that Hebrew prose completely lacks parallelism. In the section at the end of Obadiah, for example, although its lack of terseness and its frequent use of prose particles indicate its status as prose, vv 19–20 do exhibit parallelistic clauses. Moreover, not every verse of Hebrew poetry displays parallelism. It is not very evident in vv 1, 9, 15a, and 17b. Nevertheless, unlike prose Hebrew poetry structures its content by the dominant and systematic use of parallelism.

BHS prints vv 1–18 in short lines placed side by side with a space between them. Thereby the *BHS* editors intend to display on the page the sense of parallelism that readers perceive in these verses. The basic unit is the colon, or line; I use the two terms interchangeably. Although occasionally a line stands alone, usually it has one or more partners. Perhaps the most complete description of parallelism is the one given by Berlin (1985). In parallelism similarity is superimposed on contiguity. The reader perceives a basic structure of correspondence between juxtaposed elements; yet within the correspondence lies contrast as well. Parallelism activates all aspects of language; the more aspects involved, the greater the perception of parallelism. The four aspects are: grammatical, lexical, semantic, and phonological.

Obadiah 8 illustrates the phenomenon:

wĕha'ăbadtî ḥăkāmîm mē'ĕdôm	*ûtĕbûnâ mēhar 'ēśāw*
"I will destroy the wise from Edom	and understanding from Mount Esau."

Both lines have the same syntax with the verb gapped in the second line: verb + object + prepositional phrase with *min* (from). In terms of morphology there is a contrast between the masculine plural noun *ḥăkāmîm* (the wise) and the feminine singular noun *tĕbûnâ* (understanding). "The wise" and "understanding" form a lexical word pair; the former is concrete and the latter abstract. Also "Edom" and "Mount Esau" are paired. With respect to the semantic relationship between the lines, both lines are virtually equivalent in meaning. Both prepositional phrases begin with the phoneme *mē* (a sound pair), and both lines begin with the letter *waw*. Because the A-line and the B-line correspond in so many respects, the reader naturally considers them "parallel."

In v 8 the parallelism operates "horizontally" within a line pair or bicolon. However, parallelism can also function "vertically" among lines or line pairs. Sometimes a line relates to another line not immediately contiguous to it but some distance away. Verses 3–4 provide an illustration:

A	The presumption of your heart has deceived you,
B	you who dwell in the clefts of the crags,
C	in the height of your seat,
D	you who say in your heart:
E	"Who will bring me down to the earth?"
F	Even if you could exalt (your nest) like the eagle,
G	and even if among stars you could set your nest,
H	from there I will bring you down.

While A is the main clause for the sentence of A–E, the repetition of "your heart" links it especially with D. Lines D–E express the presumption of Edom's heart stated in A. H gives Yahweh's reply to Edom's boast in E by using the same verb, and the line pair of F–G intensifies the motif of Edom's lofty abode introduced in the line pair of B–C. This example illustrates that we should not focus only on the "horizontal" parallelism of a line pair but also recognize the correlations that a line may have with other lines farther removed. Although the binary pattern or line pair occurs, it is not the only or even the most common pattern in the prophetic poetry of Obadiah. One must be attentive to the other links and patterns as well, patterns that can become quite intricate.

For Obad 1–18, parallel line pairs (bicola) are easily recognized in vv 2, 8, 15b, and 17a. Larger groupings of parallel lines also occur: three in v 10; four in v 16; five in v 11 and in v 18; seven in v 7; eight in vv 3–4 and in vv 5–6; and sixteen in vv 12–14. Embedded within some of these larger groupings are line pairs: vv 3, 4, 5, 6, 11, and 16. All of this shows the predominance of parallelism in Obadiah's poetry.

D. TERSENESS

Another prominent feature of Hebrew poetry is its terseness. Kugel (1981: 88) likens terseness to the style of telegrams: "[E]verything is variable, but the standard of terseness, like the telegram-taker's word count, exerts a constant pressure toward concision and ellipsis." Although Kugel works with a broader concept of terseness, in this section I will concentrate on line length. A typical line or colon is a short phrase or clause that ranges from two to four words. However, a line's terseness can be described with more precision. Although different methods for describing it are possible, I will follow the method advocated by Freedman, that of combining syllable counts with the more traditional approach of counting stresses (cf. Culley 1970; also see Raabe 1990: 18–21; Petersen and Richards 1992: 37–47).

Let me emphasize at the start that I do not believe that Obadiah counted syllables, or stresses for that matter. I have the same doubts regarding Sophocles and Shakespeare. Highly skilled poets do not need to count mechanically. Yet in seeking to describe length the reader does need to count. The traditional approach counts only accented syllables. I count every MT accent although no more than one accent per word; I count the *metheg* with a word bound to the following word by a *maqqef*.

Given the uncertainties involved in determining stresses — commentators often differ from each other in their stress counts — the syllable count serves as an important check. I follow the Tiberian vocalization of the MT although with certain minor modifications that reflect a *pre-Masoretic pronunciation*. Thus I treat segolates as monosyllabic; I do not count a furtive *patach* or a half-vowel that substitutes for what would ordinarily be a silent *shewa* (e.g., for yaʿăqōb read yaʿqōb, two syllables), but a half-vowel that substitutes for what would ordinarily be a vocal *shewa* is counted (e.g., ḥăkāmîm, three syllables). It must be emphasized that the above minor modifications do not significantly affect the data; the same conclusions would result from simply following the Masoretic vocalization.

Even with these minor modifications this approach faces problems. It remains uncertain how accurately Masoretic Hebrew reflects the earlier Hebrew of the exilic period, although we have reason to believe that the Masoretes were preservers more than innovators. Furthermore, the text could have been modified in oral recitation by the elision of vowels. Nevertheless, the patterns that emerge should at least approximate those of the original text of Obadiah. All of this "counting business" has a purpose, that of determining the length of the lines and of the larger units. The contention here is that length matters and deserves to be included in any description of Obadiah's poetry (cf. Bartelt 1991). The syllable and stress counts of vv 1–18 follow (omitting the superscription and inserting [lōḥămê] before laḥmĕkā in v 7).

	Syllables		*Stresses*
v 1	1 + 2 + 3 + 2 + 3	= 11	5
	3 + 3 + 2 + 2	= 10	4
	2 + 3 + 2	= 7	3
	2 + 4 + 3 + 4	= 13	4
v 2	2 + 2 + 4 + 3	= 11	4
	2 + 2 + 2	= 6	3
v 3	2 + 3 + 4	= 9	3
	3 + 3 + 1	= 7	2
	2 + 2	= 4	2
	2 + 3	= 5	2
	1 + 4 + 1	= 6	3
v 4	1 + 2 + 2	= 5	2
	2 + 1 + 3 + 1 + 3	= 10	4
	2 + 4	= 6	2
	2 + 2	= 4	1
v 5	1 + 3 + 2 + 2	= 8	3
	1 + 3 + 2	= 6	2
	1 + 3	= 4	2
	2 + 3 + 2	= 7	3
	1 + 3 + 2 + 1	= 7	3
	2 + 3 + 3	= 8	3
v 6	1 + 3 + 2	= 6	3
	2 + 3	= 5	2
v 7	1 + 3 + 4	= 8	3
	1 + 2 + 4	= 7	3
	4 + 3 + 2	= 9	3

	Syllables		*Stresses*
	2 + 4	= 6	2
	[3] + 3	= 6	2
	3 + 2 + 3	= 8	3
	1 + 3 + 1	= 5	3
v 8	2 + 2 + 2	= 6	3
	2 + 2	= 4	1
	4 + 3 + 3	= 10	3
	4 + 2 + 2	= 8	3
v 9	3 + 4 + 2	= 9	3
	2 + 3 + 1 + 2 + 2 + 2	= 12	6
v 10	3 + 3 + 2	= 8	3
	4 + 2	= 6	2
	4 + 3	= 7	2
v 11	2 + 4 + 2	= 8	3
	2 + 2 + 2 + 2	= 8	4
	3 + 2 + 3	= 8	3
	2 + 4 + 2 + 2	= 10	3
	1 + 2 + 3 + 2	= 8	3
v 12	2 + 2 + 2 + 3	= 9	2
	2 + 2	= 4	2
	2 + 2 + 2 + 3	= 9	3
	2 + 2	= 4	2
	2 + 2 + 2	= 6	2
	2 + 2	= 4	2
v 13	1 + 2 + 2 + 2	= 7	3
	2 + 2	= 4	2
	1 + 2 + 1 + 2 + 4	= 10	3
	2 + 2	= 4	2
	2 + 3 + 3	= 8	2
	2 + 2	= 4	2
v 14	2 + 2 + 1 + 2	= 7	3
	3 + 1 + 3	= 7	2
	2 + 2 + 3	= 7	2
	2 + 2	= 4	2
v 15	1 + 2 + 1 + 2	= 6	3
	1 + 1 + 3	= 5	1
	3 + 3 + 3 + 1	= 10	4
	4 + 2 + 4	= 10	3
v 16	1 + 3 + 3 + 1 + 1 + 2	= 11	5
	2 + 1 + 3 + 2	= 8	4

	Syllables		Stresses
	3 + 3	= 6	2
	3 + 2 + 2	= 7	3
v 17	3 + 2 + 2 + 3	= 10	4
	3 + 1	= 4	2
	4 + 1 + 2 + 1 + 4	= 12	5
v 18	3 + 1 + 2 + 1	= 7	3
	2 + 2 + 3	= 7	3
	2 + 2 + 2	= 6	3
	4 + 2 + 4	= 10	3
	2 + 2 + 2 + 2 + 2	= 10	5
	1 + 2 + 2	= 5	3

It is clear that vv 1–18 display no consistent and predictable pattern in terms of syllables or accents and therefore no "meter" in any traditional sense. The syllable counts range from 4 to 13 and the stress counts from 1 to 6. One might dispute some of the stress counts — counting stresses is more subjective than many assume — but even so it is impossible to make them consistent without emending the text. If we examine the frequency of the different lengths and counts, we see that most lines range from 4 to 10 syllables and from 2 to 4 accents. Obadiah's line lengths are fairly evenly spread, although they tend toward the short side. Of the seventy-seven lines 40 percent are 4–6 syllables, 39 percent are 7–9 syllables, and 21 percent are 10–13 syllables. The same observation holds for the stress counts: 4 percent have 1 stress; 34 percent have 2 stresses; 45.5 percent have 3 stresses; 10 percent have 4 stresses; and 6.5 percent have 5–6 stresses. The data are presented below.

Syllables	Number of lines	Stresses	Number of lines
4	12	1	3
5	6	2	26
6	13	3	35
7	13	4	8
8	12	5	4
9	5	6	1
10	10		
11	3		
12	2		
13	1		

If we examine the line lengths and stress patterns in connection with the book's overall structure, which is established on other grounds (see below), then we see that two dominant patterns alternate from section to section. The sections are vv 1–4, 5–7, 8–15, and 16–18. The third section displays both patterns, which distinguish vv 8–11 from vv 12–15. The norms or averages for each section are as follows: vv 1–4 — a line of 8 syllables and a stress pattern of 3 + 3; vv 5–7 — a line of 6–7 syllables and a stress pattern of 3 + 2; vv 8–11 — a line of 8 syllables and a stress pattern of 3 + 3; vv 12–15 — a line of 6–7 syllables and a stress pattern of 3 + 2; vv 16–18 — a line of 8 syllables and a stress pattern of 3 + 3. The statistics are displayed below.

	Lines	Syllables	Average syllables/line	Stresses	Average stresses/line
vv 1–4	15	114	7.6	44	2.9
vv 5–7	15	100	6.7	40	2.7
vv 8–11	14	112	8.0	42	3.0
vv 12–15	20	129	6.5	47	2.35
vv 16–18	13	103	7.9	45	3.5

Thus for sections I, III, and V, the average per line is ca. 8 syllables and 3 accents, while for sections II and IV, it is ca. 6.5 syllables and 2.5 accents. The alternating character of the sections can also be seen from the frequencies of the line lengths. For vv 1–4, 8–11, and 16–18 short lines (4–6 syllables) and long lines (10–13 syllables) balance each other, whereas for vv 5–7 and 12–15 the line lengths are unbalanced. The data are given below.

	Syllables	Number of lines
vv 1–4	4–6	7
	7–9	3
	10–13	5
vv 8–11	4–6	3
	7–9	8
	10–12	3
vv 16–18	4–6	4
	7–9	4
	10–12	5
vv 5–7	4–6	7
	7–9	8
vv 12–15	4–6	10
	7–9	7
	10	3

These two patterns conform with the results of Freedman (1972; 1986) who has demonstrated on the basis of the alphabetic acrostics that Hebrew poetry has at least two underlying norms and ideal patterns: a bicolon of 8 + 8 syllables/ 3 + 3 accents and a bicolon of 9 + 4 or 8 + 5 or 7 + 6 syllables/3 + 2 accents. The former is a balanced pattern and the latter an unbalanced pattern, the so-called Qinah meter. (On the Budde hypothesis, see von Fange 1992.) These are ideal patterns and underlying norms. Nevertheless, they are not actualized on the surface of the text with consistency, since one finds considerable diversity within a section. Therefore we must reckon with the combination of underlying norms and surface deviations.

To sum up, the poetry of the book of Obadiah displays terse lines, most of which range from 4 to 10 syllables and from 2 to 4 accents. Furthermore, two different underlying patterns alternate from unit to unit.

COMPOSITIONAL HISTORY AND UNITY

At first it seems somewhat surprising that so much scholarly debate has concentrated on the question of the compositional history and unity of such a little book. But as we will see the debate is understandable. Does the book contain one multifaceted speech, all of which was composed in one historical setting by one person named Obadiah? Or should we think of the book as a collection or anthology of distinct oracles that were composed at various times by different hands? The answer depends upon the reader's overall working model. I suggest that three basic models exist — although they usually remain tacit and hidden — with each having its own set of expectations, assumptions, and criteria. Each model is internally consistent so that it becomes virtually impossible to prove or disprove any one of them.

1. If we start with the expectation that the original prophet had only one perspective, emphasis, and style, and if we assume that the book of Obadiah in its present form is the result of a lengthy process of development with additions and interpolations made along the way, and if we further assume that these different layers or strata can be identified on the basis of shifts in perspective, emphasis, and style, then we will conclude that the book had several stages in its compositional history. A further step beyond this approach would assume that the various layers were correctly identified by source criticism but then would attribute to the redactional level any coherence that the book now has.

2. If we assume that one person is responsible for the whole book and that this person had at any single time only one perspective, emphasis, and style, then we will conclude that different parts of the book stem from different

times in the prophet Obadiah's own ministry and we will seek to distinguish between its earlier and later phases.

3. If we assume that a single prophet could have set forth different perspectives, emphases, and styles within one speech composed at one time, then we will conclude that the whole book reflects one multifaceted speech written/spoken by Obadiah on one occasion.

Before discussing the issue further, we should recognize the large amount of diversity evident in the book's twenty-one verses, diversity that operates in all categories.

1. The reader sees significant shifts in the book's depiction of the relationships among Edom, the nations, Israel, and Yahweh. According to vv 1–2, the nations will campaign against Edom, while vv 4 and 8 speak of Yahweh as the one who will destroy Edom. The reader naturally relates the two by viewing Yahweh as the principal actor who uses the nations as his instrument. However, v 7 states that Edom's allies expel Edom from its land. Now Edom's enemies are no longer the unspecified nations but Edom's own allies. So far the book makes a distinction between Edom and other nations, but vv 15a and 16 change the perspective. Previously the nations were Yahweh's means to judge Edom, but now they themselves receive his judgment. Finally, v 18 presents an additional shift in viewpoint: Israel will be the party that will conquer Edom.

2. The book also gives differing portrayals of Edom's fate. Verse 6 and the first two sentences of v 7 use perfect verb forms to describe Edom's downfall, whereas the rest of the book uses imperfects and *waw*-consecutive perfects. Furthermore, v 7 pictures Edom being expelled and foreigners occupying its land, while v 19 envisions Israel possessing Edom's land. According to vv 9 and 18, every Edomite will be killed so that Edom will no longer have a remnant, but according to v 21, Israel will rule over Edom, which implies the continuing existence of Edomites in their land. Verses 12–15 present yet another perspective. A series of vetitives or negative commands warn Edom to stop its anti-Judahite hostilities before the day Yahweh comes. The implication is that Edom still has some hope for a continuing existence and that its future remains open.

3. The book views the demise of Judah from two different perspectives. Verses 10–14 speak of Judah as a victim of attacks by Edom and foreigners, whereas v 16 depicts its ruin with the metaphor of drinking Yahweh's wrath. The former gives a historical perspective, and the latter offers a theological perspective.

4. The first half of the book (vv 1–15) addresses Edom in second person — although v 6 uses the third person — while the second half at least in the

beginning addresses Judah in the second person (v 16) and promises it a future restoration (vv 17–21).

5. The book shifts from poetry in vv 1–18 to prose in vv 19–21. Also its grammatical style changes in midstream. Verses 1–7 lack any verbal strings or sequences, but vv 8–10 and vv 16–18 frequently use the imperfect + *waw*-consecutive perfect sequence. Furthermore, as noted above, the poetry section operates with two different norms regarding line length and stress pattern.

In light of such diversity and shifting, it is understandable that the issue of unity has been hotly debated. The positions of representative scholars illustrate the debate. (For surveys of views, see Fohrer 1966; Wehrle 1987: 5–9.)

1. The book is a combination of two separate compositions: vv 1–14 and 15b by the prophet and a later supplement of vv 15a and 16–21 (Wellhausen 1963; Marti 1904; Duhm 1911 — who dates the supplement to the Maccabean period; Bewer 1911).

2. The parts that represent later additions are vv 19–21 (Fohrer 1966; Kaiser 1975) or vv 19–20 (Rudolph 1971; Wolff 1977).

3. The book contains three separate compositions: vv 1–14 and 15b by Obadiah; 15a and 16–18; 19–21 by two later hands (Eissfeldt 1965). Deissler (1984) locates the second part in the 5th century and the third part ca. 400. Keller (1965) attributes vv 1–15 to the prophet, vv 16–18 possibly to another prophet living at the same time, and vv 19–21 to later readers of the book.

4. Dicou (1994) posits three stages to the book's development: vv 1–14 and 15b (and 21?) represent the original oracle composed toward the end of the exilic period; vv 15a and 16–18 are redactional extensions of the previous oracle produced a few years later; vv 19–20 constitute a later addition composed together with the appendages of Joel and Amos (Joel 4:18–21 [3:18–21]; Amos 9:13–15) in the early postexilic period. But Dicou also argues for a redactional unity in the book's final form.

5. Mason (1991) suggests four stages of growth: vv 1c–5 based on an earlier "stock" oracle; vv 1b, 6–14, and 15b dated to the exilic period; vv 15a and 16–18 dated to the postexilic period; vv 19–21 are still later.

6. Perhaps the most extreme views are those of T. H. Robinson (1938; cf. 1916) and Weimar (1985). The former sees the book as a collection of eight fragments, each of which originally circulated in isolated form, and the latter proposes a complicated development of six stages for which he atomistically subdivides single verses.

7. Some scholars propose different phases for the prophet's own ministry. According to Rudolph (1971), the second half of the book (vv 15a, 16–18, 21)

stems from a time not much later than the first half. Also Weiser (1967) attributes vv 1–15 and vv 16–18 to two different situations. Wolff (1977) suggests that each of the second half's three units belonged to a different occasion (vv 15a and 16–17; 18; 21).

8. Some scholars assume an original disunity but consider the book in its final form to reflect a redactional unity or cohesion (Childs 1979; Snyman 1989; Dicou 1994).

9. Other scholars maintain the original unity of the book as containing the prophet's own words (Condamin 1900; Isopescul 1913; Theis 1937; Aalders 1958; Allen 1976; Stuart 1987). Also Thompson (1956) posits a unity, although he sees vv 1–9 as embodying an earlier oracle.

As suggested above, one's overall working model with its set of expectations and assumptions determines to a great extent one's conclusions regarding the compositional history and unity of the book. In my view, no historical information in the book necessitates a date later than the first half of the exilic period. Moreover, there is no a priori reason why the prophet himself could not have composed the whole book including the prose section. It is precisely the nature of prophetic discourse to make sudden shifts on all levels of language, including style and imagery, and to juxtapose multiple, divergent, and even dissonant perspectives in much the same way as in the use of poetic parallelism. I consider doubtful the tacit evolutionary model assumed by some scholars: the assumption that the second half of the book must derive from a later hand because it generalizes and universalizes the judgment beyond the particular judgment of Edom presented in the book's first half. On the contrary, in speeches addressed to specific situations the prophets would often generalize and make their messages paradigmatic for other situations and audiences. Prophetic visions characteristically bring the particular into the orbit of the universal (cf. Hummel 1964). In this way the prophets transcended the level of the obvious and mundane so as to present what for them was the view of things from Yahweh's throne room. The approaches that fragment the book into separate, self-contained oracles or that posit several stages of growth for the book seem to impose a western standard of uniformity and self-consistency on an ancient text (cf. Greenberg 1986).

In my opinion, model 3 is worth considering. This would mean that the whole book was composed for one occasion. Or we might combine model 3 with model 2. In that case, perhaps vv 1–18 were composed for one occasion while vv 19–21 were added by Obadiah at a later time. Because it takes only about four minutes to read the whole book out loud at a normal pace, it does not stretch credulity to imagine either scenario as the book's origin. Or are we to believe that no individual speech lasted more than, say, thirty seconds? Another possibility is to conceive of the book as a condensation of what Obadiah said over the course of a longer ministry. In any case, the question soon becomes moot, since one can neither prove nor disprove such hypotheses. All we can deal with is the book as we now have it. And despite the amount of diversity displayed in it, the book does present itself as a literary and structural unity, a unity that invites the reader to make coherent sense of the book's contents by interpreting the parts as integrally related to each other rather than as self-contained and self-defining units. What Berlin (1994: 23) says of Zephaniah holds true for Obadiah as well: *"viewing it as a whole yields an interpretation much more interesting and compelling than viewing it as a collection of separate parts"* (emphasis in original).

STRUCTURE AND COHERENCE

Various structural outlines for the book have been proposed. The subdivisions that one makes depend on which features of the text one considers to be the most significant. I prefer to divide the book on the basis of formal and literary criteria. I begin with the most obvious markers, the speech formulas:

Thus spoke the Lord Yahweh to Edom (v 1)
utterance of Yahweh (v 4)
utterance of Yahweh (v 8)
For Yahweh has spoken (v 18)

The formulas indicate that the book has at least two divine speeches: vv 1–4 and vv 8–18. Each formulaic sequence has parallels elsewhere: "Thus spoke DN [divine name] ... utterance of DN" (Jer 2:2–3; 12:14–17; 29:21–23; 31:37; 32:42–44; Ezek 12:28; 16:59–63; 26:19–21; 29:19–20; 37:12–14); "utterance of DN ... for Yahweh has spoken" (Isa 22:25; cf. Jer 49:2; Amos 9:13–15). The formulas isolate vv 5–7 and vv 19–21 as two additional sections. Thus the book has four major sections: vv 1–4, 5–7, 8–18, and 19–21.

In keeping with the divine speech formulas the first and third sections present Yahweh as the speaker also by their use of the first person pronoun (vv 2, 4, 8, 13, 16); the phrase "the day of Yahweh" in v 15 is stereotypical and therefore not a sign of a change of speakers (cf. Ezek 30:3; Joel 3:4 [2:31]). However, embedded in v 1 between the messenger formula and the start of the divine speech in v 2 lies an interlude spoken by the prophet.

For the other two sections the identity of the speaker is not so clear. Because the last section follows a major closure formula of divine speech ("For Yahweh has spoken") and because it uses the third person to refer to Yahweh (v 21), the reader naturally identifies it as a discourse given by the prophet who steps out of his role as the mouthpiece of Yahweh. The section of vv 5–7 intervenes between two divine speech formulas (v 4 and v 8) and lacks any first person pronoun. Hence one might take it as another prophetic speech. However, it lacks any third person reference to Yahweh as well. In conformity with vv 1–4 it continues to use the second person pronoun "you." Since the pronoun presupposes the divine speech formula of v 1 for identifying the antecedent as Edom ("Thus spoke the Lord Yahweh to Edom"), it is more likely that Yahweh remains the speaker in this section. This conclusion receives support by the parallel in Jer 49:9–10 where Yahweh is the speaker.

The third section can be further subdivided on the basis of the grammatical addressee: vv 8–15 address Edom ("you" singular), whereas vv 16–18 address the Jerusalemites/Judahites ("you" plural in v 16). Verse 8 is only an apparent exception, since its reference to Edom in the third person is dictated by the grammatical construction. Also vv 17b–18 use the third person "house of Jacob" because they are referring to all of historic Israel, including both north and south (see Notes).

The length of the units reveals a noteworthy symmetry. For the first, second, and fourth sections and one subdivision of the third section, each is approximately the same size (vv 1–4, 5–7, 19–21, and 16–18), while the third section's other subdivision (vv 8–15) is a little more than double the size. And when we observe the more accurate measurement of syllable counts, a very precise symmetry of length becomes evident: vv 1–4 match vv 19–21 and vv 5–7 match vv 16–18.

	Words	Syllables
vv 1–4	48	114
vv 5–7	43	100
vv 8–15	106	241
vv 16–18	47	103
vv 19–21	46	111

Note that the combined length of the first two units is identical to the combined length of the last two units: 91 and 93 words, and 214 syllables.

The individual sections exhibit the literary device of *inclusio*. In v 1 the nations are summoned to attack Edom: "*Arise* so that we may *rise against her* for battle." The result is expressed in v 4 with the antonym of "arise": "I will *bring you down*." The preposition + pronoun "to you" brackets the next section, twice in v 5 and once in v 7. *Inclusio* becomes more prominent in the next two sections. The motif of Edom's extermination brackets vv 8–18: "everyone will be cut off from Mount *Esau* by slaughter" (v 9); "there will be no survivor for the house of *Esau*" (v 18). The same device also occurs in this section's two subdivisions: the phrase "in that day" in v 8 anticipates the phrase "the day of Yahweh" in v 15; the extermination motif of v 18 echoes that of v 16 (the nations "will be as if they had never been"), although the two clauses convey slightly different ideas. In addition note the construction *lō' hāyâ* (will not be) in v 16 and v 18. For the last section, the name "Mount Esau" appears toward the beginning of v 19 and toward the end of v 21.

The major sections are joined together by a concatenated pattern that functions like links in a chain. The first two sections are tied together by the use of "if" clauses in v 4 and v 5 and by the use of rhetorical questions in v 3 and v 5. Repetition of the noun "understanding" joins the second and third sections: "in which there is no understanding" (v 7); "I will destroy . . . understanding from Mount Esau" (v 8). The two subdivisions within vv 8–18 are linked by the recurrence of "for . . . just as" and of "all the nations" (vv 15, 16). Finally, repetitions connect the last two sections: the verb "will possess" in v 17 and v 19; the name "Esau" in v 18 and v 19. This overall concatenated pattern holds the parts together structurally and therefore encourages the reader to interpret the book in a holistic and coherent way despite all of its disparateness. In other words, the book's literary structure functions as something like centripetal force (cf. Grossberg 1989). Note also the unifying effect achieved by the repetition of key words: "Yahweh," 7 times; "Esau," 7 times; "day," 12 times; "the nations," 4 times.

THE CONCATENATED PATTERN OF OBADIAH'S STRUCTURE

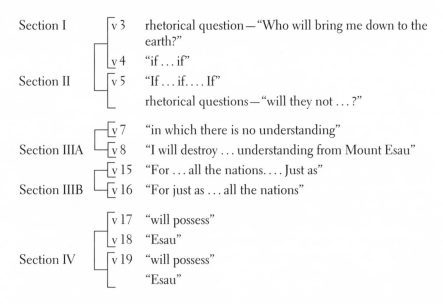

Section I	v 3	rhetorical question — "Who will bring me down to the earth?"
	v 4	"if . . . if"
Section II	v 5	"If . . . if. . . . If"
		rhetorical questions — "will they not . . . ?"
Section IIIA	v 7	"in which there is no understanding"
	v 8	"I will destroy . . . understanding from Mount Esau"
Section IIIB	v 15	"For . . . all the nations. . . . Just as"
	v 16	"For just as . . . all the nations"
Section IV	v 17	"will possess"
	v 18	"Esau"
	v 19	"will possess"
		"Esau"

The book has two chief parts: three Yahweh speeches in poetry (vv 1–18) followed by Obadiah's own expansion in prose (vv 19–21). It unfolds in a linear way in that subsequent units presuppose and further develop earlier units. The connections further prompt the reader to interrelate the contents of the various parts.

1. As noted above, the antecedent of the second person pronoun "you" in v 5 and v 7 is "Edom" mentioned in v 1.

2. Verse 7 specifies the identity of those being recruited to attack Edom (v 1), namely, Edom's covenant partners. And v 11 clarifies that these covenant partners are the "strangers" and "foreigners" who attacked Judah.

3. One of the senses of the double entendre in v 5 anticipates v 13: the exclamation, "How you have been similar" to common thieves and plunderers, receives clarification in the charge against Edom of seizing Judah's wealth.

4. Verse 8 develops the motif introduced in v 7: Edom's land will lack "understanding" because Yahweh will destroy "understanding from Mount Esau."

5. The metaphor of Judah drinking the cup of wrath in v 16 requires for its comprehension the description of Judah's fall given in v 11. Also the former verse's statement that all the nations will drink the cup of wrath develops the motif introduced in v 15, "the day of Yahweh is near against all the nations."

6. The promise of Zion's future holiness in v 17 presupposes its profanation by strangers and foreigners described in v 11.

7. The promises of Israel's victory and dominance over Edom given in v 18 and v 21 assume the reader's knowledge of Edom's hostility detailed in vv 10–14. Note especially the standard of *lex talionis* at work (v 15): just as Edom sought to eliminate Israel's "survivors" (v 14), so Israel will leave Edom without "survivor" (v 18).

8. The phrase "Mount Esau" in vv 19 and 21 requires for its comprehension its earlier appearance where it receives definition by the parallelism with "Edom" (v 8). Without v 8 (and vv 6, 9, 18) the phrase would be rather unintelligible in vv 19 and 21.

9. Verses 19–20 clarify the meaning of v 17b, "the House of Jacob will possess their own possessions."

10. The reference to the exiles of Israel and Jerusalem in v 20 recalls the mention of their captivity in v 11.

In summary, the little book of Obadiah contains a remarkable amount of diversity and divergency in perspective, emphasis, and style. Nevertheless, the last clause provides the book with a strong closure: "the kingship will belong to Yahweh." Moreover, the book's structure and linear style of thematic progression promote a kind of reading that will treat it in a holistic way. Therefore the reader should attend to both its individual variations and its overall coherence.

OBADIAH AND JEREMIAH

A great deal of overlap exists between Obadiah and Jeremiah. Many of the same motifs and much of the same vocabulary occur in both books. The closest parallels are found in Obad 1–6 and Jeremiah's Edom oracle, 49:14–16, 9–10. Of the forty-three words in Obad 1–4 (omitting the superscription and the opening messenger formula) twenty-nine occur in Jer 49:14–16 (67 percent), and twelve of the twenty-four words in Obad 5–6 appear in Jer 49:9–10 (50 percent). Furthermore, the second sentence in Obad 7 occurs in Jer 38:22. Because the overlap is too great to be coincidental, it raises the question of dependence. Did Obadiah use Jeremiah or the reverse? Or did both use a third unknown source? Each position has its supporters. (For a listing of each position's supporters, see Wehrle 1987: 12–13.) Based on Caspari's work (1842) earlier commentators considered Jeremiah dependent on Obadiah and placed the latter in the ninth century. When an exilic date for Obadiah became more favored, some scholars understood the oracle of Jer 49 or at least the verses the two have in common to be a later postexilic addition. This hypothesis enabled them to maintain the priority of Obadiah over Jeremiah 49. Perhaps the most popular view today posits a third source or oral tradition upon which both prophetic texts depend. Yet the position that considers Obadiah to have adapted Jeremiah also has some defenders.

Three questions need to be addressed. Is the Jeremiah material authentic to Jeremiah or a later addition? What is the date of the respective texts? What is the most likely direction of dependence? To the first question, Dicou (1994: 58–70) has convincingly demonstrated on the basis of vocabulary and motifs that Jer 49:14–16, 9–10 are thoroughly at home in the book of Jeremiah and need not be considered later editorial insertions.

Several clues in both Jeremiah 49 and Obadiah help us to answer the second question. Jeremiah's Edom oracle lacks any accusation of Edom for its sins or crimes against Judah. The absence is striking especially in light of Obadiah's extended list of charges laid against Edom for its anti-Judah hostilities. Moreover, Jer 49:12 speaks of Jerusalem's/Judah's drinking the cup of wrath in future tense, whereas Obad 16 speaks of it in past tense (cf. Thompson 1956). Both clues suggest a preexilic date for Jeremiah's Edom oracle, perhaps ca. 605 in light of Jer 45 and 46:2. Obadiah most likely should be placed in the early exilic period, ca. 585–555.

With respect to the third question, there is good reason to believe that Obadiah adapted Jeremiah rather than that both relied upon a third source. Obad 1–6 is not the only place in Obadiah that has parallels in Jeremiah. The second sentence of Obad 7 is virtually identical to Jer 38:22, and the last line of Obad 7 together with Obad 8 echoes Jer 49:7. Furthermore, Obadiah's use of the metaphor of drinking the cup of wrath presupposes the metaphor's extended development in Jeremiah. Without the Jeremiah background Obad 16 would be rather unintelligible. In addition to the above connections, several of Obadiah's motifs find their closest parallels in Jeremiah. For example, the rhetorical question attributed to Edom in Obad 3, which Jer 49 lacks, echoes the rhetorical questions given in Jer 21:13 and 49:4. It seems more plausible to explain this amount of overlap by assuming Obadiah's dependence upon Jeremiah than by positing a third source or tradition (so also Bonnard 1972; Dicou 1994). With respect to the objection that Jer 49 must be a later corrupted version since it evinces a more disconnected and uneven flow, the opposite hypothesis appears more likely, namely, that Obadiah modified Jeremiah's oracle to make it flow more smoothly and logically. On the basis of the working hypothesis of Jeremiah's priority we are now ready to examine the parallels more closely. (For more details, see the Notes.)

Between Obadiah and the Jeremiah parallels there are some differences that need to be explained. With respect to Obad 1–4, Obadiah has three lines that are absent from Jeremiah, while Jeremiah has two lines that Obadiah lacks (Jer = thirteen lines; Obad = fourteen lines). Other differences exist as well. They do not reflect secondary transmissional variants, which textual criticism can account for. Rather, they represent primary literary variations, some of which simply use synonyms while others seem to exhibit intentional modifications made by Obadiah. Following Obadiah's order I will present the parallels and then comment on the variations.

	Jeremiah 49		*Obadiah*
v 14	*šĕmûʿâ šāmaʿtî mēʾēt yahweh*	v 1	*šĕmûʿâ šāmaʿnû mēʾēt yahweh*
	wĕṣîr baggôyīm šālûaḥ		*wĕṣîr baggôyīm šullāḥ*
	hitqabbĕṣû ûbōʾû ʿāleyhā		*qûmû wĕnāqûmâ ʿāleyhā*
	wĕqûmû lammilḥāmâ		*lammilḥāmâ*
v 15	*kî hinnēh qāṭōn nĕtattîkā*	v 2	*hinnēh qāṭōn nĕtattîkā*
	baggôyīm		*baggôyīm*
	bāzûy bāʾādām		*bāzûy ʾattâ mĕʾōd*
v 16	*tiplaṣtĕkā hiššîʾ ʾōtāk*	v 3	*zĕdôn libbĕkā hiššîʾekā*
	zĕdôn libbekā		
	šōkĕnî bĕhagwê hasselaʿ		*šōkĕnî bĕhagwê sselaʿ*
	tōpĕśî mĕrôm gibʿâ		*mĕrôm šibtô*
			ʾōmēr bĕlibbô
			mî yôrîdēnî ʾāreṣ

kî tagbîah kannešer qinnekā

miššām 'ôrîdĕkā
nĕ'ūm yahweh

v 14 A report I have heard from
   Yahweh:
   "A messenger has been sent
     among the nations (to
     say):
   'Gather yourselves together
     and go against her,
   and arise for battle.'"
v 15 For, look! I have made you
     insignificant among the
     nations,
   despised among people.
v 16 Your terribleness has deceived
     you,
   the presumption of your
     heart,
   you who dwell in the clefts of
     the crags,
   you who hold the height of the
     hill.

   If you could exalt your nest
     like the eagle,

   from there I will bring you
     down" —
   utterance of Yahweh.

v 4 *'im tagbîah kannešer*
   wĕ'im bên kôkābîm śîm
     qinnekā
   miššām 'ôrîdĕkā
   nĕ'ūm yahweh

v 1 A report we have heard from
   Yahweh:
   "A messenger has been sent
     among the nations (to
     say):
   'Arise so that we may rise
     against her for battle.'"

v 2 Look! I have made you
     insignificant among the
     nations.
   You are utterly despised.
v 3 The presumption of your heart
     has deceived you,

   you who dwell in the clefts of
     the crags,
   in the height of your seat,

   you who say in your heart:
   "Who will bring me down to
     the earth?"

v 4 Even if you could exalt (your
     nest) like the eagle,
   and even if among stars you
     could set your nest,
   from there I will bring you
     down —
   utterance of Yahweh.

Verse 1. Unlike Jeremiah who uses the singular "I" Obadiah includes himself among the people with the plural "we." The phrase "A messenger has been sent" has a *qal* passive participle in Jeremiah but a *pu'al* perfect in Obadiah. The two represent merely stylistic and interchangeable variations that lack any noticeable semantic difference. They are the passive formations of the *qal* and *pi'el* of the verb "to send" (*šlḥ*); the *nip'al* occurs only once in Biblical Hebrew. Elsewhere the noun "messenger" (*ṣîr*) appears with this verb in the *qal* (Isa 18:2; Prov 25:13) and in the *pi'el* (Isa 57:9) but without semantic difference.

In the summons to war each of the two lines in Jeremiah expresses the same sequence, first get ready and then attack: the nations should gather together and attack; the nations should get up in order to do battle. By combining the two lines one would read: "Arise, gather yourselves together and go against her for battle." Obadiah expresses basically the same sequence, although he reduces it to one line of four words in place of Jeremiah's two lines of five words; three of the words overlap. However, Obadiah makes one significant change. Whereas Jeremiah consistently uses imperatives addressed to the nations who alone do the fighting, Obadiah has a first person plural form, "Arise so that *we* may rise against her for battle." The use of "we" includes in the military party the sender of the "messenger," namely, Yahweh who acts as commander-in-chief. In this way Obadiah heightens the dramatic effect by bringing the divine warrior motif to the fore.

The referent of "her" in Obadiah is "Edom." Since Edom is masculine throughout the rest of Obadiah, the use of the feminine pronoun is a bit awkward, although Edom can be construed with either masculine or feminine pronouns in Hebrew. In contrast, the referent of "her" in Jeremiah is "Bozrah" mentioned in the previous verse. Thus the feminine pronoun ties v 14 closely with v 13.

Verse 2. Jeremiah uses the conjunction *kî* (for), which introduces the reason why the nations will attack Edom: because Yahweh has made Edom insignificant and despised among the nations. Obadiah omits the conjunction and thereby makes the relationship between v 1 and v 2 more ambiguous. On the one hand, the relationship might still be a causal one as in Jeremiah. On the other hand, it might be that v 1 gives the evidence for the conclusion in v 2: the nations' current preparation for war provides Edom with evidence of its insignificant and despised status.

In the second line Obadiah has a verbless clause: "You are utterly despised." Thereby Obadiah emphasizes more strongly than Jeremiah the present status of Edom and the degree of its degradation.

Verse 3. Obadiah omits the *hapax* noun of Jeremiah *tiplaṣtěkā*, the sense of which remains uncertain. In light of the verb *plṣ* (to shudder, shake) perhaps it denotes "your terribleness," that is, "the terror that you inspire." Bright (1965) suggests that the noun might have the same sense as *mipleṣet* in 1 Kgs 15:13, "your horrible idol." If so, it would be a contemptuous epithet for Edom's god. By omitting it Obadiah reduces Jeremiah's line pair to a single line. Also note Obadiah's grammatical substitution of an object suffix (*hiššî'ekā*) for Jeremiah's object marker + suffix (*hiššî' 'ōtāk*) — "has deceived you."

Obadiah's third line has the phrase "in the height of your seat" with the previous verb gapped, "you who dwell." (On the translation of "your seat" instead of "his seat," see the Notes.) Jeremiah uses a parallel verb and a slightly different object, "you who hold the height of the hill." The difference seems to be merely stylistic.

Obadiah adds two more lines beyond Jeremiah in order to depict Edom's presumptuous heart. He does this by attributing to Edom the rhetorical question: "Who will bring me down to the earth?" The addition heightens the contrast between Edom's self-opinion and its self-deception. Moreover, the rhetorical question effectively sets up Yahweh's response in the next verse, which Jeremiah also has: "I will bring you down."

Verse 4. Obadiah substitutes *'im* (if) for Jeremiah's *kî*. Both particles introduce conditional clauses, but the substitution ties the "if" clauses of Obad 4 more closely with those of Obad 5. Furthermore, Obadiah adds a line not found in Jeremiah in order to intensify the motif of Edom's lofty abode: "and even if among stars you could set your nest." Note that he delays the direct object of both lines ("your nest") to the end of the second line, while Jeremiah locates it at the end of the first line. The additional line gives the deictic phrase "from there" an explicit referent, namely, "from among stars." In Jeremiah the referent is either the implied lofty location of Edom's "nest" or Edom's dwelling "in the clefts of the crags" and "the height of the hill."

Obadiah 5–6 and Jeremiah 49:9–10. Jeremianic influence on Obadiah is evident also by the close similarity between Obad 5–6 and Jer 49:9–10. A comparison reveals that Obadiah echoes and yet significantly modifies the Jeremiah text.

JEREMIAH 49:9–10c

9a	*'im bōṣĕrîm bā'û lāk*	If vintagers come to you,
9b	*lō' yaš'îrû 'ôlēlôt*	they will not leave gleanings;
9c	*'im gannābîm ballaylâ*	if thieves in the night,
9d	*hišḥîtû dayyām*	they ravage what suffices them.
10a	*kî 'ănî ḥāśaptî 'et 'ēśāw*	For I have stripped Esau;
10b	*gillêtî 'et mistārāyw*	I have exposed his secret places;
10c	*wĕnehbāh lō' yûkāl*	and he cannot conceal himself.

The vintagers and the nocturnal thieves represent Edom's enemies, the means by which God will punish "Esau" (v 8). Vintagers will thoroughly and completely harvest Edom's vineyards, unlike normal vintagers who leave gleanings, and thieves will ransack and even destroy (*hišḥîtû*) — unlike normal thieves — Edom's treasures to their hearts' content. Verse 10a–b gives the reason why it will be so easy for them. For before the vintagers arrive, God "strips bare" (*ḥāśaptî*) the foliage of the vines, making it easy for them to find and take every grape. (For this use of *ḥśp*, see Joel 1:7 and Psalm 29:9.) And before the thieves arrive, God "exposes" Edom's hiding places so that they can easily find and even destroy whatever they want. Thus verse 10a supports v 9a–b and v 10b undergirds v 9c–d. Bourguet (1987: 295–302) considers v 10a–b to be parallel with v 9 and thus to liken God to the vintagers and thieves, but this interpretation fails to recognize the significance of *kî* (for) as a connector.

Verse 10a–b also prepares for v 10c. Verse 10a employs "Esau" as a metonym in order to personify Edom; this accounts for the shift to third person (cf. verse 8, which also mentions "Esau"). The verb *ḥśp* can also be used of stripping and denuding a person (Isa 20:4; Jer 13:26). According to this usage, verse 10a–b leads into v 10c: God strips Esau naked, shaming him and making him seek cover, but he cannot conceal himself because God also uncovered his hiding places (cf. Bourguet 1987: 295–302). Verse 10a–b is the key to understanding the text. It functions as a pivot that looks backward and forward in that it supports v 9 and leads into v 10c.

OBADIAH 5–6

5a	*'im gannābîm bā'û lěkā*	If thieves come to you,
5b	*'im šôdědê laylâ*	if plunderers of the night —
5c	*'êk nidmêtâ*	How you have been similar/destroyed!
5d	*hălô' yigněbû dayyām*	— will they not steal what suffices them?
5e	*'im bōṣěrîm bā'û lāk*	If vintagers come to you,
5f	*hălô' yaš'îrû 'ōlēlôt*	will they not leave gleanings?
6a	*'êk nehpěśû 'ēśāw*	How Esau has been thoroughly searched out,
6b	*nib'û maspūnāyw*	his hidden things thoroughly sought after!

Like Jeremiah the text of Obad 5–6 employs the image of vintagers and thieves, but here a contrast is made between the vintagers/thieves and the attacking enemies. Ordinary thieves steal only what they need and want, not every single item in the whole house, and normal vintagers leave gleanings behind. However, unlike such common thieves and vintagers, Edom's enemies will thoroughly search and find all of Edom's hiding places and treasures. The reader naturally identifies the enemies with the "nations" mentioned in v 1 who are further specified in v 7 as Edom's allies.

Obadiah bases this unit on the Jeremiah text. Two similar conditional sentences and much of the same or similar vocabulary appear. The similarities can be seen when the two texts are placed side by side.

Jeremiah 49:9–10c		Obadiah 5–7	
9c	'im gannābîm ballaylâ	5a	'im gannābîm bā'û lĕkā
		5b	'im šōdĕdê laylâ
		5c	'êk nidmêtâ
9d	hišḥîtû dayyām	5d	hălô' yignĕbû dayyām
9a	'im bōṣĕrîm bā'û lāk	5e	'im bōṣĕrîm bā'û lāk
9b	lō' yaš'îrû 'ôlēlôt	5f	hălô' yaš'îrû 'ōlēlôt
10a	kî 'ănî ḥāśaptî 'et 'ēśāw	6a	'êk neḥpĕśû 'ēśāw
10b	gillêtî 'et mistārāyw	6b	nib'û maṣpūnāyw
9c	if thieves in the night,	5a	If thieves come to you,
		5b	if plunderers of the night —
		5c	How you have been similar/destroyed!
9d	they ravage what suffices them.	5d	— will they not steal what suffices them?
9a	If vintagers come to you,	5e	If vintagers come to you,
9b	they will not leave gleanings.	5f	will they not leave gleanings?
10a	For I have stripped Esau;	6a	How Esau has been thoroughly searched out,
10b	I have exposed his secret places.	6b	his hidden things thoroughly sought after!

Given the close similarities, the differences become even more noticeable. On the basis of the hypothesis that Obadiah used Jeremiah, the following section attempts to account for the divergences.

1. Obadiah reverses Jeremiah's order of vintagers-thieves. On the one hand, Jeremiah's order progresses with respect to the seriousness of the threatened disaster. Vintagers who leave no gleanings are a relatively minor worry, whereas nocturnal thieves who not only can easily steal but can even damage whatever they please are more grievous. Obadiah, on the other hand, sets up the contrast between thieves/vintagers and Edom's enemies by beginning with the most dangerous, thieves and plunderers. Even such criminals steal only what they want and no more. Next, Obadiah mentions vintagers who do in fact leave gleanings. By juxtaposing the commonplace — vintagers leaving gleanings — with Edom's enemies, Obadiah brings to the fore the thoroughgoing nature of the enemies' ransacking. Jeremiah equates Edom's enemies with vintagers and thieves who are *extraordinary* in that the former do not leave gleanings and the latter ravage and destroy. In contrast Obadiah distinguishes between Edom's enemies and *ordinary* thieves/vintagers who leave behind remainders; the enemies will carefully and thoroughly seek out every hiding place and hidden treasure (v 6).

2. Obadiah (v 5b) adds a parallel clause to Jeremiah's if-clause regarding thieves — "if plunderers of the night." Obadiah construes the genitive noun "night" with "plunderers," but Jeremiah construes the prepositional phrase "in the night" with "thieves" or with the gapped verb "come." Obadiah's extra clause intensifies the idea by using a stronger phrase: "Even if *plunderers of the night* come to you, still they will only steal what suffices them."

3. Obadiah inserts an exclamation (v 5c) between the protases and the apodosis. Although the multivalent verb *nidmêtâ* has several senses that fit, the first sense is noteworthy in this context: "How you have been similar!" The interjection is significant because it reflects the date of Obadiah. Jeremiah's oracle lacks this clause as well as any mention of Edom's specific crimes against Israel because it predates the Babylonian crisis. Obadiah, however, by using the interjection refers to the looting and plundering done by the Edomites during this crisis (see v 13). In this way Edom had been "similar" to common thieves and plunderers.

4. Obadiah lessens the destructiveness of the thieves by replacing Jeremiah's strong verb in v 9d — "they ravage" — with the more general term "they steal" (v 5d). This further sets up the contrast with the ransacking enemies of v 6.

5. Obadiah changes the indicative apodoses of Jeremiah 49:9 into interrogatives (v 5). As a result they become rhetorical questions that expect an affirmative answer and that heighten the contrast with the exclamations of v 6.

6. Obadiah makes the two conditional sentences of v 5 more closely parallel in grammatical structure. Jeremiah's second protasis in v 9c gaps the verb and the prepositional phrase of the first protasis, "come to you." Also his first apodosis in v 9b uses a negated imperfect, "they will not leave," while his second apodosis in v 9d has a perfect, "they ravage." Obadiah, however, repeats the clause, "come to you," in both protases and uses a negated imperfect with interrogative *h* in both apodoses, "will they not steal" and "will they not leave."

7. Obad 6 alludes to Jer 49:10a–b. Both use perfect verbs and both mention "Esau" in third person. It should be noted that Jeremiah 49, Obadiah, and Malachi are the only places in the Latter Prophets that refer to Edom as "Esau." Obad 6a further evokes Jer 49:10a by using something like an anagram, what J. J. Glück (1970) calls "parasonancy," punning on the basis of consonant mutation:

Jeremiah   *ky*   *'ny ḥśpty 't*   *'św*
Obadiah   *'yk*   *nḥpśw*   *'św*

The consonant sequence of the former is reversed and reordered in the latter.

Although Obadiah echoes the Jeremiah parallel, he also changes the action and the agent (by implication and context). Jeremiah has Esau "stripped" (*ḥśp*) by God, but Obadiah uses the verb "thoroughly searched out" (*ḥpś*) and implies that the agent is Esau's enemies. The respective second lines as well reflect the change of action and agent. For Jeremiah, Esau's "secret places" (*mistārāyw*) are "exposed" by God, but for Obadiah, Esau's "hidden things" (*maṣpūnāyw*) — both places and treasures — are "thoroughly sought after" and found by enemies. The next verse (Obad 7) identifies these enemies as Edom's allies.

Obadiah 7 and Jeremiah 38:22. The second sentence of Obad 7 repeats almost verbatim a line from Jer 38:22.

Jer 38:22	Obad 7
hissîtûkā wĕyākĕlû lĕkā	*hiššî'ûkā yākĕlû lĕkā*
'anšê šĕlōmekā	*'anšê šĕlōmekā*
hoṭbĕ'û babbōṣ raglekā	
nāsōgû 'āḥôr	
They have deceived you and	They have deceived you, prevailed
prevailed over you,	over you,
those of your peace.	those of your peace.
Your feet have sunk in the mire;	
they [your friends] have turned back.	

Jeremiah threatens Zedekiah that if he refuses to surrender to Babylon, the women left in the palace will be led out to the Babylonians and will taunt Zedekiah with the words cited above. Obadiah repeats the first sentence and addresses it to Edom with a reference to Edom's allies. He makes two minor changes: he uses the near-synonym *hiššî'ûkā* (to deceive) instead of Jeremiah's *hissîtûkā* and omits the *waw* (and) before *yākĕlû* (prevailed). By using *hiššî'ûkā* Obadiah recalls v 3, which has the same verb, "the presumption of your heart has deceived you."

Obadiah 7–8 and Jeremiah 49:7. Finally, there is an echo of the beginning of Jeremiah's Edom oracle in the last line of Obad 7 through Obad 8 (cf. Dicou 1994: 67–69).

Jeremiah 49:7	*Obadiah 7–8*
ha'ên 'ôd ḥokmâ bĕtêmān	'ên tĕbûnâ bô
	hălô' bayyôm hahû'
	nĕ'ūm yahweh
'ābĕdâ 'ēṣâ mibbānîm	wĕha'ăbadtî ḥăkāmîm mē'ĕdôm
nisrĕḥâ ḥokmātām	ûtĕbûnâ mēhar 'ēśāw
Is there no longer wisdom in Teman?	In which there is no understanding.
	Will it not indeed happen in that
	day —
	utterance of Yahweh
Has counsel perished from the	— that I will destroy the wise from
perceptive?	Edom,
Has their wisdom spoiled?	and understanding from Mount Esau?

The two texts share the following items in common: an interrogative *h*, the construction '*ên* + noun + *b* ("there is no N in"), the verb '*bd* followed by the preposition *min* (to perish/destroy from) and the root *ḥkm* (wise/wisdom). Note also the near-synonyms "counsel" and "understanding." Dicou observes that each text uses an ABA noun pattern: Jer — "wisdom . . . counsel . . . wisdom"; Obad — "understanding . . . the wise . . . understanding."

Conclusion. The hypothesis that Obadiah reused and adapted material from Jeremiah best accounts for the evidence. We can only speculate about how this adaptation process might have taken place. Perhaps Obadiah had access to Jeremiah's scroll. Or Obadiah might have heard and remembered Jeremiah's oracles when they were first proclaimed. In any case, the book of Obadiah particularly in vv 1–8 displays considerable overlap with parts of the book of Jeremiah. Yet Obadiah was no mere copyist. Even with respect to vv 1–8 the changes he made reveal a measure of sophistication and creativity also on his part.

OBADIAH AND OTHER
BIBLICAL PARALLELS

What Berlin (1994: 13) says of Zephaniah applies to Obadiah as well:

The Book of Zephaniah is a study in intertextuality. A highly literate work, it shares ideas and phraseology with other parts of the Hebrew Bible to such an extent that at times it may appear as nothing more than a pastiche of borrowed verses and allusions. . . . The general effect is the creation of a strong link between this otherwise obscure prophet and the rest of the canon — not only the

Prophets, but also the Torah and the Psalms. Zephaniah participates in the textual world of the Hebrew Bible. This suggests that this textual world, in one form or another, was known and accepted by the book's first audience (whether that audience was in the time of Josiah or later), for only then would invoking it be rhetorically effective.

In addition to the parallels with Jeremiah noted above, much of Obadiah's phraseology appears elsewhere in the Hebrew Bible. Here I note only the closest parallels.

v 1   Arise so that we may rise against her for battle (cf. Judg 18:9; Jer 6:4–5)

v 2   Insignificant I have made you among the nations (cf. Mal 2:9)

v 3   you who dwell in the clefts of the crags (cf. Jer 48:28; Cant 2:14)

     Who will bring me down to the earth (cf. Jer 21:13; 49:4)

v 4   Even if you could exalt (your nest) like the eagle (cf. Job 39:27)

     even if among stars you could set your nest (cf. Num 24:21; Hab 2:9)

     from there I will bring you down (cf. Amos 9:2)

v 7   those of your peace (cf. Jer 20:10; Ps 41:10 [9])

     [Those who eat] your bread (cf. Ps 41:10 [9])

     in which there is no understanding (cf. Deut 32:28)

v 9   everyone will be cut off from Mount Esau by slaughter (cf. Ezek 25:13; 35:7)

v 10 because of the violence you did to your brother Jacob (cf. Joel 4:19 [3:19])

     shame will cover you (cf. Mic 7:10)

v 11 cast lots for Jerusalem (cf. Joel 4:3 [3:3]; Nah 3:10)

v 12 do not rejoice over the Judahites . . . do not open your mouth wide (cf. Ezek 35:13, 15; Ps 35:19–21; Lam 2:16; 3:46)

v 15 For the day of Yahweh is near (cf. Isa 13:6; Ezek 30:3; Joel 1:15; 2:1; 4:14 [3:14]; Zeph 1:7, 14)

     Just as you have done, it will be done to you (cf. Jer 50:15, 29; Ezek 16:59; 35:11, 15)

     your deeds will return upon your own head (cf. 1 Kgs 2:33; Joel 4:4, 7 [3:4, 7]; Ps 7:17 [16]; Prov 12:14)

v 17 But on Mount Zion will be escape (cf. Joel 3:5 [2:32])

     and a holy place (cf. Joel 4:17 [3:17])

v 18 The house of Jacob will become fire, and the house of Joseph, flame (cf. Isa 10:17)

     and there will be no survivor for the house of Esau (cf. Num 24:19 [?])

v 19 The Negeb will possess Mount Esau (cf. Num 24:18; Amos 9:12)

v 21 and the kingship will belong to Yahweh (cf. Ps 22:29 [28]; 1 Chr 29:11)

The listing above represents twenty different books and a wide variety of genres. In most instances Obadiah seems to have been the borrower. However, with respect to Joel, which has several close parallels, the direction of influence was probably the reverse. Most scholars consider the formula in Joel 3:5 [2:32] as indicating a citation: "For on Mount Zion and in Jerusalem will be escape, just as Yahweh has said." To be sure, the idea of deliverance in Zion is found elsewhere, even in the book of Joel, but this identical sentence occurs only in Obad 17. Therefore the citation indicates that Joel depended upon Obadiah. (For a different view, see Dicou 1994: 74–87.)

Not only Obadiah's wording but also many of his motifs and themes have parallels in other books, which are noted in the commentary. All of this overlap demonstrates the extent to which the book of Obadiah is at home in the Hebrew Bible and especially among the Latter Prophets. Although it is a very small book, it offers the reader a study in intertextuality; one sees a text that both creatively adapts earlier materials and generates later reapplications.

EDOM IN THE LATTER PROPHETS

Obadiah takes its place among other prophecies against Edom. Edom receives attention in more books of the Latter Prophets than any other nation: Isaiah, Jeremiah, Ezekiel, Joel, Amos, Obadiah, and Malachi. However, this does not mean that Edom oracles occupy more space than oracles against any of the other nations; Moab oracles or Tyre oracles, for example, take up more space (cf. Stuart 1987: 404–6). This fact alone should caution us against overstating the case by claiming that the prophets hated Edom more than any other nation. "Prophetic pronouncements against Nineveh are just as bitterly worded, those against Tyre are just as graphically styled, and so on" (Stuart 1987: 404). Furthermore, Moab like Edom can also stand as a representative of all the nations (cf. Isa 25:10–12). Nevertheless, because Edom does receive a fair amount of attention among the prophets, a brief survey of the texts will assist in providing a context for Obadiah among the prophets. It will become apparent that Obadiah's extensive discourse regarding Edom is not as strange or unusual as it at first appears. I include in the survey every reference to Edom in the Latter Prophets except Jer 40:11, which speaks of the Judahites in Edom rather than of Edom as such.

Isaiah 11:14. This verse forms part of a lengthy promise regarding Israel's future restoration. A reunited Israel will extend its authority over the surrounding countries so that it need not live in fear of them anymore. The chapter describes a situation that will resemble the period of David when these countries were subject to him. Here Edom has no special significance other than being one of the nations that will come under Israel's sway:

Their hand's reach will extend to Edom and Moab,
and the Ammonites will be their subjects.

Isaiah 21:11–12. This short oracle concerns "Dumah" and constitutes the seventh member of a collection of ten oracles against foreign nations, each of which has the word *maśśā'* (oracle/burden) in its title: Babylon, Philistia, Moab, Damascus, Egypt, Babylon, Dumah, Arabia, Judah, and Tyre (Isa 13–23). It remains unclear whether Dumah refers to Dumet ej-Jendal in Arabia or presents a wordplay on the name "Edom" — *dûmâ* denotes "silence." A wordplay would not be unusual here, given that other titles for Isaiah's oracles use symbolic names (21:1, 13; 22:1). Moreover, the oracle begins with a reference to Seir, which immediately makes one think of Edom. If it does concern Edom, as seems likely, it presents a rather enigmatic oracle in keeping with the title's wordplay. Someone inquires of the prophet regarding the future and the prophet replies that "morning comes and also evening." He then invites the inquirer to come back again. Although enigmatic the general gist seems clear enough: the prophet has no consolation for Edom but can only offer silence. One should note that the oracle neither accuses Edom of any crimes nor attributes to Edom any special role; Edom is simply one nation among many.

Isaiah 34. After a call to attention (v 1), the chapter begins by announcing Yahweh's wrath against all the nations: "he has given them over to slaughter" so that "the mountains will melt from their blood" (vv 2–3). Then the prophet depicts the destruction of the heavens (v 4), and thereupon to the end of the chapter (vv 5–17) he focuses on Edom.

After envisioning a descent of Yahweh's sword from heaven to Edom, the prophet portrays Edom's judgment as a sacrifice (vv 5–6):

When my sword has become drenched [Qumran has "appears"] in the
     heavens,
behold, it will descend upon Edom,
and upon the people of my ban for judgment.
Yahweh has a sword filled with blood . . .
For Yahweh has a sacrifice in Bozrah
and a great slaughter in the land of Edom.

The imagery of a sacrificial slaughter continues in v 7, which is followed in v 8 by a brief statement of the reason for the judgment. Verses 9–17 then describe the judgment's aftermath, in which Edom's territory becomes a perpetual wasteland inhabited only by desert animals. The imagery evokes that of Sodom and Gomorrah (cf. Jer 49:18).

What is the relationship between the destruction of all the nations (vv 2–3) and the destruction of Edom (vv 5–17)? The two might simply form parallel pictures, one general and one specific. Or the reference to the sword in the heavens might suggest a sequential movement of the judgment: from the nations (vv 2–3) to the heavens (vv 4–5a) and finally to Edom (vv 5b–8). In that case Edom would stand as the last of the nations to receive judgment, but, as Mathews (1994) cautions, perhaps this reads the poetic imagery too literalistically.

The chapter notably lacks specific charges against Edom for its crimes. The only indictment given is the rather general statement of v 8: "For Yahweh has a day of vengeance, a year of repayment in Zion's lawsuit." The statement announces Yahweh's punitive retribution for violence against Zion. Yet the book of Isaiah nowhere attributes to Edom any hostile actions against Zion. The statement's generalized character shows that Edom typifies all the nations. The statement receives further clarification in chapter 35 (cf. 35:4). Yahweh's sword will clear away the nations that assail Zion or impede the return of Zion's exiles. As Peels (1995: 154) explains:

> Isa. 34 is the reverse image of Isa. 35; everything that makes Zion faint-hearted (35:4), and everything that makes the people of YHWH sorrow and sigh (35:10), will have to suffer the vengeance of God.

The name "Edom" refers to the actual nation and place with its chief city of "Bozrah." Yet Edom also functions in this chapter as illustrative and typical of the nations. Why is Edom given this role? Scholars usually explain it on historical grounds as deriving from Israel's reaction to Edom's hostilities during the Babylonian crisis. However, in light of the book's complete lack of any specific charges against Edom, a historical explanation seems unlikely. Two other explanations are more plausible.

1. The first half of the chapter connects Edom with the nations by concentrating on the similarity of their fates rather than by detailing any correspondence of their deeds. Note that the judgments of both groups are pictured as a "ban" (*ḥrm*; vv 2, 5) and a "slaughter" (*ṭbḥ*; vv 2, 6) with an abundance of blood (vv 3, 6–7). This similarity suggests a literary explanation. Because the noun *dām*, "blood," is repeated (once in v 3, twice in v 6, once in v 7), perhaps the prophet chose *'ĕdôm* for its sound play with *dām*, which in turn led to the imagery of sacrifice and slaughter (cf. *'ādōm*, "red"; Gen 25:30; 2 Kgs 3:22).

2. Perhaps an additional motivating factor was Edom's geographical location in the south. It enabled the prophet to develop in the poem's second half

the imagery of Sodom and Gomorrah as a perpetual wasteland, which served to create a stark contrast with the reverse imagery of chapter 35.

Accordingly, Edom does not constitute the most hated or hostile of all the nations but simply one typical nation whose name and location evoke its own fate and that of the other nations.

Isaiah 63:1–6. The unit consists of a dialogue between the prophet and Yahweh. The prophet begins by asking: "Who is this that comes from Edom, in crimsoned garments from Bozrah?" Yahweh replies: "It is I, who speaks in righteousness, mighty to save." The prophet then asks: "Why is your apparel red [*'ādōm*] and your garments like those of one who treads in the winepress?" Yahweh answers by stating that he has trodden the peoples in his wrath so that their lifeblood has stained his clothes. He adds: "For the day of vengeance was in my heart, and the year of my redemption [or "my redeemed ones"] has come" (cf. 59:15–20; Peels 1995: 170–76).

Isaiah 63 presupposes Isaiah 34. Note the use of the phrase "the day of vengeance" in both chapters (34:8; 63:4) and the similarity of the phrases "the year of recompense" (34:8) and "the year of my redemption" (63:4). Furthermore, both texts pair "Edom" with "Bozrah": "Bozrah" and "the land of Edom" in 34:6; "Edom" and "Bozrah" in 63:1. The relationship between the pictures of the two chapters is sequential: 34:2–7 depicts Yahweh's slaughter of the nations and Edom, while 63 portrays its aftermath when Yahweh comes from Edom. Note also the prophecy-fulfillment sequence in that the former places Edom's judgment in the future, while the latter places it in the past (cf. Mathews 1994). However, the two chapters employ different images: in 34 Yahweh has a sacrifice, but in 63 Yahweh tramples the nations as one tramples grapes.

Again, why is Edom singled out? Like chapter 34 the text does not accuse Edom of any crimes, and therefore historical reasons seem unlikely. Two other considerations appear to offer more plausible explanations.

1. The use of two pictures based on wordplays suggests a literary explanation. The prophet chose the name *'ĕdôm* not only to complete the sequence begun in chapter 34 but also to evoke the noun *'ādōm* ("red"; cf. Gen 25:30). Moreover, like 34:6 Edom is paired with its capital *boṣrâ* (Bozrah). The latter name evokes the root *bṣr*, "to gather grapes," which produces the image of Yahweh treading upon the nations like grapes. Thus the oracle's imagery is created by the very names of "Edom" and "Bozrah" (Alonso Schökel 1988: 30).

2. The ancient tradition of Yahweh's march in the south, rather than any recent historical event, motivated the prophet to mention Edom (cf. Deut 33; Judg 5; Hab 3). The prophet adapted this tradition by depicting Yahweh marching from Edom to Zion. Thus Edom is the last stop on Yahweh's triumphant march to Zion (cf. Mathews 1994).

Jeremiah 9:24–25 [25–26]. This brief oracle presents a divine speech in which Yahweh announces that he will punish the circumcised — yet really uncircumcised — nations: Egypt, Judah, Edom, the Ammonites, Moab, and (apparently) Arab tribes living in the desert. The point of the passage is that the covenant people stand under divine judgment no less than the other nations. Here Edom is only one nation among others with no additional significance.

Jeremiah 25:21. Jeremiah 25:15–29 presents an extended cup-of-wrath passage that lists the various nations destined to drink the cup (see Excursus). Edom appears in the list along with Moab, Ammon, and the other nations. Consequently, Edom has no special representative function.

Jeremiah 27. The chapter describes in narrative form Jeremiah's response to an assembly of foreign envoys gathered in Jerusalem ca. 594/3 b.c. for the purpose of establishing an anti-Babylonian alliance. The envoys represent the kings of Edom, Moab, Ammon, Tyre, and Sidon. In keeping with the prophet's basic stance, Jeremiah warns against the coalition and advocates submission to Babylon: Yahweh will permit any capitulating nation to continue dwelling in its own land, but if it refuses to surrender, it will be destroyed by Nebuchadnezzar. The context makes it clear that Edom stands only for itself.

Jeremiah 49:7–22. Jeremiah's Edom oracle stands fifth in a collection of eight oracles against foreign nations, seven smaller nations followed by Babylon as the eighth and climactic one: Egypt, Philistia, Moab, Ammon, Edom, Damascus, Kedar and Hazor (= one oracle), and Babylon (Jer 46–51 MT). It is significant that the oracle lacks any accusation of Edom for past crimes. It only describes with a variety of images Edom's appointed doom. Like the other oracles in the first group of seven, excluding Babylon, Edom plays no special representative role. As with the two previous texts in the book of Jeremiah, Edom is simply one nation among many placed under Yahweh's judgment.

Dicou (1994: 88–104), however, attributes to Edom a symbolic role in Jer 49. He contends that the overlap between parts of the Edom oracle and the Babylon oracles associates Edom with Babylon. Therefore Edom like Babylon represents the nations' and Israel's antagonist. Three considerations argue against this interpretation.

1. To be sure, the last verses of the Edom oracle occur again in the Babylon oracles. Yet the content of these repeated verses applies more appropriately to Edom than to Babylon. The imagery and the references to "Sodom and Gomorrah" and to "the Jordan" used in 49:18–21 fit better with Edom than with Babylon in 50:40, 44–46. Consequently, the prophet's point is just the reverse of Dicou's interpretation. By reapplying the Edom verses to Babylon the prophet reduces Babylon to the level of just another nation that is destined to receive the same fate as the other nations. The prophet does not

place Edom into the same category as Babylon but Babylon into the same category as Edom.

2. There are significant parallels between the Edom oracle and the Moab oracle. The last verse of the Edom oracle occurs also in the Moab oracle (48:41; 49:22), and the cup-of-wrath metaphor is applied to both countries (48:26; 49:12). Moreover, the point of 49:12 is identical with the point of 25:28–29, according to which the cup of wrath is imposed on every nation equally and without differentiation.

3. The Edom oracle unlike the Babylon oracles nowhere accuses Edom of being Israel's antagonist.

In conclusion, Jer 49 portrays Edom as one nation among many that will receive God's judgment. Edom does not stand out as more significant or representative than Moab or any other nation. The only uniqueness the chapter gives Edom is its association with "Esau" (49:8, 10), which evokes the Jacob-Esau connection. However, the association is not developed in Jer 49 as fully as it is in Obadiah.

Ezekiel 25:12–14. Ezekiel's Edom oracle occupies third position in a collection of seven oracles against foreign nations: Ammon, Moab, Edom, Philistia, Tyre, Sidon, and Egypt (Ezek 25–32). Unlike the texts we have discussed so far, here Edom receives explicit condemnation for its anti-Judah hostilities. The oracle presents a divine speech that charges Edom with acting vengefully against Judah, no doubt referring to Edom's conduct during the Babylonian crisis. In keeping with the *lex talionis* principle, Yahweh announces that he will lay his vengeance upon Edom through Israel acting as his agent. The motif resembles the one found in Obad 18, which envisages Israel destroying Edom. These are the only two texts in the prophetic Edom oracles that give Israel the role of agent in Yahweh's judgment of Edom. Also Ezek 35 has several close parallels with Obadiah (see below). Therefore it is plausible to suggest a relationship of dependence between the two books in which the direction of influence perhaps went from Ezekiel to Obadiah (so Dicou 1994: 70–73).

Some of the Edom oracle's phrases and motifs appear in the surrounding oracles as well. Note especially how the prophet treats Philistia as he does Edom; both acted vengefully and both will experience God's vengeance, although Israel functions as the agent of God's punishment only for Edom (cf. Peels 1995: 187–94). The correspondences and similarities indicate that Edom holds no extraordinary significance in Ezekiel's collection of oracles against the nations. Edom's guilt and doom are viewed as part of a series of judgments that it shares with other nations (cf. Woudstra 1968). The purpose of the punishment receives clarification in the conclusion given for the oracles against the first six nations: after Israel's future restoration Israel will no longer have malicious neighbors (28:24–26).

Ezekiel 32:29. This verse constitutes part of the prophet's mocking lament over the descent of Egypt into the netherworld. Pharaoh together with Egypt's multitudes will lie in the Pit and thus join Edom along with Assyria, Elam, Meshech, and Tubal, the princes of the north, and the Sidonians. The verse lacks any accusation of Edom. It only asserts that Edom, its mighty kings, and princes are associated with those slain by the sword; they lie with the uncircumcised and with those who descend into the Pit. The context indicates that Edom plays no representative role in the chapter.

Ezekiel 35–36. These two interconnected and contrastive chapters concern two sets of mountains. The former announces judgment against "Mount Seir" and the latter promises restoration for "the mountains of Israel." In chapter 35 the prophet lays four basic charges against Mount Seir, i.e., Edom:

1. holding "perpetual enmity" and hatred against Israel (vv 5, 11);
2. giving Israel over to the sword and pursuing bloodshed (vv 5–6);
3. desiring to possess Israel's land and rejoicing over its desolation (vv 10, 12, 15);
4. boasting against Yahweh (v 13).

In keeping with the prophetic viewpoint, such conduct calls for a divine response of judgment. Whereas the charges refer to Edom's actions in the past during the time of Judah's fall to Babylon, the announcement of judgment locates the punishments in the future. On the basis of the talionic standard, the punishments correspond with the crimes:

1. Yahweh will deal with Edom according to the anger and envy that it showed (v 11);
2. blood will pursue Edom so that its inhabitants will be killed with the sword (vv 6–8);
3. Mount Seir will become a perpetual desolation (vv 3–4, 7, 9, 14–15);
4. Yahweh will reveal himself to Edom as its judge (vv 4, 9, 11–12, 15).

Chapter 35 by itself does not clearly attribute to Edom the role of representing or typifying all the nations. However, this role becomes apparent in chapter 36. Verse 2 uses the general term "the enemy" and attributes to him what 35:10 says of Edom, namely, the desire to possess Israel's land. The next two verses clarify that "the enemy" includes "the rest of the nations round about." Then in v 5 Yahweh announces judgment "against the rest of the nations and against Edom altogether, who have given my land to themselves as a possession with whole-hearted joy and with utter contempt, in order to empty it out for booty." Although Edom is the only nation specifically named, it is closely associated with the other hostile nations (cf. v 5 with vv 6–7, 15). Here Edom exemplifies and typifies all the nations that oppose Israel and consequently face divine wrath (cf. Woudstra

1968). Edom's typical role is further indicated by the similar kinds of hostility attributed to other nations: Philistia is accused of harboring "perpetual enmity" (25:15), while Ammon (25:3, 6), Moab (25:8), and Tyre (26:2) are charged with rejoicing over Israel's desolate land.

Chapters 35–36 form two sides of the same coin. On the one hand, Israel's enemies, epitomized by Edom, receive divine wrath because of their anti-Yahweh and anti-Israel conduct. On the other hand, God devastates Israel's enemies who have possessed Israel's land so that he can restore Israel's fortunes in its land. Whereas the first side stresses the grounds for the nations' judgment, the second side emphasizes the judgment's purpose. Note 36:15: after the judgment has taken place, restored Israel will never again hear the reproach of the nations.

Joel 4:19 [3:19]. Toward the end of the book of Joel one reads this verse:

Egypt will become a desolation,
and Edom will become a desolate wilderness,
because of the violence done to the Judahites
in whose land they shed innocent blood.

There are two grammatical uncertainties in the passage. I take the antecedent for the suffix of *bĕ'arṣām* (lit., "in their land") to be "the Judahites" and the subject of the verb "they shed" to be the Edomites.

The verse announces the future destruction of Edom based on its past actions against the Judahites. The language recalls Obad 10, which uses a similar phrase to accuse Edom of violence, and Ezek 35, which accuses Edom of bloodshed and proclaims its future desolation. Although the date of Joel is debated, in light of the citation of Obad 17 in Joel 3:5 [2:32] Joel most likely depends on Obadiah (and Ezekiel).

The mention of "Egypt" and "Edom" creates a kind of chronological merismus. Egypt had been Israel's archenemy in the earliest period, while Edom had become its archenemy in more recent times. Wolff (1969) points to the presence of both names in texts dealing with "the Day of Yahweh," a prominent theme in Joel (Isa 34:8; Jer 46:10; Ezek 30:3–4). Therefore their appearance in Joel is explicable as part of the inherited prophetic tradition. The devastation of Egypt and Edom particularizes the universal judgment of "the day of Yahweh" announced in 4:14 [3:14]. Hence both nations stand as notable examples of all the nations that face condemnation. By way of contrast the next two verses refer to the future security and vindication of Judah/Jerusalem with Zion as Yahweh's dwelling place (4:20–21 [3:20–21]).

Amos 1. The Edom oracle (1:11–12) occupies fourth position in a collection of eight oracles against the nations: Aram, Philistia, Tyre, Edom, Ammon, Moab, Judah, and Israel (Amos 1–2). The collection has the overall effect of demoting

Judah and especially Israel to the level of the other neighboring countries; the covenant people of Yahweh stand under divine judgment just like the other nations (cf. Jer 9:24–25 [25–26]). Here it is clear that Edom stands for itself only, without any larger representative function.

The oracle presents a divine speech in which Yahweh announces the destruction of Teman and Bozrah by fire. The judgment is grounded in a twofold charge: first, Edom pursued his brother with the sword and destroyed his allies, and second, Edom's anger persisted always. The first charge mentions Edom's hostile actions against "his brother." The significance of the term *'āḥîyw* (his brother) is disputed but probably refers to Israel based on the Jacob-Esau connection. For the difficult word *raḥămāyw*, Andersen and Freedman (1989) translate "his allies," and understand the word to reflect both kinship and covenant associations, while Paul (1991) proposes "his womenfolk" (cf. Judg 5:30). The second charge accuses Edom of perpetually maintaining its anger and rage, a charge that resembles the one made in Ezek 35:5.

Although the Edom oracle is often considered to be a secondary addition along with the Tyre and Judah oracles, its authenticity has been recently defended by Andersen and Freedman (1989), Paul (1991), and Steinmann (1992). In that case the charges already applied to Edom in the eighth century. It remains uncertain which event(s) Amos had in mind. Perhaps he referred to Edom's revolt against Judah in the mid-ninth century as recorded in 2 Kgs 8:20–22. Or he may have thought of some cruel border raid (cf. Paul 1991). Two other oracles in Amos 1 mention Edom, namely, the oracles against Philistia and Tyre (1:6, 9). They name Edom as the recipient of slaves, possibly acting as the middleman in a slave-trade network (see Notes for v 14). At any rate, the strained relations between the two nations were longstanding and did not first begin in the sixth century (cf. 2 Kgs 14:7, 22).

Amos 9:12. Amos 9:11–15 presents a divine speech that announces Israel's future restoration in its own land. Within this promise there is a reference to Edom. The statement says that Yahweh will rebuild David's booth so that restored Israel "will possess the remnant of Edom and of all the nations upon whom my name has been called — utterance of Yahweh who is about to do this."

Although space prohibits an extensive treatment of the section, a few exegetical remarks are necessary. I take the phrase "all the nations" as a second juxtaposed genitive of "the remnant" (cf. Joüon 1991 § 129b). "The remnant of Edom" designates the Edomites who will survive the judgment announced in 1:11–12, while "the remnant . . . of all the nations" refers to the survivors of the other nations mentioned in chapters 1–2. Although the verb *yrš*, when it takes a personal object, usually denotes "to dispossess," here it means "to possess" in the sense of incorporate or own; the statement expresses more the idea of Israel controlling and ruling the survivors of the nations than that of occupying their lands. (For a similar idea, see Isa 14:2 and 54:2–3.)

41

Amos 9 promises Israel a reversal of its fortunes. Instead of being attacked by Edom as in the past (1:11–12), Israel will possess and dominate Edom's remnant. The statement then expands to include the remnant of all the nations; they too will be subject to Israel. But lest one think only of a military rule, the relative clause adds a further qualification. Edom and the nations are those upon whom Yahweh will have pronounced his name. The idiom "to have one's name called upon an object" denotes ownership (cf. 2 Sam 12:28; Isa 4:1). When Yahweh's name is the subject, it also connotes a privileged status. In the Hebrew Bible only Israelite entities have "Yahweh's name pronounced upon them": Israel (Deut 28:10; Isa 63:19; Jer 14:9; Dan 9:19; 2 Chr 7:14); Jerusalem (Jer 25:29; Dan 9:18, 19); the temple (1 Kgs 8:43 = 2 Chr 6:33; Jer 7:10, 11, 14, 30; 32:34; 34:15); the ark (2 Sam 6:2); and the prophet Jeremiah (Jer 15:16). That Edom and the nations would be given such a status is quite striking and brings to mind the idea expressed in Isa 19:24–25. (For a different interpretation of the verse, see Andersen and Freedman 1989.)

Amos 9 juxtaposes "Edom" with "all the nations." Why does the passage single Edom out? Several reasons are possible.

1. Of the six non-Israelite nations listed in Amos 1–2, Edom is mentioned most often. In addition to the Edom oracle itself, the Philistia and Tyre oracles implicate Edom in the practice of slave trade (1:6, 9), while the Moab oracle charges Moab with burning the bones of the king of Edom to lime (2:1). Therefore the reason for the special mention of Edom in chapter 9 might be nothing more than the name's frequent occurrence in the oracles against the nations.

2. The reason might be that the prophet considered it the most implacable of the nations, because only Edom receives condemnation for maintaining its fierce anger and rage (1:11).

3. Perhaps Edom receives special mention because of its status as a brother nation (1:11; cf. Koch 1983: 69).

4. Possibly a literary explanation applies. The name 'ĕdôm evokes the common noun 'ādām, "humanity," which naturally leads into the next phrase, "all the nations" (cf. LXX; G. V. Smith 1988: 169–70).

The verse moves from the particular to the general so that Edom functions as one specific illustration of all the nations. If the verse is genuine to Amos, then Edom receives a more general typifying role — at least, in incipient form — already in the early eighth century. However, the authenticity of Amos 9:11–15 is disputed. Many scholars deny it (e.g., Wolff 1969), while other scholars support it (e.g., Paul 1991); for a thorough discussion, see Hasel (1991).

Obadiah. The book of Obadiah deals with Edom at length; only three verses lack any reference to Edom (vv 16–17, 20). That is not to say, however, that the book can be characterized as simply one long tirade against a "hated" nation. On the contrary, the book reflects some obvious and many subtle differences in the way it treats Edom.

The book begins with the announcement of Edom's coming doom, portrayed with a variety of images (vv 1–9). Verses 10–14 have a twofold function. First, they ground the judgment in accusations of Edom for its past violence against Judah. The prophet makes basically three charges: Edom gloated over Judah's fall, looted its wealth, and captured and handed over its survivors. In these ways Edom sided with Judah's enemies and virtually became one with the Babylonians (v 11). Second, the grammar of vv 12–14 (eight vetitives, or negative commands, "do not . . .") and the concluding motivation clause in v 15 ("For the day of Yahweh is near . . .") indicate that vv 12–14 also function as warnings for Edom to stop its anti-Judah hostilities before it is too late.

The second half of the book contains promises of Israel's restoration (vv 16–21), within which Edom is also mentioned. Verse 18 states that a reunited Israel will totally annihilate Edom so that Edom will have no survivors. According to v 19, the Negeb will occupy Edom's land, while according to v 21, deliverers on Mount Zion will rule over Edom.

More than any other prophet Obadiah emphasizes the Edom-Esau equation and the Esau-Jacob relationship. As a reference to Edom the name "Esau" occurs seven times: "Esau" (v 6), "Mount Esau" (vv 8, 9, 19, 21), and "the house of Esau" (v 18a, b). Also v 10 and v 12 designate Jacob as Edom's "brother." Unlike Amos 1 and Ezek 35, the book of Obadiah does not treat Edom as a traditional enemy of Israel. On the contrary, it is precisely their relationship as "brothers" that accounts for the tone of bewilderment and horror that underlies much of the book. Verse 11 illustrates this "et-tu-Brute" tone:

> On the day when you stood opposite,
> on the day when strangers took captive his [Jacob's] power,
> while foreigners entered his gates
> and cast lots for Jerusalem,
> also you were like one of them.

Because the book so strongly evokes the Jacob-Esau narratives, which end with the reconciliation of the two brothers (Gen 33; cf. Deut 23:8 [7]), and because vv 12–15 function as warnings in addition to accusations, it would be misleading to characterize the book as an expression of national hatred against Edom (*pace* Haller 1925) or "damn-Edom theology" (*pace* Cresson 1963; 1972). To be sure, v 9 and v 18 speak of Edom's total annihilation. But this is based on the talionic standard of judgment operative throughout the book and in fact throughout the Latter Prophets: just as Edom sought to eliminate Judah (v 14), so Edom will be eliminated. In addition to this depiction of Edom's future, v 21 posits a continued existence of Edom in its own land albeit under Zion's aegis, while vv 12–15 offer Edom an implicit opportunity to avoid the universal condemnation of the day of Yahweh. Thus the book sets forth different portrayals of Edom's future destiny, which can neither easily be harmonized nor simply reduced to one depiction.

With the names "Edom," "Esau," and "Teman" the prophet refers to the historical nation and land. But does Edom also play a representative role in the book? The evidence is mixed. In v 1 and v 7 Edom is distinguished from the nations; the nations and specifically Edom's treaty partners will attack Edom. According to vv 12–16, Edom faces the threat of being condemned together with all the nations. So far the reader concludes that Edom represents only itself as one nation among many. However, some of the statements announcing Edom's doom portray it in a way that resembles the appointed destiny of the nations. According to vv 9 and 18, Edom will be annihilated so that it lacks any survivor or remnant, and according to v 10, Edom "will be cut off forever." With this motif compare the statement made in v 16 regarding all the nations: "they will be as if they had never been." In light of this resemblance, the reader rightly thinks of Edom's fate as an illustration that typifies the fate of all the nations (cf. Hummel 1979: 320). Yet even here Edom retains its uniqueness vis-à-vis the nations in that only Edom is considered Jacob's "brother."

Malachi 1. Malachi 1:2–5 presents a dialogue between Yahweh and Israel in which the names "Esau" and "Jacob" occur. The text uses each name to designate the patriarch himself and at the same time his descendants. The dialogue begins with Yahweh's assertion, "I have loved you," which Israel disputes, "In what way have you loved us?" Yahweh defends his assertion by pointing to the distinction he made between Esau/Edom and Jacob/the Israelites: "Was not Esau a brother of Jacob? Yet I have loved Jacob, but Esau I have hated." The statement concerns their role in history. Although Esau (and therefore Edom) by right of primogeniture had claim to the birthright and preferential treatment, Yahweh freely chose Jacob (and therefore the Israelites) to bear the promise and the blessing. The next statement refers to recent history as proof of the assertion: "I have made his [Esau's] mountains into a wasteland and his inheritance (into a wasteland) for the jackals of the desert." The hearers should be able to recognize in recent history Yahweh's discriminating love for Jacob and his descendants, given their continuing existence in contrast to the fate of Esau/Edom. Yahweh further supports his defense by arguing that Edom's fate is sealed; if Edom rebuilds its ruins, he will tear them down. Thus "they will be called a territory of wickedness, and the people with whom Yahweh is indignant forever." According to the text's final statement, Edom's destruction not only demonstrates indirectly Yahweh's love for Jacob but also reveals Yahweh's lordship over the other nations, "Yahweh is great beyond the territory of Israel."

In this text Edom represents only itself. The prophet considers Edom to be wicked and therefore under divine wrath. Unlike the other prophetic texts that we have examined, Mal 1 speaks of Edom's destruction as having taken place in the past. The specific historical event in view remains unclear. Although the date of Malachi is debated, a date somewhere between 500 and 450 seems likely (cf. Hill 1983; Glazier-McDonald 1987: 14–18). In light of this time frame, Edom's devastation might have been caused by the campaign of Nabonidus in 553 (so Bartlett 1989: 160–61) or by that campaign together with the subsequent Nabatean settlement (so Glazier-McDonald 1987: 34–41). In any case, by the time of Malachi Edom's political history had for all intents and purposes come to an end. However, Malachi indicates and archaeology provides further evidence that some Edomites continued to live in their land during the Persian period (cf. Bartlett 1989: 147–74).

Conclusions. From the sixteen texts surveyed above emerge several overall conclusions.

1. The texts treat Edom in a variety of ways. All of the texts except Mal 1 locate Edom's judgment in the future. Six of the texts speak only of Edom's doom (Isa 34; 63; Jer 9; 25; 49; Ezek 32), and six texts both accuse Edom of crimes and pronounce doom (Ezek 25; 35; Joel; Amos 1; Obad; Mal 1, which calls Edom "a territory of wickedness"). Isaiah 21 and Jeremiah 27 are unique. The former offers Edom only silence regarding its future, while the latter holds open the possibility of Edom's continued existence in its land if it submits to Babylon. In four texts the announcement of Edom's doom is matched with a corresponding promise of Israel's restoration (Isa 34–35; Ezek 35–36; Joel, Obad). Several texts mention Edom within a promise of Israel's restoration: Isa 11, Amos 9, and Obad 21 foresee Edom's continued existence under the authority of Israel, while Ezek 36 proclaims Edom's judgment within a promissory context. Two texts envisage Edom's destruction at the hands of Israel (Ezek 25; Obad 18). Finally, four texts refer to the Esau-Jacob connection (Jer 49; Amos 1; Obad; Mal 1).

2. When the prophets mention Edom within lists that specify other nations by name, Edom stands only for itself (Isa 11; Jer 9; 25; 27; Ezek 32). This limited role of Edom also applies to the longer Edom oracles that appear in collections of oracles against foreign nations (Isa 21; Jer 49; Ezek 25; Amos 1). In these contexts the name "Edom" refers to the historical nation and land, and it functions as only one nation and land among many.

3. When the prophets associate Edom closely with all the nations seen as an undifferentiated whole, Edom both represents itself and serves as a special illustration of all the nations. Edom has this more extensive function in texts that occur outside of lists and collections of oracles against the nations (Isa 34; 63; Ezek 35–36; Amos 9; Obad). Each of these texts — excluding

Obadiah — appears in a book containing a collection of oracles against the nations in which there is an Edom oracle. That is to say, in the books of Isaiah, Ezekiel, and Amos, Edom first plays a more limited role within the collection and then a more general role outside the collection.

4. The more extensive role that Edom has in the second set of texts needs further definition. These texts speak of Edom together with all the nations; it is a case of "both-and," Edom and the nations. This usage and the content of these texts indicate that the name "Edom" is not used as a mere symbol or cipher for all the nations. The name still refers to the historical nation and land. Yet Edom also exemplifies and typifies all the nations. Prophetic discourse often prefers to speak of a whole category by vividly depicting and dramatizing one specific instance of it rather than by making abstract statements about the whole category. Edom functions in like manner as a classic example or an inclusive representative. For most of the texts, the point of comparison lies in the judgment: the doom Edom will experience illustrates the doom awaiting all the nations (Isa 34; 63; Ezek 35–36; Obad). For Ezek 35–36 it also lies in the correlation between Edom's crimes and those of the other nations. In Amos 9 Edom represents one of the nations that will be possessed by restored Israel.

5. In the effort to determine what might have motivated the prophets to choose Edom as their classic example, we should not reduce every possible cause to the level of political history. On the contrary, several considerations were at work.

(a) Literary considerations played a role. A poet starts with a name and then "develops" the ideas and imagery generated by the sound of the name. (On "development" in poetry, see Alonso Schökel 1988: 180–89.) For example, the psalmist in Ps 122 develops the name of "Jerusalem" according to its two components (*yĕrû* and *šālayim*), which evoke the motifs of the "city" (*'îr*) and "peace" (*šālôm*). More than other names, such as "Philistia," the name "Edom" was conducive to creating a wordplay and then developing its associated imagery. "Edom" evokes the noun *dām* (blood), which can then be developed in association with slaughter and sacrifice (Isa 34). Or it evokes the noun *'ādōm* (red; cf. Gen 25:30), which leads into the picture of Yahweh's garments stained red with the nations' blood (Isa 63). In Isa 63 the prophet also works the name "Bozrah," from *bṣr* (to harvest grapes), by portraying Yahweh as trampling the nations as one tramples grapes. Note that the oracle in Isa 21, which probably refers to Edom, plays with the word *dûmâ* (silence). With respect to Amos 9, perhaps "Edom" is mentioned because it evokes the noun *'ādām* (humanity) and thus leads naturally into the next phrase, "all the nations."

(b) Another factor was geography. Edom's location encouraged the imagery associated with Sodom and Gomorrah (Isa 34; cf. Jer 49:18) and called to mind the tradition of Yahweh marching in the south (Isa 63). Its mountainous terrain made it an appropriate match for the mountains of Israel (Ezek 35–36; cf. Ezek 6).

(c) Historical reasons sometimes motivated the prophet. This is clearly the case for Ezek 35–36: Edom's hostile actions against Israel made it the paradigm of all the enemy nations who must be defeated in order for Israel to be restored. Obadiah correlates Edom's doom with that of all the nations. Here as well, Edom's conduct in history motivated the prophet to focus on Edom. What made Edom's actions doubly blameworthy for Obadiah was its status as Jacob's brother; of the texts that attribute to Edom a representative role only Obadiah explicitly makes the Edom-Esau connection.

In summary, the prophets occasionally give Edom a prominent and exemplary role. Because theoretically any nation could have played this role, why was Edom chosen? Most scholars propose that the choice was motivated by historical events, specifically the Edomites' hostility during the fall of Judah and their possession of Judahite territory (Haller 1925; Cresson 1963; 1972; Hoffmann 1972; Dicou 1994). To be sure, recent history constituted one motivating factor: Edom became Israel's most dangerous neighbor. But geographical and literary considerations also played important roles so that the motivation for giving Edom a typifying role did not always derive from Israel's reaction to past injuries. In many of the texts Edom represents only itself as one nation among many. Moreover, some texts treat Edom less harshly by positing for it a continuing existence albeit under Israel's aegis. Consequently, it would be misleading to characterize the prophetic judgments against Edom — or, for that matter, against the other nations — as expressions of Israelite nationalistic "hate literature" or "xenophobia." The oracles against Edom and the rest of the nations served purposes other than merely giving vent to hatred (cf. Raabe 1995).

DATE AND HISTORICAL SETTING

One might question whether we should attempt to identify the book's historical setting, given the book's use of conventional language and its stereotypical pattern as an oracle against the nations (so Carroll 1990). However, such a view wrongly pits conventionality against history. It is rather the case that prophets addressed particular historical occasions by using conventional phraseology and generalizing forms of speech. The contents of the book itself promote a historical reading, one that locates it in a specific situation within space and time. First, the book projects a geographical location for the author within Judah; the prophet does not place himself among the nations (v 1) or among the exiles (v 20). Second, the book projects a specific temporal position for the author; it speaks of some events in the past tense and of other events in the future tense but not of "timeless" events (*pace* Bič [1951; 1953] who considered the book unhistorical and treated it as a cultic drama for the so-called enthronement festival). For example, the tone of shock expressed in vv 10–11 suggests that recent events evoked the prophet's response. In other words, the book's contents encourage the reader, on the one hand, to think of a historical occasion giving rise to the prophecy and, on the other hand, to understand the prophet to be addressing a specific situation by using what is in some places — but not everywhere — rather general and conventional language. Therefore it remains in keeping with the nature of the text to inquire after its historical setting (see above under "Preliminary Observations").

Unfortunately, the superscription gives us only the prophet's name without any additional information. We must therefore infer the historical circumstances from the book's contents and from known history. The process consists of two steps. First, we will use the basic data from the book to envision an occasion for the prophecy, and then we will correlate this occasion with historical data derived from other sources.

The book places certain events in the past:

1. the attack of "strangers/foreigners" against Judah and Jerusalem (v 11) and the experience of Yahweh's wrath undergone by Judah/Jerusalem (v 16);
2. Edom's acts of "violence" (v 10) on the day of Judah's ruin, which vv 12–14 describe — although with negative commands rather than indicative verbs — as gloating over Judah's demise, looting Judah's towns, and capturing Judah's fugitives;
3. by promising Israel's restoration, v 17 and v 19 presuppose Israel's loss of territory, including Ephraim, Samaria, and Gilead (vv 17, 19); perhaps we should also assume the loss of "the cities of the Negeb" (v 20).

Obadiah locates other events in the future, some of which are admittedly more cosmic and "eschatological" in nature:

4. the attack upon Edom by the nations (v 1) and specifically by Edom's allies who will drive Edom out of its land (v 7) — the use of perfect verbs in v 6 and the first half of v 7 should be taken as prophetic perfects in the context;
5. the total extermination of Edom (vv 8–9) and its end as a nation (v 10); v 18 speaks of a reunited Israel that will annihilate Edom;
6. the restoration of Israel within its traditional borders and the return of Judah's exiles together with Jerusalem's exiles located in Sepharad (vv 19–20);
7. the day of Yahweh's universal judgment (vv 15–16) and the manifestation of his kingship when Zion will rule over Edom (v 21).

Various proposals have been made for the date of the book, the most important of which are discussed below (see also Wehrle 1987: 9–12). The book's placement in the canon is not a determining factor. It was located after Joel and Amos in the MT most likely because of thematic considerations rather than chronological ones, particularly its connection with Joel 4:19 [3:19] and Amos 9:12 (cf. Wolff 1977). In the LXX the three undated books were placed together (following Hosea, Amos, Micah): Joel, Obadiah, Jonah.

1. Locate Obadiah in the early ninth century. Early Jewish traditions, followed by Jerome, identified Obadiah with the "Obadiah" mentioned in 1 Kgs 18, the official in charge of Ahab's palace who hid 100 prophets of Yahweh in two caves and provided them with food and water in order to save them from Jezebel. They suggested that he was an Edomite proselyte who was given the gift of prophecy for his generous act. They further connected him with the man from the company of the prophets who had been the husband of the widow helped by Elisha (2 Kgs 4:1). The basis for the combination is that both men are said to have "feared Yahweh" (1 Kgs 18:3, 12; 2 Kgs 4:1). Some early church fathers equated Obadiah both with the third captain sent by Ahaziah to Elijah (2 Kgs 1:13) and with the widow's husband. Saadiah on the Jewish side (882–942) and Rupert of Deutz on the Christian side (1075/80–1129) identified Obadiah with Ahab's palace official (1 Kgs 18) and connected him with the war of Jehoshaphat (= Ahab's contemporary in Judah) depicted in 2 Chr 20. This connection established an association with Edom, since 2 Chr 20 includes men from Mount Seir among Jehoshaphat's opponents. In contrast to the above attempts to relate the prophet to a known figure, some Jewish exegetes of the Middle Ages, such as Ibn Ezra (1089–1164) and Kimhi (1160?–1235?), concluded that there is insufficient evidence for any equation. (For details of the early traditions, see Caspari 1842; Elowsky 1992.)

2. Date Obadiah ca. 845. According to the biblical accounts, with David's conquests Edom came under the rule of Israel (2 Sam 8; 1 Kgs 11; 1 Chr 18; cf. Hauer 1980). Edom remained subject until ca. 845 when Edom successfully rebelled against Judah's authority and reestablished its own monarchy (2 Kgs 8:20–22; 2 Chr 21:8–10). In response Jehoram (= Joram) of Judah went to Zair (= Zoar at the southern tip of the Dead Sea?) and attacked the Edomites who had surrounded him and his chariot officers, but Jehoram's army fled back home (cf. Cogan and Tadmor 1988). According to 2 Chr 21:16–17, at about the same time Philistines and Arabs attacked Judah, invaded it, and "took captive" all the possessions that they found belonging to the palace along with the king's sons and wives, except Jehoahaz, his youngest son.

   Some commentators locate Obadiah in this setting (e.g., Keil 1888;

Isopescul 1913; Theis 1937; Laetsch 1956; Spaude 1987; Niehaus 1993). Delitzsch (1851) suggested that the prophet was the "officer" named "Obadiah" under Jehoshaphat in 2 Chr 17:7 and that this officer may have participated in the war of Jehoram against Edom (cf. 2 Chr 21:9). According to this historical setting, the "strangers/foreigners" who attacked and "took captive" Jacob's goods and people (Obad 11) were the invading Philistines and Arabs. Note the use of the same verb *šbh* (to take captive) in 2 Chr 21:17 and Obad 11. However, this proposal has several problems. First, 2 Kgs 8 makes no mention of Edomites in Judah as Obad 12–14 presupposes; Jehoram fought them at Zair. Second, it is doubtful that the metaphor of Jerusalem/Judah drinking the cup of Yahweh's wrath (Obad 16) would appropriately apply to this event. Third, the promise given in Obad 19 presupposes the loss of the northern territories in 732 and 722. Finally, 2 Chr 21, unlike Obad 20a, does not speak of the exiles of Judah; the commentators usually relate Amos 1:6, 9 to this event but the connection remains uncertain.

3. Date Obadiah ca. 735. If we read "Edom" for MT "Aram" in 2 Kgs 16:6, then Edom regained Elath from Judah during the early years of Ahaz (cf. 2 Kgs 14:22; Cogan and Tadmor 1988). However, it should be noted that *'ĕdôm* is always spelled *plene* in the MT, so that any confusion of "Edom" and "Aram" must have occurred before this spelling became standard (cf. Andersen and Freedman 1989: 259). According to the parallel in 2 Chr 28, when Syria and Israel invaded Judah, the Edomites also attacked Judah and "took captives," while the Philistines raided towns in the Shephelah and the Negeb. Some scholars place Obadiah in this setting during the reign of Ahaz (e.g., G. L. Robinson 1926; Young 1949; Davis 1972). Raven (1906) suggested that Obad 11 refers to the events of Jehoram's reign (2 Chr 21) but that the prophet lived during the time of Ahaz (2 Chr 28). Two arguments speak against relating Obadiah to 2 Chr 28. Although 2 Chr 28:10 refers to Jerusalemites becoming prisoners of northern Israel, Obadiah would hardly have called northern Israel's army "strangers/foreigners" (Obad 11); nor does 2 Chr 28 mention any attack upon Jerusalem by the Edomites or the Philistines. Against Raven's suggestion, the tone of Obad 11 gives the impression that it refers to recent events rather than events having occurred more than a century earlier.

4. Date Obadiah ca. 450. Some scholars place at least the core of the book in the mid-fifth century near the time of Malachi and Nehemiah (e.g., Wellhausen 1963; Nowack 1897; Bewer 1911; Thompson 1956; Kodell 1982). They connect the book with the Nabatean settlement in Edom and understand the attack upon Edom depicted in vv 1–7 as descriptive of past events, namely, the Arab incursions. However, in light of vv 1, 4, 7b, 8–10, the first

part of the book is meant to be taken as an announcement of future events; thus the perfect verbs in vv 6–7 a function as prophetic perfects.

5. Date Obadiah during the exilic period. Luther and Calvin were the first to locate the prophet after the fall of Jerusalem in 587/6. Luther considered Obadiah to be a contemporary of Jeremiah. Most recent scholars agree in placing at least the core of the book within the exilic period (e.g., Janssen 1956; Keller 1965; Eissfeldt 1965; Weiser 1967; Rudolph 1971; Kaiser 1975; Wolff 1977; Hummel 1979; Boadt 1984; Deissler 1984; Armerding 1985; Stuart 1987). Some propose a slightly later date during the early post-exilic period (e.g., Watts 1969; Allen 1976; Limburg 1988; Pazdan [1989] suggests ca. 535–435; Peckham [1993] dates it to ca. 535; Dicou [1994] sees the development of the book taking place ca. 550–500). Based on linguistic and statistical criteria, Adams and Adams (1977) place the writing of the book in the period between 586 and 458 B.C.

In my view the book fits best in the first half of the exilic period, ca. 585–555; the terminus a quo is the fall of Judah and Jerusalem to the Babylonians (587/6), while the terminus ad quem is the campaign of Nabonidus against Edom (553). Clues in the book and information from other sources help to determine the prophet's location between these two termini.

1. Verse 11 speaks of non-Israelites entering the towns of Judah, taking captive both people and goods, and casting lots for Jerusalem. The description points to the Babylonian attack and the fall of Jerusalem. In some other texts the verb *šbh* (to take captive) applies to the Babylonians (Jer 13:17; 50:33; Ezek 6:9; Ps 137:3). Although the book does not specify the Babylonians by name, this absence can be explained. First, the purpose of v 11 is to condemn Jacob's brother, Edom, for siding with the invading "strangers" and "foreigners" rather than with Edom's own brother; the political identity of the invaders is beside the point. Second, the exilic book of Lamentations and some exilic psalms (Pss 74, 79, 102) refer to the Babylonians with terms such as "enemy" and "foe" but do not mention them by name.

2. Verses 12–14 refer to the day of Judah's "adversity," "ruin," "distress," and "ordeal." The phrase in v 12 is especially strong, "on the day of their [the Judahites'] ruin," literally, "on the day of their perishing." This suggests a time when Judah was destroyed, which best fits the Babylonian attack. Furthermore, note the close parallel of Obad 13, "on the day of their ordeal," in Ezek 35:5, "at the time of their ordeal."

3. Verse 16 states that Judah/Jerusalem has drunk the cup of divine wrath. In light of the way the metaphor is employed elsewhere, it most naturally applies to the Babylonian destruction (see Excursus). Although the book does not explicitly mention the destruction of the temple, v 16 implies it. Also

the statement in v 17, that "(on Mount Zion) will be a holy place," intimates a future rebuilt temple.

4. The promise given in v 19 presupposes the loss of the territories of Ephraim, Samaria, and Gilead, which happened during the Assyrian campaigns of 732 and 722. Thus the book must postdate those events.

5. Although the reference in v 20 to the exiles of Israel and Jerusalem could apply to other periods, it most naturally points to the Babylonian exile.

6. The book accuses the Edomites of taking advantage of the crisis within Judah. According to vv 12–14, at the time of Judah's ruin they gloated, stole property (cf. v 5), and captured fugitives. Unlike other parts of the book that employ figurative language and imagery, these verses use realistic language and make specific accusations. Only if the Edomites actually engaged in such activities does the prophet's expression of shock and disbelief make sense. Therefore we should understand vv 12–14 as an accurate description of Edom's behavior rather than as the prophet's poetic imagination (*pace* Bartlett 1989: 154–55).

In fact, similar charges are made in other texts that refer to this period (Ezek 25:12–14; 35–36; Ps 137; Lam 4:21–22). Bartlett (1989: 151–57) calls into question the historical accuracy of these texts. To be sure, other narrative accounts of the Babylonian attacks provide no corroboration of Edom's involvement during this period. (2 Kgs 24:2 should not be emended to read "Edom" for MT "Aram"; see Cogan and Tadmor 1988.) Nevertheless, we need not doubt the historical and referential value of the above texts. They would have lacked any persuasive power, if they had not accurately referred to Edomite activity. Psalm 137 mentions both Edom and Babylon, and certainly the reference to Babylon is historically accurate. Furthermore, there is no reason to think that the author of Lam 4 falsely accused Edom of rejoicing over Zion's fall. The same observation applies to the charges that Ezekiel leveled against Edom, especially in light of the fact that the Latter Prophets do not uniformly speak of Edom's conduct (see above under "Edom in the Latter Prophets"). In other words, Ezekiel's anti-Edom material was not simply created by literary convention; it can only be explained as a prophetic response to Edom's historical actions, although, as the prophet emphasized, Edom was not alone in its anti-Judahite sentiments (cf. Ezek 25). The above four texts accuse Edom of the same types of anti-Judahite hostilities as the book of Obadiah: rejoicing and gloating over Judah's demise (Ezek 35–36; Ps 137; Lam 4); taking possession of Judah's property, although Ezekiel more explicitly refers to Edom's desire to occupy Judah's territory (Ezek 35–36); and giving Israelites over to the power of the sword (Ezek 35). A reference in the late second-century-B.C. book of 1 Esdras speaks of the Edomites burning the temple (4:45), perhaps under the influence of Ps 137:7; however, the other accounts and even 1 Esdras elsewhere (1:52 [55]) attribute the burning of the temple solely to Babylon.

Data from other sources assist us in reconstructing the historical situation. Recent archaeological work has revealed a growing Edomite presence in the Negeb during the seventh to early sixth centuries B.C. (see Beit-Arieh 1989; Bartlett 1989: 141–43; King 1993: 53–63). Edomite presence is indicated by several types of evidence coming from sites in the eastern Negeb between Beersheba and Arad. (a) The Arad ostraca testify to the Edomite threat. For example, ostracon 24, dated to early in the sixth century, contains an order that troops be sent from Arad and Qinah to Ramath-negeb for reinforcement "lest Edom come there" (Aharoni 1970; 1981: 46–49; Lindenberger 1994: 104–5). (b) An Edomite ostracon found at the fort of Horvat 'Uza gives a message that was sent by a high Edomite official to Blbl, probably the Edomite commander of the fort. The message instructs Blbl to give a supply of foodstuff to the messenger(s) bearing the letter (Beit-Arieh and Cresson 1985; cf. 1991). (c) An Edomite sanctuary was uncovered at Horvat Qitmit. (d) Edomite pottery and inscriptions with Edomite names have been found at several Negeb sites. This evidence shows that Edomites resided in the southern parts of Judah during the upheavals of the early sixth century. Thus they could very well have engaged in the activities that Obadiah and the other texts mention. Perhaps Edomite presence in the Negeb also provides the background of the statement in Obad 20: "and the exiles of Jerusalem who are in Sepharad will possess the cities of the Negeb." If so, the statement envisages that the returning exiles will retrieve the Negebite towns from Edomite control (cf. 1 Esdras 4:50). The process of Edomite settlement in southern Judah continued so that by the late fourth century B.C. the area was called "Idumea."

How should we account for Obadiah's tone of shock and disbelief at the Edomites' conduct? It is plausible to suppose that in the preceding century the relationship between Judah and Edom had become amicable. Although Zephaniah's oracles against the nations condemn the Transjordanian countries of Moab and Ammon, Edom is noticeably absent. Glazier-McDonald (1995) argues that its absence is significant, because it points to friendly relations between Edom and Judah during the last part of the seventh century. Perhaps by cooperating when Assyria's power was on the decline they hoped to exploit the trade routes to their mutual benefit. Even as late as 594/3 the governments of Edom and Judah were on good enough terms that the king of Edom was considering the prospect of joining Zedekiah's anti-Babylonian coalition (Jer 27). However, the coalition did not materialize or hold, because in 589 only Judah, Tyre, and apparently Ammon rebelled against Nebuchadnezzar (see Malamat 1987). Perhaps

Edom recognized that its survival required dissociation from Jerusalem, and therefore it took Jeremiah's advice and withdrew. In any case, Edom appears to have been spared from Nebuchadnezzar's campaigns (cf. Jer 40:11; Josephus *Ant.* X.9.7; Lindsay 1976).

If the supposition is correct that the relations between Edom and Judah had improved during the final decades of the seventh century and the first decade of the sixth century, then the Judahites could have expected Edomite support during the 587/6 catastrophe. When instead they experienced betrayal and hostility, Obadiah's expression of dismay and disbelief becomes understandable. From Edom's point of view, however, a pro-Babylonian stance, which Edom seems to have taken (cf. Obad 11), offered certain political and economic advantages. First, Edom was able thereby to guarantee the preservation of its Transjordanian state and its port of Elath. Second, the Edomites could secure permission to enlarge their landholdings in the Negeb and thus maintain an interest in the trade route passing through the Negeb to Philistia and the port of Gaza (cf. Lindsay 1976: 30–31). All things considered, what the book of Obadiah says regarding the activities of the Edomites within Judah points to the early exilic period as the historical background.

7. The terminus ad quem is the fall of Edom, which the book treats as a future event. Although the Nabonidus Chronicle is badly preserved in places, it appears to refer to a campaign of Nabonidus against Edom. According to the text's most likely reconstruction and interpretation, in December 553 Nabonidus on his way south through the Transjordan to Teima in Arabia "encamped [against? the land of E]dom," [... $^{kur}\acute{u}$]-*du-um-mu it-ta-du-ú* (Beaulieu 1989: 165–69; cf. Eph'al 1982: 185–88). Archaeology seems to attest to this campaign; the Edomite sites of Buseira, Tawilan, and Tell el-Kheleifeh give evidence of destruction apparently in the sixth century (cf. Bartlett 1989: 157–59). Thus Edom's existence as an independent state probably came to an end in the middle of the sixth century. However, there are signs of occupation continuing into the Persian period, which suggests that Nabonidus was interested in subjugation — rather than annihilation — in order to control the trade of the region. After the takeover of Babylon by Cyrus in 539, Edom most likely came under Persian rule (cf. Bartlett 1989: 163–74). During the Persian period the Nabateans migrated into Edom so that by the end of the fourth century they were securely established at Petra. The location of their original homeland is debated. Although southern Arabia is often favored, northeast Arabia and the Persian Gulf region seem equally possible (cf. Graf 1990; 1992).

Obad 7 speaks of Edom's covenant partners turning against the Edomites by expelling them from their homeland and establishing a place of foreigners in their stead. Many scholars identify the covenant partners as neighboring Arab tribes with whom Edom might have had commercial ties. However, in light of v 11, which indicates that the Edomites took the side of the Babylonians, it is more plausible to suppose that from the prophet's point of view the allies were the Babylonians (so Lindsay 1976; Bartlett 1989: 159–61; Bartlett earlier favored the hypothesis of Arab trading partners [1972]). Whether a formal treaty or an informal agreement, v 7 uses covenantal language to refer to what was no doubt a vassal-suzerain relationship rather than one of parity between Edom and Babylon. In addition to taking greedy advantage of Judah's distress, the Edomites apparently functioned as something like "a police force in Babylon's pay" by apprehending and handing over Judahite fugitives (Lindsay 1976: 29; cf. Ezek 35:5; Obad 14).

In 553 Babylon turned against Edom in fulfillment of Obadiah's prophecy; there is no need to see it as a *vaticinium ex eventu*, a prophecy after the fact. The specifics of Nabonidus's campaign are unknown. Presumably he drove out Edom's officials and set up his own governor. Perhaps some Edomites were deported. In any case, the kingdom of Edom came to an end, and its land eventually became "a place of foreigners."

The book of Obadiah fits best within the first half of the exilic period, between 587/6 and 553. The rhetorical nature of the book's language suggests that it was orally delivered, whether spoken first and later written down or written first and read aloud (cf. Conrad 1992). But were people to whom the prophecy could have been addressed living in Judah at the time? We should not think of Judah as totally depopulated by Babylon (see Janssen 1956). The biblical texts themselves state that some Judahites were left to remain in the land following the Babylonian deportations (2 Kgs 24:14; 25:12; Jer 39:10; 40:6). According to Jer 40:11–12, the Judahites who had fled to the Transjordan returned. In addition to the biblical data, archaeological work increasingly reveals the continuation of life in Judah during the exile, as illustrated by the following evidence (cf. Barkay 1992: 372–73): sites in the territory of Benjamin escaped the 587/6 destructions (Malamat 1987: 299–300); the Ketef Hinnom tombs indicate that people continued to live in Jerusalem and to bury their dead nearby along with precious artifacts (Barkay 1986); and perhaps the Hebrew cave inscriptions near Khirbet Beit Lei, east of Lachish, were written by a refugee fleeing from the Babylonians (so Cross 1970; Naveh [1963] prefers to date them ca. 700 B.C.). Also note the discussion of exilic material culture given by Lapp (1981: 81–101).

Is it possible to identify more precisely a setting in which Obadiah proclaimed his prophecy? A plausible setting is provided by the lamentation services held at the ruined temple site (so Wolff 1977; Ogden 1982; for a discussion, see Dicou 1994: 188–97, who also cites Kellermann in support of this view). Jeremiah 41:5 and especially Zech 7–8 indicate that lamentation services occurred regularly during the exilic period (cf. Janssen 1956: 94–104; Meyers and Meyers 1987:

386–89, 433–35; Williamson 1990). Perhaps the important fast of the Ninth of Ab in Jewish tradition has its roots in these exilic fasts. These occasions present the natural setting for the materials gathered in the book of Lamentations as well as for some exilic psalms (Pss 44; 74; 79; 102).

Obadiah's prophecy very well could be a prophetic response to exilic prayers and thus could function in a way similar to the statements made against Edom in Lam 4:21–22 (cf. Wolff 1977). On the basis of similarities in vocabulary, Ogden (1982) suggests that Obadiah responded to the communal lament expressed in Ps 137. Note especially the prayer of v 7:

> O Yahweh, remember *the day of Jerusalem* with respect to the Edomites,
> who were saying "Lay bare! Lay bare to its foundation!"

Obadiah's announcement of judgment upon Edom and his tenfold use of the word "day" to refer to the fall of Judah/Jerusalem (vv 11–14) make a fitting response to this kind of petition. Furthermore, as I note in the commentary, many of Obadiah's themes address the concerns expressed in the exilic laments.

To sum up: the original setting for the book of Obadiah can best be placed in Judah during the first half of the exilic period, and perhaps the book presents a prophetic response to the laments given at the ruined temple site in Jerusalem.

THEOLOGY AND RHETORICAL PURPOSE

The book of Obadiah illustrates some of the main types of discourse that one finds in the Latter Prophets: announcements of coming doom (vv 1–9), accusations (vv 10–14), warnings (vv 12–15), and promises of restoration (vv 16–21). (For introductory discussions with surveys of research, see Tucker 1978; 1985: 335–42.) The first three types listed are addressed to Edom and the fourth to Judah. Obadiah's discourse needs to be examined not only in terms of what it says, namely, its content, but also in terms of why it says what it does, namely, its rhetorical or persuasive function. That is to say, Obadiah, like other prophets, should be thought of as somewhat like an orator or preacher who attempted to persuade and influence others by what he said.

For discovering the rhetorical purpose of a given unit, the area of speech act theory is helpful (for discussions, see Houston 1993; Raabe 1995). Basically it seeks to determine an utterance's "illocutionary force" and "perlocutionary force." The former addresses the question "What is the prophet doing in saying this?" and suggests speech acts such as warning or promising. The latter addresses the question "What effect does the prophet seek to produce in the hearers by saying this?" and proposes effects such as sorrow or hope. Admittedly, these questions are difficult to answer, but plausible suggestions can be made in light of the nature of the language used and the proposed historical setting.

As noted above, the book has two grammatical addresses: Edom in vv 1–15 (= two-thirds of the book; 197 words and 455 syllables) and Judah in vv 16–21 (= one-third of the book; 93 words and 214 syllables). In light of the proposed historical setting, which sees the book as a prophetic response to the laments and prayers given at the ruined temple site, one assumes that the real, extratextual hearers were Judahites. Yet why does so much of the book grammatically address Edom? One might consider this simply an example of "apostrophe," that is, a literary device that addresses an absent party to make a point to the real hearers. In that case Ezekiel's speech to Mount Seir in chapter 35 would provide a parallel. However, vv 12–15, which address Edom with a series of exhortations followed by a motivation clause, represent persuasive speech rather than simply a vivid literary device. This style of persuasion suggests that the prophet actually intended to influence the Edomites. Moreover, the prophet's emphasis on Edom as Jacob's brother and his expression of shock at Edom's behavior would have had full effect only if he had meant for Edomites to hear or to hear of his words. To be sure, presumably only Judahites had any interest in attending the commemorations at the temple site. Yet reports of the prophet's pronouncements could easily have spread. Especially given that Edomites were present in southern Judah at the time, it does not stretch credulity to suppose that Obadiah's message was actually intended for the ears of Edomites as well as Judahites. (On the possibility that some of the other oracles against foreign nations were intended for non-Israelites, see Raabe 1995; cf. Jer 27.)

In light of the considerations mentioned above, we are ready to correlate the book's themes with their rhetorical purposes. In vv 1–9 Obadiah uses a variety of motifs to announce Edom's impending doom. Thereby the prophet places Edom under Yahweh's judgment, under the divine king's death sentence as it were (for this function of announcements of doom, see Houston 1993). The rhetorical purpose is to convince the Edomites that their defenses will be of no avail. None of the strengths that give Edom self-confidence and a sense of security can fend off the coming destruction: Edom's status among the nations (vv 1–2), inaccessible location in the mountains (vv 3–4), hiding places and wealth (vv 5–6), allies (v 7), wisdom (v 8), and military might (v 9).

In vv 10–11 the prophet grounds the coming destruction in Edom's past acts of "violence" against Jacob. Instead of defending its brother Jacob, Edom took the side of the attacking Babylonians. In light of vv 10–11 the reader takes vv 12–14, first of all, as further specifying these acts of violence: gloating over Judah's fall, looting Judah's property, and capturing Judah's fugitives. These acts manifest hostility against not only a "brother" but also Yahweh's own "people" (v 13) and therefore implicitly against Yahweh himself. Thus vv 10–14 function as accusations and give the reason for Edom's future doom.

Obadiah closely correlates Edom's crimes with its impending judgment. The standard of the judgment is the *lex talionis* principle stated in v 15: "Just as you

have done, it will be done to you; your deeds will return upon your own head."
In fact, the book of Obadiah presents a classic study of this standard at work.

1. Just as Edom gloated over Judah (vv 12–13), so it is already "despised" by the nations (vv 1–2) and will wear "shame" as its garment (v 10).
2. Just as Edom acted like "thieves" and "plunderers of the night" (vv 5, 13), so its own hidden treasures will be ransacked (vv 5–6).
3. Just as Edom betrayed its brother Jacob (vv 10, 12), so its own allies will "deceive" and betray it (v 7).
4. Just as Edom sought to "eliminate" Israel's "escapees" and "survivors" (v 14), so Israel like fire will consume Edom until it has no "survivors" (v 18). Also note the use of the root *krt* (to cut off) for the punishment in vv 9–10 and for the crime in v 14.

The correlations show that Edom's fall should be understood not as something occurring by mere happenstance but as a divine punishment, a punishment that mirrors the offense and therefore is deserved, appropriate, and just. (On this theme, see Miller 1982.) Because the punishment corresponds with Edom's sins, it reveals the retributive justice of God, the God of Israel who as "the Lord" (v 1) has claims on all the nations including Edom.

In addition to their function as accusations against Edom for its past crimes, vv 12–14 function as warnings or exhortations for Edom to stop its anti-Judahite hostilities. This second function is evident from their grammatical form as a series of eight vetitives, e.g., "But do not gaze upon the day of your brother, on the day of his adversity" (v 12). This series of vetitives is followed by a *kî*-clause (for) in v 15, which serves as a motivation clause:

For the day of Yahweh is near
against all the nations.
Just as you have done, it will be done to you;
your deeds will return upon your own head.

We may conceive of the rhetorical device in one of two ways: either the prophet imaginatively locates himself in the past, during or slightly before the time of Judah's catastrophe, or he projects the past into his present situation. Then he commands the Edomites not to engage in the activities of gloating, looting, and capturing fugitives. But what kind of sense does it make that a speaker would prohibit another party from doing something yesterday? By using vetitives instead of perfects to refer to the Edomite offenses, Obadiah can simultaneously accuse regarding the past and exhort regarding the present. In the latter role the vetitives together with the motivation clause of v 15 function as warnings for the Edomites, urgently calling them to cease from acting in these sorts of hostile ways before it is too late, "For the day of Yahweh is near."

So far we have seen that the prophet addresses Edom in different and yet inter-related ways. The utterances of vv 1–15 suggest several types of "illocutionary force": the prophet places Edom under God's coming judgment (vv 1–9); he accuses Edom of past crimes (vv 10–14); and he warns Edom to cease from its anti-Judahite hostilities before the impending day of Yahweh (vv 12–15). The corresponding "perlocutionary" effects would seem to include the following kinds of intended responses: Edom should become convinced that its defenses cannot protect it from the destruction to come; it should acknowledge its own guilt and the justice of Yahweh's sentence; and it should change its ways before it is too late.

One sees that vv 1–15 have a built-in tension. On the one hand, because of Edom's guilt its future doom is certain; vv 1–11 offer Edom no hope of escape. On the other hand, the nature of vv 12–15 implies that Edom's future remains open, that it can escape the day of Yahweh's universal condemnation, provided that it alters its policy and instead (by implication) sides with its brother Jacob and the God of Jacob. What would happen then the book does not say. Judging from the Jacob-Esau connection that Obadiah stresses, one might speculate concerning his answer: Edom would then benefit from the promise of blessing conveyed through Yahweh's chosen bearer of the promise (cf. Gen 27:29; 28:14; 33:10–11). Or on the basis of the next book in the canonical order, that of Jonah, one might think of Yahweh repenting from the decreed destruction. In any case, the divergent perspectives of a closed future and an open future are so tightly interwoven that one would do violence to the book's message by separating them or by emphasizing one at the expense of the other.

For Judahite hearers the pronouncement of judgment against Edom in vv 1–15 would have functioned as an indirect promise giving them hope for their future. The surprising hostilities of their neighbors and "brothers" will not go unpunished. The impending defeat of their most hostile neighbor will bring about the preliminary stage that is necessary for their future restoration. The promise of future restoration now becomes the central focus of the last third of the book, which directly addresses the Judahites (vv 16–21). In this section Edom also figures prominently, but it is treated from a different perspective. Whereas vv 1–15 create a tight nexus between Edom's doom and its own sins, vv 16–21 speak of Edom's fate in the context of Israel's restoration. The tables will be turned so that Israel will conquer Edom (v 18) and Zion will rule over Edom (v 21). Thus the first part announces Yahweh's judgment to Edom and thereby stresses his justice, while the second part announces Yahweh's promise to Judah and thereby reveals his commitment to his people.

The one party will experience woe and the other party weal. At first glance the speeches to Edom and to Judah appear to be mirror images of each other. Yet the promissory speech differs from the judgment speech in one crucial way: it is not grounded in or based on Judah's behavior. The prophet simply proclaims unconditionally Israel's future restoration. It has no other basis than Yahweh's undeserved commitment and faithfulness to Jacob and Zion.

Verse 16 begins the address to Judah by proclaiming that the Judahites/Jerusalemites "have drunk" the cup of God's wrath. Although the reason is not explicitly stated, one can reasonably infer from the exilic laments — to which Obadiah responded — that the prophet agreed with their confessions of sin. Such an inference also remains in keeping with the other cup-of-wrath texts (see Excursus). However, the prophet's goal was not to call the Judahites to repentance. They had already experienced Yahweh's just wrath, and, judging from the laments, the experience had broken their spirit and left them without hope as they struggled to survive in the face of powerful foes. He therefore performs the speech act of setting forth promises (i.e., "illocutionary force") in order to instill in them hope for their future life (i.e., "perlocutionary force").

In the prophet's address to Judah he attempts to convince the Judahite listeners of several things. First and foremost is the basic belief that Yahweh has not rejected his people or forgotten his promises to Jacob. In response to the exilic laments, such as those expressed in Ps 79 and Lam 5, he proclaims in v 16 that Zion's experience of Yahweh's wrath will not last forever nor will the nations who do not acknowledge Yahweh maintain their position of power in the world and over his people. Although the cup of wrath began with Zion, it will soon move to the nations; they are not exempt from Yahweh's royal judgment (cf. Jer 25:15–29). The nations, which first serve as Yahweh's agent to judge Zion (v 11) and Edom (vv 1, 7), then receive judgment themselves.

Second, Obadiah stresses that Judah's future will not simply be a continuation of the present status quo, for Yahweh will reverse the fortunes of his people. Although the nations will drink the full measure of the cup of wrath on the day of Yahweh (vv 15–16), Zion will be delivered from the coming wrath and will become a holy place, never again to be profaned by the nations (v 17a). Furthermore, Israel will be restored, including the northern tribes (v 18) and the exiles (v 20), and it will repossess the full extent of its allotted territories (vv 17b, 19–20).

Third, lest the Judahites fear that Edom will rise again and oppress them (cf. Mal 1:4), Obadiah precludes the possibility with two pictures: Israel like fire will so thoroughly consume Edom that it will have no remnant (v 18), and Zion will rule over Edom (v 21).

Finally, the book ends appropriately with a climactic promise: "the kingship will belong to Yahweh" (v 21). Although it appeared to the Judahites that other nations were currently exercising dominion, the prophet sought to lead his hearers from despair to hope in their God by announcing the future definitive manifestation of Yahweh's rule over the whole world. This promise not only brings the book to closure, but it expresses the basic presupposition of Obadiah's entire vision. In fact, the book can be seen as simply unfolding and unpacking what Yahweh's future rule will mean for Edom, the nations, Zion, and Israel.

BIBLIOGRAPHY

◆

Aalders, G. C.
  1958   *Obadja en Jona*. COut. Kampen: J. H. Kok.
Ackroyd, P. R.
  1968   *Exile and Restoration: A Study of Hebrew Thought of the Sixth Century B.C.* OTL. London: SCM.
  1992   "Obadiah, Book of." *ABD* 5: 2–4.
Adams, W. J., Jr., and Adams, L. La Mar.
  1977   "Language Drift and the Dating of Biblical Passages." *HS* 18: 160–64.
Aejmelaeus, A.
  1986a   "Function and Interpretation of *ky* in Biblical Hebrew." *JBL* 105: 193–209.
  1986b   *The Traditional Prayer in the Psalms*. BZAW 167. Berlin: Walter de Gruyter.
Aharoni, Y.
  1970   "Three Hebrew Ostraca from Arad." *BASOR* 197: 16–42.
  1973   *Beer-Sheba I: Excavations at Tel Beer-Sheba 1969–1971 Seasons*. Tel Aviv: Tel Aviv University.
  1981   *Arad Inscriptions*. Judaean Desert Studies. Trans. J. Ben-Or, ed. and rev. A. F. Rainey. Jerusalem: Israel Exploration Society.
Albright, W. F.
  1944   "The Oracles of Balaam." *JBL* 63: 207–33.
Allen, L. C.
  1976   *The Books of Joel, Obadiah, Jonah and Micah*. NICOT. Grand Rapids: Eerdmans.

Alonso Schökel, L.
1988   A Manual of Hebrew Poetics. Trans. A Graffy. Subsidia biblica 11. Rome: Biblical Institute.

Alter, R.
1985   The Art of Biblical Poetry. New York: Basic Books.

Andersen, F. I.
1970   The Hebrew Verbless Clause in the Pentateuch. SBLMS 14. Nashville: Abingdon.
1974   The Sentence in Biblical Hebrew. Janua linguarum, Series practica 231. The Hague: Mouton.

Andersen, F. I., and Forbes, A. D.
1983   "'Prose Particle' Counts of the Hebrew Bible." Pp. 165–83 in The Word of the Lord Shall Go Forth: Essays in Honor of David Noel Freedman in Celebration of His Sixtieth Birthday, ed. C. L. Meyers and M. O'Connor. Winona Lake: Eisenbrauns.
1986   Spelling in the Hebrew Bible. BibOr 41. Rome: Biblical Institute.

Andersen, F. I., and Freedman, D. N.
1980   Hosea. AB 24. Garden City: Doubleday.
1989   Amos. AB 24A. New York: Doubleday.

Armerding, C. E.
1985   "Obadiah." Pp. 335–57 in The Expositor's Bible Commentary. Vol. 7. Ed. F. E. Gaebelein. Grand Rapids: Zondervan.

Astour, M. C.
1976   "Sepharad." IDBSup: 807.

Aufrecht, W. E.
1989   A Corpus of Ammonite Inscriptions. Ancient Near Eastern Texts and Studies 4. Lewiston: Edwin Mellen.

Austin, J.
1962   How To Do Things With Words. Oxford: Clarendon.

Bach, R.
1962   Die Aufforderungen zur Flucht und zum Kampf im alttestamentlichen Prophetenspruch. WMANT 9. Neukirchen: Neukirchener.

Baker, D. W.
1988   "Obadiah." Pp. 17–44 in Obadiah, Jonah, Micah. TOTC 23a. Downers Grove: Inter-Varsity.

Ball, I. J., Jr.
1988   A Rhetorical Study of Zephaniah. Berkeley: BIBAL.

Baloian, B. E.
1992   Anger in the Old Testament. American University Studies Series 7, Theology and Religion 99. New York: Peter Lang.

Barkay, G.

1986   *Ketef Hinnom: A Treasure Facing Jerusalem's Walls.* Catalogue No. 274. Jerusalem: Israel Museum.

1992   The Iron Age II–III. Pp. 302–73 in *The Archaeology of Ancient Israel,* ed. A. Ben-Tor. Trans. R. Greenberg. New Haven: Yale University.

Barr, J.

1989   *The Variable Spellings of the Hebrew Bible.* Oxford: Oxford University.

Barré, M. L.

1986   "The Meaning of *l' 'šybnw* in Amos 1:3–2:6." *JBL* 105: 611–31.

Bartelt, A. H.

1991   *Style and Structure in Prophetic Rhetoric: Isaiah 2–12.* Ph.D. diss., The University of Michigan (Winona Lake: Eisenbrauns, forthcoming).

Barthélemy, D.

1986   *Critique textuelle de l'Ancien Testament 2: Isaïe, Jérémie, Lamentations.* OBO 50/2. Fribourg: Éditions Universitaires.

1992   *Critique textuelle de l'Ancien Testament 3: Ézéchiel, Daniel et les 12 Prophètes.* OBO 50/3. Fribourg: Éditions Universitaires.

Barthélemy, D., et al.

1980   *Prophetical Books II: Ezekiel, Daniel, Twelve Minor Prophets.* Preliminary and Interim Report on the Hebrew Old Testament Text Project 5. New York: United Bible Societies.

Bartlett, J. R.

1969   "The Land of Seir and the Brotherhood of Edom." *JTS* 20: 1–20.

1972   "The Rise and Fall of the Kingdom of Edom." *PEQ* 104: 26–37.

1989   *Edom and the Edomites.* JSOTSup 77. Sheffield: JSOT.

Bauer, H., and Leander, P.

1962   *Historische Grammatik der hebräischen Sprache des Alten Testamentes.* Hildesheim: Georg Olms.

Baumann, A.

1978   "*dāmāh II.*" *TDOT* 3: 260–65.

Beaulieu, P. -A.

1989   *The Reign of Nabonidus, King of Babylon, 556–539 B.C.* YNER 10. New Haven: Yale University.

Beit-Arieh, I.

1989   "New Data on the Relationship between Judah and Edom toward the End of the Iron Age." Pp. 125–31 in *Recent Excavations in Israel: Studies in Iron Age Archaeology.* AASOR 49, ed. S. Gitin and W. G. Dever. Winona Lake: Eisenbrauns.

Beit-Arieh, I., and Cresson, B. C.
  1985   "An Edomite Ostracon from Ḥorvat 'Uza." *TA* 12: 96–101.
  1991   "Ḥorvat 'Uza: A Fortified Outpost on the Eastern Negev Border." *BA* 54: 126–35.
Bekel, H.
  1907   "Ein vorexilisches Orakel über Edom in der Klageliederstrophe: Die gemeinsame Quelle von Obadja 1–9 und Jeremiah 49: 7–22." *TSK* 80: 315–43.
Benz, F. L.
  1972   *Personal Names in the Phoenician and Punic Inscriptions.* Studia Pohl 8. Rome: Biblical Institute.
Ben Zvi, E.
  1991   *A Historical-Critical Study of the Book of Zephaniah.* BZAW 198. Berlin: Walter de Gruyter.
  1993   "Historical Audiences and Prophetic Texts: Obadiah 19–21." Paper presented at the American Academy of Religion/Society of Biblical Literature annual meeting in Washington, D.C.
Bergman, J., and Ottosson, M.
  1974   "'ereṣ." *TDOT* 1: 388–405.
Berlin, A.
  1985   *The Dynamics of Biblical Parallelism.* Bloomington: Indiana University.
  1992   "Zephaniah's Oracle against the Nations and an Israelite Cultural Myth." Paper presented at the American Academy of Religion/Society of Biblical Literature annual meeting in San Francisco.
  1994   *Zephaniah.* AB 25A. New York: Doubleday.
Bewer, J. A.
  1911   *A Critical and Exegetical Commentary on Obadiah and Joel.* ICC. Edinburgh: T. & T. Clark.
Beyer, K.
  1984   *Die aramäischen Texte vom Toten Meer.* Göttingen: Vandenhoeck & Ruprecht.
Bič, M.
  1951   "Ein verkanntes Thronbesteigungsfestorakel im Alten Testament." *ArOr* 19: 568–78.
  1953   "Zur Problematik des Buches Obadja." VTSup 1: 11–25.
Black, M.
  1962   *Models and Metaphors: Studies in Language and Philosophy.* Ithaca: Cornell University.
  1979   "More About Metaphor." Pp. 19–43 in *Metaphor and Thought,* ed. A. Ortony. Cambridge: Cambridge University.

Boadt, L.
1984   *Reading the Old Testament: An Introduction.* New York: Paulist.
Bonnard, P. -E.
1972   "Abdias." *DBSup* 8: 693–701.
Borowski, O.
1989   "The Negev — The Southern Stage for Biblical History." *BRev* 5:
        40–44.
Bourguet, D.
1987   *Des métaphores de Jérémie.* EBib 9. Paris: J. Gabalda.
Braver, A. J.
1973   "The Name ʿbdyh-ʿbdyhw: Its Punctuation and Explanation." *Beth
        Mikra* 54: 418–19 (Hebrew), 427 (English summary).
Bretón, S.
1987   *Vocación y misión: Formulario profético.* AnBib 111. Rome: Bibli-
        cal Institute.
Brettler, M. Z.
1989   *God Is King: Understanding an Israelite Metaphor.* JSOTSup 76.
        Sheffield: JSOT.
Briggs, C. A.
1907   *A Critical and Exegetical Commentary on the Book of Psalms.* Vol.
        2. ICC. Edinburgh: T. & T. Clark.
Bright, J.
1965   *Jeremiah.* AB 21. Garden City: Doubleday.
Brongers, H. A.
1969   "Der Zornesbecher." *OTS* 15: 177–92.
1973   "Die Partikel *lĕmaʿan* in der biblisch-hebräischen Sprache." *OTS*
        18: 84–96.
1981   "Some Remarks on the Biblical Particle *hălōʾ*." *OTS* 21: 177–89.
Brownlee, W. H.
1979   *The Midrash Pesher of Habakkuk.* SBLMS 24. Missoula: Scholars.
Cannon, W. W.
1927   "Israel and Edom: The Oracle of Obadiah." *Theology* 15: 129–40,
        191–200.
Carroll, R. P.
1990   "Obadiah." Pp. 496–97 in *A Dictionary of Biblical Interpretation,*
        ed. R. J. Coggins and J. L. Houlden. London: SCM.
Caspari, C. P.
1842   *Der Prophet Obadja.* Leipzig: R. Beyer.
Cathcart, K. J.
1992   "Day of Yahweh." *ABD* 2: 84–85.

Cathcart, K. J., and Gordon, R. P.
1989   *The Targum of the Minor Prophets.* The Aramaic Bible 14. Wilmington: Michael Glazier.

Černý, L.
1948   *The Day of Yahweh and Some Relevant Problems.* Prague: Nákladem Filosofické Fakulty University Karlovy.

Childs, B. S.
1979   *Introduction to the Old Testament as Scripture.* Philadelphia: Fortress.

Clark, D. J., and Mundhenk, N.
1982   *A Translator's Handbook on the Books of Obadiah and Micah.* New York: United Bible Societies.

Clifford, R. J.
1972   *The Cosmic Mountain in Canaan and the Old Testament.* HSM 4. Cambridge: Harvard University.

Coelho Dias, G. J. A.
1990   "Filisteus em Canaã, uma cultura desaparecida?" *Did* 20: 199–210.

Cogan, M., and Tadmor, H.
1988   *II Kings.* AB 11. New York: Doubleday.

Condamin, A.
1900   "L'unité d'Abdias." *RB* 9: 261–68.

Conrad, E. W.
1992   "Heard But Not Seen: The Representation of 'Books' in the Old Testament." *JSOT* 54: 45–59.

Craigie, P. C.
1976   *The Book of Deuteronomy.* NICOT. Grand Rapids: Eerdmans.
1983   *Psalms 1–50.* Word Biblical Commentary 19. Waco: Word.
1984   *Twelve Prophets.* Vol. 1. Philadelphia: Westminster.

Cresson, B. C.
1963   *Israel and Edom: A Study of the Anti-Edom Bias in Old Testament Religion.* Ph.D. diss., Duke University.
1972   "The Condemnation of Edom in Postexilic Judaism." Pp. 125–48 in *The Use of the Old Testament in the New and Other Essays: Studies in Honor of William Franklin Stinespring,* ed. J. M. Efird. Durham: Duke University.

Cross, F. M.
1953   "The Council of Yahweh in Second Isaiah." *JNES* 12: 274–77.
1966   "An Aramaic Inscription from Daskyleion." *BASOR* 184: 7–10.
1970   "The Cave Inscriptions from Khirbet Beit Lei." Pp. 299–306 in *Near Eastern Archaeology in the Twentieth Century: Essays in Honor of Nelson Glueck,* ed. J. A. Sanders. Garden City: Doubleday.
1988   "A Report on the Samaria Papyri." *VTSup* 40: 17–26.

Culley, R. C.
1970   "Metrical Analysis of Classical Hebrew Poetry." Pp. 12–28 in *Essays on the Ancient Semitic World*. Toronto Semitic Texts and Studies, ed. J. W. Wevers and D. B. Redford. Toronto: University of Toronto.

Dahood, M.
1965   *Psalms I*. AB 16. Garden City: Doubleday.
1970   *Psalms III*. AB 17A. Garden City: Doubleday.

Dandamayev, M. A.
1984   *Slavery in Babylonia: From Nabopolassar to Alexander the Great (626–331 B.C.)*. Rev. ed. Trans. V. A. Powell. De Kalb: Northern Illinois University.
1992   "Slavery: Ancient Near East." *ABD* 6: 58–62.

Davies, E. W.
1989   "Land: Its Rights and Privileges." Pp. 349–69 in *The World of Ancient Israel: Sociological, Anthropological and Political Perspectives*, ed. R. E. Clements. Cambridge: Cambridge University.

Davies, G. I.
1977   "A New Solution to a Crux in Obadiah 7." *VT* 27: 484–87.

Davis, J. D.
1972   *Davis Dictionary of the Bible*. 4th rev. ed. Grand Rapids: Baker [1st ed. 1898].

Deissler, A.
1984   *Zwölf Propheten II: Obadja, Jona, Micha, Nahum, Habakuk*. Würzburg: Echter.

Delitzsch, F.
1851   "Wann weissagte Obadja?" *Zeitschrift für die lutherische Theologie und Kirche* 12: 91–102.
1877   *Isaiah I and II*. Trans. J. Martin. Repr. Grand Rapids: Eerdmans, 1976.

Del Olmo Lete, G.
1981   *Mitos y leyendas de Canaan según la tradición de Ugarit*. Madrid: Cristiandad.

De Vries, S. J.
1975   *Yesterday, Today, and Tomorrow: Time and History in the Old Testament*. Grand Rapids: Eerdmans.

Dick, M. B.
1984   "A Syntactic Study of the Book of Obadiah." *Semitics* 9: 1–29.

Dicou, B.
1994   *Edom, Israel's Brother and Antagonist: The Role of Edom in Biblical Prophecy and Story*. JSOTSup 169. Sheffield: JSOT.

Dohmen, C., and Rick, D.
　　1993　　"r'." *TWAT* 7: 582–612.
Dothan, M.
　　1992　　"Ashdod." *ABD* 1: 477–82.
Driver, G. R.
　　1957　　"Difficult Words in the Hebrew Prophets." Pp. 52–72 in *Studies in Old Testament Prophecy, Presented to Theodore H. Robinson*, ed. H. H. Rowley. Edinburgh: T. & T. Clark.
Duhm, B.
　　1911　　"Anmerkungen zu den Zwölf Propheten. VIII Buch Obadja." *ZAW* 31: 175–78.
Edelkoort, A. H.
　　1946–1947　　"De profetie van Obadja." *NedTTs* 1: 276–93.
Eising, H.
　　1980　　"ḥayil." *TDOT* 4: 348–55.
　　1986　　"ne'um." *TWAT* 5: 119–23.
Eissfeldt, O.
　　1965　　*The Old Testament: An Introduction*. Trans. P. R. Ackroyd. New York: Harper & Row.
　　1974　　"'ādôn; 'ădōnāi." *TDOT* 1: 59–72.
Elowsky, J.
　　1992　　*The Annals of Obadiah: A Record of the Wars and Peace Treaties in the History of Its Interpretation*. Master of Sacred Theology thesis, Concordia Seminary, St. Louis.
Emerton, J. A.
　　1982　　"New Light on Israelite Religion: The Implications of the Inscriptions from Kuntillet 'Ajrud." *ZAW* 94: 2–20.
Eph'al, I.
　　1982　　*The Ancient Arabs: Nomads on the Borders of the Fertile Crescent, 9th–5th Centuries B.C.* Jerusalem: Magnes.
Erlandsson, S.
　　1970　　*The Burden of Babylon: A Study of Isaiah 13:2–14:23.* ConBOT 4. Lund: Gleerup.
Esse, D. L.
　　1992　　"Ashkelon." *ABD* 1: 487–90.
Everson, A. J.
　　1974　　"The Days of Yahweh." *JBL* 93: 329–37.
Ewald, G. H. A. von.
　　1876　　*Commentary on the Prophets of the Old Testament*. Vol. 2. Trans. J. F. Smith. London: Williams and Norgate.
Fabry, H. -J.
　　1989　　"ṣar I." *TWAT* 6: 1113–22.

Fishbane, M.
    1970   "The Treaty Background of Amos 1:11 and Related Matters." *JBL* 89: 313–18.

Fitzmyer, J. A.
    1971   *The Genesis Apocryphon of Qumran Cave I: A Commentary.* 2nd rev. ed. BibOr 18A. Rome: Biblical Institute.

Fitzsimmonds, F. S.
    1982   "Wine and Strong Drink." Pp. 1254–55 in *New Bible Dictionary.* 2nd ed. Ed. J. D. Douglas, N. Hillyer, et al. Leicester: Inter-Varsity.

Fohrer, G.
    1966   "Die Sprüche Obadjas." Pp. 81–93 in *Studia Biblica et Semitica: T. C. Vriezen dedicata.* Wageningen: H. Veenman & Zonen.

Fowler, J. D.
    1988   *Theophoric Personal Names in Ancient Hebrew: A Comparative Study.* JSOTSup 49. Sheffield: JSOT.

Freedman, D. N.
    1960   "Archaic Forms in Early Hebrew Poetry." *ZAW* 72: 101–7.
    1972   "Acrostics and Metrics in Hebrew Poetry." *HTR* 65: 367–92.
    1985   "Prose Particles in the Poetry of the Primary History." Pp. 49–62 in *Biblical and Related Studies Presented to Samuel Iwry,* ed. A. Kort and S. Morschauser. Winona Lake: Eisenbrauns.
    1986   "Acrostic Poems in the Hebrew Bible: Alphabetic and Otherwise." *CBQ* 48: 408–31.

Fretheim, T. E.
    1984   *The Suffering of God: An Old Testament Perspective.* OBT. Philadelphia: Fortress.
    1988   "The Repentance of God: A Key to Evaluating Old Testament God-Talk." *HBT* 10: 47–70.

Frey, H.
    1948   *Das Buch der Kirche in der Weltwende: Die kleinen nachexilischen Propheten.* BAT 24. Stuttgart: Calwer.

Frymer-Kensky, T.
    1980   "Tit For Tat: The Principle of Equal Retribution in Near Eastern and Biblical Law." *BA* 43: 230–34.

Gammie, J. G.
    1989   *Holiness in Israel.* OBT. Minneapolis: Fortress.

Gelston, A.
    1987   *The Peshiṭta of the Twelve Prophets.* Oxford: Clarendon.

Gilse, J. van.
    1913   "Tijdsbepaling der profetie van Obadja." *NTT* 2: 293–313.

Gitin, S.
 1987 "Urban Growth and Decline at Ekron in the Iron II Period." *BA* 50: 206–22.
Glazier-McDonald, B.
 1987 *Malachi: The Divine Messenger.* SBLDS 98. Atlanta: Scholars.
 1995 "Edom in the Prophetical Corpus." Pp. 23–32 in *You Shall Not Abhor An Edomite For He Is Your Brother: Edom and Seir in History and Tradition*, ed. D. V. Edelman. Archaeology and Biblical Studies 3. Atlanta: Scholars.
Glück, J. J.
 1970 "Paronomasia in Biblical Literature." *Semitics* 1: 50–78.
Glueck, N.
 1940 *The Other Side of the Jordan.* New Haven: American Schools of Oriental Research.
Goldenberg, G.
 1991 "On Direct Speech and the Hebrew Bible." Pp. 79–96 in *Studies in Hebrew and Aramaic Syntax Presented to Professor J. Hoftijzer on the Occasion of His Sixty-Fifth Birthday*, ed. K. Jongeling, H. L. Murre-Van den Berg, and L. van Rompay. Studies in Semitic Languages and Linguistics 17. Leiden: E. J. Brill.
Good, R. M.
 1983 *The Sheep of His Pasture: A Study of the Hebrew Noun ʿAm(m) and Its Semitic Cognates.* HSM 29. Chico: Scholars.
Görg, M.
 1975 "*bāzāh.*" *TDOT* 2: 60–65.
 1990 "*yāšab.*" *TDOT* 6: 420–38.
Gowan, D. E.
 1975 *When Man Becomes God: Humanism and Hybris in the Old Testament.* Pittsburgh: Pickwick.
 1986 *Eschatology in the Old Testament.* Philadelphia: Fortress.
Graf, D. F.
 1990 "The Origin of the Nabataeans." *ARAM* 2: 45–75.
 1992 "Nabateans." *ABD* 4: 970–73.
Gray, J.
 1953 "The Diaspora of Israel and Judah in Obadiah v. 20." *ZAW* 65: 53–59.
 1965 *The Legacy of Canaan: The Ras Shamra Texts and Their Relevance to the Old Testament.* 2nd rev. ed. VTSup 5. Leiden: E. J. Brill.
Greenberg, M.
 1983 *Ezekiel 1–20.* AB 22. Garden City: Doubleday.
 1986 "What Are Valid Criteria for Determining Inauthentic Matter in Ezekiel?" Pp. 123–35 in *Ezekiel and His Book: Textual and Literary*

Criticism and Their Interrelation, ed. J. Lust. BETL 74. Leuven: Leuven University.

Greene, J. T.
1989   *The Role of the Messenger and Message in the Ancient Near East.* BJS 169. Atlanta: Scholars.

Gressmann, H.
1929   *Der Messias.* FRLANT 43. Göttingen: Vandenhoeck & Ruprecht.

Gröndahl, F.
1967   *Die Personennamen der Texte aus Ugarit.* Studia Pohl 1. Rome: Biblical Institute.

Grossberg, D.
1989   *Centripetal and Centrifugal Structures in Biblical Poetry.* SBLMS 39. Atlanta: Scholars.

Gruber, M. I.
1980   *Aspects of Nonverbal Communication in the Ancient Near East.* Studia Pohl 12/2. Rome: Biblical Institute.

Gusmani, R.
1964   *Lydisches Wörterbuch.* Heidelberg: Carl Winter.

Haag, H.
1980   "ḥāmās." *TDOT* 4: 478–87.

Haak, R. D.
1992   *Habakkuk.* VTSup 44. Leiden: E. J. Brill.

Habel, N. C.
1985   *The Book of Job: A Commentary.* OTL. Philadelphia: Westminster.

Hadley, J. M.
1987   "Some Drawings and Inscriptions on Two Pithoi from Kuntillet 'Ajrud." *VT* 37: 180–213.

Halévy, J.
1907   "Recherches bibliques: Le livre d'Obadia." *RevSém* 15: 165–83.

Haller, M.
1925   "Edom im Urteil der Propheten." Pp. 109–17 in *Vom Alten Testament* (Festschrift for Karl Marti). BZAW 41. Ed. K. Budde. Giessen: Töpelmann.

Hallo, W. M.
1983   "The First Purim." *BA* 46: 19–29.

Hals, R. M.
1989   *Ezekiel.* FOTL 19. Grand Rapids: Eerdmans.

Hamp, V.
1978   "gānab." *TDOT* 3: 39–45.

Hanfmann, G. M. A., et al.
1983   *Sardis from Prehistoric to Roman Times: Results of the Archaeological Exploration of Sardis 1958–1975.* Cambridge: Harvard.

Hanson, A. T.
1957   *The Wrath of the Lamb.* London: S.P.C.K.

Haran, M.
1968   "Observations on the Historical Background of Amos 1:2–2:6." *IEJ* 18: 201–12.
1985   "Book Size and the Device of Catch-Lines in the Biblical Canon." *JJS* 36: 1–11.

Hart, S.
1986   "Selaʿ: The Rock of Edom?" *PEQ* 118: 91–95.

Hasel, G. F.
1974   *The Remnant: The History and Theology of the Remnant Idea from Genesis to Isaiah.* Andrews University Monographs, Studies in Religion 5. Berrien Springs: Andrews University.
1984   "*kārat.*" *TWAT* 4: 355–67.
1991   *Understanding the Book of Amos: Basic Issues in Current Interpretations.* Grand Rapids: Baker.

Hauer, C. E.
1980   "David's Battles." *CJ* 6: 150–54.

Hayes, J. H.
1963   "The Tradition of Zion's Inviolability." *JBL* 82: 419–26.

Held, M.
1969   "Rhetorical Questions in Ugaritic and Biblical Hebrew." *EI* 9: 71–79.

Herion, G. A.
1992   "Wrath of God (OT)." *ABD* 6: 989–96.

Herr, L. G.
1993   "What Ever Happened to the Ammonites?" *BARev* 19: 26–35, 68.

Hill, A. E.
1983   "Dating the Book of Malachi: A Linguistic Reexamination." Pp. 77–89 in *The Word of the Lord Shall Go Forth: Essays in Honor of David Noel Freedman in Celebration of His Sixtieth Birthday*, ed. C. L. Meyers and M. O'Connor. Winona Lake: Eisenbrauns.

Hillers, D. R.
1964   *Treaty-Curses and the Old Testament Prophets.* BibOr 16. Rome: Biblical Institute.
1972   *Lamentations.* AB 7A. Garden City: Doubleday.
1983   "*Hôy* and *Hôy*-Oracles: A Neglected Syntactic Aspect." Pp. 185–88 in *The Word of the Lord Shall Go Forth: Essays in Honor of David Noel Freedman in Celebration of His Sixtieth Birthday*, eds. C. L. Meyers and M. O'Connor. Winona Lake: Eisenbrauns.

Hitzig, F.
  1838   *Die zwölf kleinen Propheten.* KEHAT 1. Leipzig: Weidmannsche Buchhandlung.
Hoffmann, Y.
  1972   "Edom as a Symbol of Wickedness in the Prophetic Literature." Pp. 76–89 in *Bible and Jewish History: Studies in Bible and Jewish History Dedicated to the Memory of Jacob Liver*, ed. B. Uffenheimer. Tel Aviv: Tel Aviv University (Hebrew with English summary).
  1981   "The Day of the Lord as a Concept and a Term in the Prophetic Literature." ZAW 93: 37–50.
Hoftijzer, J.
  1973   "The Nominal Clause Reconsidered." *VT* 23: 446–510.
Holladay, W. L.
  1986   *Jeremiah 1.* Hermeneia. Philadelphia: Fortress.
  1989   *Jeremiah 2.* Hermeneia. Minneapolis: Fortress.
Homès-Fredericq, D.
  1987   "Possible Phoenician Influences in Jordan in the Iron Age." Pp. 89–96 in *Studies in the History and Archaeology of Jordan III*, ed. A. Hadidi. Amman: Department of Antiquities; London: Routledge & Kegan Paul.
Honeyman, A. M.
  1936   "Hebrew *sap* 'Basin, Goblet.'" *JTS* 37: 56–59.
Houston, W.
  1993   "What Did the Prophets Think They Were Doing? Speech Acts and Prophetic Discourse in the Old Testament." *Biblical Interpretation* 1: 167–88.
Huesman, J.
  1956   "Finite Uses of the Infinitive Absolute." *Bib* 37: 271–95.
Huffmon, H. B.
  1992   "Lex Talionis." *ABD* 4: 321–22.
Hummel, H. D.
  1964   "The Old Testament Basis of Typological Interpretation." *BR* 9: 38–50.
  1979   *The Word Becoming Flesh: An Introduction to the Origin, Purpose, and Meaning of the Old Testament.* St. Louis: Concordia Publishing House.
Isopescul, S. O.
  1913   "Historisch-kritische Einleitung zur Weissagung des Abdias." *WZKM* 27: 141–62.
  1914   "Übersetzung und Auslegung des Buches Abdiae." *WZKM* 28: 149–81.

Janssen, E.
1956   *Juda in der Exilszeit: Ein Beitrag zur Frage der Entstehung des Judentums.* FRLANT 69. Göttingen: Vandenhoeck & Ruprecht.

Jenni, E.
1967   "Faktitiv und Kausativ von *'bd* 'zugrunde gehen.'" Pp. 143–57 in *Hebräische Wortforschung: Festschrift zum 80. Geburtstag von Walter Baumgartner.* VTSup 16. Leiden: E. J. Brill.

Jepsen, A.
1980   "*ḥāzāh.*" *TDOT* 4: 280–90.

Johnson, A. R.
1962   *The Cultic Prophet in Ancient Israel.* Cardiff: University of Wales.

Johnson, M., ed.
1981   *Philosophical Perspectives on Metaphor.* Minneapolis: University of Minnesota.

Jongeling, K.
1991   "On the VSO Character of Hebrew." Pp. 103–11 in *Studies in Hebrew and Aramaic Syntax Presented to Professor J. Hoftijzer on the Occasion of His Sixty-Fifth Birthday,* ed. K. Jongeling, H. L. Murre-Van den Berg, and L. van Rompay. Studies in Semitic Languages and Linguistics 17. Leiden: E. J. Brill.

Joüon, P.
1920   "Études de morphologie hébraïque." *Bib* 1: 353–71.
1991   *A Grammar of Biblical Hebrew.* Trans. and rev. T. Muraoka. Subsidia biblica 14. Rome: Biblical Institute.

Kaiser, O.
1975   *Introduction to the Old Testament.* Trans. J. Sturdy. Minneapolis: Augsburg.

Kalluveettil, P.
1982   *Declaration and Covenant.* AnBib 88. Rome: Biblical Institute.

Katzenstein, H. J.
1992   "Gaza (Prehellenistic)." *ABD* 2: 912–15.

Kaufman, S. A.
1977   "An Assyro-Aramaic *egirtu ša šulmu.*" Pp. 119–27 in *Essays on the Ancient Near East in Memory of Jacob Joel Finkelstein.* Memoirs of the Connecticut Academy of Arts and Sciences 19, ed. M. de Jong Ellis. Hamden: Archon Books.

Kedar-Kopfstein, B.
1993   "*śārîd.*" *TWAT* 7: 879–82.

Keil, C. F.
1888   *Die zwölf kleinen Propheten.* Leipzig: Dörffling und Franke. Translation, *Minor Prophets.* Trans. J. Martin. Keil and Delitzsch Commentary on the Old Testament 10. Grand Rapids: Eerdmans, 1977.

Keller, C. -A.
    1965   "Abdias." Pp. 251–62 in *Commentaire de l'Ancien Testament* 11a. Neuchâtel: Delachaux & Niestlé.

Kelso, J. L.
    1948   *The Ceramic Vocabulary of the Old Testament.* BASORSup 5–6. New Haven: American Schools of Oriental Research.

Kennedy, J. M.
    1992   "Obadiah." *ABD* 5: 1–2.

King, P. J.
    1993   *Jeremiah: An Archaeological Companion.* Louisville: Westminster/ John Knox.

Kingsbury, E. C.
    1964   "The Prophets and the Council of Yahweh." *JBL* 88: 279–86.

Kitchen, K. A.
    1992   "The Egyptian Evidence on Ancient Jordan." Pp. 21–34 in *Early Edom and Moab: The Beginning of the Iron Age in Southern Jordan,* ed. P. Bienkowski. Sheffield Archaeological Monographs 7. Sheffield: J. R. Collis Publications.

Klein, R. W.
    1968   "The Day of the Lord." *CTM* 39: 517–25.
    1979   *Israel in Exile: A Theological Interpretation.* OBT. Philadelphia: Fortress.

Klopfenstein, M. A.
    1972   *Scham und Schande nach dem Alten Testament.* ATANT 62. Zürich: Theologischer.

Knauf, E. A.
    1992a   "Teman." *ABD* 6: 347–48.
    1992b   "Uz." *ABD* 6: 770–71.

Knauf, E. A., and Lenzen, C. J.
    1987   "Edomite Copper Industry." Pp. 83–88 in *Studies in the History and Archaeology of Jordan III,* ed. A. Hadidi. Amman: Department of Antiquities; London: Routledge & Kegan Paul.

Koch, K.
    1955   "Gibt es ein Vergeltungsdogma im Alten Testament?" *ZTK* 52: 1–42.
    1983   *The Prophets I: The Assyrian Period.* Trans. M. Kohl. Philadelphia: Fortress.
    1984   *The Prophets II: The Babylonian and Persian Periods.* Trans. M. Kohl. Philadelphia: Fortress.

Kodell, J.
    1982   *Lamentations, Haggai, Zechariah, Malachi, Obadiah, Joel, Second Zechariah, Baruch.* OTM 14. Wilmington: Michael Glazier.

Köhler, L.
1923   *Deuterojesaja (Jesaja 40–55) stilkritisch untersucht.* BZAW 37. Giessen: Töpelmann.
1945   "Der Botenspruch." Pp. 13–17 in *Kleine Lichter.* Zwingli Bücherei 47. Zürich: Zwingli.

Köhler-Rollefson, I. U.
1985   "Eagle." P. 232 in *Harper's Bible Dictionary,* ed. P. J. Achtemeier. San Francisco: Harper & Row.

Kraabel, A. T.
1983   "Impact of the Discovery of the Sardis Synagogue." Pp. 178–90 in Hanfmann et al.

Krašovec, J.
1984   *Antithetic Structure in Biblical Hebrew Poetry.* VTSup 35. Leiden: E. J. Brill.

Kronholm, T.
1986   *"nešer." TWAT* 5: 680–89.

Kugel, J. L.
1981   *The Idea of Biblical Poetry: Parallelism and Its History.* New Haven: Yale University.

Labuschagne, C. J.
1966   *The Incomparability of Yahweh in the Old Testament.* Pretoria Oriental Series 5. Leiden: E. J. Brill.

Laetsch, T.
1956   *The Minor Prophets.* St. Louis: Concordia Publishing House.

Lambdin, T. O.
1971   *Introduction to Biblical Hebrew.* New York: Charles Scribner's Sons.

Lampe, G. W. H., ed.
1961   *A Patristic Greek Lexicon.* Oxford: Clarendon.

Lang, B., and Ringgren, H.
1986   *"nkr." TWAT* 5: 454–63.

Lapp, N. L., ed.
1981   *The Third Campaign at Tell el-Fûl: The Excavations of 1964.* AASOR 45. Cambridge: American Schools of Oriental Research.

LaSor, W. S.
1988   "Sepharad." *ISBE* 4: 399.

Lawton, R.
1984   "Israelite Personal Names on Pre-Exilic Hebrew Inscriptions." *Bib* 65: 330–46.

Layton, S. C.
1990   *Archaic Features of Canaanite Personal Names in the Hebrew Bible.* HSM 47. Atlanta: Scholars.

Leeuwen, C. van.
1973   "Die Partikel *'im*." *OTS* 18: 15–48.

Leiman, S. Z.
1976   *The Canonization of Hebrew Scripture: The Talmudic and Midrashic Evidence.* Transactions of the Connecticut Academy of Arts and Sciences 47. Hamden: Archon Books.

Leupold, H. C.
1959   *Exposition of the Psalms.* Wartburg: Wartburg. Repr., Grand Rapids: Baker, 1969.

Levenson, J. D.
1985   *Sinai and Zion: An Entry into the Jewish Bible.* New Voices in Biblical Studies. San Francisco: Harper & Row.
1992   "Zion Traditions." *ABD* 6: 1098–1102.

Levine, B. A.
1987   "The Language of Holiness: Perceptions of the Sacred in the Hebrew Bible." Pp. 241–55 in *Backgrounds for the Bible,* ed. M. O'Connor and D. N. Freedman. Winona Lake: Eisenbrauns.

Lillie, J. R.
1979   "Obadiah — A Celebration of God's Kingdom." *CurTM* 6: 18–22.

Limburg, J.
1988   *Hosea-Micah.* IBC. Atlanta: John Knox.

Lindblom, J.
1924   *Die literarische Gattung der prophetischen Literatur: Eine literargeschichtliche Untersuchung zum Alten Testament.* Uppsala: A. Lundequistska bokhandlen.
1962   "Lot-Casting in the Old Testament." *VT* 12: 164–78.

Lindenberger, J. M.
1994   *Ancient Aramaic and Hebrew Letters,* ed. K. H. Richards. SBLWAW 4. Atlanta: Scholars.

Lindsay, J.
1976   "The Babylonian Kings and Edom, 605–550 B.C." *PEQ* 108: 23–39.

Lipiński, E.
1973   "Obadiah 20." *VT* 23: 368–70.
1975   *Studies in Aramaic Inscriptions and Onomastics I.* OLA 1. Leuven: Leuven University.

Lohfink, N.
1981   "Textkritisches zu *jrš* im Alten Testament." Pp. 273–88 in *Mélanges Dominique Barthélemy: Études bibliques offertes a l'occasion de son 60 anniversaire,* ed. P. Casetti, O. Keel, and A. Schenker. OBO 38. Fribourg: Éditions Universitaires.
1990   "*yāraš.*" *TDOT* 6: 368–96.

Luciani, F.
  1983   "Il verbo *bô'* in Abd. 13." *RivB* 31: 209–11.
MacDonald, B.
  1993   *Ammon, Moab and Edom: Early States/Nations of Jordan in the Biblical Period (End of the 2nd and during the 1st Millennium B.C.).* Amman: Al Kutba.
Macintosh, A. A.
  1980   *Isaiah XXI: A Palimpsest.* Cambridge: Cambridge University.
Macky, P. W.
  1990   *The Centrality of Metaphors to Biblical Thought: A Method for Interpreting the Bible.* Studies in the Bible and Early Christianity 19. Lewiston: Edwin Mellen.
Maier, J.
  1982   "'Siehe, ich mach(t)e dich klein unter den Völkern . . .' Zum rabbinischen Assoziationshorizont von Obadja 2." Pp. 203–15 in *Künder des Wortes,* ed. L. Ruppert, P. Weimar, and E. Zenger. Würzburg: Echter.
Malamat, A.
  1987   "The Last Years of the Kingdom of Judah." Pp. 287–314 in *Archaeology and Biblical Interpretation: Essays in Memory of D. Glenn Rose,* ed. L. G. Perdue, L. E. Toombs, and G. L. Johnson. Atlanta: John Knox.
Mallon, E. D.
  1990   "Joel, Obadiah." Pp. 399–405 in *The New Jerome Biblical Commentary,* ed. R. E. Brown, J. A. Fitzmyer, and R. E. Murphy. Englewood Cliffs: Prentice Hall.
Mare, W. H.
  1992   "Zion." *ABD* 6: 1096–97.
Marti, D. K.
  1904   *Das Dodekapropheton erklärt.* KHC 13. Tübingen: J. C. B. Mohr.
Martin-Achard, R.
  1976   "*nēkār,* Fremde." *THAT* 2: 66–68.
Mason, R.
  1991   *Micah, Nahum, Obadiah.* OTG. Sheffield: JSOT.
Mathews, C. R.
  1994   *Defending Zion: Edom's Desolation and Jacob's Restoration (Isaiah 34–35) in Context.* Ph.D. diss., Yale University (BZAW, forthcoming).
Mayer, G.
  1990   "*yārad.*" *TDOT* 6: 315–22.

Mayes, A. D. H.
: 1989   *The Old Testament in Sociological Perspective.* London: Marshall Pickering.

McCarter, P. K.
: 1973   "The River Ordeal in Israelite Literature." *HTR* 66: 403–12.
: 1976   "Obadiah 7 and the Fall of Edom." *BASOR* 221: 87–91.
: 1987   "Aspects of the Religion of the Israelite Monarchy: Biblical and Epigraphic Data." Pp. 137–55 in *Ancient Israelite Religion: Essays in Honor of Frank Moore Cross,* ed. P. D. Miller, P. D. Hanson, and S. D. McBride. Philadelphia: Fortress.

McConville, J. G.
: 1993   *Judgment and Promise: An Interpretation of the Book of Jeremiah.* Winona Lake: Eisenbrauns.

McCreesh, T. P.
: 1991   *Biblical Sound and Sense: Poetic Sound Patterns in Proverbs 10–29.* JSOTSup 128. Sheffield: JSOT.

McKane, W.
: 1980   "Poison, Trial by Ordeal and the Cup of Wrath." *VT* 30: 474–92.

McKenzie, J. L.
: 1968   *Second Isaiah.* AB 20. Garden City: Doubleday.

McLauchlin, B. K.
: 1992   "Lydia (Place)." *ABD* 4: 423–25.

Meier, J. P.
: 1994   *A Marginal Jew: Rethinking the Historical Jesus.* Vol. 2. Anchor Bible Reference Library. New York: Doubleday.

Meier, S. A.
: 1988   *The Messenger in the Ancient Semitic World.* HSM 45. Atlanta: Scholars.

Mendelsohn, I.
: 1949   *Slavery in the Ancient Near East: A Comparative Study of Slavery in Babylonia, Assyria, Syria, and Palestine, from the Middle of the Third Millennium to the End of the First Millennium.* New York: Oxford University.

Mendenhall, G. E., and Herion, G. A.
: 1992   "Covenant." *ABD* 1: 1179–1202.

Meyers, C. L., and Meyers, E. M.
: 1987   *Haggai, Zechariah 1–8.* AB 25B. Garden City: Doubleday.
: 1993   *Zechariah 9–14.* AB 25C. New York: Doubleday.

Milgrom, J.
: 1991   *Leviticus 1–16.* AB 3. New York: Doubleday.

Miller, P. D.
1968   "The Divine Council and the Prophetic Call to War." *VT* 18:
        100–7.
1973   *The Divine Warrior in Early Israel.* HSM 5. Cambridge: Harvard
        University.
1982   *Sin and Judgment in the Prophets: A Stylistic and Theological Analy-
        sis.* SBLMS 27. Chico: Scholars.
1987   "Cosmology and World Order in the Old Testament: The Divine
        Council as Cosmic-Political Symbol." *HBT* 9: 53–78.

Mirsky, A.
1977   "Stylistic Device for Conclusion in Hebrew." *Semitics* 5: 9–23.

Mitchell, C. W.
1987   *The Meaning of BRK "To Bless" in the Old Testament.* SBLDS 95.
        Atlanta: Scholars.

Muenchow, C.
1989   "Dust and Dirt in Job 42:6." *JBL* 108: 597–611.

Muilenburg, J.
1940   "The Literary Character of Isaiah 34." *JBL* 59: 339–65.

Mullen, E. T.
1980   *The Divine Council in Canaanite and Early Hebrew Literature.*
        HSM 24. Chico: Scholars.

Munch, P. A.
1936   *The Expression bajjôm hahu'. Is It an Eschatological Terminus Tech-
        nicus?* ANVAO II.2. Oslo: Dybwad.

Muraoka, T.
1985   *Emphatic Words and Structures in Biblical Hebrew.* Jerusalem:
        Magnes.
1991   "The Biblical Hebrew Nominal Clause with a Prepositional
        Phrase." Pp. 143–51 in *Studies in Hebrew and Aramaic Syntax Pre-
        sented to Professor J. Hoftijzer on the Occasion of His Sixty-Fifth
        Birthday,* ed. K. Jongeling, H. L. Murre-Van den Berg, and L. van
        Rompay. Studies in Semitic Languages and Linguistics 17. Leiden:
        E. J. Brill.
1993   *A Greek-English Lexicon of the Septuagint: Twelve Prophets.* Leu-
        ven: Peeters.

Myers, J. M.
1971   "Edom and Judah in the Sixth–Fifth Centuries B.C." Pp. 377–92 in
        Near Eastern Studies in Honor of William Foxwell Albright, ed. H.
        Goedicke. Baltimore: Johns Hopkins.

Naveh, J.
1963   "Old Hebrew Inscriptions in a Burial Cave." *IEJ* 13: 74–92.

Neiman, D.
1963   "Sefarad: The Name of Spain." *JNES* 22: 128–32.

Newsom, C.
1984   "A Maker of Metaphors — Ezekiel's Oracles against Tyre." *Int* 38: 151–64.

Niehaus, J. J.
1993   "Obadiah." Pp. 495–541 in *The Minor Prophets*. Vol. 2. Ed. T. E. McComiskey. Grand Rapids: Baker.

Nielsen, K.
1989   *There Is Hope for a Tree: The Tree as Metaphor in Isaiah.* JSOTSup 65. Sheffield: JSOT.

Nowack, D. W.
1897   *Die kleinen Propheten.* HKAT 3/4. Göttingen: Vandenhoeck & Ruprecht.

O'Connor, M.
1980   *Hebrew Verse Structure.* Winona Lake: Eisenbrauns.

Odell, M. S.
1991   "An Exploratory Study of Shame and Dependence in the Bible and Selected Near Eastern Parallels." Pp. 217–33 in *The Biblical Canon in Comparative Perspective: Scripture in Context IV*, ed. K. L. Younger, W. W. Hallo, and B. F. Batto. Ancient Near Eastern Texts and Studies 11. Lewiston: Edwin Mellen.

Odendaal, D. H.
1970   *The Eschatological Expectation of Isaiah 40–66 with Special Reference to Israel and the Nations.* Philadelphia: Presbyterian and Reformed.

Oesterley, W. O. E., and Robinson, T. H.
1934   *An Introduction to the Books of the Old Testament.* New York: Macmillan.

Ogden, G. S.
1982   "Prophetic Oracles against Foreign Nations and Psalms of Communal Lament: The Relationship of Psalm 137 to Jeremiah 49:7–22 and Obadiah." *JSOT* 24: 89–97.

Orlinsky, H. M.
1940–1941
        "On the Cohortative and Jussive after an Imperative or Interjection in Biblical Hebrew. *JQR* 31: 371–82.
1941–1942
        "On the Cohortative and Jussive after an Imperative or Interjection in Biblical Hebrew." *JQR* 32: 191–205, 273–77.

Otto, E.
1989   "ṣiyyôn." *TWAT* 6: 994–1028.

1991   "Die Geschichte der Talion im Alten Orient und Israel." Pp.
         101–30 in *Ernten, was man sät: Festschrift für Klaus Koch zu seinem
         65. Geburtstag*, ed. D. R. Daniels, U. Glessmer, and M. Rösel.
         Neukirchen-Vluyn: Neukirchener.

Ottosson, M.
1969   *Gilead: Tradition and History*. Trans. J. Gray. ConBOT 3. Lund:
         Gleerup.
1975   "*gĕbûl.*" TDOT 2: 361–66.
1984   "The Prophet Elijah's Visit to Zarephath." Pp. 185–98 in *In the
         Shelter of Elyon: Essays on Ancient Palestinian Life and Literature
         in Honor of G. W. Ahlström*, ed. W. B. Barrick and J. R. Spencer.
         JSOTSup 31. Sheffield: JSOT.

Overholt, T. W.
1989   *Channels of Prophecy: The Social Dynamics of Prophetic Activity*.
         Minneapolis: Fortress.

Padilla, W.
1989   *Amos-Abdias*. Comentario Bíblico Hispanoamericano. Miami: Ed-
         itorial Caribe.

Parpola, S.
1970   *Neo-Assyrian Toponyms*. AOAT. Neukirchen-Vluyn: Butzon &
         Bercker Kevelaer.

Parunak, H. van Dyke.
1983   "Transitional Techniques in the Bible." *JBL* 102: 525–48.

Paul, S. M.
1991   *Amos*. Hermeneia. Minneapolis: Fortress.
1992   "Polysensuous Polyvalency in Poetic Parallelism." Pp. 147–63 in
         *Sha'arei Talmon: Studies in the Bible, Qumran, and the Ancient
         Near East Presented to Shemaryahu Talmon*, ed. M. Fishbane and
         E. Tov. Winona Lake: Eisenbrauns.

Pazdan, M. M.
1989   "Obadiah." Pp. 586–91 in *The Collegeville Bible Commentary*, ed.
         D. Bergant and R. J. Karris. Collegeville: Liturgical.

Peckham, B.
1993   *History and Prophecy: The Development of Late Judean Literary
         Traditions*. Anchor Bible Reference Library. New York: Double-
         day.

Pedley, J. G.
1972   *Ancient Literary Sources on Sardis*. Archaeological Exploration of
         Sardis Monograph 2. Cambridge: Harvard University.
1992   "Sardis." *ABD* 5: 982–84.

Peels, H. G. L.
1995   *The Vengeance of God: The Meaning of the Root NQM and the*

Function of the NQM-Texts in the Context of Divine Revelation in the Old Testament. OTS 31. Leiden: E. J. Brill.

Petersen, D. L., and Richards, K. H.
1992   *Interpreting Hebrew Poetry.* Minneapolis: Fortress.

Pfeiffer, R. H.
1926   "Edomitic Wisdom." *ZAW* 44: 13–25.

Pope, M.
1952   "Isaiah 34 in Relation to Isaiah 35, 40–66." *JBL* 71: 235–43.
1977   *Song of Songs.* AB 7C. Garden City: Doubleday.

Prinsloo, W. S.
1985   *The Theology of the Book of Joel.* BZAW 163. Berlin: Walter de Gruyter.

Pritchard, J. B.
1978   *Recovering Sarepta, A Phoenician City.* Princeton: Princeton University.

Procksch, O.
1930   *Jesaia I.* KAT 9. Leipzig: A. Deichertsche Verlagsbuchhandlung.

Raabe, P. R.
1990   *Psalm Structures: A Study of Psalms with Refrains.* JSOTSup 104. Sheffield: JSOT.
1991   "Deliberate Ambiguity in the Psalter." *JBL* 110: 213–27.
1995   "Why Prophetic Oracles against the Nations?" Pp. 236–57 in *Fortunate the Eyes That See: Essays in Honor of David Noel Freedman in Celebration of His Seventieth Birthday,* ed. A. B. Beck, A. H. Bartelt, P. R. Raabe, and C. A. Franke. Grand Rapids: Eerdmans.

Rabinovitz, I.
1968   "Sepharad." *EncMiqr* 5: 1100–3 (Hebrew).

Rainey, A. F.
1976   "Sela (of Edom)." *IDBSup:* 800.

Raven, J. H.
1906   *Old Testament Introduction: General and Special.* New York: Fleming H. Revell.

Revell, E. J.
1981   "Pausal Forms and the Structure of Biblical Poetry." *VT* 31: 186–99.
1990   "Conjunctive *Dagesh:* A Preliminary Study." Pp. 95–101 in *VIII International Congress of the International Organization for Masoretic Studies: Chicago 1988,* ed. E. J. Revell. SBLMasS 6. Atlanta: Scholars.

Richards, I. A.
1936   *The Philosophy of Rhetoric.* New York: Oxford University.

Richter, W.
1966   *Recht und Ethos: Versuch einer Ortung des weisheitlichen Mahn-spruches.* SANT 15. München: Kösel.

Ricks, S. D.
1988   "The Prophetic Literality of Tribal Reconstruction." Pp. 273–81 in *Israel's Apostasy and Restoration: Essays in Honor of Roland K. Harrison,* ed. A. Gileadi. Grand Rapids: Baker.

Ricoeur, P.
1977   *The Rule of Metaphor: Multi-disciplinary Studies of the Creation of Meaning in Language.* Trans. R. Czerny with K. McLaughlin and J. Costello. Toronto: University of Toronto.

Ringgren, H.
1953   "Vredens kalk." *SEÅ* 17: 19–30.
1966   *Israelite Religion.* Trans. D. E. Green. Philadelphia: Fortress.
1984   "*kāsāh.*" *TWAT* 4: 272–77.
1986a   "*ḥmr.*" *TDOT* 5: 1–4.
1986b   "*sāpaq.*" *TWAT* 5: 909–10.
1986c   "*nśʾ I.*" *TWAT* 5: 657–58.

Ringgren, H., Seybold, K., and Fabry, H. -J.
1984   "*melek.*" *TWAT* 4: 926–57.

Roberts, J. J. M.
1991   *Nahum, Habakkuk, and Zephaniah: A Commentary.* OTL. Louisville: Westminster/John Knox.

Robertson, D.
1969   "The Morphemes *-y (-î)* and *-w (-ô)* in Biblical Hebrew." *VT* 19: 211–23.
1972   *Linguistic Evidence in Dating Early Hebrew Poetry.* SBLDS 3. Missoula: SBL.

Robinson, G. L.
1926   *The Twelve Minor Prophets.* New York: Harper & Brothers.

Robinson, H. W.
1944   "The Council of Yahweh." *JTS* 45: 151–57.

Robinson, R. B.
1988   "Levels of Naturalization in Obadiah." *JSOT* 40: 83–97.

Robinson, T. H.
1916   "The Structure of the Book of Obadiah." *JTS* 17: 402–8.
1938   *Die zwölf kleinen Propheten: Hosea bis Micha.* HAT 14/1. Tübingen: J. C. B. Mohr.

Ross, J. F.
1962   "The Prophet as Yahweh's Messenger." Pp. 98–107 in *Israel's Prophetic Heritage: Essays in Honor of James Muilenburg,* ed. B. W. Anderson and W. Harrelson. New York: Harper & Row.

1970   "Prophecy in Hamath, Israel, and Mari." *HTR* 63: 1–28.

Roth, W.
1989   "'ll." *TWAT* 6: 151–60.

Rouillard, H.
1985   *La péricope de Balaam (Nombres 22–24): la prose et les "oracles."* EBib 4. Paris: J. Gabalda.

Rudolph. W.
1931   "Obadja." *ZAW* 49: 222–31.
1971   *Joel-Amos-Obadja-Jona.* KAT 13.2. Gütersloh: Gerd Mohn.

Sagarin, J. L.
1987   *Hebrew Noun Patterns (Mishqalim): Morphology, Semantics, and Lexicon.* Atlanta: Scholars.

Sasson, J. M.
1990   *Jonah.* AB 24B. New York: Doubleday.

Sauer, J. A.
1986   "Transjordan in the Bronze and Iron Ages: A Critique of Glueck's Synthesis." *BASOR* 263: 1–26.

Sawyer, J.
1965   "What Was a *Mošiaʿ*?" *VT* 15: 475–86.

Scharbert, J.
1980   "*zûd.*" *TDOT* 4: 46–51.

Schmidt, H.
1934   *Die Psalmen.* Tübingen: J. C. B. Mohr.

Schmitz, P. C.
1992   "Canaan (Place)." *ABD* 1: 828–31.

Schunck, K. -D.
1980   "*ḥēmāh.*" *TDOT* 4: 462–65.
1992   "Benjamin." Trans. P. R. Callaway. *ABD* 1: 671–73.

Seebass, H.
1975   "*bôš.*" *TDOT* 2: 50–60.

Seybold, K.
1978   "*gāmal.*" *TDOT* 3: 23–33.

Silva, M.
1983   *Biblical Words and Their Meaning: An Introduction to Lexical Semantics.* Grand Rapids: Zondervan.

Smend, R.
1963   *Die Bundesformel.* ThStud 68. Zürich: EVZ.

Smith, G. V.
1988   "Alienation and Restoration: A Jacob-Esau Typology." Pp. 165–74 in *Israel's Apostasy and Restoration: Essays in Honor of Roland K. Harrison,* ed. A. Gileadi. Grand Rapids: Baker.

Smith, J. M. P.
  1939   *The Complete Bible: An American Translation, The Old Testament.*
          Chicago: University of Chicago.
Snijders, L. A.
  1954   "The Meaning of *zār* in the Old Testament." *OTS* 10: 1–154.
  1980   "*zûr/zār.*" *TDOT* 4: 52–58.
Snyman, S. D.
  1989   "Cohesion in the Book of Obadiah." *ZAW* 101: 59–71.
Soderlund, S.
  1985   *The Greek Text of Jeremiah: A Revised Hypothesis.* JSOTSup 47.
          Sheffield: JSOT.
Soggin, J. A.
  1980   "Observations on the Root *špṭ* and the Term *šôpĕṭîm* in Biblical
          Hebrew." *BA* 43: 208.
Sonsino, R.
  1980   *Motive Clauses in Hebrew Law: Biblical Forms and Near Eastern
          Parallels.* SBLDS 45: Chico: Scholars.
Soskice, J. M.
  1985   *Metaphor and Religious Language.* Oxford: Clarendon.
Spaude, C. W.
  1987   *Obadiah, Jonah, Micah.* The People's Bible. Milwaukee: North-
          western.
Sperber, A.
  1973   *The Bible in Aramaic IV B: The Targum and the Hebrew Bible.*
          Leiden: E. J. Brill.
Steinmann, A. E.
  1992   "The Order of Amos's Oracles against the Nations: 1:3–2:16." *JBL*
          111: 683–89.
Stern, E.
  1982   *Material Culture of the Land of the Bible in the Persian Period 538–
          332 B.C.* Warminster: Aris & Phillips.
Stoebe, H. J.
  1971   "*ḥāmās*, Gewalttat." *THAT* 1: 583–87.
Stuart, D.
  1987   *Hosea-Jonah.* Word Biblical Commentary 31. Waco: Word.
Swart, I.
  1991   "In Search of the Meaning of *ḥamas*: Studying an Old Testament
          Word in Context." *Journal for Semitics* 3: 156–66.
Swiggers, P.
  1981   "The Meaning of the Root *lḥm* 'Food' in the Semitic Languages."
          UF 13: 307–8.
  1991   "Nominal Sentence Negation in Biblical Hebrew: The Grammati-

cal Status of *'yn*." Pp. 173–79 in *Studies in Hebrew and Aramaic Syntax Presented to Professor J. Hoftijzer on the Occasion of His Sixty-Fifth Birthday*, ed. K. Jongeling, H. L. Murre-Van den Berg, and L. van Rompay. Studies in Semitic Languages and Linguistics 17. Leiden: E. J. Brill.

Talmon, S.
    1978   "*har.*" *TDOT* 3: 427–47.

Tångberg, K. A.
    1987   *Die prophetische Mahnrede: Form- und traditionsgeschichtliche Studien zum prophetischen Umkehrruf.* FRLANT 143. Göttingen: Vandenhoeck & Ruprecht.

Theis, J.
    1937   "Der Prophet Abdias." Pp. 140–54 in J. Lippl and J. Theis, *Die zwölf kleinen Propheten.* Die Heilige Schrift des Alten Testaments 8.3/1. Bonn: Peter Hanstein.

Thompson, J. A.
    1956   "The Book of Obadiah." Pp. 855–67 in *The Interpreter's Bible.* Vol. 6. New York: Abingdon.

Tov, E.
    1992   *Textual Criticism of the Hebrew Bible.* Minneapolis: Fortress.

Travis, S. H.
    1992   "Wrath of God (NT)." *ABD* 6: 996–98.

Tucker, G. M.
    1978   "Prophetic Speech." *Int* 32: 31–45.
    1985   "Prophecy and the Prophetic Literature." Pp. 325–68 in *The Hebrew Bible and Its Modern Interpreters*, ed. D. A. Knight and G. M. Tucker. SBLBMI 1. Philadelphia: Fortress.

Ullendorff, E.
    1956   "The Contribution of South Semitics to Hebrew Lexicography." *VT* 6: 190–98.

Van der Merwe, C. H. J.
    1990   *The Old Hebrew Particle gam: A Syntactic-Semantic Description of gam in Gn-2 Kg.* ATAT 34. St. Ottilien: EOS.

Van der Toorn, K.
    1988   "Ordeal Procedures in the Psalms and the Passover Meal." *VT* 38: 427–45.

Vanoni, G.
    1993   "*śāmaḥ.*" *TWAT* 7: 808–22.

de Vaux, R.
    1969   "Téman, ville ou région d'Édom?" *RB* 76: 379–85.

Vetter, D.
    1976   "*ne'um*, Ausspruch." *THAT* 2: 1–3.

Von Fange, E. A.
  1992   "Budde Hypothesis." *ABD* 1: 783–84.
Von Soden, W., Bergman, J., and Saebø, M.
  1990   "*yôm.*" *TDOT* 6: 7–32.
Waltke, B. K., and O'Connor, M.
  1990   *An Introduction to Biblical Hebrew Syntax.* Winona Lake: Eisen-
          brauns.
Watson, D. F., and Hauser, A. J.
  1994   *Rhetorical Criticism of the Bible: A Comprehensive Bibliography
          with Notes on History and Method.* Leiden: E. J. Brill.
Watts, J. D. W.
  1969   *Obadiah: A Critical Exegetical Commentary.* Grand Rapids:
          Eerdmans.
Wehrle, J.
  1987   *Prophetie und Textanalyse: Die Komposition Obadja 1–21 interpre-
          tiert auf der Basis textlinguistischer und semiotischer Konzeptionen.*
          ATAT 28. St. Ottilien: EOS.
Weimar, P.
  1985   "Obadja: Eine redaktionskritische Analyse." *BN* 27: 35–99.
Weingreen, J.
  1954   "The Construct-Genitive Relation in Hebrew Syntax." *VT* 4:
          50–59.
Weiser, A.
  1967   *Das Buch der zwölf kleinen Propheten I: Die Propheten Hosea, Joel,
          Amos, Obadja, Jona, Micha.* 5th ed. ATD 24. Göttingen: Vanden-
          hoeck & Ruprecht.
Wellhausen, J.
  1963   *Die Kleinen Propheten übersetzt und erklärt.* 4th ed. Berlin: Walter
          de Gruyter [3rd ed. Berlin: Georg Reimer, 1898].
Westermann, C.
  1967   *Basic Forms of Prophetic Speech.* Trans. H. C. White. Philadel-
          phia: Westminster.
  1991   *Prophetic Oracles of Salvation in the Old Testament.* Trans. K.
          Crim. Louisville: Westminster/John Knox.
Whybray, R. N.
  1971   *The Heavenly Counsellor in Isaiah xl 13–14: A Study of the Sources
          of the Theology of Deutero-Isaiah.* SOTSMS 1. Cambridge: Cam-
          bridge University.
Wiesenberg, E.
  1954   "A Note on *mizzeh* in Psalm 75:9." *VT* 4: 434–39.
Williams, R. J.
  1976   *Hebrew Syntax: An Outline.* 2nd ed. Toronto: University of Toronto.

Williamson, H. G. M.
1990 "Laments at the Destroyed Temple: Excavating the Biblical Text Reveals Ancient Jewish Prayers." *BRev* 6: 12–17, 44.

Willis, W., ed.
1987 *The Kingdom of God in 20th-Century Interpretation.* Peabody: Hendrickson.

Wilson, R. W.
1980 *Prophecy and Society in Ancient Israel.* Philadelphia: Fortress.

Wiseman, D. J.
1958 *The Vassal-Treaties of Esarhaddon.* London: The British School of Archaeology in Iraq.
1982 "'Is It Peace?'—Covenant and Diplomacy." *VT* 32: 311–26.
1985 *Nebuchadrezzar and Babylon.* Oxford: Oxford University.

Wolff, H. W.
1969 *Dodekapropheton 2: Joel und Amos.* BKAT 14/2. Neukirchen-Vluyn: Neukirchener.
1977 *Dodekapropheton 3: Obadja und Jona.* BKAT 14/3. Neukirchen-Vluyn: Neukirchener.

Woudstra, M. H.
1968 "Edom and Israel in Ezekiel." *CTJ* 3: 21–35.

Yaron, R.
1958 "A Ramessid Parallel to 1 K ii 33, 44–45." *VT* 8: 432–33.

Yeivin, I.
1980 *Introduction to the Tiberian Masorah.* Trans. and ed. E. J. Revell. SBLMasS 5. Missoula: Scholars.

Young, E. J.
1949 *An Introduction to the Old Testament.* Grand Rapids: Eerdmans.

Zeitlin, S.
1969 "The Origin of the Term Edom for Rome and the Roman Church." *JQR* 60: 262–63.

Zevit, Z.
1983 "A Chapter in the History of Israelite Personal Names." *BASOR* 250: 1–16.

Ziegler, J.
1971 *Sylloge: Gesammelte Aufsätze zur Septuaginta.* MSU 10. Göttingen: Vandenhoeck & Ruprecht.

NOTES
AND
COMMENTS

◆

SUPERSCRIPTION (v 1a)

◆

Obadiah's Vision.

NOTES

1a. Obadiah's Vision. The book begins with the phrase *ḥăzôn ʿōbadyāh*, which clearly serves as the book's heading and title. It provides the reader with an extremely brief superscription, only the designation of the following material as a prophetic "vision" and the prophet's name. It is the shortest heading of the Latter Prophets, but then again the book itself is the shortest prophetic book. Unlike other superscriptions in the Book of the Twelve, all of which give further information such as the prophet's place of origin, father's name, occupation, date, or the prophecy's addressee, here we learn only the prophet's name. Wolff (1977) suggests that the text may have been written down shortly after it had been proclaimed so that a heading with more information was unnecessary. However, surely people like Isaiah and Jeremiah were well known, yet their books have complete superscriptions. Perhaps lack of information in the heading reflects lack of knowledge on the part of the writers of the headings. Or perhaps the compiler(s) felt that this brief heading supplied readers with sufficient information to understand the following block of material.

The superscription consists of the noun *ḥāzôn* (vision) in construct and the prophet's personal name. This sequence of *ḥāzôn* + personal name also occurs in the heading of the book of Isaiah ("The Vision of Isaiah"—1:1) and the book of Nahum ("the *maśśāʾ* of Nineveh, the Book of the Vision of Nahum the Elkoshite"—1:1). To it one should relate the headings of Isa 2:1; 13:1; Amos 1:1; Mic 1:1; and Hab 1:1, all of which use the verbal form *ḥāzâ*. Consequently, the title

"The Vision of Obadiah" leads one to anticipate finding prophetic utterances spoken by a historical individual whose name was Obadiah.

Vision. The noun *ḥāzôn* is a *qāṭôn* formation from the verbal root *ḥzh*. Including nominal derivatives the root occurs 174 times in the Hebrew Bible, 129 in Hebrew and 45 in Aramaic. The vast preponderance of the Hebrew passages associate the root with prophecy, at least 75 percent according to Jepsen (1980: 282). The Hebrew verb itself can be used in a secular sense denoting natural eyesight (Ps 58:9 [8]; Isa 33:20) or close inspection (Job 15:17; Prov 24:32), and sometimes it applies to "seeing God" (Exod 24:11; Ps 17:15; 63:3 [2]; Job 19:26–27). This last usage brings us close to its most common sense, that of prophetic vision.

The range of contexts and applications of *ḥzh* overlaps with that of *r'h*. The latter can apply to prophetic "seeing," such as *rō'eh* (seer), and *ḥzh* can be used for natural eyesight. Nevertheless, *ḥzh* usually serves as a technical term for a revelation of a "prophet." The relationship between the two is what lexical semantics terms "hyponymy" (Silva 1983: 126–29). Whereas *r'h* is the larger circle, the more inclusive and general term, which in the *qal* occurs over 1100 times, *ḥzh* is the smaller circle within the other circle, whose usage is commonly more limited and specialized. Thus *r'h* is the "superordinate" of *ḥzh* and *ḥzh* is a "hyponym" of *r'h*, much like the relationship between the senses of "flower" and "rose" or between "to speak" and "to preach." Another example in Hebrew is the relationship between *bārûk* and *'ašrê*, both of which mean "blessed" (Mitchell 1987: 179–81).

Perhaps the oldest passage with *ḥzh* and one where it designates prophetic revelation is found in Numbers 24, the oracles of Balaam son of Beor:

"The oracle of one who hears the words of El,
and who knows the knowledge of Elyon,
who sees [*ḥzh*] the vision [*maḥăzēh*] of Shadday,
who falls prostrate and whose eyes are uncovered:
I see [*r'h*] him, but not now;
I behold him, but not near." (vv 16–17a; cf. v 4)

An interesting extrabiblical parallel comes from the Balaam text of Deir 'Allah:

He was one who saw [*ḥzh*] the gods,
and the gods came to him in the night.

These two passages speak of the prophet "seeing" but the Numbers passage also refers to the prophet "hearing"; the clause "sees the vision of Shadday" parallels the clause "hears the words of El." Both the visual and the auditory senses operate as the prophet receives the revelation from God, a combination that makes sense given that eyes and ears are the two primary means by which a person receives information and encounters another person.

The noun *ḥāzôn* refers to a prophetic revelation. It occurs thirty-five times in the Bible, twelve of which come from Daniel. In the Daniel passages it denotes a visual image that is described, such as the ram and he-goat of chapter 8. However, this Danielic usage seems to have been influenced by the Aramaic noun *ḥezwā'* (apparition), which occurs twelve times in the Aramaic section of Daniel 2–7. Therefore it is best to omit the Daniel passages from consideration here. Of the remaining twenty-three passages, twenty-two refer to the "visions" of the prophets. Isaiah 29:7 presents the only non-prophetic application, the multitude "will be like a dream, a vision of night."

What is the precise meaning of *ḥāzôn?* Does it denote the act of seeing, the event in which a divine revelation comes, or the content of the prophetic message itself? It is never used as a verbal noun to denote the act of seeing, and in only one passage does it designate the event or subjective experience in which a divine message comes to the recipient, Ps 89:20 [19]: "Once you [Yahweh] spoke in a vision to your devoted ones and said . . ."

In all the other passages the noun designates the content of the prophetic revelation, the message itself. This becomes evident by the way it is used. Often the texts parallel or collocate *ḥāzôn* with *dābār* (word). 1 Sam 3:1 supplies a good example, "The *word* of Yahweh was rare in those days, there was no frequent *vision*." Ezek 7:26 states that the Israelites "will seek (in vain) a *vision* from the prophet, and instruction will perish from the priest and counsel from the elders," but its parallel in Jer 18:18 reads, ". . . and a *word* from the prophet." 1 Chr 17:15 summarizes the account of the divine promise to David by saying that Nathan spoke to David "according to all these *words* and according to all this *vision*." Verse 3 indicates that what came to Nathan in the night was "the *word* of God." Thus Nathan's "vision" consisted of the divine *speech* recorded in verses 4–14. The nature of *ḥāzôn* as prophetic utterance is also indicated by the fact that *ḥāzôn* can be the direct object of a speaking-verb. According to Jer 23:16, false prophets "*speak* the vision of their own heart, not from the mouth of Yahweh" (cf. Jer 14:14). The last phrase implies that a legitimate *ḥāzôn* comes from Yahweh's *mouth*, which also points to its nonvisual nature (cf. Ezek 12:21–28).

The passage just quoted illustrates a distinction the biblical texts make as to the sources of a prophetic "vision." According to the texts, true prophets receive their "vision" from Yahweh (1 Sam 3:1; Hos 12:11 [10]; Mic 3:7; Hab 2:2–3; 1 Chr 17:15; Lam 2:9), whereas the source of false "visions" lies in the prophet's own heart (Jer 14:14; 23:16).

All of this makes plain the meaning of the title "Obadiah's Vision." It designates the following textual material as utterances and speeches from Yahweh spoken by Obadiah. Perhaps a more accurate translation of *ḥāzôn* would be "revelation" (Allen 1976; Stuart 1987) or "observation" (A. R. Johnson 1962: 14,37) or "prophecy" (TEV; Wolff 1977). The Targum characteristically uses Aramaic *nbw't* (prophecy) to translate the noun (Cathcart and Gordon 1989: 99).

Obadiah. The only piece of information the title provides about the prophet is his name, and even with that there is some uncertainty. The MT vocalizes it as *'ōbadyāh*, which apparently derives from the participle *'ōbēd*, "one who serves/ worships Yahweh." The same formation is found in the biblical name *'ōbēd*, probably a shortened form of *'ōbadyāh*, and the name *'ōbēd 'ĕdōm*. In contrast the Septuagint manuscripts (except Vaticanus, which reads *Obdeiou*) read *Abdiou* or *Abdeiou* and the Vulgate has *Abdiae*. This vocalization is based on the form *'abdiyyāh* from the noun *'ebed*, "the servant of Yahweh." According to Stuart (1987: 406) the two forms "reflect perhaps bi-forms of the same name, comparable to Bert and Burt or Beth and Betty." This explanation is reinforced by comparing the names in 1 Chr 9:16 and Neh 11:17. They both refer to the same person, but the former vocalizes the name *'ōbadyāh* whereas the latter reads *'abdā'*.

Braver (1973) suggests that the name be vocalized *'ăbādyāh* on the basis of the Septuagint and Vulgate and the parallel *'ăśāh'ēl* (God has made — 2 Sam 2:18– 32). The theophoric *-yāh* would be the subject of the perfect verb *'bd*, which in this case according to Braver means "to make"; hence "Yahweh has made [him]." This view, however, is quite unlikely. The Septuagint and Vulgate were thinking of the noun *'ebed* and not the perfect of *'bd*, since in the latter case they would have preserved a vowel between *b* and *d*. Moreover, it is doubtful that Yahweh would be the subject of *'bd* (Wolff 1977).

The name "Obadiah" denominates twelve persons in the Hebrew Bible (Kennedy 1992). Three persons, all preexilic, bear the name with the long form *'ōbadyāhû* (1 Kgs 18:1–16; 1 Chr 27:19; 2 Chr 34:12), but for the other nine we find the short form *'ōbadyāh*. Of these nine, four persons are preexilic (1 Chr 7:3; 8:38 = 9:44; 12:10 [9]; 2 Chr 17:7), one is exilic (Obad 1) and four are postexilic (1 Chr 3:21; 9:16 = Neh 11:17; Ezra 8:9 = [?] Neh 10:6 [5]; Neh 12:25).

Zevit (1983) has demonstrated that whereas names with the theophoric *-yhw* are characteristically preexilic, names with *-yh*, which he argues developed in the ninth–eighth centuries B.C., span both the preexilic and postexilic periods. The short form interchanged freely with the long form in Judah from the seventh century to the early postexilic period and then became dominant in the postexilic period. Consequently, one cannot date the prophet Obadiah simply on the basis of the name's spelling.

Hebrew names built with *'bd* are common in the Bible and in Hebrew seals and inscriptions (Lawton 1984; Fowler 1988). They occur in full form with a theophoric suffix or as hypocoristica. The following provides a complete listing.

Hebrew Bible
'abdĕ'ēl
'abdî'ēl
'ōbadyāhû
'ōbadyāh
'ōbēd 'ĕdōm/'ōbēd 'ĕdôm
'ōbēd/'ôbēd
'ebed
'abdā'
'abdî
'abdôn

Hebrew Inscriptions and Seals
'bdyhw
'bdyh (reading uncertain, Aharoni 1973: 75, and plate 32:1)
'bdyw
'bd'
'bdy

That the name "Obadiah" with its variations would be so popular is not surprising, since one finds the nominal formation *'bd* + DN (the servant of divine name) well attested in Semitic, including Pre-Islamic Arabic, Amorite, Akkadian (which uses *[w]ardu*), Aramaic, and Canaanite (Layton 1990: 122, 130–31; Fowler 1988: 282). It is attested throughout the Levant, in Ugaritic (Gröndahl 1967: 104–6), Phoenician and Punic (Benz 1972: 369–72), Ammonite (Aufrecht 1989: 371), and Edomite (Bartlett 1989: 203, 205–6, 211).

It has been suggested that "Obadiah" might not be a personal name but a symbolic title ("worshiper of Yahweh") substituted to identify a nameless prophetic text (Oesterley and Robinson 1934: 370–71; Watts 1969: 44; Ackroyd 1992). One might compare "Malachi" (Ackroyd 1992), which many argue is a symbolic title ("my messenger") and not a personal name on the basis of its usage in 3:1. Bič (1953) argues that "worshiper of Yahweh" signifies worshiping Israel during an enthronement festival.

However, given the popularity of the personal name "Obadiah" in Israel and of the same type of name throughout the ancient Near East there can be little doubt that it is a personal name here. This is reinforced by the parallel book headings in Isa 1:1 ("The Vision of Isaiah") and Nah 1:1 ("The Book of the Vision of Nahum the Elkoshite"), both of which have a personal name following *ḥāzôn*. Moreover, the Malachi comparison does not apply since, unlike *mal'ākî*, the root *'bd* never occurs elsewhere in the book of Obadiah. We might not know much about the prophet but at least we are given his name. This seems to be the minimal amount of biographical information that the editor(s) of the book believed was necessary for the reader (cf. Hab 1:1).

COMMENT

The superscription identifies for the reader the genre of the following textual material and thus places the book into a literary context that restricts its possible meanings. Just as a book cover today raises certain expectations in the mind of the reader who will then expect to find a novel or a science textbook and will read the text according to the conventions appropriate to that genre, so the superscription "Obadiah's Vision" orients one's interpretation (cf. R. B. Robinson 1988: 88). It specifies a single vision and thereby encourages the reader to interpret the book as a unified whole. It also designates the material as prophetic discourse, as utterances spoken by Yahweh through his mouthpiece, Obadiah. That the prophet's personal name is recorded signifies something about the nature of divine utterances in the Hebrew Bible. They were not thought of as abstract and timeless ideas suspended in the air. On the contrary, they came into concrete historical situations within space and time and were proclaimed through specific persons, whose personal names are usually given. Furthermore, the record of the prophet's name served to hold the prophet accountable for his words in accordance with the test given in Deut 18:20–22 and with what appears to be the practice of the ancient Near East (cf. Roberts 1991: 165). Perhaps one reason why Obadiah's prophecy was preserved in exilic and postexilic Judah is that Edom's demise in the mid-sixth century provided confirmation and verification.

I. YAHWEH'S FIRST UTTERANCE: ANNOUNCEMENT OF DOOM ADDRESSED TO EDOM (vv 1b–4)

◆

1b Thus spoke the Lord Yahweh to Edom —
> A report we have heard from Yahweh:
>> "A messenger has been sent among the nations (to say):
>> 'Arise so that we may rise against her for battle.'"

2 — Look! Insignificant I have made you among the nations.
> You are utterly despised.

3 The presumption of your heart has deceived you,
> you who dwell in the clefts of the crags,
>> in the height of your seat,

you who say in your heart:
>> "Who will bring me down to the earth?"

4 Even if you could exalt (your nest) like the eagle,
> and even if among stars you could set your nest,
>> from there I will bring you down —
>> utterance of Yahweh.

EXCURSUS: THE MESSENGER FORMULA

The clause *kōh ʾāmar* N consists of the demonstrative adverb *kōh* (thus, the following), the perfect verb *ʾāmar* (spoke), and the name or title of the speaker. It means, "The following is what N has said," and is commonly designated "the messenger formula" (*Botenformel*).

To understand the formula one should begin by examining the nineteen occurrences in the Hebrew Bible (not counting parallel texts) where the formula has a human subject (see Bretón 1987: 81–82):

Thus spoke your servant Jacob (Gen 32:5 [4])
Thus spoke your son Joseph (Gen 45:9)
Thus spoke Pharaoh (Exod 5:10)
Thus spoke your brother Israel (Num 20:14)
Thus spoke Balak the son of Zippor (Num 22:16)
Thus spoke Jephthah (Judg 11:15)
Thus spoke the king [Solomon] (1 Kgs 2:30)
Thus spoke Ben-Hadad (1 Kgs 20:3, 5 [2, 5])
Thus spoke the king [Ahab] (1 Kgs 22:27)
Thus spoke the king [Ahaziah] (2 Kgs 1:11)
Thus spoke the king [Joram] (2 Kgs 9:18, 19)
Thus spoke the great king, the king of Assyria (2 Kgs 18:19 // Isa 36:4)
Thus spoke the king [Sennacherib] (2 Kgs 18:29 // Isa 36:14)
For thus spoke the king of Assyria (2 Kgs 18:31 // Isa 36:16)
Thus spoke Hezekiah (2 Kgs 19:3 // Isa 37:3)
For thus spoke Amos (Amos 7:11)
Thus spoke Cyrus, the king of Persia (2 Chr 36:23 // Ezra 1:2)

Except for Amos 7:11 where Amaziah's messenger reports to Jeroboam what Amos said, the formula always heads a message delivered by a messenger whom a sender dispatches to another party. Thus three parties are always involved, the sender and author of the message, the messenger, and the recipient of the message. The narratives provide a clear picture of the communication process, which Genesis 32:4–7 [3–6] illustrates.

Commission:	Jacob sends messengers to Esau, instructing them, "Thus you will say to my lord Esau:
Formula:	'Thus spoke your servant Jacob:
Message:	"I have sojourned with Laban . . . and I have sent to tell my lord, in order that I may find favor in your sight."'"
Messengers travel to addressee:	To be assumed since the messengers return to Jacob, saying, "We came to your brother Esau."

Messengers deliver the message:	To be assumed as above.
Messengers return to sender and report:	And the messengers return to Jacob, saying, "We came to your brother Esau, and he is coming to meet you, and four hundred men with him."

The essentials of the process consist of the sender's commissioning of the messengers, the message in direct discourse, its delivery, and their return trip to the sender with a report. In this process the formula "Thus spoke the sender" is spoken by the messenger and precedes the message. Consequently, it is commonly designated the "messenger formula." It functions to authorize and legitimate the messenger and to authenticate the message as one coming from the sender.

Not all of the secular texts with the formula describe the whole chain of communication as completely as Genesis 32. Some texts record only the commissioning scene and others only the messenger's delivery of the message, so as to avoid unnecessary redundancy. Consequently, the messenger formula is located in either the commissioning scene where the formula is spoken by the sender (3 times) or in the delivery scene where it is spoken by the messenger (12 times). In four texts the situation remains unclear because the narratives simply report that messengers were sent and then record the message. The following presents the data:

Formula in commissioning scene:	Gen 32:5 [4]; 45:9; 1 Kgs 22:27
Formula in delivery scene:	Exod 5:10; Num 22:16; 1 Kgs 2:30; 20:3, 5 [2, 5]; 2 Kgs 1:11; 9:18, 19; 18:19, 29, 31; 19:3
Formula in nonspecific report:	Num 20:14; Judg 11:15; Amos 7:11; 2 Chr 36:23

In the first set of texts the *sender* orders the messenger to say to the recipient "Thus spoke N," whereas in the second set the *messenger* speaks the formula to the recipient. In either case the messenger was to speak the formula, and we can safely assume the same for the last set. We can also assume that in each case the messenger was commanded by the sender to begin the message with the formula. Since from the narrative's perspective the messenger is the one who either will or does speak the formula, the perfect verb *'āmar* in the formula should be translated as a past tense, "Thus spoke N." The messenger repeats what the sender has already spoken.

In addition to the 19 cases where the sender is human, the formula occurs 406 times. (The statistics used here derive from Bretón 1987: 70–82. In his calculation he omits the duplicates, such as the Chronicles texts that repeat those of Kings, and the expression *kōh 'āmar Yahweh 'ēlay*, "Thus spoke Yahweh to me." This expression begins an autobiographical report rather than a messenger speech addressed to a third party.) In all 406 occurrences the sender is Israel's deity, not another deity, and the formula always introduces divine speech in direct discourse. The formula *kōh 'āmar* + divine name is typically prophetic, located in the Latter Prophets 353 times of the total 406 (87 percent). If we include the 41 occurrences in prophetic narratives from Samuel, Kings, and Chronicles, then the percentage increases to 97 percent for the formula's association with prophetic speech. The following presents the data for *kōh 'āmar* + divine name in the Latter Prophets.

Isaiah	39
Jeremiah	145
Ezekiel	126
(The Twelve	43)
Amos	14
Obadiah	1
Micah	2
Nahum	1
Haggai	5
Zechariah	19
Malachi	1
Total:	353

The formula is used throughout the corpus of the Latter Prophets, except for Hosea, Joel, Jonah, Habakkuk, and Zephaniah. Its absence from Jonah and Habakkuk is understandable, since the book of Jonah records only a five-word prophetic oracle (3:4) and the book of Habakkuk consists of a dialogue between the prophet and Yahweh followed by the prophet's prayer. Hosea, Joel, and Zephaniah signal divine speech in other ways by using formulas such as *nĕ'ūm yahweh* and *'āmar yahweh*.

One finds the formula located in an account depicting the prophet's commission or at the head of the prophet's actual delivery of the oracle. Sometimes the lines between the two become blurred and the commissioning scene merges into the delivery (e.g., Isa 7:3–12). In every case divine speech in direct discourse follows the formula although not always immediately.

It was noted above that in every biblical instance where the formula has a human subject, a messenger (or messengers) proclaims the formula at the beginning of the message after receiving the message from the sender. The phrase "thus spoke N" and similar formulas that introduce messages are attested also in other ancient Near Eastern literature (see the most recent treatments by Meier

1988; Greene 1989). In light of this, it is generally accepted that the formula *kōh ʾāmar* + divine name in the prophetic corpus functions as a messenger formula and that the biblical prophets claimed to be Yahweh's messengers (Köhler 1923: 102–9; Lindblom 1924; Ross 1962; Westermann 1967).

Other evidence supports this conclusion.

1. According to Isa 37:1–7 (= 2 Kgs 19:1–7), Hezekiah's messengers proclaimed to Isaiah a message with the introductory "Thus spoke Hezekiah" (v 3). Isaiah responded "Thus you will say to your master: 'Thus spoke Yahweh: Do not fear . . .'" (v 6). The reader naturally understands the phrase "Thus spoke Yahweh" to be a messenger formula spoken by Yahweh's messenger, patterned after the similar clause spoken by Hezekiah's messengers.

2. One finds similar terminology associated with both the commissioning of a human messenger and the commissioning of a prophet. In both cases the originator of the utterance "sends" (*šlḥ*) others to deliver it to the recipient. Often both commissions begin "Go and say to N."

3. A parallel exists between the commissioning scene of heavenly "messengers" and that of the canonical prophets. The biblical texts portray both groups as being commissioned in the heavenly council. That the members of the divine council were messengers and were designated as such (*malʾākîm*) is clear from Ps 103:20; 104:4; and elsewhere. Ugaritic texts provide ample parallels. Biblical prophets also received their commissions in the divine council — Isa 6; Jer 23:18, 22; Ezek 1–3; Amos 3:7. (Mullen 1980: 209–26 provides a thorough discussion of this parallel.)

4. Biblical prophets are explicitly called Yahweh's "messengers" (*malʾākîm*) in some texts. 2 Chr 36:15–16 states, "Yahweh, the God of their fathers sent persistently to them by his messengers . . . but they kept mocking the messengers of God, despising his words, and scoffing at his prophets . . ." The prophet Haggai is designated "the messenger of Yahweh" (Hag 1:13). Mal 1:1 mentions *malʾākî*, which — whether a personal name or title — means "my messenger" (cf. 3:1). Isa 44:26 seems to refer to prophets as Yahweh's "messengers," who are contrasted with the false omens and diviners mentioned in v 25. A possible extrabiblical parallel appears in the Aramaic eighth-century-B.C. Zakir inscription. In side A, lines 11–12 it reads:

> Baalshamayn [spoke] to me
> through seers [*ḥzyn*] and through messengers [*ʿddn*].

Although the precise meaning of *ʿddn* is uncertain, it probably is to be related to Ugaritic *tʿdt*, "messengers" (*DISO*: 204; Ross 1970: 1–11). If so, the sentence equates or at least associates seers with "messengers."

All of this evidence would seem to lead naturally and persuasively to the conclusion that the Hebrew Bible portrays the prophets as Yahweh's messengers. They participated in the heavenly council from which they were sent to a third party to proclaim Yahweh's message — which consisted of an announcement of doom, a promise, or a command given by Yahweh in his throne room — and to speak in his name and with his authority. Often, although not always, they signaled their role as messengers delivering a message with the introductory formula "Thus spoke Yahweh."

However, this generally accepted understanding has recently been called into question by Greene (1989). He provides a thorough study of the nature of ancient messengers and messages and demonstrates that messengers were an essential part of the communication system throughout the ancient Near East. They existed primarily to extend temporally and geographically the power of the sender's words and will. In light of this nearly ubiquitous phenomenon in the ancient world, Greene questions whether biblical prophets can be considered "messengers" and their oracles "messages." Although he concedes that the functions of messengers and prophets overlap to some extent — and his comparison in this regard helps to clarify the prophetic functions — nevertheless he disputes the equation of prophet and messenger with five primary arguments.

1. Messengers were always sent to bridge a geographical distance that existed between sender and recipient, but the component of travel is generally absent from the accounts of the Latter Prophets. Nor do the prophets return to the sender (i.e., Yahweh) with a report of the recipient's response.

2. The biblical texts that designate prophets as "messengers" come from late sources and therefore cannot be used to define how preexilic prophets were understood.

3. According to the biblical texts, some prophets contended with other prophets and disputed the others' claims and authority. Such a contest between ancient Near Eastern messengers is unattested.

4. Biblical prophets were far more than simply "messengers," since they also interceded for Israel, lamented their prophetic calling, performed "action prophecies," and so on.

5. The so-called messenger formula does not occur in several prophetic books (Hosea, Joel, Jonah, Habakkuk, and Zephaniah), and some prophetic "messages" have no formula of any kind.

The methodology Greene follows, that of first defining and delineating "messengers" of human senders and then comparing and contrasting these characteristics with those of biblical prophets, is, in my opinion, the proper approach. Too often scholars speak of prophets as "messengers" and their oracles as "messages" in a general and vague sort of way. Consequently, Greene's work is much needed and contributes toward clarifying the issue. Certainly the biblical prophets were more than Yahweh's messengers; they also functioned as mediators of the covenant between Yahweh and Israel. His observation concerning the formula "Thus spoke Yahweh" is well taken. Other formulas beside this one, such as "utterance of Yahweh" (*nĕ'ūm yahweh*), designate divine speech and should be considered messenger formulas as well.

Nevertheless, his arguments in my opinion do not overthrow the equation of prophets with "messengers." That was, at least, part of their role and function, to deliver the divine sender's decrees to the human recipients. With respect to point 2 above, not all secular "messengers" were so designated either. That preexilic prophets were considered messengers can be seen in other ways; they were "sent" by Yahweh and often with a commission similar to that of secular messengers, such as "Go and say to N."

Perhaps the most telling arguments against the equation are points 1 and 3. However, the differences between prophets and messengers are due to the nature of the case. When a human being claims to have been sent by a deity with a "message" that calls for a radical change of behavior on the part of the recipients, especially when the recipients are ruling officials, one naturally expects to find disagreements and disputes. The recipients will often seek a "second opinion" and usually one more conducive to their own point of view. The legitimacy of the prophet and the authenticity of the speech as in fact originating with the deity cannot easily be verified, unlike messages from human senders.

The absence of travel by the prophet from divine sender to human recipient raises doubts for Greene, since bridging the geographical distance was essential to a messenger's task. Where was the heavenly council located? Did the prophet literally travel from the divine council to the human recipient? Admittedly, the biblical texts do not give precise scientific answers to these sorts of questions. The prophets were understood as mediators between Israel's God and Israel, and one important aspect of their calling was simply to announce to the people what their God had said. The same questions can be posed for Yahweh's heavenly angelic messengers as well, yet they are explicitly designated "messengers." Moreover, some texts do portray the prophets being commissioned to travel (e.g., Jer 1:7; Amos 7:12–15).

In conclusion, the majority viewpoint is still persuasive and convincing. Obadiah claimed to have been Yahweh's messenger, commissioned to proclaim the heavenly king's decree to human hearers. He signaled his messenger role with the introductory words "Thus spoke the Lord Yahweh" and in this way authenticated the following speech as Yahweh's word. With this formula Obadiah announced that he was speaking in the name and by the command of the Lord Yahweh and not by virtue of his own authority.

NOTES

1b. *kōh 'āmar 'ădōnāy yahweh le'ĕdôm.*
Thus spoke the Lord Yahweh to Edom.
The demonstrative adverb *kōh* begins a new sentence following the book's superscription. The Masoretic accentuation reflects this with the *athnach* under the name *'ōbadyāh*. The clause means "The following is what the Lord Yahweh has said" and is usually termed "the messenger formula" (see Excursus). By it Obadiah indicates that he has been commissioned by the Lord Yahweh to deliver the following divine speech.

the Lord Yahweh. The Masoretes vocalize *'dny yhwh* as *'ădōnāy yĕh(ō)wīh* in order to read aloud *'ădōnāy 'ĕlōhîm* (the Lord God) and thus avoid the redundancy *'ădōnāy 'ădōnāy* (Lord Lord). This is a standard *Kethib-Qere* variation. Some translations follow the *Qere* and translate "the Lord GOD" (e.g., RSV), whereas others in effect create a hendiadys of the redundancy that the Masoretes avoided and translate "the Sovereign LORD" (e.g., NIV, TEV). The Hebrew is not so complicated; *'ădōnāy* is a title and *yahweh* is a personal name.

The title *'ădōnāy* is usually parsed as the plural form of *'ādōn* (lord) — a plural of excellence or majesty — with the first person singular pronominal suffix *-ay*; the suffix is written with a lengthened vowel *-āy* (cf. Joüon 1991 § 136d). This unique form always refers to Yahweh. Although perhaps it was originally a vocative, "my Lord," it has become ossified as a nominative, "the Lord." The suffix clearly does not have the semantic value of "my" in several kinds of texts: texts with the divine self-identification formula, "I am *'ădōnāy* Yahweh" (Ezek 13:9; 23:49; 24:24; 28:24; 29:16); divine speeches (2 Kgs 19:23 = Isa 37:24; Job 28:28); texts with more than one speaker (1 Kgs 22:6; Ps 44:24 [23]); texts by a third-person narrator (1 Kgs 3:10). According to Eissfeldt (1974), the ending *-āy* is not a first person possessive suffix but a nominal afformative that reinforces the meaning of the word. He cites the Ugaritic afformative *-āy* as a parallel. Accordingly, *'ădōnāy* means in at least the great majority of cases "the Lord of all" rather than "my Lord." Either explanation of *'ădōnāy* yields the same translation, "the Lord." The title identifies Yahweh as the master and ruler of the world, by virtue of which he has the authority to place demands on Edom and the nations and to judge them. Edom together with all nations is accountable to "the Lord Yahweh."

The phrase *'ădōnāy yahweh* occurs 280 times, 261 of which (93 percent) appear in the Latter Prophets (KB: 11). The vast majority of instances come from Ezekiel, 211 occurrences. The full formula "Thus spoke the Lord Yahweh" appears 133 times, always in the Latter Prophets (see Bretón 1987: 80–81). Again, Ezekiel employs it the most, 123 times (92 percent). In light of the phrase's popularity, especially with Ezekiel who was contemporaneous with Obadiah, there is no need to posit *'ădōnāy* as a later addition (*pace* Wolff 1977).

to Edom. The preposition *l* of *le'ĕdôm* is generally taken by commentators and translators in a loose sense as a *lamed* of specification, "with respect to/concerning Edom." Since the rest of v 1 and vv 2–4 parallel 49:14–16, they naturally look to Jer 49 for clarification of the opening clause in Obad 1b and claim to find it in Jer 49:7.

However, Jer 49:7 does not provide a very good parallel. In fact, its meaning and function are quite different. Jeremiah 49:7 reads:

Concerning Edom [*le'ĕdôm*]:
Thus spoke Yahweh of Hosts:
"Is there no longer wisdom in Teman . . ."

Here the prepositional phrase precedes the messenger formula and functions as the heading of the collection of Edom oracles in vv 7–22. The messenger formula then introduces the immediately following divine speech. The same sequence of *l* + name followed by the messenger formula occurs elsewhere in Jeremiah's oracles against the nations (48:1; 49:1, 28). In each case the construction *l* + name serves as the heading of the collection and the messenger formula introduces the first divine speech. There are also collections of oracles against the nations preceded only by *l* + name without the following messenger formula (Jer 46:2; 49:23; cf. 23:9). In these cases the *lamed* is a *lamed* of specification, "with respect to/concerning."

In Obadiah, however, the phrase *le'ĕdôm* follows the messenger formula, and the Masoretic accentuation construes both together. In this syntactic sequence or syntagm, it is much more natural to understand the preposition *l* as indicating the indirect object of the verb and the addressee of the divine speech, "Thus spoke the Lord Yahweh *to* Edom." In fact, in every instance except one in the Hebrew Bible with the sequence of the messenger formula followed by *l* + name/noun, the prepositional phrase designates the addressee of the divine speech. This is indicated by the use of the second person for the addressee. The pertinent passages are: Isa 45:1; 49:7; Jer 4:3; 29:4; Ezek 6:3; 7:2; 16:3; 26:15; 36:4; 37:5; Amos 5:4; and 2 Chr 20:15. In all of these cases one should translate "Thus spoke divine name *to* name." The only exception occurs in Jer 14:10, "thus spoke Yahweh concerning this people [*lā'ām hazzeh*]: 'They have loved to wander thus, they have not restrained their feet.'" Usually, however, when the divine speech concerns a group but does not address it directly, the preposition *'al* is used.

The issue here is of no small importance but has ramifications for one's interpretation of the whole book. I argue in the Introduction that Edom is not only the grammatical addressee of vv 2–15 but also the actual, historical, extratextual addressee. The weight of the linguistic usage cited above tips the scales toward seeing Edom as the addressee and not simply as the topic under consideration in the following material. Hence, the translation "Thus spoke the Lord Yahweh *to* Edom." This raises the next question, that of the clause's role and function in its present location.

Thus spoke the Lord Yahweh to Edom. It has been argued above that this clause serves to introduce divine speech in direct discourse addressed to Edom. What causes commentators difficulty is that the divine speech to Edom does not immediately follow but begins later in v 2. In the next line the prophet speaks of Yahweh in the third person, "we have heard from Yahweh." How should one understand the introductory formula in light of the rest of v 1? The following survey presents various options and cites representatives of each.

1. The formula "Thus spoke the Lord Yahweh" is a later addition to an original heading that had only the prepositional phrase (Eissfeldt 1965: 402). The question then becomes why this was added and placed before the prepositional phrase.

2. The clause "Thus spoke the Lord Yahweh to Edom" originally preceded v 2 (Theis 1937; Watts 1969; Deissler 1984). A difficulty with this view is that it leaves the pronoun of "against her" at the end of v 1 without an antecedent. Wolff (1977) avoids this problem by keeping the reference to Edom in its present position and transposing only "Thus spoke [the Lord] Yahweh" after v 1. Again, one wonders why the original sequence was altered. Wolff suggests that the messenger formula was accidentally omitted by a copyist, then added in the margin, and from there it strayed into its present location. Deissler hypothesizes that the rest of v 1 was inserted between the messenger formula and v 2 by a redactor — who derived it from Jer 49:14 — in order to provide a context for the following divine speech. Watts argues that the editor or compiler moved the formula to its present position to form part of the book's heading. This enabled the book to be identified as a true prophecy — since the messenger formula was a common prophetic idiom — and as a prophecy against Edom.

3. Transpose the messenger formula to immediately before the last line of v 1, "Arise so that we may rise against her for battle" (Mallon 1990). Rudolph (1971) argues that the editor moved the formula from this its original location to the front of v 1 in order to serve as a heading for the whole book. The difficulty with this option is twofold. First, linguistic usage shows that one should understand "Edom" as the direct addressee of the divine speech rather than simply the topic under consideration. But the command in the last line of v 1 is addressed to nations other than Edom. Second, the messenger formula introduces what the *prophet* was commanded to speak rather than what the dispatched "messenger" (*ṣîr*) of v 1 speaks.

4. The introductory formula, which should be kept in its present location, designates the following lines as a quotation of an older oracle (Bewer 1911; Cannon 1927: 192). The older oracle is also reflected in Jer 49:14–16. Against this view is the standard usage of the messenger formula. It commonly introduces divine speech spoken by a prophet and does not function as a technical designation of a quotation from an earlier prophetic oracle.

5. Keep the messenger formula in its present position and construe it with v 1a ("Obadiah's Vision") as the second half of a bipartite heading. Accordingly, it introduces the whole book and identifies the following twenty-one verses as Yahweh's word concerning Edom. This is perhaps the most common interpretation (Keil 1888; Halévy 1907; Allen 1976). However, there are several problems with this view. First, the prepositional phrase most likely should be translated "to Edom" rather than "concerning Edom." But the grammatical addressee of vv 16–21 is Judah and not Edom. Second, even if one prefers the latter rendition, not all twenty-one verses concern Edom, such as vv 16–17 and 20. Third, the Masoretic accentuation construes the messenger formula with the following lines rather than with the preceding superscription. Fourth, the messenger formula elsewhere always introduces divine speech in direct discourse, which does not begin until v 2. This standard usage makes it at least a strange introduction to the prophet's report in the rest of v 1. Finally, no other prophetic book employs the messenger formula as an introduction to its entire collection of oracles.

There is no textual evidence that supports either omitting or transposing the formula, as all the ancient versions agree with the MT. Nor is there any need for emendation. The easiest and most natural way to understand its function is to consider it the messenger formula introducing the divine speech of vv 2–4. Verses 2–4 consist of the divine utterance that Obadiah was commissioned to proclaim. He signals his role as messenger with the prefatory words "Thus spoke the Lord Yahweh to Edom." However, before he begins the divine speech addressed to Edom, he provides background information necessary for understanding it.

That there would be such a delay or gap between the messenger formula and the divine message itself is not as unusual as commentators assume. One encounters the phenomenon on occasion, especially in the oracles of Jeremiah. Intervening between the formula and the divine speech is material that supplies the addressee and reader with an explanatory context. The intervening material represents not so much an unrelated parenthesis as a delay necessary for comprehension. In the gap one finds information that expands on the nature of the divine speaker or of the addressee or of the topic under consideration. The following examples illustrate these three kinds of intervening material.

A. Expansion concerning the speaker (Jer 31:35–36):

v 35 "Thus spoke Yahweh —
who gives the sun for light by day
and the fixed orders of the moon and the stars for light by night,
who stirs up the sea so that its waves roar;
Yahweh of hosts is his name —
v 36 'If these fixed orders depart from before me,'
utterance of Yahweh,
'then will the seed of Israel cease from being a nation before me all the
days.'"

The gap between the messenger formula (v 35a) and the divine speech (v 36) is filled with an interlude that characterizes the speaker as the creator. It also supplies information necessary for understanding the comparison made in the divine speech. Compare Jer 33:2 and 42:9.

B. Expansion concerning the addressee (Jer 45:2–5):

v 2 "Thus spoke Yahweh, the God of Israel, concerning you, Baruch —
v 3 You said, 'Woe is me! For Yahweh has added
sorrow to my pain; I am weary with my groaning,
and rest I have not found.'
v 4 Thus you will say to him —
'Thus spoke Yahweh:
Look! What I have built I am breaking down . . .
v 5 As for you, do you seek for yourself great things?
Do not seek [them]. . . .'"

Before continuing with the divine speech (vv 4–5), Jeremiah quotes Baruch in the intervening material (v 3) in order to provide a context for the message. Another example where the text in the interlude between formula and speech clarifies the situation of the addressee appears in Ezek 36:4–5:

v 4 "Thus spoke the Lord Yahweh
to the mountains and the hills, the ravines and
the valleys, the desolate wastes and the deserted cities —
which have become a prey and derision to the
rest of the nations that are round about —
v 5 Therefore thus spoke the Lord Yahweh:
'In my hot jealousy I have spoken against the rest
of the nations and against all Edom . . .'"

Compare also Jer 31:2–6.

C. Expansion concerning the topic of the divine speech (Jer 27:19–22):

v 19 "For thus spoke Yahweh of hosts
    concerning the pillars, the sea, the stands, and the rest of the vessels left
        in this city —
v 20 which Nebuchadnezzar king of Babylon did not take away, when he took
        into exile from Jerusalem to Babylon Jeconiah the son of Jehoiakim,
        king of Judah, and all the nobles of Judah and Jerusalem —
v 21 for thus spoke Yahweh of hosts, the God of Israel,
    concerning the vessels left in the house of Yahweh and in the house of
        the king of Judah, and in Jerusalem:
v 22 'To Babylon they will be carried and there they will remain until the day
        when I attend to them,' utterance of Yahweh.
    'Then I will bring them back and restore them to this place.'"

Verse 19 gives the messenger formula and the topic under consideration, which is clarified further in v 20. After the repetition of the formula and the topic in v 21, the divine speech finally appears in v 22. One finds the same type of topic-clarification between formula and speech in Jer 29:16–19; 33:4–9; Mic 3:5–7; and Zech 2:12–13 [8–9]. Another noteworthy example, one that contains a quotation in the gap, occurs in Jer 32:36–37:

v 36 "Now therefore thus spoke Yahweh, the God of Israel,
    concerning this city —
    of which you say, 'It is given into the hand of the king of Babylon by
    sword, by famine, and by pestilence' —
v 37 'Behold, I will gather them . . .'"

The above examples reveal that an interlude or delay between the messenger formula and the divine speech is not unprecedented. The intervening material provides information that serves to clarify the subsequent message from Yahweh. Occasionally this material contains a quotation. Obad 1–2 corresponds with this type of sequence. Verse 1b gives the messenger formula and vv 2–4 record the divine message. Intervening between the two is the prophet's report that clarifies the addressee's situation, and embedded in this lies a quotation of Yahweh by a "messenger" recruiting the nations. Technically the prophet speaks in v 1 whereas the words of Yahweh addressed to Edom do not begin until v 2.

The closest parallel to the sequence of Obad 1–2 occurs in Jer 30:5–7:

v 5 "For thus spoke Yahweh —
    A voice of panic we have heard,
    of terror and no peace. —

v 6 'Ask and see:
　　Can a man bear a child?
　　Why then do I see every man
　　with his hands on his loins like a woman in labor,
　　and every face turned pale?
v 7 Alas! For that day is so great
　　there is none like it;
　　it is a time of distress for Jacob;
　　yet he will be saved from it.'"

Here we encounter between the messenger formula and the divine speech a delay in which a report is made by Jeremiah, "A voice of panic we have heard." It is difficult to say where the divine speech begins. It might be delayed until v 10 or v 8, but the use of imperatives and the switch to a first person singular verb in v 6 suggest it begins with v 6. At any rate, the sequence is much the same as in Obad 1–2; the same first person plural verb "we have heard" appears in the gap between the formula and the divine speech.

Granted that the sequence — messenger formula + intervening material + divine speech — is not so unusual, one might still inquire into the reason why Obadiah adopted this sequence here. Since Obadiah was drawing upon traditional material for v 1b–4, probably directly from Jer 49:14–16 rather than from a third source (see the Introduction), it is likely that he did not want to weaken the connection between v 1b and v 2 (= Jer 49:14–15). Compare Jer 26:18, where the formula introduces the quote of Mic 3:12 even though the quoted source lacks the formula. By placing the phrase "Thus spoke the Lord Yahweh to Edom" first, Obadiah also supplies the pronoun of the phrase "against her" at the end of v 1 with an antecedent, namely "Edom." In the Jer 49 parallel its antecedent is "Bozrah" mentioned in v 13.

šĕmû'â šāma'nû mē'ēt yahweh.
A report we have heard from Yahweh.
The line begins with the alliterative and assonant clause *šĕmû'â šāma'nû* in which *šĕmû'â* is a "cognate accusative" of the verb (lit., "a hearing we have heard"). The noun *šĕmû'â* follows the *qāṭûl / qĕṭûlâ* noun pattern from the root *šm'* (to hear). Its basic meaning is simply "something that is heard." By itself the noun does not convey positive or negative connotations; to be qualified further it needs an adjective such as "good" (Prov 15:30; 25:25) or "bad" (Jer 49:23; Ps 112:7). Its precise sense is supplied by the given context. It can be used to denote a vague "rumor" (2 Kgs 19:7; Jer 51:46; Dan 11:44) or factual "news" (1 Sam 4:19; 2 Sam 13:30; 1 Kgs 2:28). It can also designate a "report" from Yahweh (Isa 28:19; 53:1; Ezek 21:12 [7]; cf. Jer 6:22–24). This last usage corresponds with what is found in Obad 1 and its parallel in Jer 49:14.

What exactly is the "report" that Obadiah heard from Yahweh? Bewer (1911) suggests that it consists of the divine decree addressed to Edom and recorded in Obad 2–4 and Jer 49:15–16. What speaks against this view is that it leaves the next two lines unrelated to the "report." How can the prophet quote the summons to war unless somehow he heard of it? More likely the content of the "report" is stated in the next two lines (so Watts 1969):

> "A messenger has been sent among the nations (to say):
> 'Arise so that we may rise against her for battle.'"

Dick (1984: 8, 27 n. 19) suggests that the next line actually quotes Yahweh, a quotation that is introduced with *waw* (see Exod 2:20; 2 Sam 18:11; 24:3; 2 Kgs 4:14; 2 Chr 25:9; GKC § 154b for this use of *waw*). Or one might take the *waw*-clause as an object clause (cf. Joüon 1991 § 177h):

> "A report we have heard from Yahweh,
> *that* a messenger has been sent . . ."

It is curious that the parallel in Jer 49 has the singular "I have heard" in contrast to Obadiah's plural "we have heard." The plural subject in Obadiah might simply be an editorial "we" (Spaude 1987); or Obadiah might be identifying himself with the people as their representative so that when he "heard" the report they "heard" it in and through him (Keil 1888; Allen 1976). Unlike Jeremiah, who distinguishes himself from the people by using the singular "I," Obadiah includes Israel in *his* hearing. Perhaps the plural subject is used to refer to Obadiah and the people who "heard" what Jeremiah had "heard" and announced some years earlier (cf. Hitzig 1838; see the Introduction on the relationship between Jer 49 and Obadiah).

The clause indicates that Yahweh is the source and speaker of what was heard (cf. Isa 21:10; 28:22). When prophets say that they "heard" something from Yahweh, they usually state its content in the preceding or the following section (Isa 6:8; Jer 6:24; Ezek 1:28; 2:2; 43:6). Here we see its content given in the next two lines.

wĕṣîr.
A messenger.
Although the noun *ṣîr* occurs only six times in the Hebrew Bible, its basic sense is clear, that of a "messenger" or "envoy." (Wiseman [1982: 315–16] relates it to the Akkadian verb **ṣîru*, "to go to and fro," and the noun *ṣîru*, "envoy" or "chieftain.") In Isa 18:2 and Prov 13:17 *ṣîr* parallels *mal'āk* (messenger). In five texts *ṣîr* is construed with the verb *šlḥ* (to send): the object of the *qal* in Isa 18:2 and Prov 25:13; the object of the *pi'el* in Isa 57:9; the subject of the *qal* passive participle in Jer 49:14; and the subject of the *pu'al* in our text. Although the textual basis is small, one can perhaps specify more precisely that a *ṣîr* is an offi-

cial envoy sent by an authority figure to deliver a message. In Isa 18:2 the sender is Cush and in Isa 57:9 the sender is apostate Israel. According to Prov 25:13, a faithful envoy refreshes those sending him, who are called "his lords."

In Obad 1 and the parallel of Jer 49:14 is the ṣîr a human messenger or a heavenly one? The answer depends on the prior decision of whether the sender is an unspecified nation or Yahweh. In the other four texts it refers to a human messenger, but that is so only because in those texts the sender happens to be human. Below it will be argued that in Obad 1 and Jer 49 the sender is Yahweh. Therefore the "messenger" spoken of here is a celestial being, a member of Yahweh's heavenly council. Because ṣîr parallels mal'āk (Isa 18:2; Prov 13:17), which can designate both a human and an angelic "messenger," there is no reason why ṣîr cannot have the same range of reference.

baggôyīm šullāḥ.
has been sent among the nations (to say).

The prepositional phrase "among the nations" should be construed with the following verb "to send," which often takes the preposition b. The phrase "among the nations" states the destination to which the messenger was sent rather than the location of his origin. The nations are the recipients of the war summons stated in the next line that is to be delivered by the messenger. Frequently after the verb šlḥ comes the message in direct discourse, which often is construed with lē'mōr (saying) but on occasion lacks it, as is the case here (cf. Num 20:14; 1 Sam 20:21; 2 Sam 11:6; Isa 18:2 [with ṣîr]; 2 Chr 2:10 [11]).

The passive verb (puʻal) does not specify who sent the messenger. Bewer (1911) and Watts (1969) argue that some unidentified nation sent the messenger. Bewer bases this upon the next line in which the messenger supposedly identifies himself with the nations he addresses, "Arise so that we may rise against her for battle." However, two factors weigh against this view. First, one would expect an active form of the verb "to send" with the sending nation identified, if the sender were someone other than Yahweh, the author of the "report" mentioned in the previous line. Second, the recipients of the message are viewed as an undifferentiated whole. The simple phrase "among the nations" does not encourage one to distinguish between a summoning nation and other summoned nations. That Yahweh is the sender is the easiest and most natural understanding. With this the LXX, the Vulgate, and most commentators agree.

Biblical texts often speak of Yahweh "sending" heavenly messengers to announce and enact his decrees. One usually finds the verb in the qal (Gen 24:7, 40; Exod 23:20; 33:2; Num 20:16; Judg 13:8; Zech 1:10; 1 Chr 21:15; 2 Chr 32:21), but the piʻel (Gen 19:13) and puʻal (Dan 10:11) occur as well. In keeping with this usage the reference here is to a heavenly messenger, and v 1 narrates his commission by Yahweh in the divine assembly to recruit the nations for war against Edom. Thus v 1 portrays in typical poetic terseness the commissioning scene of one of Yahweh's celestial agents. The next line states the message he was commissioned to announce. For treatments of the divine council, see H. W. Robinson (1944), Cross (1953), Whybray (1971), Mullen (1980), Miller (1987), and Brettler (1989: 100–9).

The motif of Yahweh recruiting the nations for war against a targeted city or nation occurs fairly often in the Latter Prophets (Bach 1962). It is particularly popular in Jeremiah's oracles against the nations (Jer 46–51). One of the ways that Yahweh recruits the nations according to the prophetic texts is through the agency of the divine council members (Miller 1968). For example, according to Joel 4:9 [3:9] Yahweh commands his angelic hosts to call the nations to arms:

"Proclaim this among the nations:
'Consecrate war!
Stir up the warriors!
Let all the men of war draw near, let them go up!'"

In the first line Yahweh addresses the divine assembly with the plural imperative "proclaim." The following lines then give the message that the divine assembly is to proclaim among the nations. The divine council also may be the context for understanding Jer 51:27–28 (Miller 1968: 104–5). There Yahweh commands with plural imperatives an unspecified group, possibly the members of his council, to summon the nations for war against Babylon:

"Raise a signal in the earth!
Sound the trumpet among the nations!
Consecrate nations against her!
Summon kingdoms against her,
Ararat, Minni, and Ashkenaz. . . ."

Perhaps we should think of the individual angelic princes who are assigned to the different nations, an idea reflected in Deut 32:8 (Qumran, LXX) and Daniel. Yet the biblical texts generally do not clarify exactly how the angelic hosts of Yahweh's council are to summon nations. They only emphasize that Yahweh through his agents recruits nations to do his bidding. This is one way that the God of Israel is portrayed as exercising his kingship over the whole world.

However, there is one text that perhaps clarifies the way the communication process was conceived in ancient Israel. In 1 Kgs 22:19–23 the prophet Micaiah describes his vision of the divine council. While sitting on his throne and surrounded by the heavenly host, Yahweh asked, "Who will entice Ahab, that he may go up and fall at Ramoth-gilead?" After some discussion a "spirit" volunteered to entice Ahab by becoming a "lying spirit" in the mouth of Ahab's prophets. Yahweh then commissioned the "spirit" to do just that. According to this account, a member of the divine council incited Ahab to attack Ramoth-gilead by deceiving Ahab's prophets into recommending this military action. It is noteworthy that the same verb, "to go up, advance," is found in other prophetic texts that record a divine summons to war (Isa 21:2; Jer 46:9; 49:28, 31; 50:21; Joel 4:9, 12 [3:9, 12]).

One might interpret Obad 1 along the same lines, that Yahweh sent an angelic messenger to persuade a nation's officials into recommending a military campaign against Edom (Laetsch 1956). However, unlike the lengthy and detailed portrayal of the heavenly council's commissioning scene in 1 Kgs 22, Obad 1 and its parallel in Jer 49:14 give only the basic information concerning *who* ("a messenger"), *what* ("has been sent"), and *where* ("among the nations"). That suffices to indicate that Yahweh as the "Lord" over all the nations is the one behind the impending attack on Edom. He is the one who "stirs up the spirit of the kings" to execute his plan (Jer 51:11).

qûmû.
Arise.

The summons to war addressed to the nations by Yahweh through his messenger begins with the plural imperative "arise." The imperative of *qwm* occurs seventeen times in a military context in the Bible (Deut 2:24; Josh 8:1; Judg 4:14; 5:12; 7:9, 15; 9:32; 18:9; 1 Sam 23:4; Isa 21:5; Jer 6:4, 5; 49:14, 28, 31; Mic 4:13; Obad 1). In these contexts it is the initial verb of a call to attack a military enemy. Usually a verb of motion follows, such as *hlk* (to go) or *'lh* (to go up). The basic sense of *qwm* in these texts is therefore "arise from inaction, get up, get ready" for the purpose of embarking on a military campaign. In nine of these texts the speaker is Yahweh who addresses either Israelites — all Israel (Deut 2:24), Zion (Mic 4:13), individual military leaders, such as Joshua (Josh 8:1), Gideon (Judg 7:9), and David (1 Sam 23:4) — or the nations (Jer 49:14; Obad 1), such as Babylon (Jer 49:28, 31).

wěnāqûmâ 'āleyhā lammilḥāmâ.
so that we may rise against her for battle.

In the syntactic sequence of imperative + simple *waw* + cohortative, the second clause usually signals a purpose or result clause (Lambdin 1971: 119; cf. Orlinsky 1940–1941; 1941–1942). In this case we have a purpose clause: "Get up for the purpose that we may attack her." The sequence with the imperative of *qwm* + *waw* + first person plural cohortative is found also in Judg 19:28; 2 Sam 15:14; and Jer 31:6; 46:16. The closest parallels, which also represent summons to war, occur in Judg 18:9 and Jer 6:4–5. In the former the Danite spies call the Danites to attack the people of Laish:

qûmâ wěna'āleh 'ālêhem

"Arise so that we may go up against them."

In the Jeremiah text the foe from the north prepares to attack Jerusalem:

qûmû wĕnaʿăleh baṣṣohŏrāyim
qûmû wĕnaʿăleh ballāyĕlâ
wĕnašḥîtâ ʾarmĕnôteyhā

"Arise so that we may go up at noon . . .
Arise so that we may go up at night
and destroy her citadels."

When it has a personal object, the construction *qûm ʿal* means "to rise up against, attack" with the connotation of unexpected suddenness. The sense can be illustrated by 1 Sam 17:35. There David argues that Saul should allow him to fight Goliath, because previously David demonstrated his ability to kill a lion or a bear whenever it would *"rise up against"* him. The sense is further clarified by Deut 19:11 and Judg 9:43. The former designates the case of a man who "hates his neighbor, lies in wait for him, *rises up against him*, and smites him so that he dies." According to the latter, Abimelech with his men set an ambush in the open field for the Shechemites and *"rose up against them* and smote them." In both texts the idiom refers to the action that comes between lying in wait and actually smiting another party. Thus it designates a surprise attack against an enemy. Usually the subject of the idiom is human, but occasionally it is God (Isa 14:22; 31:2; Amos 7:9). In Obadiah those attacking Edom consist of both divine and human actors, both Yahweh and the nations acting in concert (see below).

In the Jer 49 parallel we find only second person plural imperatives, which are addressed to the nations (v 14). Although Yahweh is the one recruiting the nations, the nations alone are the party that will actually fight Edom. In contrast Obadiah heightens the dramatic effect with the first person plural verb.

Who are the referents included in the "we" subject? Certainly "the nations" constitute part of the attackers, since they are the addressees of the initial imperative and of the whole line. We do not learn more precisely of the identity of these nations until v 7, but they do not include Jerusalem (*pace* Wolff 1977). Obadiah consistently distinguishes between the "nations" (*gôyīm*) and Judah/Jerusalem as Yahweh's "people" (*ʿam* — v 13: cf. vv 2, 11, 15–17). Verse 1 distinguishes between the "we" who "heard" and "the nations" to whom Yahweh issued the war summons. The other referent of the first person pronoun is the speaker. The "messenger" is the one being commissioned to communicate the summons. But as is generally the case with messengers, he does not speak in his own name but in the name of the sender. The sender and the speaker of the "report" is Yahweh. By employing the first person plural "we" Yahweh includes himself in the warring party. The divine "Lord" not only recruits the coalition but also intends to participate in the battle as their leader and commander-in-chief (so Keil 1888; Thompson 1956; Wolff 1977).

her. One should read with the MT the feminine pronominal suffix '*āleyhā*; the antecedent is "Edom." In contrast vv 2–15 have masculine pronouns throughout. Why is "Edom" considered feminine in v 1? Bič (1953: 14) in keeping with his view of Obadiah as reflecting a cult drama argues that Edom is feminine here because she is compared with the primeval foe Tiamat, but such an interpretation is quite unlikely and unnecessary.

Place names "frequently lose their head nouns (the grammatical process of 'beheading'), while the head noun continues to control the gender of the phrase" (Waltke and O'Connor 1990: 103). "Beheading" is evident in English when we say, for example, "California" for "the state of California." In languages with grammatical gender systems one often finds this "beheading" process. It explains why names of countries, cities, rivers, and the like are assigned one gender or another (Waltke and O'Connor 1990: 103–4).

In some cases in Biblical Hebrew, the same place name can vary between masculine and feminine genders because the underlying and implied head noun varies. Examples include "Assyria," "Judah," and "Edom." "Edom" can be considered a "land" (*'ereṣ* — feminine) since the phrase "the land of Edom" is common (Gen 36:16, 17, 21, 31; Num 20:23; 21:4; 33:37; Judg 11:18; 1 Kgs 9:26; Isa 34:6; 1 Chr 1:43; 2 Chr 8:17), yet "Edom" is also spoken of as a "nation" (*gôy* / *'am* — masculine; Gen 25:23; Isa 34:5; Jer 9:25 [26]; 25:17, 21) and as "Esau" (Gen 36:1, 8, 19; Jer 49:8, 10; Mal 1:3; cf. Amos 1:11). Consequently, one is not surprised to find the gender of "Edom" as masculine (Num 20:14–21; 24:18; 2 Sam 8:14; 2 Kgs 8:20–22 = 2 Chr 21:8–10) and feminine (Ezek 25:13; 32:29; 35:15; 36:5; Joel 4:19 [3:19]; Lam 4:21–22 — "daughter Edom").

Occasionally the gender of "Edom" varies in the same context. Mal 1:3 uses the masculine pronoun in "his mountains" and "his inheritance" to refer to "Esau" mentioned previously, but verse 4 takes "Edom" as a feminine. In Jer 49:8–12 we find the masculine pronoun referring to Edom apparently under the influence of "Esau" mentioned in vv 8 and 10. In vv 14–16, which parallel Obad 1–4, v 14 has the feminine pronoun because its antecedent is the feminine city name "Bozrah" mentioned in v 13, but vv 15–16 change to masculine pronouns either because of the influence of the name "Esau" or because Edom is considered a "nation." However, feminine pronouns are used in vv 17–21 where Edom is probably thought of as a "land."

Therefore, it need not come as a surprise that "Edom" is designated in Obad 1 by the feminine pronoun but by masculine pronouns in the following verses. If Obadiah based the opening words on Jer 49:14, it was unnecessary for him to change '*āleyhā* (against her) there to '*ālāyw* (against him) since "Edom" can be a feminine as well as a masculine place name. Verse 1 probably considers "Edom" a "land" and therefore feminine (Bewer 1911). Furthermore, the feminine suffix promotes assonance of the final vowel -*a*: *qûmû wĕnāqûmâ 'āleyhā lammilḥāmâ* (Dick 1984: 8). The following verse switches to masculine pronouns because "Edom" is reckoned a "nation" among nations (v 2). Later in v 6 it is equated with "Esau."

for battle. The preposition *l* signals purpose (cf. 2 Sam 18:32; 1 Kgs 22:6; 1 Chr 12:20 [19]; 2 Chr 20:1). The phrase specifies the intent and goal of the attack against Edom. Jer 49:14 joins "for battle" with the imperative "arise."

2. *hinnēh qāṭōn nĕtattîkā baggôyīm.*
  Look! Insignificant I have made you among the nations.
  The deictic-exclamatory particle *hinnēh* can mark an unexpected turn of events by introducing what Andersen labels "surprise clauses" (Andersen 1974: 94–96). It primarily functions to draw the hearers'/readers' attention to the following word or statement (Muraoka 1985: 137–40). The usual translation "Behold!" or "Look!" conveys this function, although the particle does not denote "to see." Here *hinnēh* focuses attention on the following and surprising adjective that is placed forward for emphasis, "insignificant."
  The parallel in Jer 49:15 makes explicit a causal connection between the following statement and the preceding by using *kî hinnēh* (For, look!), but *hinnēh* alone can also function to make such a connection (Waltke and O'Connor 1990: 677–78). The following statement by Yahweh explains why the nations will not hesitate to attack Edom, namely, because Yahweh has already made Edom insignificant in their estimation. Yet the omission of Jeremiah's "for" opens up another connection between v 1 and v 2. The very fact that the nations are currently preparing for war against Edom provides Edom with evidence of its present insignificant status.

  Insignificant. The adjective *qāṭōn* has the basic sense of "small" in contrast to "great" (*gādôl*), but further precision depends on the context and the noun or pronoun it modifies. It can be used to characterize a reality that is "small" in terms of time, such as "young in age" (Gen 42:13) and a "brief period" (Isa 54:7), or in terms of size, such as a "small house" (Amos 6:11) and a "small robe" (1 Sam 2:19), or in terms of status, such as a "trivial matter" (Exod 18:22) and an "insignificant person" (1 Sam 15:17). However, it does not mean "few in number"; for that sense one uses *mĕ'aṭ* (Num 13:18; Deut 7:7; Dan 11:23; Neh 7:4).
  In Obad 2 *qāṭōn* modifies the pronoun "you," which refers to "Edom" (v 1). When used to qualify a place, the adjective designates either its size or its status. On the one hand, in Eccl 9:14 it refers to the size of a city, "a small [*qĕtannâ*] city and few [*mĕ'āṭ*] men in her." On the other hand, in Amos 7:2, 5 it designates an insignificant status. There Amos responds to the visions of impending destruction shown him by Yahweh, "Please forgive/cease! How can Jacob survive, for he is small?" "Small" does not denote Jacob's territorial size, especially since, as Andersen and Freedman argue, "Jacob" refers to all the descendants of the patriarch, both the northern and the southern kingdoms (Andersen and Freedman 1989: 114–15; cf. Paul 1991: 229 n. 33). Rather, the adjective points to Jacob's

insignificant, weak, and feeble status, its inability to survive the threatened catas-trophe. Possibly Amos alludes to the patriarch's prayer, "I am too insignificant [qṭnty] for all the kindness and for all the faithfulness that you have shown your servant" (Gen 32:11 [10]). The significance of qṭn is unclear in 1 Sam 9:21, where Saul says that he is "a Benjaminite of the smallest [mqṭny] of the tribes of Israel" and that his family is "the least [hṣ'rh] of all the families of the tribe of Benjamin." The reference could be to Benjamin's territorial size or its low esteem or both (cf. Mic 5:1 [2]; Ps 68:28 [27]; Judg 6:15).

On the basis of these parallels and if Obad 2a were isolated from its context, one could interpret Edom as "small" either in size or in status. However, the next colon clarifies the ambiguity by paralleling qāṭōn with bāzûy, "despised." Consequently, the adjective refers to Edom's "small" status, that it is insignificant and weak in the eyes of the nations and hence vulnerable to an attack. The fol-lowing lines contrast Edom's low esteem among the nations with its own lofty self-opinion. The contrast does not lie in the domain of size, as if Edom considers itself "great" in territorial dimensions or population. Rather, according to v 3 Edom proudly feels itself secure from hostile attack due to its geographical loca-tion. The adjective qāṭōn is employed to contradict this false sense of security. In addition, there might be another though more indirect reason for the use of this adjective. Because v 6 begins to evoke the Esau-Jacob narratives, possibly "small" alludes to and represents a reversal of Esau's status as the "great" (haggādōl) or "older" son (Gen 27:1, 15). The rabbis developed this association extensively (Maier 1982).

I have made you. The subject of the first person verb is Yahweh and the pronoun "you" refers to Edom. The pronoun is masculine here in contrast to the feminine in v 1 because "Edom" is considered a "nation" (gôy) among other nations. Whereas in the last line of v 1 Yahweh addresses the other nations, here he addresses Edom through the prophet. Thus v 2 begins the divine speech intro-duced by the messenger formula of v 1.

The verb ntn frequently takes double accusatives. When the first accusative is a pronoun, the other accusative is usually a noun (Gen 17:5; Exod 7:1; Deut 1:15; Jer 1:5; etc.) but occasionally an adjective, as is the case here (cf. Deut 28:25; Lam 1:13). In this construction the verb means "to make, appoint" and the accusatives designate the object and the object's changed status, "I have made/appointed you an insignificant status" (cf. BDB; Waltke and O'Connor 1990: 174–75; GKC § 117ii). A close parallel occurs in Mal 2:9 where Yahweh says to the priests, "I have made you despised and low before all the people."

The use of the perfect raises the issue of whether this is a "prophetic perfect" threatening a future event or a "past perfect" announcing a completed action and a present reality. Most commentators take it to be a "prophetic perfect" signi-fying that Edom's diminution is as good as done since Yahweh has already decreed it. According to this view, v 2 expresses the purpose, whereas the impending attack by the nations in v 1 constitutes the means for achieving this end. Yahweh is currently recruiting the nations against Edom because he intends to "make [it] small among the nations." This interpretation assumes that the phrase *qāṭōn nětattîkā* designates a diminution of Edom's population and living space (e.g., Wolff 1977; Rudolph 1971; Stuart 1987). Indeed, if that assumption were correct, the interpretation would be preferred (*pace* Wellhausen 1963; Ewald 1876; Nowack 1897 and others who think that Edom's size and population have already been decimated). However, to express the idea of "reducing size or population" Hebrew uses a different construction, the *hip'il* of *m't*.

The phrase designates, rather, the insignificant and feeble status that Yahweh has given Edom among the nations. Accordingly, the perfect verb indicates a completed and present situation, completed and present not only from the speaker's perspective but also in historical reality. At least that is the text's claim. The next colon further emphasizes that Edom's low status is a current reality. Now the nations neither fear Edom nor hesitate to embark on a military campaign against it. The reduction of Edom's status forms the basis for the impending attack because it removed any deterrence capability Edom might have. Moreover, the very fact that the nations are currently preparing for war reveals their lack of respect for Edom's strength. The following verse develops the motif of Edom's inflated self-opinion in order to contrast it with the nations' low esteem of Edom.

among the nations. The repetition of the phrase serves to link v 2 with v 1. Both phrases refer to the same nations, but their identity is left unspecified until v 7.

bāzûy 'attâ mě'ōd.
You are utterly despised.
When the predicate of a verbless clause classifies or describes a definite subject, the predicate usually is indefinite and the word order usually is Predicate + Subject (Andersen 1970: 31–34; Waltke and O'Connor 1990: 132–35). Obad 2b corresponds with this pattern. Classifying clauses answer the question "What is the subject like?" Here the statement declares not only that Edom is "despised" but also heightens the statement with the intensifier "utterly."

The parallel in Jer 49:15 reads *bāzûy bā'ādām* (despised among humankind) and gaps the verb:

"Insignificant I have made you among the nations,
despised (I have made you) among humankind."

Obadiah in contrast creates a separate sentence and pairs a nominal clause with a verbal clause. Possibly Obadiah intentionally changed Jeremiah's text by inserting the pronoun *'attâ* after *bāzûy*, omitting the preposition *b* of *bā'ādām*, and transposing the consonants of 'dm to m'd. If so, what was Obadiah's intent? With these changes Obadiah echoes Jeremiah but also emphasizes more strongly than Jeremiah the magnitude ("utterly") and the present reality ("you are") of Edom's despised status. The changes create a progression from what "I" have done to what "you" are.

The form bāzûy is a qal passive participle of bzh with the same sense as the nip'al participle nbzh, "one who has been/is despised." Although the colon does not identify the despisers, one assumes ellipsis of "among the nations" in light of Jeremiah's version.

The roots bzh and bwz mean "to despise, disdain, hold contempt for" (Görg 1975). The semantic field clarifies the sense. Note the following near-synonyms: l'g, "to deride, ridicule" (2 Kgs 19:21 = Isa 37:22; Pss 22:8 [7]; 123:4), ḥerpâ, "reproach, scorn" (Pss 22:7 [6]; 119:22), t'b, "to abhor" (Isa 49:7), and šqṣ, "to detest" (Ps 22:25 [24]). Words with senses antithetical to bzh include: yr', "to fear, respect" (Prov 13:13; 14:2; Mal 1:6; cf. v 14), kibbēd, "to honor" (1 Sam 2:30; Mal 1:6), and hll, "be commended" (Prov 12:8). In all cases the word denotes an intense attitude of disdain that a person has toward another person or object.

In both Obadiah and Jeremiah bāzûy parallels qāṭōn of the previous colon (cf. Ps 119:141, "I am insignificant and despised [ṣā'îr 'ānōkî wĕnibzeh]"). It well illustrates the intensifying semantic structure that appears frequently in poetic parallelism, in which the second colon advances and heightens the sense of the first colon (cf. Kugel 1981; Alter 1985). Not only do the nations consider Edom "insignificant" and feeble, which could signify simply a neutral indifference, but they "utterly despise" it in an active and hostile sense. Their lack of respect for Edom's inaccessible location and defensive capabilities (v 3), their lack of esteem for its friendship (v 7), and their utter disdain for it as a nation motivate them to prepare a military attack. Thus v 2b connects well with v 2a and with v 1.

The line has links with the following material as well. Occasionally one finds bwz associated with pride in the sense of being haughty and contemptuous of others (Pss 31:19 [18]; 123:4), and that association forms a fitting antithesis to the next verse. Edom's heart might be proud, but in reality, so the text claims, Edom is in no position to "despise" others. Quite the opposite is the case. Furthermore, like its paired word qāṭōn, bāzûy perhaps anticipates the Esau connection established in v 6, as it evokes Gen 25:34, "And Esau despised [bzh] the birthright."

3. zĕdôn libbĕkā.
The presumption of your heart.
The normal word order of verb + subject for a verbal clause is reversed here in order to contrast the initial noun "presumption" with the initial adjectives of the previous two cola, "insignificant" and "despised" (cf. Muraoka 1985: 28–33; Jongeling 1991). Also note that the vowel sequence of zĕdôn (reduction of origi-

nal *zādôn*) echoes that of *qāṭōn* and *bāzûy*. Whereas the nations consider Edom "insignificant" and "despised," "presumption" characterizes Edom's own self-opinion.

The word *zādôn* is a *qālôn* noun formation of the root *zyd*. The root with its derivatives seems to fall into the general semantic field of "pride," traditionally one of the seven deadly sins (cf. Gowan 1975: 19–23). Yet unlike normal pride or even excessive pride that can be based on genuine superiority, *zyd* suggests "claims that are totally unjustified — the arrogation of rights to which one is not entitled, a refusal to recognize the limits set by God and the legal or moral order" (Scharbert 1980: 51). The noun *zādôn* conveys more the sense of "presumption" and "unwarranted boldness" than simply "pride." Deut 18:22 illustrates the sense. A prophet who speaks a word in the name of Yahweh when Yahweh did not speak is said to speak "in presumption." 1 Sam 17:28 provides another clarifying example. David had left his flock and had come to Israel's military camp as they faced Goliath. When Eliab, David's oldest brother, overheard David speaking with some of the men, he accused David of neglecting his responsibilities and meddling in affairs that did not concern him, "I know your presumption and the evil of your heart."

In Obad 3 the thought assigned to Edom gives expression to its *zādôn*, "you who say in your heart, 'Who will bring me down to the earth?'" Edom supposes that it is secure and invulnerable to enemy attack. By using the word *zādôn* Obadiah expresses the irony that in spite of its mountainous and lofty abode, this bold assumption is totally unwarranted and unfounded. Because Edom refuses to recognize the limits set by the Lord Yahweh, "the presumption of [its] heart has deceived" Edom. As is usually the case in the Bible, "heart" denotes the inner life, one's self-awareness, the mind and will more than the seat of emotions.

hiššî'ekā.
has deceived you.

The *hipʿil* of *nšʾ* II (sometimes designated *nšʾ* I) occurs at least thirteen times in the sense of "to deceive, give false hopes" (Ringgren 1986c). The basic sense can be seen from the verb's collocations: *tʿh*, "to go astray" (Isa 19:13), *swt*, "to lead astray, seduce" (2 Chr 32:15), *ḥălōmôt*, "dreams," and *šeqer*, "falsehood" (Jer 29:8–9).

Perhaps the best-known occurrence is Eve's reply in Gen 3:13, "The serpent deceived me and I ate." In several instances one finds a sequence with a quote spelling out what the deceived are led to think followed by the opposing view. In Jer 4:10 the prophet laments, "Ah, Lord Yahweh, surely you have utterly deceived this people and Jerusalem by saying 'You will have peace,' when the sword has reached to the throat." According to Jer 37:9, Yahweh says, "Do not deceive yourselves by saying 'The Babylonians will surely leave us,' for they will not leave." And in 2 Kgs 19:10 (= Isa 37:10) Sennacherib's messengers say to Hezekiah,

"Do not let your god in whom you trust deceive you by saying 'Jerusalem will not be given into the hand of the king of Assyria.'" The message goes on to say that no god delivered any of the other nations or cities (cf. 2 Kgs 18:29 = Isa 36:14).

These texts reveal the sense of the verb, that of giving a false hope and a false object of trust. To be "deceived" is to believe and hope in a lie. Obad 3–4 follows the same pattern as the above texts by attributing a quoted thought to Edom and then providing a contrary claim on the part of Yahweh:

The presumption of your heart has deceived you . . .
you who say in your heart:
"Who will bring me down to the earth?" . . .
I will bring you down!

The claim is that Edom's presumptuous heart has given Edom a false hope and a false sense of security in thinking no one can bring it down.

šōkĕnî bĕhagwê ssela'.
you who dwell in the clefts of the crags.

The masculine singular participle šōkĕnî lies in apposition to the preceding pronominal suffix -kā and could be considered — although not necessarily — a bound form. The participle is written with the affixed -î morpheme, the so-called ḥireq compaginis. In addition to this occurrence and the parallel in Jer 49:16, the same verb in participial form with ḥireq compaginis appears three times (Deut 33:16; Jer 51:13-Kethib; Mic 7:14), and its synonym yšb also in participial form with ḥireq compaginis occurs six times (Jer 10:17-Kethib; 22:23-Kethib; Ezek 27:3-Kethib; Pss 113:9; 123:1; Lam 4:21-Kethib).

Robertson (1969) provides a helpful study of the ḥireq compaginis. In the Hebrew Bible there are thirty-three instances of this morpheme and all but two appear in poetry, including archaic poetry. Twenty-seven instances have it affixed to a participle and the other six to a noun. We find the same pattern as Obad 3 and Jer 49:16 twelve other times, participle -î + prepositional phrase. In the vast majority of cases (twenty-nine out of thirty-three) the -î morpheme is affixed to a participle/noun that lies in apposition to a pronoun or noun. This explains why it so often occurs with participles (twenty-six out of these twenty-nine), since participles lend themselves to being used in apposition to another element. For the other four instances the ḥireq compaginis seems to reinforce a bound structure.

The noun ḥagwê is the plural bound form of the absolute *ḥāgû or *ḥagweh and derives from the root *ḥgh. It occurs only three times in the Bible, all of which have the same phrase (Obad 3 = Jer 49:16; Cant 2:14); the root never occurs elsewhere in Biblical Hebrew. Therefore its meaning must be determined by the context, Semitic cognates, and the ancient versions.

The context indicates that the noun has something to do with places in rocky terrain in which to dwell securely. One naturally thinks of the clefts, crevices, caves, and inaccessible hiding places that abound in the Edomite hills. The rock-cut city of Petra, the "rose-red city half as old as time," provides a well-known illustration of the terrain. Cant 2:14 clarifies the sense:

> *yônātî bĕḥagwê hasselaʿ*
> *bĕsēter hammadrēgâ*

> "My dove in the *ḥagwê* of the crags
> in the covert of the steeps."

The noun *madrēgâ* designates either rugged passes between mountains or hill-side terraces (cf. Ezek 38:20). Here the phrase *ḥagwê hasselaʿ* refers to the cliff-side clefts and caves where doves hide their nests (Pope 1977: 400–1). Jer 48:28 offers a close parallel to both the Obadiah/Jeremiah and the Canticles texts:

> *ʿizbû ʿārîm wĕsiknû basselaʿ*
> *yōšĕbê môʾāb*
> *wihyû kĕyônâ*
> *tĕqannēn bĕʿebrê pî pāḥat*

> "Abandon the cities and dwell in the crags,
> O inhabitants of Moab!
> And become like the dove
> that nests in the sides of the mouth of the gorge."

Here as well the reference is to the ravines and precipitous cliffs that are perforated with caves and crevices (cf. Job 39:27–28). Note the related phrases "the cleft of the crag" (*nĕqîq hassālaʿ* [Jer 13:4]) and "the clefts of the crags" (*nĕqîqê hasselāʿîm* [Isa 7:19; Jer 16:16]).

With the root **ḥgh* one can compare Arabic *ḥajja*, "to split, rend," or more likely *ḥajaʾa*, "to flee for refuge" (*maḥjaʾ* / *ḥajān* / *ḥajayn*, "place of refuge"). Also note Arabic *wajaḥ*, "cave." The ancient versions translate Obad 3, Jer 49, and Cant 2 with words denoting "caves, clefts" or less concretely "protection, fortification."

The genitive of the phrase is *sselaʿ* — the *samek* is doubled by a conjunctive *dagesh* (see Yeivin 1980: 289–96; Revell 1990). Here *selaʿ* is not written with the definite article *h* but with *h* in Jer 49:16 and Cant 2:14 where the same phrase occurs. This illustrates a common feature of Hebrew poetry: although the definite article *h* might not appear on a noun — it is generally rare in poetry — the noun might still be considered definite. Such is the case here.

One could understand *selaʿ* as the place name Sela, an Edomite site captured by Judah in the early eighth century (2 Kgs 14:7). Frequently Sela has been identified with Petra, the subsequent Nabatean capital, and more specifically Umm el-Biyara in Petra. But another site has also been suggested, Khirbet Sil' located a few kilometers northwest of Buseira (Bozrah) in the northern part of Edom (see Rainey 1976; Bartlett 1989: 51–52). Both sites are isolated rock massifs with steep slopes, and each has only one approach that can be easily defended. The archaeological evidence does not yet settle the question (Hart 1986).

With *sela'* Obadiah and Jeremiah probably allude to the place name Sela, but the Canticles parallel indicates that *sela'* technically is used here as the common noun meaning "crag" or collective "crags." The text attributes to the Edomites a strong sense of security and invulnerability based on the many crevices and caves where they could hide in times of danger and the nearly inaccessible location of their cities in high rock formations.

měrôm šibtô.
in the height of your seat.
The phrase is a construct chain that matches the previous construct chain "in the clefts of the crags" (cf. Isa 22:16 where "height" is paired with "crag"). The verb *škny* (dwell), which is gapped here, can take an accusative noun of location (Mic 7:14; Job 39:28) or the preposition *b* with a noun of location (Jer 48:28). Consequently, one can construe the phrase as an accusative (cf. Isa 33:5, 16; 57:15) or consider the preceding preposition *b* to be gapped.

The ancient versions suggest two possible alternatives for MT *měrôm*. First, following the LXX (*hypsōn*) and the Vulgate (*exaltantem*), one could posit that MT misread an original *hip'il* participle of *rwm*, *mērîm*, "[you] who exalt your seat." But more likely the translators, motivated by the desire to have a participle that parallels the previous and subsequent participles *šōkĕnî* and *'ōmēr*, misread *mrwm*. Thereby they alleviated the problem of the *škny . . . šbtw* sequence. Second, one could assume an original absolute form *mārôm* rather than the construct *měrôm* in light of the Targum *brwm' mwtbyh* and the Peshiṭta *wbrwm' mwtbh*, "whose dwelling is on high." But again, it is more likely that the translators attempted to simplify the verse by creating a clause independent of the previous colon's verb *škny*. Therefore MT is to be preferred. Jeremiah's use of the same form *měrôm* supports this conclusion (cf. Barthélemy 1992: 697–98).

The pronominal suffix of *šibtô* is third person (lit., "his seat"), a switch from the second person object suffix of the main verb *hišši'ekā* (has deceived you). Such a change in person happens frequently in Biblical Hebrew. Biblical Hebrew like classical Arabic commonly uses third person pronouns in relative or appositional clauses that modify a preceding second person reference (Hillers 1983). Isa 22:16 illustrates the phenomenon:

ḥāṣabtā llĕkā pōh qāber
ḥōṣĕbî mārôm qibrô
ḥōqĕqî bassela' miškān lô

"You have hewn out for yourself a tomb here,
you who hew out on high your [lit. his] tomb,
you who hollow out in the crag an abode for yourself [lit. himself]."

Other examples include: Isa 44:1, 23; 47:8; 54:1; Jer 5:21–22; 49:4–5; Ezek 21:30 [25]; Mic 1:2; 3:9–12; 7:18–20; Ps 18:50–51 [49–50]. The change in person is morphological and syntactic but not semantic; direct discourse continues throughout the sequence. To reflect this continuity, my translation maintains the second person throughout verse 3.

The noun *mārôm*, a *maqtal noun formation of the middle weak root *rwm*, means "height, elevated place." It can refer to the heavens, the abode reserved for Yahweh, and possibly that idea is implied here; Edom claims to inhabit the heavenly heights with Yahweh (cf. Isa 14:12–14). Compare the Ugaritic expression *mrym ṣpn*, "the heights of Ṣapān," the abode of Baal. But the primary reference here is to the lofty Edomite mountains, as the parallel in Jer 49:16 makes clear:

tōpĕśî mĕrôm gibʿâ

"(you) who seize the height of the hill."

Most Edomite sites were located on the high plateau southeast of the Dead Sea, which was bordered by the deep-cut Wadi el-Ḥasā (biblical Zered) to the north, the Rift Valley of the Arabah to the west, the Wadi Ḥismā to the south, and the gentle slope of the Arabian desert in the east. This ridge reached heights of 4,000 to 5,600 feet. The heights are particularly impressive from a vantage point in the west.

The genitive *šibtô* is a nominal derivative of *yšb*, technically the infinitive construct form *šebet* with pronominal suffix. The verb *yšb* can mean either "to take a seat" or "to be in the state of sitting," what Görg (1990) terms "sedative" and "mansive" respectively. With the infinitive the mansive sense dominates. But occasionally, five times in addition to Obad 3 according to BDB, *šebet* loses its verbal sense completely and instead functions as a noun with the sense of "abode, seat, location." 1 Kgs 10:19 (= 2 Chr 9:18) uses *šebet* to denote Solomon's throne. In Amos 6:3 *šebet* seems to have the sense of "seat, throne" or the extended sense of "reign" -*šebet ḥāmās*, "the reign of lawlessness" (Andersen and Freedman 1989: 562; cf. *kissēʾ hawwôt*, "a seat of injustice" [Ps 94:20]). One also finds *šebet* with the sense of "location" (Num 21:15; 2 Sam 23:7). Ugaritic attests to this nominal usage as well, *tbt*, "seat, throne" (KTU 1.6 VI 27–28): *ʾalt tbtk* // *ksʾa mlkk* "the support of your seat // the throne of your kingship."

With *mĕrôm šibtô* compare the following similar phrases: *mĕqôm šibtĕkā* (1 Kgs 8:30 = 2 Chr 6:21); *mĕkôn šibtekā* (1 Kgs 8:39, 43, 49 = 2 Chr 6:30, 33, 39); *mĕkôn šibtô* (Ps 33:14); and *mākôn lĕšibtĕkā* (Exod. 15:17; 1 Kgs 8:13 = 2 Chr

6:2). It is difficult to tell in each of these cases whether the phrase means "the place where you dwell" or "the place of your abode/throne." But in Obad 3 *šibtô* lacks the verbal idea of "being in the state of dwelling" since *měrôm šibtô* represents the *location* rather than the *activity* of Edom's "dwelling"; the latter is conveyed by the governing verb *šōkěnî*. Hence *šibtô* here denotes Edom's "location," "abode," "seat," or even "throne." Compare the Vulgate, *solium suum*, "his throne."

'ōmēr bělibbô.
you who say in your heart.
The phrase, a participle + the preposition *b* and noun, syntactically matches the clause of v 3a. Both participial phrases modify the object "you." On the switch to the third person pronominal suffix of *bělibbô*, see the Note above.

The phrase "to say in the heart" is a common idiom used to denote thinking, reflecting, intending, believing, and the like. The "heart" designates the locus of such cognitive and volitive activity. Technically the verb '*mr* does not mean "to think"; that is not the sense evoked by the signifier '*mr*. However, since a person naturally thinks by subvocalizing with language in the mind, the use of a verb that means "to speak" is understandable. Here as elsewhere the content of the thought is expressed in direct discourse immediately following this idiom. The contrast between this line and the next verse is noteworthy. Whereas Edom privately and inaudibly "speaks in the heart," Yahweh through his prophet responds openly and publicly.

mî yôrîdēnî 'āreṣ.
Who will bring me down to the earth?
From the speaker's point of view, in this case Edom, this type of question is intended to be rhetorical, an indirect way of making a statement and even belaboring the obvious: "Of course no one will or possibly can bring me down." Here the question is designed to reveal Edom's presumptuous heart with its defiant claims of autonomy and security due to its mountainous location. Such rhetorical questions are frequently attributed to opponents and enemies in order to express their pride, self-confidence, wicked plans, and so forth. Naturally such claims often provoke a divine response that challenges them (Labuschagne 1966: 27).

Although the Jeremiah parallel lacks this colon and the previous colon, the following two texts from the book of Jeremiah provide close parallels. The first is directed to Jerusalem and the second to Ammon:

"Behold, I am against you,
O inhabitant of the valley,
O rock of the plain — utterance of Yahweh —
those who say:

'Who will march down against us?
Who will enter our habitations?'
I will punish you according to the fruit of your deeds . . ."(21:13–14)

"Why do you boast in the valleys,
though your valley flows,
O faithless daughter;
you who trust in your treasures:
'Who will come against me?'
Behold, I will bring against you terror . . ." (49:4–5)

The syntax of the clause is unique. Elsewhere with the verb *yrd* there is either a preposition before *'ereṣ* (earth) such as *'el* (Ezek 31:18; 32:18, 24) and *l* (Isa 63:6; Ezek 26:11; Eccl 3:21; Lam 2:10) or a directive *h*, *'arṣāh* (Gen 44:11). Here in contrast the noun *'ereṣ* stands alone as an accusative of place, designating the goal to which descent is made.

The noun is polysemous with senses that include the following: "habitable land" in contrast to "sea"; "territory"; "ground"; "earth" in contrast to "heavens"; and "underworld" (Bergman and Ottosson 1974). In the context of Obad 3 the first two senses do not apply, but it is difficult to decide among the other three. It is possible that *'ereṣ* here denotes "the underworld." Compare the Ugaritic expression *yrdm 'arṣ*, "those who descend to the underworld." In Ezekiel, we find the expression "descend to the netherworld" (32:18, 24; cf. 31:18), but there *'ereṣ* is qualified with *taḥtiyyôt*. One might also compare Jonah 2:7 [6] where *BHS* construes *yrd* with *hā'āreṣ*, "I descended to the underworld." However, Sasson (1990: 185–88) persuasively argues for separating the two words by connecting *yrd* with the preceding clause and *hā'āreṣ* with the following clause. Although possible it seems unlikely that *'ereṣ* in Obad 3 has this sense. Would Obadiah intend for Edom to claim that no one could bring it down "to the underworld"?

More likely Obadiah intended one or both of the other two senses. The easiest and most obvious interpretation takes *'ereṣ* as designating the "ground" in distinction to Edom's location in the mountainous heights. This is the meaning of *'ereṣ* when *lā'āreṣ* (Isa 63:6; Ezek 26:11; Eccl 3:21; Lam 2:10) and *'arṣāh* (Gen 44:11) are joined with the verb *yrd*. Compare other similar expressions that speak of being cut down or thrown "to the ground" (Bergman and Ottosson 1974: 398–99). For example, Isa 26:5 says:

"For he [Yahweh] has brought low
the inhabitants of the height,
the lofty city.
He lays it low, lays it low to the ground [*'ad 'ereṣ*],
casts it to the dust [*'ad 'āpār*]."

The meaning of "earth" applies as well. In this case Edom's rhetorical question exhibits irony. Even though Edom dwells "in the clefts of the crags" and "the height" of the mountains, a location that might be lofty but certainly still on "earth," Edom thinks it dwells in the heavens. Therefore Edom proudly asks, "Who will bring me down to the earth?" The next verse takes Edom up on its claim: "even if *among stars* you could set your nest, from there I will bring you down!" A parallel occurs in Isa 14:12, part of the prophet's taunt against the king of Babylon:

> "How you have fallen *from heaven*,
> O morning star, son of dawn!
> You have been cut down *to the earth*,
> you who bring defeat upon the nations."

4. *'im tagbîah kannešer*
   wĕ'im bên kôkābîm śîm qinnekā
   Even if you could exalt (your nest) like the eagle,
   and even if among stars you could set your nest.

Verse 4 consists of two protases introduced by the particle *'im* and of a subsequent apodosis. Usually *'im* signals a real conditional, a situation capable of fulfillment, in contrast to *lû*, which introduces an irreal conditional (Leeuwen 1973: 16–27). But the semantic content of the two protases undermines one's expectation generated by the use of *'im*. It is at least doubtful that Edomites could locate their homes at the same altitude as eagles, and certainly "among stars" would have been impossible. Even eagles cannot do that! Occasionally *'im* appears where one expects *lû*, and perhaps Obad 4 provides an example of such an interchange (cf. Hos 9:11–12; Pss 50:12; 139:8; GKC § 159m; Joüon 1991 § 167f, i). In that case we may take the two *'im* clauses as irreal conditionals.

Yet perhaps the *'im* clauses are intended in the normal way as introducing real conditionals. Note that the LXX and Vulgate use the future-more-vivid instead of the contrary-to-fact or the future-less-vivid construction. Leeuwen (1973: 29) interprets the *'im* clauses as concessive clauses that stress the hypothetical force more than the irreal force. The purpose then would be for rhetorical effect; the speaker attributes to Edom a capability that even Edom would probably deny. The idea can be paraphrased as follows:

> If you exalt your nest like the eagle,
> and if you locate it among stars —
> and I recognize that you can and might do this —
> then from the stars I will bring you down.

Even if you could exalt (your nest). The verb *tagbîah*, a *hip'il* imperfect of *gbh*, poses a problem. One can construe it as an internal *hip'il*, "Even if you could go high/exalt yourself." On the surface this seems to be the case, since the colon contains no expressed nominal object nor does the verb have an object suffix. The LXX (*meteōristhēs*, "you are exalted"), the Vulgate (*exaltatus fueris*, "you will be exalted"), and the Peshitta (*ttrym*, "you are exalted") apparently took it this way—or did they (mis)read the *qal, tigbah?* Some modern versions adopt this view as well (RSV, JB, NIV; cf. Ewald 1876; Allen 1976; Deissler 1984). Or one can interpret the verb as a causative *hip'il*, a transitive verb for which "your nest" at the end of the second colon serves as its delayed direct object (so Keil 1888; Wellhausen 1963; Marti 1904; Halévy 1907; Edelkoort 1946–1947). The Targum apparently understood the verb this way since it uses the causative form *trym* (you raise up).

Because the *qal* of *gbh* is intransitive, "to be high, lofty," we expect the *hip'il* to have a transitive and causative sense, "to cause X to become high." In at least seven of our root's ten *hip'il* occurrences this is the case (Isa 7:11; Jer 49:16; Ezek 17:24; 21:31; Job 5:7; Prov 17:19; 2 Chr 33:14). The other two cases besides Obad 4 are debatable. In Ps 113:5 the *hip'il* participle might be internal (Dahood 1970: 131):

Who is like Yahweh our God,
the One who is enthroned on high [*hammagbîhî lāšābet*].

Or the verb might be causative with *lāšābet* functioning as the object, "the One who exalts his dwelling" (BDB). The second passage, Job 39:27, closely resembles Obad 4:

'im 'al pîkā yagbîah nāšer
wěkî yārîm qinnô

"At your command does the eagle elevate
and raise his nest?"

Again, we can take the *hip'il* imperfect to be internal ("go high, elevate himself") or transitive with the unwritten but implied object *'ûp* ("elevate his flight," cf. Job 5:7; BDB). A third possibility presents itself as well; perhaps "his nest" functions as the object of both verbs. In that case the verse splits the word pair "eagle—nest" and creates two parallel cola out of the underlying sentence "At your command does the eagle elevate/raise his nest?" This third option corresponds with the preferred interpretation of Obad 4 (see below).

The existence of an internal *hip'il* of *gbh* is debatable, since it is possible to understand the previous two occurrences as causative in conformity with the other instances. In any case, the decisive evidence for Obad 4 derives from the parallel passage in Jer 49:16:

kî tagbîah kannešer qinnekā
miššām 'ôrîdĕkā
nĕ'ūm yahweh

"Even if you could exalt your nest like the eagle,
from there I will bring you down" —
utterance of Yahweh.

Here *tagbîah* is a causative *hip'il* with "your nest" as its object.

In light of the Jeremiah parallel we should construe "your nest" at the end of the second colon as the object of *tagbîah* in the first colon. O'Connor (1980: 122–29, 401–7) designates this "leftward gapping"; an element is gapped in the first colon and written in the second colon. Isa 42:2 provides an example of leftward object gapping. The noun "his voice" functions as the object of both "he will lift up" and "he will make heard," but it is gapped in the A-colon:

"He will not cry out or lift up (his voice),
and he will not make heard in the streets his voice."

(Compare also Ps 57:4 [3]; Judg 5:4; Hab 3:2.)

This interpretation of Obad 4 conforms well with the immediate context. The previous verse stresses the height of Edom's dwelling and verse 4 intensifies the motif. It compares Edom with the eagle not in terms of flight but in terms of the lofty location of the home.

like the eagle. The noun *nešer* can designate either a "vulture" (Mic 1:16; Prov 30:17) or an "eagle" (Ezek 17:3, 7); in most texts either one is possible. The vulture involved is probably a griffon-vulture (*gyps fulvus*), while a number of eagle species are possible: the imperial eagle (*aquila heliaca*), the golden eagle (*aquila chrysaetos*), the booted eagle (*hieraaetus penatus*), Bonelli's eagle (*hieraaetus fasciatus*), and the tawny eagle (*aquila rapax*). Among other characteristics the *nešer* was noted for its speed (2 Sam 1:23; Jer 4:13; Lam 4:19), its high flying (Jer 49:22; Prov 23:5; 30:19), and the elevation of its nest (Job 39:27–30). In Obadiah and the Jeremiah parallel the comparison between Edom and the *nešer* focuses on the height of the dwelling along with its inaccessibility and invulnerability. (On *nešer*, see Greenberg 1983: 56, 310; Köhler-Rollefson 1985; Kronholm 1986.)

and even if among stars. Obadiah intensifies the previous colon by mentioning the stars, which represent the upper limits of the cosmos (Job 22:12). The Ugaritic texts locate the stars at one end of a polarized expression (*KTU* 1.3 III 24–25):

"The whispering of the heavens with the earth,
of the deeps with the stars."

Also Mot's tongue extends "to the stars" (*KTU* 1.5 II 3).

According to the biblical view, to dwell in the heavens among the stars is to attain divine status. Yet Yahweh, who is always higher, brooks no rivals. Those who attempt to storm the heavens will experience a sudden fall. The Tower of Babel story provides the classic example of the motif. The people try to build a tower that reaches into the heavens, but Yahweh spoils their plans (Gen 11:1–9). In Isa 14:12–15 mythological language describes the king of Babylon's attempt to "ascend into heaven" and exalt his throne even "above the stars of El" so that he becomes like the Most High. But again, Yahweh brings him down. Daniel's vision of the he-goat portrays a "little horn" (= Antiochus IV) that grew "even to the host of heaven" and cast down to the earth "some of the host of the stars." Thereby it magnified itself, even up to the level of God, but in the end it is broken by God (8:9–11, 25).

Although this motif seems implicit, Obadiah does not develop it extensively or explicitly. Rather, he focuses attention on Edom's lofty dwelling place in the mountains and the inaccessibility associated with such a location. Even if Edom could nest "among stars," which represent the highest and most inaccessible location possible, Edom would still not dwell beyond the reach of Yahweh (cf. Jer. 51:53; Amos 9:2).

you could set your nest. Although the form of the MT verb *śîm* is problematic, it is to be preferred over reading *tāśîm* (cf. Barthélemy 1992: 698–99). Usually it is parsed as a passive participle and is cited in connection with Num 24:21, 1 Sam 9:24, and 2 Sam 13:32 — *Kethib* (GKC § 73f). If this is correct, then the following noun "your nest" is still an accusative; passive forms can take the accusative (GKC § 116k, 121; Joüon 1991 § 128). Caspari (1842) parses it as an infinitive construct so that the whole phrase *śîm qinnekā* functions as the delayed object of the verb in the A-colon: "Even if you could exalt . . . the setting of your nest."

Neither interpretation is very satisfying. Second *yodh* verbs are unstable in that the base form vacillates between medial *yodh* and *waw*. Normally their infinitive absolute forms are written **qôl* but one finds **qîl* as well: *šôt* (Isa 22:7) and *šît* (Jer 13:16 — *Qere*; cf. Holladay 1986: 405); *rôb* (Judg 11:25) and *rîb* (Jer 50:34). Prov 23:24 has *gôl* according to the *Kethib* but *gîl* according to the *Qere*, and in Prov 23:1 we find *bîn*. With respect to *śym*, the infinitive construct usually appears as *śûm*, but *śîm* occurs twice, in 2 Sam 14:7 (*Qere*) and Job 20:4. (Joüon [1920: 362–63] parses *śîm* in these two passages as a *qal* passive infinitive.)

In light of this instability, the infinitive absolute form likewise might be written as both *śôm* and *śîm*. If so, then *śym* in Obad 4 is an infinitive absolute that functions as a finite verb equivalent to the previous verb and takes "your nest" as its object. On the finite use of the infinitive absolute, see Huesman (1956) and Joüon (1991 § 123u–y). This understanding might also apply to *śym* in Num 24:21, Balaam's oracle to the Kenites:

'êtān môšābekā
wĕśîm bassela' qinnekā

"Your abode is perpetual,
and you set in the crag your nest."

However, the question must be left open, since there are no certain cases of *śîm* as an infinitive absolute form; the form *śôm* is attested in Deut 17:15; Jer 42:15; and Neh 8:8 — a finite usage.

Whether *śîm* is parsed as an infinitive absolute or a passive participle (an infinitive construct is unlikely), Obadiah probably constructed his phrase on the basis of the Numbers passage (Albright 1944: 222). By using *śîm* Obadiah prepares the hearer/reader for the phrase *miššām* (from there) in the next colon, since *śîm* and *miššām* form a sound pair.

your nest. The noun "your nest" forms a word pair with "like the eagle" of the first colon, a pair that occurs elsewhere as well (Deut 32:11; Job 39:27). Both Jeremiah and Obadiah combine a simile with a metaphor. Whereas Jer 49:16 includes both in one colon — "Even if you could exalt your nest like the eagle" — Obadiah splits the pair by placing "like the eagle" in the A-colon and "your nest" in the B-colon. This produces an intensifying and heightening effect from A to B: Edom progresses from being "like the eagle" to becoming the eagle itself; the "nest" belongs to Edom and not to the "eagle."

The metaphorical identification of Edom's home with an eagle's nest focuses attention on the location's height, inaccessibility, and security. These are features commonly associated with an eagle's nest, as Job 39:27–28 illustrates:

"At your command does the eagle exalt
and raise his nest?
He inhabits the crag and spends the night,
upon the peak of the crag as a mountain stronghold."

Other texts evoke the same associations by metaphorically designating a human home a "nest" (cf. Rouillard 1985: 453–55). Num 24:21 uses the image to signify the seeming security enjoyed by the Kenites:

"Your abode is perpetual,
and you set in the crag your nest."

Hab 2:9 pronounces woe to the person who greedily oppresses "in order to set on high his nest to be delivered from the reach of harm." Obadiah picks up on these associations and hyperbolically extends them by locating Edom's nest "among stars." Since the other texts locate a nest in the "crag" and "on high," perhaps the literal reference to Edom's dwelling "in the clefts of the crags" and in the "height" (v 3) brought to mind the eagle-nest image.

miššām 'ôrîdĕkā.
from there I will bring you down.

The adverbial deictic phrase "from there, from that place" refers to the hypothetical location of Edom's nest "among stars." Since the parallel in Jer 49:16 lacks the reference to the "stars," the phrase "from there" in Jeremiah points to either the implied lofty location of Edom's "nest" or Edom's dwelling "in the clefts of the crags" and "the height of the hill."

The verb is a *hip'il* of *yrd*, literally "I will cause you to descend." On the literal level it denotes a physical descent from Edom's abode in the mountain heights and even from the stars if Edom should reach that altitude. On this level the clause closely parallels and perhaps is based on Amos 9:2:

wĕ'im ya'ălû haššāmayim
miššām 'ôrîdēm

"And even if they [Israel] ascend to the heavens,
from there I will bring them down."

But the clause also operates on a figurative level. The *hip'il* of *yrd* can be used to express the humiliation and defeat of nations, and such a usage applies here as well: although Edom proudly feels secure and invulnerable, Yahweh will debase and conquer it (cf. 2 Sam 22:48; Isa 10:13; Pss 56:8 [7]; 59:12 [11]; Zech 10:11 — *hop'al*; Mayer 1990: 319).

The line presents Yahweh's response as antithetical to Edom's claim in v 3, "Who will bring me down to the earth?" Accordingly, the divine reply uses a *hip'il* imperfect with suffix of *yrd* to correspond with Edom's use of the same form. The sequence represents a speech//anti-speech antithetical structure and expresses the pride-humiliation type of contraposition that frequently appears in the Hebrew Bible (cf. Krašovec 1984). The literary effect is powerful. From Edom's perspective its question is intended to be strictly rhetorical, but the response attributed to Yahweh treats it as a serious question intended to be answered: "I will bring you down." Also striking from a rhetorical point of view is the contrast in length between this line and the previous line:

and even if among stars you could set your nest [5 words, 10 syllables],
from there I will bring you down [2 words, 6 syllables].

The short line has the effect of bringing Edom to a sudden and quick end already in the speech.

nĕʾūm yahweh.
utterance of Yahweh.

This formula frequently is used to introduce or conclude a prophetic oracle. Here it concludes the first divine speech of verses 2–4 as well as the parallel in Jer 49:14–16. It occurs again in Obad 8 to introduce another section. It presents Yahweh as the speaker and the prophet as Yahweh's mouthpiece, one commissioned to speak in Yahweh's name and by his authority (cf. Jer 23:31–32; Ezek 13:6–7). The formula has the effect of blurring the distinction between the deity and his prophet. (On the formula, see Vetter [1976], Eising [1986], and Bretón [1987: 213–26].)

The formula *nĕʾūm* + divine name is almost exclusively prophetic. According to Bretón, it occurs 357 times and all but seven appear in the Latter Prophets. Only two instances are spoken by a non-prophet: Gen 22:16 by the angel of Yahweh and Num 14:28 by Moses (although he is probably considered a prophet here). The statistics follow:

Genesis 1	Joel 1
Numbers 1	Amos 21
Samuel 2	Obadiah 2
Kings 3	Micah 2
Isaiah 25	Nahum 2
Jeremiah 172	Zephaniah 5
Ezekiel 83	Haggai 12
(The Book of the Twelve 70)	Zechariah 20
Hosea 4	Malachi 1

All of the Latter Prophets have the formula except Jonah and Habakkuk. They understandably lack the expression, since neither book consists of a collection of prophetic oracles. The specific formula *nĕʾūm yahweh* occurs 227 times, most frequently in Jeremiah (161 times).

COMMENT

Verses 1–4 repeat with a few modifications parts of Jeremiah's oracle against Edom (Jer 49:14–16; see the Introduction). For Obadiah, Jeremiah's prophecy remained alive and valid. Therefore Obadiah reiterated it, built upon it, and updated it.

The book begins with Obadiah as Yahweh's messenger addressing Edom. In conformity with a common convention of prophetic discourse, he regards Edom as a collective whole and personifies it. Thus he uses singular pronouns. Furthermore, in this first section he treats Edom as one "nation" among other "nations." It is the next section that introduces the Edom-Esau connection. Before proclaiming the divine utterance addressed to Edom in vv 2–4, the prophet provides some background information that is necessary for appreciating the full force of the divine utterance. Yahweh has sent an angelic messenger among the nations to recruit them for war against Edom. Not only is Yahweh currently recruiting them, but he plans to participate in the attack as the commander-in-chief: "Arise so that *we* may rise against her for battle."

The divine warrior motif in the Bible and the ancient Near East is well known (see the classic study by Miller 1973). The Bible usually portrays Yahweh as leading the heavenly armies and/or Israel in wars against Israel's enemies. What is striking about Obad 1 is that Yahweh leads the "nations" in a military campaign against another "nation." Here Yahweh acts as commander-in-chief and fellow combatant with the armies of earthly nations other than Israel. (Compare Isa 13:2–5 where Yahweh goes out to war leading apparently both heavenly and earthly armies, the latter of which are identified in v 17 as the Medes.) By including Yahweh in the actual military attack — which the Jer 49 parallel does not do — Obadiah heightens the drama and increases the certainty of Edom's eventual downfall. The text also reveals in a powerful way that "the Lord Yahweh" is considered lord of the nations as well as of Israel and that he exercises his lordship not only by making decrees from a distance but also by participating personally in human affairs and international events, in this case the military campaign of the nations against Edom.

The divine speech begins in v 2 by explaining why the nations will not hesitate to attack: Yahweh has already made Edom insignificant among the nations; in fact, they currently despise Edom. Verse 3 then portrays Edom's self-confidence: in contrast to Edom's disesteem among others, Edom thinks that it remains safe because of its lofty and mountainous abode. Verse 3 illustrates this belief by attributing to Edom the rhetorical question, which the Jeremiah parallel lacks: "Who will bring me down to the earth?" The rhetorical question also functions as Edom's defiant response to the previously announced military threat. Yet, although a nation dwelling in the mountains might reasonably consider itself secure from enemy attack, the prophet labels this belief "presumption," that is, unwarranted boldness. Thus vv 2–3 create a contrast by juxtaposing the nations' estimation of Edom with Edom's own self-opinion. Obadiah's purpose here is not so much to condemn Edom of pride as it is to convince Edom of its own vulnerability.

Verse 3 stated that Edom's presumptuous heart "has deceived" Edom. Now v 4 defends the claim: Edom's hopes are false because Yahweh himself intends to bring it down. What Edom did not imagine could possibly happen will happen. Although from Edom's point of view the question "Who will bring me down to the earth?" is intended to be rhetorical, Yahweh breaks the literary convention by answering it, "I will bring you down." Thus v 4 provides the divine response to Edom's self-confidence.

With respect to structure, the divine speech of vv 2–4, linked to v 1 by the opening messenger formula and the repetition of the phrase "among the nations," displays a high degree of literary artistry. It is bracketed by two first person verbs with second person object suffixes: "I have made you" and "I will bring you down." The switch in verbal aspect from perfect to imperfect indicates a two-stage process in the divine actions: Yahweh first brought Edom into disrepute among the nations, and next through the agency of the nations he will bring Edom down geographically from its lofty abode and thereby metaphorically debase it.

Furthermore, within the speech vv 3–4 are intricately interwoven.

> v 3   A   The presumption of <u>your heart</u> has deceived you,
>   B   you who dwell in the clefts of the crags,
>   B   in the height of your seat,
>   A   you who say in <u>your heart</u>:
>   C   "Who <u>will bring me down</u> to the earth?"
> v 4   B   Even if you could exalt (your nest) like the eagle,
>   B   and even if among stars you could set your nest,
>   C   from there I <u>will bring you down</u>.

With respect to syntax, v 3 consists of a main clause followed by four subordinate clauses. The subordinate clauses divide into two bicola (or line pairs), each of which begins with a participle, "you who dwell . . . you who say . . ." Verse 4 reverses the order with two conditional clauses (a bicolon) followed by a main clause. Thus the unit can be parsed as a single colon, three bicola, and another single colon.

However, with respect to the meaning of the lines, the unit also exhibits an interlocking combination of two halves, each of which has four lines arranged symmetrically: ABBA CBBC. The height of Edom's dwelling is the focus of the two bicola labeled B, the first of which is enclosed by references to Edom's "heart" (A) and the second by Edom's rhetorical question and Yahweh's reply (C). The description of Edom's elevated location progresses from a realistic portrayal (with a participle) in v 3 to an unrealistic one (with conditional clauses) in v 4. Edom does in fact dwell "in the clefts of the crags" on high, but it cannot elevate its metaphorical nest "like the eagle" nor place its home "among stars"; even eagles cannot do that! Thus the unit displays grammatical and semantic patterns that overlap and intricately bind its parts together.

II. YAHWEH'S SECOND UTTERANCE: ANNOUNCEMENT OF DOOM ADDRESSED TO EDOM (vv 5–7)

◆

5 If thieves come to you,
   if plunderers of the night—
      How you have been similar/destroyed!
        —will they not steal what suffices them?
   If vintagers come to you,
      will they not leave gleanings?
6   How Esau has been thoroughly searched out,
        his hidden things thoroughly sought after!
7 To the very border they have expelled you,
    all those of your covenant.
  They have deceived you, prevailed over you,
     those of your peace.
     [Those who eat] your bread
  will establish a place of foreigners in your stead,
        in which there is no understanding.

NOTES

v 5. *'im gannābîm bā'û lĕkā*
    'im šôdĕdê laylâ
    'êk nidmêtâ
    hălô' yignĕbû dayyām.
    If thieves come to you,
    if plunderers of the night—
    How you have been similar/destroyed!
    —will they not steal what suffices them?

The basic sentence consists of two protases introduced by *'im* (if) and one apodosis in the form of an interrogative introduced by *hălô'* (will they not). The interrogative expects an affirmative answer (Brongers 1981: 179). An exclamatory interjection intervenes between the protases and the apodosis. The verb of the first protasis, which together with the prepositional phrase "to you" is gapped in the second protasis, is a perfect, whereas the verb of the apodosis is an imperfect. The same verbal sequence appears in the following sentence as well. This verbal sequence indicates that the action of the if-clause temporally precedes the action of the then-clause: if they will have "come," then they will "steal" (Leeuwen 1973: 21–22).

thieves. The root *gnb*, well known by its occurrence in the Decalog, is used in a general way to denote various kinds of theft, but always theft done in secret. The stealing can take place either in the day or the night (Gen 31:39); the parallel in Jer 49:9 construes "thieves" with "in the night." The noun *gannāb* designates the habitual thief (Hamp 1978: 41); the *qaṭṭāl* formation often indicates profession or repeated activity.

plunderers of the night. The construct chain *šôdĕdê laylâ*, a plural participle used as a substantive followed by a genitive noun, parallels and intensifies the previous noun, *gannābîm*. Whereas *gannābîm* is used as a general term to designate thieves who steal in secret but without any accompanying violence, *šôdĕdê laylâ* is a much stronger and more forceful expression that refers to those who violently plunder and destroy at night. Depending on the context, the root *šdd* can be translated in various ways: "destroy," "ravage," "lay waste," "assail," and "plunder" (BDB, *HALAT*). Potential objects include persons, homes, fields, cities, and nations. Basically it denotes acts of physical violence done to property and persons, taking the desired items and destroying the rest (cf. Jer 49:28–29; 51:56; Mic 2:4). The mention of "night" heightens the threatening force of the hypothetical possibility expressed in the if-clauses. Since the victims are asleep and therefore defenseless during the night, the plunderers have unhindered freedom to do as they please.

How you have been similar/destroyed! Some commentators transpose the verse's second and third cola to the end of v 5: "If plunderers of the night (come to you), how you have been destroyed" (T. H. Robinson 1938; Frey 1948; Watts 1969). This would produce three distinct conditional sentences. However, in addition to the gratuitous repositioning of lines, it is doubtful that *'êk* (how) would begin an apodosis and that this apodosis would use a second person perfect verb in contrast to the other apodoses' third person imperfect verbs. Other scholars suggest that the exclamatory clause be relocated either after the first apodosis (Rudolph 1971; Allen 1976) or before the first protasis (Bewer 1911), but such repositioning of the line is unnecessary.

The most natural interpretation understands the clause with most commentators as a parenthetical interjection that intervenes between the first two protases and their apodosis. Such interjections are not unprecedented in prophetic rhetoric (cf. Isa 51:19; Ezek 16:23; Joel 4:11 [3:11]; Hab 2:6). Moreover, the clause is appropriately located after the two if-clauses (see below).

How. The word *ʾêk*, technically an interrogative adverb, can introduce a real question, a rhetorical question, or an exclamation. Sometimes the lines between them become blurred. Stuart (1987) takes it as an interrogative, "How could you be destroyed?" This has the advantage of forming grammatical parallelism with the next interrogative clause, "will they not steal what suffices them?" However, in that case one would expect the verb to be imperfect, especially with the sense he gives it.

More likely *ʾêk* is used here as well as in v 6 to introduce an exclamatory declaration (GKC § 148; BDB). Its purpose is to express the intensity of the emotion, but the specific emotion can vary depending on the following verb and the context (see Alonso Schökel 1988: 152–54).The *ʾêk*-clause can indicate surprise (Isa 14:4, 12), lamentation (2 Sam 1:19, 25, 27), reproach (Judg 16:15), horror (Jer 51:41), and delight (Jer 3:19). In light of the multivalent verb *nidmêtâ* (see below), the clause seems to express both amazement and indignant scorn:

How could it be that you have been similar to thieves and plunderers!
Oh how you have been destroyed and justly so!

you have been similar/destroyed! The verb *nidmêtâ* is a *nipʿal* perfect of *dmh*. It is unclear to what extent the different senses of *dmh* reflect homonymy or polysemy. Some lexicons (BDB; *TDOT*) list two roots: *dmh* I, "to be like," and *dmh* II, "to be silent, to cease, to be destroyed"; others (*HALAT*; *CHAL*) list three: *dmh* I, "to be like," *dmh* II, "to be silent," *dmh* III, "to be destroyed." The last two overlap in meaning in that the sense "to be silent" can easily merge into the sense "to be put to silence" or "to be destroyed." Baumann (1978) treats *dmh* II together with *dmm* and *dwm* because of the difficulty in differentiating the roots.

In any case, the *nipʿal* of *dmh* — whether considered *dmh* II or *dmh* III — can convey the senses "to be silenced, to cease to exist, to be destroyed," and its use in Obad 5 is generally interpreted along these lines (cf. Isa 15:1; Jer 47:5; Hos 10:7, 15; Zeph 1:11). According to this view, the exclamation "How you have been destroyed!" is evoked by the mention of "plunderers" in the previous clause — *ndmh* is paired with *šdd* in Isa 15:1 and collocated with *šdd* in Jer 47:4–5 — and the verb is taken as a prophetic perfect to anticipate the impending doom announced in vv 6–7 and 8–10.

The above interpretation conforms well with the usage of the verb and fits the context. But taking *nidmêtâ* as a *nipʿal* of *dmh* I is equally plausible (cf. Gilse 1913: 294). It has the same sense as the *nipʿal* of *mšl* I: "How you have become similar!" or "How you have made yourself similar!" That the *nipʿal* of *dmh* can have this sense is evident from Ezek 32:2, where Yahweh commands Ezekiel to say to Pharaoh:

kĕpîr gôyīm nidmêtā
wĕ'attâ kattannîm bayyammîm

"*You have likened yourself* to a lion among the nations,
but you are like a monster in the seas."

If we parse the verb as the *nip'al* of *dmh* I, then Obadiah expresses his indignation and shock upon seeing the way the Edomites acted toward Judah, like common "thieves" and violent "plunderers of the night." The exclamation anticipates the crimes described more thoroughly in vv 11–14. The fact that "Esau" mentioned in v 6 was the twin brother of Jacob adds to the emotional force of the outburst.

Thus, both *dmh* I and *dmh* II (or III?) appropriately apply to Obad 5. Should we choose one over the other? It seems best to take the verb as a case of deliberate ambiguity; the prophet plays on its multivalence (cf. Glück 1970; Raabe 1991; Paul 1992). The verb acts "Janus-like," retrospectively — "How you have become similar!" — and prospectively — "How you have been destroyed!" The use of the root *dmh* also forms a phonological play on the name "Edom" (*'ĕdôm*); note the possibility of a similar wordplay in Isa 21:11. A play on the *nip'al* of *dmh* I and *dmh* II (or III) also seems to occur in Ezek 27:32 (reading *ndmh* with the versions instead of MT *kdmh*, a confusion of *n* and *k*):

mî kĕṣôr [nidmâ]
bĕtôk hayyām

"Who has become like Tyre/Who has been destroyed like Tyre
in the midst of the sea?"

will they not steal what suffices them? This clause forms the apodosis of the two previous protases. Since both the verb *ygnbw* (steal) and the noun *gnbym* (thieves) are based on the same root, this line is closely tied with the first protasis. Yet it also applies to the second protasis; although "plunders of the night" ravage and destroy property and persons, still they "steal" only what they want and need.

The word *dayyām* is the noun **day* with the third person masculine plural suffix, literally "their sufficiency," "their necessary supply." It refers to the property that "thieves" and "plunderers" consider sufficient and useful for themselves. In light of the next bicolon the point is that they steal only what they want and no more, certainly not every single item in the house or city (cf. Prov 25:16). Thus it sets up a contrast with the thoroughgoing ransacking that Edom will experience according to v 6. Allen (1976) distinguishes between two ideas, "to their hearts' content" (JB) and "only as much as they need," and he opts for the former. He also takes the next bicolon to signify that the invading vintagers will leave *only* gleanings. Then v 5 would refer to the enemies who will easily and thoroughly strip house and vineyard. But the mention of vintagers in fact leaving gleanings and the switch from conditional sentences in v 5 to exclamations in v 6 suggest rather that a contrast between the two verses is being made.

'im bōṣĕrîm bā'û lāk
hălô' yaš'îrû 'ōlēlôt.
If vintagers come to you,
will they not leave gleanings?

This sentence has the same grammatical structure and some of the same words as the first protasis and apodosis: *'im* + subject + *bā'û* + *lāk*, for the protasis, and *hălô'* + imperfect verb + object, for the apodosis. The interrogative expects an affirmative answer. On the verbal sequence of perfect-imperfect, see the earlier Note.

vintagers. The subject *bōṣĕrîm*, a participle of *bṣr* I, designates "grape-gatherers" (cf. Lev 25.5), "vineyard harvesters" (cf. Deut 24:21). The image of vintagers working in Edom is apt because of the many good vineyards on Edom's lower slopes (cf. Num 20:17).

will they not leave gleanings? According to Lev 19:9–10 and Deut 24:19–22, Israelite harvesters were to leave gleanings for the poor and needy. Yet typically gleanings would remain after a harvest even apart from such commands and any religious motives. Here the noun "gleanings," which also can apply to olives, refers to the grapes that would be left for various reasons: they fell to the ground; they were rotten, unripe, or too small; they were simply overlooked because excessively thorough picking of the first crop would allow the rest to spoil given that crop ripening generally occurs rapidly (cf. Roth 1989: 152; Stuart 1987).

v 6. *'êk nehpĕśû 'ēśāw*
nib'û maṣpūnāyw.
How Esau has been thoroughly searched out,
his hidden things thoroughly sought after!

The two cola grammatically match: the word order is the standard order of verb + subject; *'êk* (how) is gapped in the B-colon; and both verbs are *nip'al* perfects. The pronoun "his" in B takes "Esau" in A as its antecedent. Also note the phonological parallelism with both verbs and subjects ending with *w*. The grammatical and phonological parallelism supports the semantic parallelism of the two cola.

Verse 6 presents a contrast with v 5. Thieves normally take only what they can carry and only what is immediately visible since they must hurry, and vintagers likewise tend to pick hurriedly only the good grapes and those easily seen. In contrast v 6 focuses all attention on the thoroughness of the ransacking that

Edom will experience. The Edomites located "in the clefts of the crags" (v 3) and their treasures hidden in secret places will be hunted down and found. By implication everything will be taken and nothing will be left.

The two sentences of v 6 are exclamations, introduced by *'êk* (how). The use of *'êk* stresses the speaker's emotional intensity (see the Note under v 5). On the one hand, it expresses surprise at the thoroughness of Edom's despoliation given the apparent security of Edom's location (v 3), and on the other hand, it reveals satisfaction at Edom's fate. Furthermore, the sequence of *'êk* + *nip'al* perfect verbs corresponds with the same sequence in the third colon of v 5. There Edom was accused of acting like thieves and plunderers. Here Edom is sentenced to experience for itself a similar plundering. As the prophetic corpus so often highlights (Miller 1982), the punishment fits the crime. This correspondence also explains the use of perfect verbs in v 6 in that the *'êk* + *nip'al* perfect sequence cements the link with v 5. Yet, in light of v 1 and v 4 Edom's fate still lies in the future. Hence the perfects of v 6 are "prophetic perfects" (*pace* Bewer 1911 and others who consider the event to lie in the historical past).

Esau. In v 6 the name Esau appears for the first time in Obadiah; it occurs seven times in the book (vv 6, 8, 9, 18a, b, 19, 21). According to biblical tradition, Esau was the eponymous ancestor of the Edomites (Gen 36). Consequently, the name Esau could be used as a metonym for Edom (Gen 36:1, 8; Deut 2:5; Jer 49:8, 10; Mal 1:3–4). Yet its appearance here is somewhat surprising. It can be explained partly by the hypothesis that Obadiah adapted Jer 49:9–10 since the name occurs there (see the Introduction).

Why does Obadiah put "Esau" in the third person rather than use the second person and make "Esau" vocative? That would conform with the second-person references in v 5 and v 7. Again, the switch to third person can be explained partly on the basis of the Jer 49 parallel where one finds the second person in v 9 (= Obad 5) but the third person in v 10 (= Obad 6). However, an additional reason suggests itself. By referring to Esau in the third person Obadiah invites the reader to think not only of Edom, the oracle's direct addressee, but also of the patriarch himself, Jacob's older twin brother. It evokes in the reader's mind the Jacob-Esau narratives, especially Jacob's supplanting of Esau by stealing his birthright (Gen 25) and his rightful blessing (Gen 27). What happened to the patriarch Esau, that he was "searched out" and his prized treasures were "sought after," will also happen to Esau's descendants.

The grammar is difficult. According to the MT, "Esau" is construed as a plural with a plural verb in the A-colon but as a singular with the singular pronoun "his" in the B-colon. The disparity might be the result of a scribal mistake; the final *w* of *nḥpśw* in A was perhaps added by assimilation to the verb *nb'w* in B or by dittography of the *w* of *'św* (Esau). Then both cola would treat "Esau" as a singular. If the MT is to be preferred, the switch from plural to singular might

144

mean that the A-colon treats "Esau" as a collective plural (GKC § 145b), as a metonym for the Edomites who hide "in the clefts of the crags" (v 3), whereas the B-colon has Esau the patriarch in view. Freedman (private communication) proposes another explanation. The underlying sentence is: "The hidden things of Esau have been thoroughly searched out/sought after." The prophet made this sentence into two parallel sentences by splitting the underlying genitive phrase "the hidden things of Esau" and apportioning "Esau" to the A-colon and "his hidden things" to the B-colon (cf. O'Connor 1980 on the trope of "combination"). Thus the verb in A is plural under the influence of the plural noun "hidden things."

has been thoroughly searched out. The verb *neḥpĕśû* is the *nip'al* of *ḥpś*. Although this is the only attested case of the *nip'al*, the verb's meaning is clear by its use in the *qal* and *pi'el*. It basically means "to conduct a thorough search" and further entails a search of hidden areas in a purposeful effort to find a particular object or person.

The sense can be seen first of all by the uses of the *qal*. In Prov 2:4–5 it parallels *bqš*:

If you seek [*bqš*] it [i.e., understanding, wisdom] like silver,
and *search it out* as for hidden treasures;
then you will understand the fear of Yahweh,
and the knowledge of God you will find.

Prov 20:27 also reveals the sense "to thoroughly search":

A human's spirit is Yahweh's lamp
that *searches* all the dark chambers of the inner self.

In Lam 3:40 the verb is collocated with *bqr*:

Let us *search out* our ways and investigate [*bqr*] them,
and let us turn to Yahweh.

The components of meaning, those of carefully searching secret places and intentionally looking for a desired object or person, are particularly evident from the use of the verb in narration. In the following texts the *pi'el* occurs, but it does not appear to differ significantly from the *qal* in sense. The verb can take inanimate items as its stated or implied object. Laban "searched" for the household gods by "rummaging through" (*mšš*) Rachel's whole tent, but he did not "find" them (Gen 31:34–35). Joseph's steward "searched" for Joseph's silver bowl in the sacks of Joseph's brothers and "found" it in Benjamin's sack (Gen 44:12). For his terms of peace, Ben-hadad proposes to send his servants to Ahab so that they can "search" Ahab's house and the houses of Ahab's servants and "seize" (*lqḥ*) whatever Ahab values (1 Kgs 20:6).

The object of the search can also be persons. According to Amos 9:3, Yahweh intends to "search out" and "seize" (*lqḥ*) the Israelites even if they should hide themselves on the top of Carmel. A similar motif appears in Zeph 1:12 where Yahweh threatens to "search" Jerusalem with lamps, looking for those who treat him with cynicism. After the Ziphites inform Saul of David's hiding places, Saul plans to "search him out among all the clans of Judah" (1 Sam 23:23). And according to 2 Kgs 10:23, Jehu ordered the servants of Baal to "search and see" that no servant of Yahweh remained in Samaria's temple of Baal.

In light of the verb's usage, its meaning in Obad 6 is clear. A deliberate and thorough search will be carried out, and the object of the search will be the descendants of Esau and their treasures. Both the nature and the object of the search present a contrast with v 5. Unlike property or grapes that can be overlooked by thieves or vintagers, the Edomites and their riches cannot go unnoticed; they will be "thoroughly searched out" even though the Edomites hide themselves and their valuables in their land's caves and coverts (v 3; cf. Josh 10:16–27). Moreover, the verb usually implies a successful search (the only exception is Gen 31:35); the Edomites and their hidden possessions will be "found" and "seized."

his hidden things. The meaning of *maṣpūnāyw*, a plural noun with pronominal suffix, is not totally certain, as it is a *hapax legomenon*. It is a *maqṭāl* nominal formation of the root *ṣpn*, "to hide" (persons or things). Therefore the noun might refer to either "secret places" (and therefore "hiding-places") or "hidden treasures." The former is suggested by the parallel in Jer 49:10, *mistārāyw*, "his [Esau's] hiding-places," and the latter can be defended on the basis of the similar noun *maṭmôn* (hidden treasures), from *ṭmn*, "to hide." The LXX (*autou ta kekrymmena*) and the Vulgate (*abscondita eius*) render it with the neuter plural, literally "his hidden things"; they probably intend "hidden treasures." Perhaps it is unnecessary to choose since both "hiding-places" and "hidden treasures" belong together (cf. Isa 45:3). Neither the descendants of Esau nor their riches will go undetected by the enemies in spite of their hiding-places. Ordinary thieves and plunderers might not have the time necessary to discover such secret places (v 5), but Edom's enemies will painstakingly and extensively seek after them and find them.

thoroughly sought after. The verb *nbʿw* is a *nipʿal* perfect of *bʿh* I (*bʿh* II, "to swell, boil," does not apply here). *HALAT* lists a third entry under *bʿh* based on Jewish Aramaic, Syriac, and postbiblical Hebrew, "to feed on, graze," and suggests that it might apply to Obad 6. However, its existence in Biblical Hebrew is doubtful. Besides, what would it mean that "his hidden things have been grazed"?

Because verse 6 pairs *nibʿû* with *neḥpĕśû*, we expect the two to relate semantically. In addition to v 6, *bʿh* I occurs only once in Biblical Hebrew, Isa 21:12. There it appears in the oracle concerning "Dumah," which is either a place name — the oasis in Arabia known today as Dûmet ej-Jendal — or a wordplay on "Edom" in that *dûmâ* means "silence." The oracle of Isa 21:11–12 reads:

> One calls to me from Seir,
> "Guard, what is left of the night?
> Guard, what is left of the night?"
> The guard said,
> "Morning comes and also night.
> If you would investigate (further), investigate [*'im tibʿāyûn bĕʿāyû*].
> Come back again."

This little oracle bristles with difficulties and enigmas, which cannot be discussed here, but the sense of *bʿh* is clear, "to investigate, seek information." Compare the usage of *bʿh / bʿʾ* in Biblical Aramaic, "to request, make petition" (Dan 2:18; 6:8 [7], 12–14 [11–13]). Note too that the verbal forms *tibʿāyûn* and *bĕʿāyû* reflect Aramaic influence and possibly represent the Edomite dialect (cf. Procksch 1930: 269–70). Macintosh (1980: 48–52, 139) argues that *bʿh* has the sense of "engaging in aggressive (military) action," but this cannot be sustained as the sense of *bʿh* per se, especially when the verb lacks any accompanying prepositional phrase or object.

The verb is well attested in Semitic: Aramaic including Biblical Aramaic, Akkadian, and Arabic. Its basic sense is "to seek" with nuances that include "wishing," "asking," "praying," "demanding," "investigating," and "thoroughly searching," depending on the context. Like the parallel *ḥpś*, *bʿh* can imply a search that is successful. This can be seen, for example, in a fifth-century-B.C. Aramaic inscription that warns anyone who damages the relief (*KAI* 258.5):

wybʿh lh šhr wšmš

Shahar and Shamash will seek him out.

Here the verb's usage also suggests a hostile intent, that the perpetrator will be found and punished. Frequently a successful search is implied by the use of *buʾû* in Akkadian texts (CAD, B/2:360–65). For example, in the following Neo-Babylonian text the sequence "seek . . . and send" implies that the sought items will be found (CAD, B/2:362):

> "Rare tablets that are known to you but
> not available in Assyria *seek* and
> send (them) to me."

The verb is also attested in Ugaritic (*bġy*) but the sense is uncertain. In one text Baal bids Anat to hasten to him in order to learn a secret (*KTU* 1.3 III 28–29): "Come and I myself will seek/reveal [?] it [*'ibġyh*]." In light of the context the verb *'ibġyh* (G or D?) appears to mean "to show, reveal" (so *UT*; Gray 1965: 47; Del Olmo Lete 1981: 529). Gray relates it to Arabic *baġā*, which in the Fourth Form means "to help to attain." Or *'ibġyh* might simply mean "I will seek it" with the implication of finding and then revealing.

The possibility that *b'h* might have the sense of "reveal" is attractive (cf. Targum). In that case Obad 6 would read:

> How Esau has been thoroughly searched out,
> > his hidden things revealed!

This would produce a closer semantic correspondence with the parallel in Jer 49:10:

> "For I have stripped Esau,
> I have exposed [*gillêtî*] his secret places."

However, in light of the uncertainty of the Ugaritic usage and in light of the parallel verb *ḥpś*, the established sense of "seek" for *b'h* is more likely. Thus Obad 6b asserts that Edom's secret places and hidden riches will be "thoroughly sought after" and by implication found and rifled.

v 7. *'ad haggĕbûl šillĕḥûkā*
  kōl 'anšê bĕrîtekā
  hiššî'ûkā yākĕlû lĕkā
  'anšê šĕlōmekā
  [lōḥămê] laḥmĕkā
  yāśîmû māzôr taḥteykā
  'ên tĕbûnâ bô.

A   To the very border they have expelled you,
B   all those of your covenant.
C   They have deceived you, prevailed over you,
D   those of your peace.
E   [Those who eat] your bread
F   will establish a place of foreigners in your stead,
G   in which there is no understanding.

Before we examine each phrase in more detail, a comment on the lineation of the verse is in order. The lineation of *BHS*, which is followed here, can be defended on several grounds.

First, the second sentence (C–D) is based on Jer 38:22:

hissîtûkā wĕyākĕlû lĕkā
'anšê šĕlōmekā

"They have deceived you and prevailed over you,
those of your peace."

The two sentences are almost identical; the only differences consist of Jeremiah's verb *hissîtûkā*, a synonym of Obadiah's verb *hiššî'ûkā*, and the presence of *waw* between the two verbs in Jeremiah but its absence from Obadiah. This parallel reveals that the nominal phrase "those of your peace" is the subject of the two immediately preceding verbs. Therefore the nominal phrase in B must be the subject of the verbal clause in A (*pace* Wellhausen 1963; Wolff 1977; Stuart 1987; and others who construe "all those of your covenant" with "have deceived you" and "those of your peace" with "prevailed over you," thereby splitting the two verbs of C).

Second, the lineation of *BHS* provides each verbal clause (A, C, F) with a prepositional phrase in addition to its own nominal subject, producing an excellent example of grammatical parallelism.

Third, this lineation results in each colon ending with -*kā* (except for the final colon that breaks the pattern with *bô*). Although not very common in biblical poetry such a final rhyming scheme is noteworthy.

Finally, the Masoretic accentuation supports the lineation of *BHS*. Moreover, in light of Revell's (1981) interpretation of pausal forms as ancient markers of poetic lineation, one should take the pausal forms of *bĕrîtekā* and *šĕlōmekā* as indicating major breaks at the end of B and D. It is possible to treat A–B and C–D as only one colon each rather than two, but at least both halves of each pair belong together (cf. Dick 1984: 27 n. 20).

To the very border they have expelled you. The unexpected word order of prepositional phrase + verb enables the colon to conclude like the following cola with the morpheme -*kā* (you/your). The preposition *'ad* when used with verbs of motion and specifically with *šlḥ* has a terminative sense, "toward, up to" (cf. 2 Kgs 2:2; Isa 57:9; Ps 80:12 [11]). Although the noun *haggĕbûl* can mean either "territory" or "border/boundary," with the preposition *'ad* it conveys the latter sense (Deut 3:14; Josh 12:5; 1 Sam 6:12; Ezek 29:10; 48:21; cf. Ottosson 1975: 364). What is not clear is whose border is in view, that of Edom or of the allies. The ambiguity results from the absence of a pronominal suffix such as "their border" or of a qualifying genitive such as "the border of Edom." The issue is closely bound up with the next, which concerns the denotation and connotation of the *pi'el* verb *šillĕḥûkā*.

The *pi'el* of *šlḥ* has a wide semantic range: "to commission" (cf. v 1 — *pu'al*); "to send"; "to let go"; "to stretch out" a hand; "to escort"; and "to expel" (*HALAT*). For v 7 three major interpretations have been proposed.

1. The allies refuse to grant asylum to Edomite refugees and instead "send" them back to the allies' border where they become vulnerable to enemy attack (Hitzig 1838; Rudolph 1971; Wolff 1977).

2. Edomite envoys sue for help against an enemy attack but the allies rebuff them and "escort" them back to the allies' border (Caspari 1842; Keil 1888). As mentioned above, the verb can denote "to escort, give a send-off" (Gen 12:20; 18:16; 31:27). However, the difficulty with this interpretation as well as with the first one is that both presuppose a step in the sequence taking place before v 7, that Edom's fugitives or envoys first travel to the allies before they are "sent" back.

3. The allies "expel" the Edomites from their cities and homes to the extremities of Edom's land (Bewer 1911; Frey 1948; Thompson 1956). The *pi'el* of *šlḥ* can denote "to forcefully send away, expel" and can have a hostile connotation (Gen 3:23; Lev 18:24; 20:23; 2 Sam 13:16; Jer 24:5; 28:16; 29:20). Milgrom (1991: 1023) notes that the *pi'el* can imply the impossibility of return on the part of the sent object.

On the whole the last interpretation fits best with the rest of v 7. It also agrees with Jeremiah's Edom oracle, which to a great extent serves as a source for Obadiah's motifs in addition to his vocabulary and idioms. In Jer 49:19 God announces:

"Look! Like a lion rises
from the thicket of Jordan to a perennial pasturage,
so will I suddenly chase him [Edom] away from it."

Compare Jer 49:5. The point of Obad 7 is not that the allies slaughter or take captive the Edomites but only that upon entering the land, instead of acting like allies they push the Edomites out of their dwellings and make them roam or settle in the outlying areas of Edomite territory. "The border" is that of Edom (Wehrle 1987: 49–50).

all those of your covenant. The phrase *kōl 'anšê bĕrîtekā* (lit., "all the men of your covenant") never occurs elsewhere — the closest parallel is "the woman of your covenant" referring to one's wife (Mal 2:14) — but the construct chain *kōl 'anšê* + noun is fairly common in Biblical Hebrew (fifteen occurrences). The phrase refers to Edom's partners and allies. Usually when *bĕrît* carries a pronominal suffix, the suffix is a subjective genitive that designates the initiating party although not necessarily the superior party (the only exceptions occur in Ezek 16:61 and Zech 9:11 — "covenant with you," an objective genitive). Therefore we may assume that Edom took the initiative in making peace with the other group, which probably is to be identified historically with the Babylonians as the superior party. The alliance could be either a formal treaty or an informal agreement.

They have deceived you. The verb, a *hipʿil* perfect with object suffix of *nš'* II, has the sense "to deceive, give false hopes." The same verb also appears in v 3, "The presumption of your heart has deceived you" (see Note). The verb's subject, "those of your peace," helps clarify the nature of the deception in v 7. An essential component of Edom's covenant was *šālôm*, from which we can infer that its covenant partner promised to maintain "peace" with Edom in a nonaggression pact and to help Edom keep "peace" in its own territory by offering, for example, military assistance in case of enemy attack (Kalluveettil 1982: 34–42). Yet such a promise of *šālôm* by the allies becomes a false hope for Edom because the allies instead attack and prevail over Edom.

prevailed over you. The verbal clause *yākĕlû lĕkā* and the preceding verb *hiššî'ûkā* together might form a henidays, "They have deceived you in order to overpower you" (McCarter 1976: 88). Freedman (private communication) notes that *yākĕlû* creates a sound play with *kōl* (all) of the previous colon.

The idiom *ykl* + *l* occurs eleven times in Biblical Hebrew (including Obad 7) and means "to overcome, prevail over" the object (BDB). It appears in contexts where two parties engage in a contest or a fight with each other (Gen 32:26 [25]; Num 13:30; Judg 16:5; 1 Sam 17:9; Jer 1:19; 15:20; 20:10; 38:22; Ps 129:2; Esth 6:13). In the context of Obad 7 the allies overpower the Edomites by forcing them to the border so that their land becomes inhabited by others.

those of your peace. Because "those of your peace" parallels "all those of your covenant," it is possible to understand "all" to be gapped here (cf. Isa 41:11). What speaks against it, however, is the parallel in Jer 38:22, which lacks "all."

Expressions similar to the genitive construction *'anšê šĕlōmekā* occur in other texts where they denote one's "friends." In Jer 20:10 the prophet refers to his friends as:

kōl 'ĕnôš šĕlômî
šōmĕrê ṣalʿî

all those of my peace
who watch for my stumbling.

Similarly, the psalmist of Ps 41:10 [9] speaks of a perfidious friend as:

gam 'îš šĕlômî
'ăšer bāṭaḥtî bô

even the one of my peace
whom I trust.

Also note the following: *šôlĕmî* — participle with suffix — "the one at peace with me" (Ps 7:5 [4]); *šĕlōmāyw* — noun with suffix — "those at peace with him"

(Ps 55:21 [20]). The antonym of this type of phrase can be expressed by a similar genitive construction, *'îš / 'anšê milḥāmâ* + objective genitive (the one/those at war with another party): "For Hadadezer was a man frequently at war with Toi" (2 Sam 8:10 = 1 Chr 18:10); "They will be as nothing and as nought, those at war with you" (Isa 41:12).

The phrase "those of your peace" refers to the same group as "all those of your covenant," Edom's treaty partners with whom Edom had friendly and peaceful relations. One finds "peace" frequently associated with "covenant." The two can be paired (Josh 9:15; 1 Kgs 5:26 [12]; Mal 2:5; Ps 55:21 [20]; cf. Job 5:23 where "covenant" is paired with the verb *šlm*) or form a construct chain — "covenant of peace" (Num 25:12; Isa 54:10; Ezek 34:25; 37:26). In light of this usage, "your covenant" and "your peace" might represent either a word pair or what O'Connor (1980) terms the trope of "combination" in which the underlying genitive phrase "your covenant of peace" has been broken up.

The noun "peace" denotes the wholeness of the relationship between two parties. It can designate the attitude of nonhostility necessary for two persons or groups when beginning negotiation or the mutual harmony and friendship that a pact establishes (Wiseman 1982; Kalluveettil 1982: 34–42). Kalluveettil notes that *šālôm*, like Akkadian *salīmum* (friendship, alliance) and *šulmum* (peace, well-being), can by itself metonymically denote a treaty or pact.

In Obad 7 "peace" expresses the mutual harmony that flows from the covenant relationship, a harmony both parties have obligated themselves to maintain. This would typically entail certain concrete obligations, such as mutual nonaggression, military assistance, extradition of rebels and fugitives, and reports of insurrection. In short, Edom's covenant partners were supposed to further Edom's prosperity, security, and orderly way of life (Kalluveettil 1982: 34–35).

[Those who eat] your bread. The isolated noun with suffix *laḥmĕkā* is difficult and probably reflects a scribal error. Of the various suggested emendations the most plausible is the one proposed by Davies (1977); read *lōḥămê laḥmĕkā*, "those who eat your bread" (cf. Prov 4:17; 23:6; Ps 41:10 [9]). In this case the scribe accidentally omitted the first of these two similar words by virtue of homoioarkton. This suggestion finds support in the Codex Venetus and the Lucianic recension of the LXX, Symmachus, the Vulgate, and the Targum. The MT has the support of Aquila and the Peshiṭta.

However, a case for the the MT can be made (cf. Armerding 1985). If we assume that "all" of the first subject, "all those of your covenant," has been gapped from the second subject, "(all) those of your peace," then we may further assume that the words "all those" have been gapped from the third subject: (*kōl 'anšê*) *laḥmĕkā* — "(all those) of your bread." A one word colon is admittedly very rare in Hebrew poetry but not impossible (cf. Bartelt 1991: 66 on Isa 5:19d). Here it would serve a rhetorical purpose: Edom's allies disappear both from history and from the page itself; the deceptive grammar signals the historical "deception" Edom is about to experience. What speaks against this understanding is that the phrase *'îš / 'anšê lehem* (the one/those of bread) never occurs elsewhere. The close parallel in Ps 41:10 [9] supports the emendation. Although the decision is difficult and cannot be made with any degree of certainty, Davies' suggestion seems more likely.

In Semitic languages the noun *lḥm* bears the sense of "common food" and refers to various victuals depending on the sociocultural situation. For example, Arabic *laḥmu* refers to "meat" or "pulp of a fruit" and the South-Arabian dialect of the island Soqotri uses *lehem* to refer to "fish." In ancient Israel *lehem* always referred to "bread" (Ullendorff 1956: 192; Swiggers 1981).

Regardless of whether one follows Davies or the MT, v 7e provides the subject of the subsequent verbal clause. It refers to the same group as the other nominal phrases, the covenant partners who have peace and table fellowship with Edom. The term "bread" operates within the same orbit as "covenant" and "peace."

Offering another party bread expressed hospitality, and eating a meal together signaled mutual friendship (cf. Gen 18; 24:33, 54; Deut 23:5 [4]; Judg 19:21; 1 Kgs 2:7). Ps 41:10 [9] illustrates the idea and offers a close parallel to our text:

gam 'îš šělômî 'ăšer bāṭaḥtî bô
'ôkēl laḥmî higdîl 'ālay 'āqēb

Even the one of my peace whom I trusted,
the one eating my bread has raised his heel against me.

Here "the one eating my bread" is paired with "the one of my peace."

Furthermore, a meal is often associated with a covenant or pact made between two parties. The meal enacts and expresses the covenant relationship. The Hebrew Bible in several places attests to covenant meals:

Gen 26:28–31	Abimelech-Isaac
Gen 31:44–54	Jacob-Laban
Exod 24:3–11	Yahweh-Israel
Josh 9:14–15	Israel-Gibeonites
2 Sam 3:12–21	Abner-David

The custom of meals associated with agreements or treaties is also well attested in the ancient Near East (Kaufman 1977: 126–27; Mendenhall and Herion 1992: 1194). Examples can be found in the Mari texts (ARM VIII, 13), Amarna letters (EA 162:22–25), Neo-Assyrian treaties (Wiseman 1958: 39–40, lines 153–54), Assyro-Aramaic legal documents (Kaufman 1977: 120, line 5), and Aramaic texts (Sefire III:5, 7; Ahiqar 33–34).

will establish a place of foreigners in your stead. The sentence posits that after the allies expel Edomites from their dwellings, non-Edomites will settle in their place (cf. Zech 9:6).

The noun *māzôr* is difficult. It occurs three times apart from Obad 7 and in all three cases denotes a "wound, sore" (Jer 30:13; Hos 5:13a, b); its root is uncertain — perhaps *zwr*, "to press" (BDB), or **mzr*, "to be foul" (*HALAT*). Some commentators — following the medieval Jewish exegetes (see Caspari 1842) — attribute the same sense to *māzôr* in Obad 7. For example, Keil (1888) construes *laḥměkā* and *māzôr* as a double object, "they make your bread into a wound under you." He understands this as a figure of speech meaning that the allies use their trading relations with Edom, from which they draw their sustenance, as an opportunity to wound Edom. The wound's location "under" Edom symbolizes its dangerous nature as one that can be healed only with difficulty. Laetsch (1956) also interprets the expression in a figurative way. According to him, Edom's "bread" stands for its metallurgical industry. The metals exported to neighboring countries will return as instruments of war used to attack Edom. Thus the allies will make Edom's "bread" (i.e., metals) to be like a festering wound sapping Edom's very life. Niehaus (1993) translates the sentence: "They have rendered your covenant meal a wound in your under parts." He compares it with the doom of Jehoram (2 Chr 21:15, 18–19). These interpretations are rather implausible.

Most commentators take *māzôr* to mean "snare, trap, net." One can construe the words in two ways: either treat *laḥměkā* and *māzôr* as a double object — "they make your bread into a snare under you" (cf. Ps 69:23 [22]) — or, as is more commonly done, consider *laḥměkā* as part of the subject and *māzôr* as the object "[those who eat] your bread place a snare under you." The sense of "snare" enjoys the support of at least some of the ancient versions:

(LXX) *enedra*	snare, ambush
(Vulgate) *insidias*	snare, ambush
(Targum) *tql'*	snare
(Peshiṭta) *km'n'*	ambush
(Theodotion) *desmon*	bonds, fetters
(Aquila) *epidesin*	bonds

It is doubtful that the versions reflect a different *Vorlage*, one that had *māṣôd* (snare, net) or *māṣôr* (siege). Yet it is unclear precisely how they derived their translations, whether they reflect guesses from the context or have a linguistic basis. Bewer (1911) derives the sense of "cord, rope, snare" from the postbiblical Hebrew verb *mzr* (to twist, weave, spin) and the Syriac verb *mzr* (to bind). Compare Syriac *'tmzr* (to stretch oneself), Arabic *mzr* (to extend evenly), and Akkadian *mazūru* (fuller's stick). The root *mzr* with the meaning "to spread out" might appear in Biblical Hebrew if in Prov 1:17 we read *mĕzūrâ* (*qal* passive participle) rather than *mĕzōrâ* (*puʻal* of *zrh*):

kî ḥinnām mĕzūrâ hārāšet
bĕʻênê kol baʻal kānāp

for in vain is the net *spread out*
in the sight of any bird.

However, McCarter (1976) offers the most plausible and satisfying explanation. He derives the noun *māzôr* from *zwr* (to be a stranger, foreigner; cf *zārîm* in v 11) and notes that nouns of the type **maqṭal* from middle weak roots are commonly nouns of place: *mābôʾ* (place of entering), *māgôr* (place of sojourning), *mākôn* (fixed place), *mālôn* (place of lodging), *mānôaḥ* (place of rest), *mānôs* (place of escape), *māqôm* (place), and *mārôm* (place of elevation). Accordingly, *māzôr* would mean "place of foreignness," that is, "place of foreigners." Symmachus is one ancient version that interprets *māzôr* in a similar way — *allotriōsin*, "estrangement, alienation."

McCarter renders the prepositional phrase *taḥteykā* "in your stead" rather than "under you." The preposition *taḥat* frequently has the substitutionary sense, and this sense can also apply to the sequence we find in Obad 7f: *śym* + object + *taḥat* (2 Sam 17:25; 1 Kgs 20:24; Ps 109:5). The above understanding was already anticipated by J. M. P. Smith (1939), who translated the sentence: "Your associates have put a foreign people in your place."

in which there is no understanding. The verbless clause does not mean "there is no understanding *of it.*" For that sense Hebrew uses the verb *byn* + *b* + object. Rather, the sequence *ʾên* + noun + *b* + noun/pronoun indicates the nonexistence or absence of a person or thing within a location. A well-known refrain in the book of Judges provides an illustration (17:6; 18:1; 21:25):

ʾên melek bĕyiśrāʾēl

"There was no king in Israel."

Therefore our clause in Obad 7 means "understanding is absent in it/him." Parallels with the same construction confirm this interpretation:

wĕʾên bāhem tĕbûnâ

"and there is no understanding in them [Israelites]." (Deut 32:28)

haʾên ʻôd ḥokmâ bĕtêmān

"Is there no longer wisdom in Teman?" (Jer 49:7)

wĕ'ên da'at 'ĕlōhîm bā'āreṣ

"and there is no knowledge of God in the land." (Hos 4:1)

kî 'ên ma'ăśeh wĕḥešbôn
wĕda'at wĕḥokmâ biš'ôl

For there is no work or thought
or knowledge or wisdom in Sheol. (Eccl 9:10)

There is some doubt regarding the antecedent of the pronominal suffix of *bô.* It could be "Esau" mentioned in v 6 ("in him") or "the border" to which Edom is expelled, but more likely it is *māzôr* in the preceding clause ("in it"). This is supported both by the following verse and by the parallel in Jeremiah's Edom oracle (49:7). The clause is an unmarked relative clause with ellipsis of *'ăšer;* hence "in which." Zech 9:11 exhibits a comparable syntax:

šillaḥtî 'ăsîrayik mibbôr
'ên mayim bô

"I have released your prisoners from the pit
in which there is no water."

The last clause of Obad 7 as the only verbless clause in vv 5–7 signals the end of the unit (Wehrle 1987: 30). It functions as a catch-line that anticipates the following unit. (On the device, see Haran 1985). Because non-Edomites will settle in the land, nothing of Edom's renowned wisdom will be present there. What appears first as a minor detail becomes expanded in verse 8, which expresses the divine intention to remove wisdom from the land of Edom.

COMMENT

In verses 5–6 Obadiah continues to use parts of Jeremiah's Edom oracle (Jer 49: 9–10), but here he modifies the material more freely than in vv 1–4. Also part of v 7 borrows from Jer 38:22 (see the Introduction). Within the context of Obadiah, the second divine utterance in vv 5–7 begins to clarify the nature of Edom's appointed destiny announced in vv 1–4: Edom will be ransacked and driven from its homeland.

The section has links with the previous one. In terms of grammar, the two if-clauses at the start of v 5 recall the two if-clauses of v 4. Also the use of two rhetorical questions given in v 5 provide Yahweh's response as it were to Edom's employment of a rhetorical question in v 3. Furthermore, just as vv 2–3 juxtaposed Edom with the nations, so vv 5–6 juxtapose Edom with other groups. Only here a similarity is made in addition to a contrast. On the one hand, Edom's secret places and hidden treasures will be thoroughly searched out, found, and plundered, unlike the leftovers that would remain if normal thieves/plunderers and grape gatherers passed through Edom's land. On the other hand, Edom has acted just like thieves and plunderers of the night (v 5). Obadiah will specify the nature of this crime more precisely later in vv 10–14, but already here he intimates it with an interjection and wordplay: "How you have been similar/destroyed!" Because Edom has acted like plunderers, it is only fitting that Edom should in turn be plundered. It is significant that Obadiah adds this interjection, which does not occur in the Jeremiah parallel. With it he anticipates the talionic standard of judgment that he will expressly state in v 15.

The identity of the party that will seek out Edom's hiding places is left unspecified in v 6 in order to emphasize the verbal action and its object. In light of v 4, one might assume that Yahweh himself will be the one to "search out" Edom (cf. Amos 9:3; Zeph 1:12 where this verb occurs with Yahweh as subject); but in light of v 1 and v 7, one sees the nations and specifically Edom's own allies as the enemy. The object of the search will be "Esau//his hidden things." For the first time in the book Obadiah equates Edom with Esau. By using the name "Esau" and by referring to him in the third person — in contrast to the second-person references to Edom in v 5 and v 7 — Obadiah also encourages the reader to think of the patriarch Esau and the Jacob-Esau narratives. The linking of Edom with Esau in this verse suggests a correspondence: the treasures of Esau's descendants will be sought just as were those of Esau.

Verse 7 changes the picture of Edom's impending doom: Edom's allies will drive the nation from its land and foreigners will settle in its place. The verse brings to a climax the sequence begun in verse 1. The unspecified nations being recruited to attack Edom (v 1), the agents by which Yahweh will bring Edom down (v 4), and those who will ransack Edom's hidden treasures (v 6) turn out to be Edom's own covenant partners. In light of v 11 they should be identified as the Babylonians. Obad 1–7 found its fulfillment, at least in principle, in 553 B.C. when Nabonidus of Babylon campaigned against Edom while on his way to Teima in Arabia. According to the most likely reconstruction, Nabonidus's campaign brought an end to Edom's existence as an independent state (see the Introduction). Several Edomite sites show evidence of destruction about this time, although some occupation and activity continued into the Persian period. In all likelihood Nabonidus maintained control over the land and the Edomites who remained (cf. Mal 1:3–4). Then after 539 jurisdiction probably transferred to Persia. By the end of the fourth century the Nabateans had occupied the territory of Edom.

The section of vv 5–7 displays two tightly interwoven units of the same size: vv 5–6 = 8 lines and 51 syllables; and v 7 = 7 lines and 49 syllables. The grammatical structure ties the 8 lines of vv 5–6 together with three protases, two apodoses, and three exclamations. They form an AABC ACBB pattern:

v 5   A   protasis   "if" (*'im*) + subject + perfect verb (*bā'û*) + preposition with suffix (*lĕkā*)

         A   protasis   "if" (*'im*) + subject

         B   exclamation   *'êk* + *nip'al* perfect verb

         C   apodosis   interrogative (*hălô'*) + imperfect verb + object

         A   protasis   "if" (*'im*) + subject + perfect verb (*bā'û*) + preposition with suffix (*lāk*)

         C   apodosis   interrogative (*hălô'*) + imperfect verb + object

v 6   B   exclamation   — *'êk* + *nip'al* perfect verb + subject

         B   exclamation   *nip'al* perfect verb + subject

Note the interlocking sequence of the introductory particles — ABC ACB:

v 5	A	*'im . . . 'im*	(if . . . if)
	B	*'êk*	(how)
	C	*hălô'*	(will they not)
	A	*'im*	(if)
	C	*hălô'*	(will they not)
v 6	B	*'êk*	(how)

Verse 5 has two sentences (plus an interjection) as does v 6. However, the sentences in v 5 are rhetorical questions with the subject positioned before the verb, whereas v 6 contains exclamations with the subject following the verb. The grammatical contrast supports the semantic contrast: Edom will be completely robbed and harvested unlike what ordinary thieves and vintagers would do. Also the use of *'êk* and of the *nip'al* perfects in v 6 (prophetic perfects) encourages the reader to connect v 6 with the interjection in v 5:

v 5 How you have been similar/destroyed!

v 6 How Esau has been thoroughly searched out,
       his hidden things thoroughly sought after!

The semantic relationship is twofold based on the double meaning of the verb in v 5. First, the verb states the crime: Edom has "been similar" to thieves/plunderers and therefore will be robbed itself; the punishment corresponds with the crime. Second, the verb expresses Edom's fate: Edom will be "destroyed," the nature of which then begins to receive clarification in v 6 — it will be ransacked.

Verse 7 forms the second unit of the section. With respect to grammatical structure, it consists of three sentences (two bicola and one tricolon), each with a verbal clause, a prepositional phrase, and a nominal phrase serving as subject:

a. prepositional phrase + verb;
b. subject;
c. verb + verb + prepositional phrase;
d. subject;
e. subject;
f. verb + object + prepositional phrase;
g. relative clause.

The first two sentences follow the standard verb-subject order, whereas the final sentence reverses the order and adds a nominal object and a relative clause. The shift in pattern signals the end of the unit (cf. Mirsky 1977). The morpheme *-kā* (you/your) occurs seven times, appearing at the end of each of the first six lines with the seventh occurring within the third line. In other words, the epistrophe of the morpheme displays a symmetrical arrangement: twice in the first sentence, twice in the third sentence, and three times in the middle sentence.

Each sentence has its own subject:

7b all those of your covenant
7d those of your peace
7e [those who eat] your bread

(On the text-critical question of v 7e, see the Note.) The three subjects refer to one and the same group of allies. The three absolute nouns are closely associated; they refer to the *covenant or pact* that Edom has with another people, a covenant that guarantees *peaceful* relations between the two and one that is expressed by table-fellowship or a covenant *meal*. Obadiah concentrates on this relationship, because for him these features should have applied to the relationship between Edom and Israel as brothers (see below).

With respect to the verbs, the perfect verbs in v 7a and v 7c should be taken as "prophetic perfects" in light of the imperfect used in v 7f. This corresponds with the overall outlook of the book in that it portrays Edom's fall as a future event (cf. vv 1, 4, 8–10). The sequence of the actions is noteworthy. The first and the third verbal clauses relate to each other chronologically. The allies expel the Edomites to the border (v 7a) and then establish their ancestral home as a place where non-Edomites live (v 7f). The intervening two verbs provide a summary of the activity. Edom's allies give the (false) hope of aid in case of enemy attack but instead turn out themselves to be the feared enemies who prevail over Edom (v 7c). Edom, noted for its wisdom and understanding (v 8), ends up ironically being "deceived" not only by its own presumption (v 3) but also by its covenant partners. The final colon (v 7g) picks up this motif and also anticipates the next verse: "understanding" will not even exist in Edom's territory.

In ancient Israel as well as the Near East in general failing to keep one's covenant obligations was considered bad enough, but for a covenant partner to become one's enemy was regarded a great offense (cf. Isa 33:8; Amos 1:9; Ps 55:21 [20]). Yet verse 7 presents an extended discussion of precisely such an offense by allotting seven lines to the matter. The purpose is again to evoke the talionic standard of judgment. Although Edom as "Esau" (v 6) should have treated Israel as a brother, Edom instead acted as Israel's enemy (vv 10–14). Therefore the hostile attack Edom will experience from its trusted allies matches the treachery Edom did to its "brother" (v 10).

The sevenfold repetition of the morpheme -kā and the threefold repetition of the subject focuses the attention on the two parties involved. The identity of the one party is clear, namely Edom. But what is the extratextual identity of the other party? Obadiah nowhere explicitly names the group but only offers a hint. Many scholars posit Edom's allies to be neighboring Arab tribes with whom Edom might have had commercial ties. However, this identification overlooks a significant clue that the book does provide. According to v 11, the Edomites became partners with those who attacked Judah and Jerusalem. These attackers were probably the Babylonians and the event was the catastrophe of 587/6 B.C. In all likelihood, therefore, the Edomites chose to become the vassals of the Babylonians. (On the question, see the Introduction.)

III. YAHWEH'S THIRD UTTERANCE (vv 8–18)

A. ANNOUNCEMENT OF DOOM, ACCUSATION AND WARNING ADDRESSED TO EDOM (vv 8–15)

◆

8 Will it not indeed happen in that day —
    utterance of Yahweh
  — that I will destroy the wise from Edom,
                and understanding from Mount Esau,
9 and your warriors will be panic-stricken, O Teman,
  with the result that everyone will be cut off from Mount Esau by slaughter?
10 Because of the violence you did to your brother Jacob
        shame will cover you,
        and you will be cut off forever.
11 On the day when you stood opposite,
  on the day when strangers took captive his power,
            while foreigners entered his gates
            and cast lots for Jerusalem,
                also you were like one of them.
12 But do not gaze upon the day of your brother,
        on the day of his adversity.
  And do not rejoice over the Judahites,
        on the day of their ruin.
  And do not open your mouth wide,
        on the day of distress.
13 Do not enter through the gate of my people,
        on the day of their ordeal.

Do not gaze, also you, upon its misfortune,
>on the day of its ordeal.
And do not reach out (your hands) for its wealth,
>on the day of its ordeal.
14 And do not stand at the fork in the road
>in order to eliminate its escapees.
And do not hand over its survivors,
>on the day of distress.
15 For the day of Yahweh is near
>against all the nations.
Just as you have done, it will be done to you;
>your deeds will return upon your own head.

NOTES

v 8. *hălô' bayyôm hahû'*
nĕ'ūm yahweh.
Will it not indeed happen in that day — utterance of Yahweh.

The initial phrase functions as a temporal clause with the main clause signaled by *w* + perfect, "that I will destroy." The composite particle — interrogative *h* + negative *lô'* — introduces a question that expects an affirmative answer (cf. v 5). Here it also seems to indicate emphatic stress, "Indeed the following event will happen in that day." The closest parallels to this syntax occur in Ezek 24:25 and 38:14, which read respectively:

hălô' bĕyôm qaḥtî mēhem 'et mā'ûzzām . . .

"Will it not indeed happen in the day when I take from them their
>stronghold . . . ?"

hălô' bayyôm hahû'
bĕšebet 'ammî yiśrā'ēl lābeṭaḥ
tēda' [or *tē'ōr*]

"Will it not indeed happen in that day
when my people Israel dwell in safety
that you will know [you will bestir yourself]?"

In both parallels *hălô'* gives emphatic force to the sentence (Brongers 1981: 183–84).

According to DeVries (1975: 324–25), the formula "in that day" designates a future time period in 111 occurrences, of which 102 appear in the Latter Prophets. Only four prophetic books lack the formula: Jonah, Nahum, Habakkuk, and Malachi. Its function has been debated. Gressmann (1929: 82–84) claimed that it is a technical term with an eschatological meaning. In response Munch (1936) opposed the eschatological interpretation by arguing that it can always be understood simply as a temporal adverb ("on the same day," "then"). It synchronizes the events mentioned in contiguous passages. DeVries (1975) attributes to the futuristic "in that day" the basic functions of synchronizing and epitomizing.

What function does the phrase have in Obad 8? The verse permits two interpretations and both fit the context. On the one hand, the repetition of "understanding" in v 7 and v 8 promotes seeing the formula as a device that further connects the two verses by synchronizing the events announced in them. The divine action declared in v 8 will happen *at the same time* as the attack by the allies depicted in v 7. On the other hand, the formula anticipates the reference to "the day of Yahweh" in v 15 (R. B. Robinson 1988: 91). "In that day," namely, in the day when Yahweh intervenes to judge the nations, he will destroy Edom's wisdom. Thus the temporal phrase "in that day" links the preceding verses with the subsequent verses and thereby brings the particular and historical judgment against Edom (vv 1–7) into the orbit of the cosmic day of judgment (v 15).

On the divine speech formula "utterance of Yahweh," see Note under v 4. Whereas in v 4 the formula concludes a unit, here it introduces one. Its location after the phrase "in that day" interrupts the syntactic sequence of temporal clause + main clause ("Will it not indeed happen in that day . . . that I will destroy"). However, this placement of the formula is not uncommon (cf. Isa 22:25; Jer 4:9; 30:8; Hos 2:18, 23 [16, 21]; Amos 8:9; Mic 4:6; 5:9 [10]; Zeph 1:10; Hag 2:23; Zech 3:10; 12:4; 13:2).

wĕha'ăbadtî ḥăkāmîm mē'ĕdôm.
that I will destroy the wise from Edom.
The clause (lit., "I will cause the wise to perish from Edom") is based on the construction *'bd* + *min*, which occurs forty-two times, including nine that use the *hip'il* (Wehrle 1987: 120). When the verb takes a personal object, the construction denotes both death and removal (cf. Lev 23:30; Jer 49:38; Ezek 25:7). Hence, the wise will die and consequently vanish from Edom's land.

It might seem odd that v 8 refers to Edom in the third person in contrast to the surrounding verses, which refer to Edom in the second person. But the same oscillation occurs in v 6. Furthermore, the presence of the third person is dictated by the construction itself (*'bd* + *min*), which normally is used with a place name rather than with a pronoun.

The closest parallel to v 8 (and the last line of v 7) occurs in Jer 49:7:

ha'ên 'ôd ḥokmâ bĕtêmān
'ābĕdâ 'ēṣâ mibbānîm
nisrĕḥâ ḥokmātām

"Is wisdom no longer in Teman?
Has counsel perished from those who understand?
Has their wisdom spoiled?"

That both passages share much of the same vocabulary and use the construction *'bd* + *min* provides further evidence of the close relationship between Obadiah and Jeremiah.

The motif of God rendering human wisdom futile is common in wisdom literature (e.g., Job 12:17, 20, 24–25; Prov 21:30). One also finds it in prophetic judgment oracles against Israel (Isa 3:1–3; 5:21; 29:14; Jer 8:8–9) and against the nations (Egypt — Isa 19:11–13; Babylon — Isa 44:25; 47:10; Jer 50:35; 51:57; Phoenicia — Ezek 28:2–7, 17; Zech 9:2).

This literary motif appropriately applies to Edom since Edom was notable for its wisdom. Job came from the land of Uz, which probably is to be connected with southern Edom and northern Arabia (Knauf 1992b; cf. Lam 4:21). Eliphaz was a Temanite (Job 2:11); Agur (Prov 30:1) and Lemuel (Prov 31:1) perhaps had an origin in northern Arabia. Edom's wisdom is also mentioned elsewhere (Jer 49:7; Job 15:17–19; Baruch 3:22–23). The tradition of Edom's wisdom was apparently still alive in the days of Muhammad (Pfeiffer 1926: 14).

The specific kind of wisdom in view here remains unknown. Pfeiffer (1926) argued for the existence of Edomite wisdom literature, which he characterized as agnostic and pessimistic in outlook. It is more natural, in the context of Obad 8 at least, to think of a wisdom that served Edom's national security, either political and diplomatic acumen (Rudolph 1971; cf. 1 Kgs 2:6; Isa 19:11–13) or technological skill in copper production (Knauf and Lenzen 1987; cf. Exod 31:2–5; 1 Kgs 7:14).

ûtĕbûnâ mēhar 'ēśāw.
and understanding from Mount Esau.
The verb of the previous colon is gapped. The feminine singular noun *tĕbûnâ* (understanding) parallels the masculine plural noun *ḥăkāmîm* (the wise), a good example of a concrete-abstract lexical pair. One finds *tĕbûnâ* frequently paired with the related noun *ḥokmâ* (wisdom), either located in parallel cola (Jer 10:12; 51:15; Ps 49:4 [3]; Job 12:12, 13; Prov 2:2, 6; 3:13, 19; 5:1; 8:1; 24:3) or collocated in the same sentence (Exod 31:3; 35:31; 36:1; 1 Kgs 5:9 [4:29]; 7:14; Ezek 28:4; Prov 10:23; 21:30).

Outside of Obadiah the name "Edom" is associated with "Esau" (Gen 25:30; 36:1, 8, 19; Jer 49:8, 10; Mal 1:3–4) or with "Mount Seir" (Gen 36:8–9; Ezek 35:2–3, 7, 15) but the term "Mount Esau" never occurs. Obadiah coined the term to create a wordplay on "Mount Seir" by transposing the letters *śin* and *'ayin: śē'îr > 'ēśāw.* The wordplay achieves two effects. It evokes "Mount Seir," a term that — regardless of its original referent — is often used in the Hebrew Bible to designate the territory in which the Edomites lived (cf. Bartlett 1969; 1989:

41–44). Thus it harks back to the mention of Edom's mountainous abode in v 3. The wordplay also keeps alive for the reader the Edom-Esau connection that was introduced in v 6 and will be further developed in v 10. The statement that "understanding" will vanish from "Mount Esau" reminds the reader of Esau's folly in selling his birthright (Gen 25).

v 9. *wĕḥattû gibbôreykā têmān.*
  and your warriors will be panic-stricken, O Teman.

The plural noun *gibbôreykā* refers to Teman's military, its trained soldiers (cf. 2 Sam 23:8–39; 1 Chr 11:11–47). Warriors are noted for their fearless courage, their determination to fight to the death in defense of their nation. But according to this verse, when Yahweh intervenes Teman's warriors will be filled with terror so as to become helpless before the attackers.

The verbal root *ḥtt* basically means "to be broken, shattered," used of bows (1 Sam 2:4; Jer 51:56), the oppressor's rod (Isa 9:3 [4]), the ground cracked by drought (Jer 14:4), and idols (Jer 50:2). When the verb applies to people, the sense transfers to the psychological domain and denotes a paralysis that renders one unable to function (Holladay 1986: 44). The precise nuance varies from being "frustrated" (Job 32:15) and "demoralized" (Isa 20:5; Jer 8:9) to being "terrified" (Job 7:14).

The verb's collocations clarify its sense: *bwš* — "to be ashamed" (e.g., Isa 20:5; Jer 8:9; 48:20); *qiṣrê yād* — "short of strength" (2 Kgs 19:26 = Isa 37:27); *paḥad* — "terror" (Job 39:22); and the antonym *'zr* — "to gird" oneself (Isa 8:9; Jer 1:17). Fifteen times the *nip'al* is paired with *yr'* — "to fear" (e.g., Deut 1:21; Josh 8:1). Perhaps the most revealing expression is the quasi-formulaic exhortation that Joshua gives Israel's warriors (Josh 10:25; cf. 1 Chr 22:13; 28:20; 2 Chr 32:7):

'al tîrĕ'û wĕ'al tēḥāttû
ḥizqû wĕ'imṣû

"Do not fear or *be panicked*;
be strong and brave."

In Obad 9 and elsewhere the root *ḥtt* is used to designate the panic and terror experienced by warriors (1 Sam 17:11; Isa 31:9; Jer 46:5; 50:36). The same motif appears in Akkadian omen texts, where the noun *ḫattu* denotes "panic, fear" (CAD 6:150). Note also the related motif of "warriors becoming like women" that occurs in the Hebrew Bible (Isa 19:16; Jer 48:41; 50:37; 51:30; Nah 3:13) and in extrabiblical literature (Hillers 1964: 66–68). A good example comes from Jeremiah's Edom oracle (49:22):

The heart of Edom's warriors will be in that day
like the heart of a woman in labor.

O Teman. The original identification of Teman remains uncertain. The noun *têmān*, derived from the root *ymn* designating the right hand, denotes the "south" (directions presuppose an eastward orientation). Yet in the Latter Prophets "Teman" is clearly a toponym (Jer 49:7, 20; Ezek 25:13; Amos 1:12; Hab 3:3).

Nelson Glueck (1940: 21–26) cited Amos 1:12, which pairs "Teman" with "Bozrah," as indicating that Teman was a city in southern Edom to match Bozrah, Edom's capital in the north (= Buseirah). He identified Teman with Tawilan in the Petra area. However, Tawilan was unfortified and therefore not an urban site comparable to Bozrah. Roland de Vaux (1969) proposed that "Teman" originally designated a region instead of a city. Gen 36:34 (= 1 Chr 1:45) mentions "the land ['*eres*] of the Temanites," and Hab 3:3 parallels "Teman" with "Mount Paran." Also Eusebius calls biblical Teman a "region." On the basis of the name's etymology and the Habakkuk passage, de Vaux located the region in southern Edom. Knauf (1992a), in contrast, places the region in northern Edom for two reasons: in light of Amos 1:12 Teman is the area surrounding Bozrah, and the phrase in Ezek 25:13 — "from Teman to Dedan" — identifies Edom's northern and southern borders respectively.

The debate illustrates the difficulty of building firm conclusions solely on the basis of poetic parallelism. For example, the pair "Teman — Bozrah" in Amos 1:12 can be understood in three ways: (1) two city names (Glueck); (2) a region in northern Edom together with its leading city (Knauf); (3) "Teman" used by synecdoche to refer to the entire territory together with its leading city (de Vaux). The similar oracles against Moab (Amos 2:2) and Judah (Amos 2:5) lend support to the third option:

Moab — Kerioth

Judah — Jerusalem

Furthermore, the phrase "from Teman to Dedan" is amenable to different interpretations. At face value one would expect Teman to be a northern city corresponding with Dedan, a city in the far south (= el-'Ula in northern Arabia). But Teman might instead designate a region, either in Edom's north (Knauf) or south (de Vaux).

To further complicate the issue, inscriptions from Kuntillet 'Ajrud, dating to the early eighth century B.C., have the phrases "Yahweh of Teman" and "Yahweh of Samaria." The site, a stop along the ancient route from Gaza to Elat, is located about fifty kilometers south of Kadesh-barnea. On the basis of the similarity of the constructions, one might assume that Teman was a city like Samaria. But again, Teman might refer to a region in southern Edom, to which wayfarers journeyed, or to a larger southern area that included 'Ajrud itself (see Emerton 1982; Hadley 1987; McCarter 1987).

At any rate, the usage of "Teman" in Obad 9 is unambiguous. Regardless of its

original identity, here it refers to the whole land of Edom by virtue of synecdoche. Note the pairs in vv 8–9:

Edom — Mount Esau
Teman — Mount Esau

The same phenomenon occurs in Jer 49:7 and 20; both verses pair "Teman"
with "Edom."

lĕmaʿan yikkāret ʾîš mēhar ʿēśāw miqqāṭel.
with the result that everyone will be cut off from Mount Esau by slaughter.

Here the conjunction *lĕmaʿan* introduces a result clause (Joüon 1991 § 169g;
Brongers 1973: 90–91). The common noun *ʾîš* often has a distributive sense
(BDB). The specific group or referent is unclear. Does *ʾîš* refer to "each" of Te-
man's "warriors" (Rudolph 1971; Allen 1976)? Or does it cover "everyone" in
Edom (Caspari 1842; Wolff 1977)? The second option seems more likely in view
of the progression of verses 8–9: "the wise" . . . "warriors" . . . "everyone." Because
Edom's wisdom and military will fail, the populace will be left defenseless. The
total extermination declared in v 9 anticipates the same idea expressed in v 18.

The construction *krt* + *min* (to cut off from) appears frequently in the Hebrew
Bible, usually with the *nipʿal* or *hipʿil* (Wehrle 1987: 121). When the prepositional object is a geographical location, the construction means "to eliminate N
so that N no longer exists in the location" (*nipʿal* — Joel 1:16; Obad 9; Zech 14:2;
Prov 2:22; Ruth 4:10; *qal* — Jer 11:19; 50:16; *hipʿil* — Exod 8:5 [9]; Josh 7:9;
11:21; 1 Sam 20:15; 28:9; 1 Kgs 9:7; Ezek 14:13, 17, 19, 21; 25:13; 35:7; Amos
1:5, 8, 2:3; Nah 1:14; 2:14 [13]; Zeph 1:3, 4; Zech 9:10; 13:2; Pss 34:17 [16];
101:8; 109:15). The expression by itself does not specify the precise nature of the
elimination process. The process might simply involve removal (1 Sam 20:15;
Joel 1:16). When people are "cut off from" a place, the event could happen by
exile and banishment (1 Kgs 9:7; Zech 14:2) or by death (Josh 11:21; Amos 2:3;
Ps 101:8). Sometimes the expression implies the extermination of the object's
memory or remnant (Jer 11:19; Zech 13:2; cf. Jer 44:7).

Related to this construction is the *kārēt* formula of the priestly legislation:

"That person will be cut off from his people."

The formula has engendered much debate among early Jewish and modern exegetes (on the formula, see Good 1983: 85–90; Milgrom 1991: 457–60). It most
likely refers to a penalty enacted by God, probably involving death (cf. Good).
Perhaps it also entails the extirpation of the offender's line and/or the denial of
afterlife (cf. Exod 31:14; Lev 20:2–6, 17).

Unlike the *kārēt* formula, however, there is no doubt about the sense of the clause in Obad 9, especially in light of the concluding phrase "by slaughter" (see below); every Edomite will be killed and thus eliminated from the land. The clause furthermore seems to imply the eradication of the Edomites' remnant and memory. Two passages in Ezekiel's oracles against Edom provide close parallels:

"Therefore thus spoke the Lord Yahweh:
'I will stretch out my hand against Edom,
and I will *cut off from it* humans and animals,
and I will make it desolate;
from Teman to Dedan they will fall by the sword.'" (25:13)

"I will make Mount Seir a waste and a desolation;
and I will *cut off from it* those who come and go." (35:7)

by slaughter. Read with the MT against the ancient versions in concluding v 9 with the prepositional phrase *miqqāṭel*. The preposition *min* marks the means by which "everyone will be cut off from Mount Esau" (cf. Williams 1976 § 320). Thus the phrase serves to specify the nature of the "cutting off" — not by exile but "by slaughter." Note the similar construction in Gen 9:11.

wĕlōʾ yikkārēt kol bāśār ʿôd mimmê hammabbûl

"All flesh will never again be *cut off by* the waters of the flood."

The Hebrew noun *qeṭel* (*miqqāṭel* is a pausal form) is a *hapax*. Moreover, the verb *qṭl*, "to kill," occurs only three times in Biblical Hebrew (Ps 139:19; Job 13:15; 24:14), even though it is well known to Hebrew students as the root used in the strong verb paradigm. Nevertheless, the basic sense of the noun is clear. It denotes "killing, slaughter"; compare the synonym *hereg*. The noun *qṭl* is also attested in Aramaic texts with the sense of "slaying, execution" (Beyer 1984: 682). The verse does not reveal the agent of the action. Theoretically it could be God (Ps 139:19; Job 13:15), but in the context of Obad 9 one naturally thinks of a human agent, specifically enemy armies (cf. vv 1, 7; cf. Job 24:14).

v 10. *mēḥămas ʾāḥîkā yaʿăqōb.*
    Because of the violence you did to your brother Jacob.
    The prepositional phrase literally reads, "From the violence of your brother Jacob." The preposition *min* is causal (cf. Ezek 12:19; Joel 4:19 [3:19]; Hab 2:8, 17), and *ʾāḥîkā* (your brother) is an objective genitive (cf. Gen 16:5; Judg 9:24; Jer 51:35; Joel 4:19 [3:19]; Hab 2:8, 17). The addressee is Edom.
    In contrast to vv 8 and 9, each of which begins with a verb, v 10 locates the prepositional phrase in the initial position (cf. v 7a). This alteration of normal word order achieves two effects. First, it juxtaposes two *min*-phrases — *miqqāṭel*

at the end of v 9 and *mēḥāmas* at the beginning of v 10. It thereby correlates the "slaughter" that the Edomites will experience with the "violence" that Edom inflicted upon Jacob. Second, it focuses the reader's attention on the initial phrase in order to emphasize the reason for Edom's coming judgment. Not only was Edom guilty of violence but it was violence toward Edom's own brother Jacob. The phrase expresses Obadiah's strong emotional shock at the crimes recently committed by Edom.

violence. The noun *ḥāmās* occurs sixty times (and the verb *ḥms* eight times) in the Hebrew Bible (see Stoebe 1971; Haag 1980; Swart 1991). It denotes "violent activity" including moral, judicial, and structural violence as well as physical violence. In most instances *ḥāmās* is done by human beings — with the exception of Job 19:7 for the noun and Lam 2:6 for the verb where God is the actor. The nearest synonym *šōd* (violence, havoc, devastation) forms with *ḥāmās* what appears to be a case of hendiadys, "violent destruction" — *ḥāmās wāšōd* (Jer 6:7; 20:8; Ezek 45:9; Amos 3:10) or *šōd wĕḥāmās* (Hab 1:3).

A variety of specific actions receive the rather general label *ḥāmās:* murder (Gen 49:5–6; Judg 9:24); rape (verb — Jer 13:22); unjust acquisition of wealth by exploiting the socially helpless (Amos 3:10; Zeph 1:9); self-aggrandizement that humiliates another person (Gen 16:5); unjust accusation and judgment that intends injury (Exod 23:1; Deut 19:16; Ps 35:11); distorting the law to the disadvantage of the powerless (verb — Ezek 22:26; Zeph 3:4); and ecological abuse (Hab 2:17). Non-Israelites besides Edom who are accused of *ḥāmās* include the Egyptian Hagar (Gen 16:5), Tyre (Ezek 28:16), the Ninevites (Jonah 3:8), and Babylon (Jer 51:35; Hab 1:9).

In some contexts translations other than "violence" seem more appropriate, such as "injustice" or "wickedness" (Swart 1991). In Obad 10, however, the term "violence" applies in light of the particular acts involved, which the following verses specify. Note especially the references to looting (v 13) and capturing survivors (v 14). The close parallel in Joel 4:19 [3:19] mentions bloodshed in connection with the "violence" of Edom. In this respect Joel echoes both Obad 10 and Ezek 35:5–6:

"Egypt will become a desolation,
and Edom will become a desolate wilderness,
because of the violence done to the Judahites [*mēḥāmas bĕnê yĕhûdâ*],
in whose land they shed innocent blood."

your brother Jacob. The addressee, that is, the referent of the pronoun "your," is still Edom. As the following verses make clear, the name "Jacob" refers to the people of Israel. The prophets frequently designate the people by the name of their patriarchal ancestor (cf. "Esau"). In v 10 and v 12 Obadiah speaks of the people of Jacob as Edom's "brother." The term "brother" can occasionally designate a treaty-partner (1 Kgs 9:13; 20:32–34; Amos 1:9). But in the context of Obadiah, which stresses the Edom-Esau connection, the term has its usual sense of a fraternal bond. Elsewhere the biblical writers mention this kinship between the two peoples (Gen 25:23; Num 20:14; Deut 2:4, 8; 23:8 [7]; Mal 1:2–4). Another relevant text is Amos 1:11, but its use of *'āḥ* (brother) is disputed. Although it might refer to a treaty connection (Fishbane 1970; Barré 1986), more likely it points to the tradition of Edom and Israel as brothers (Paul 1991: 63–64).

tĕkassĕkā bûšâ.
shame will cover you.

The clause might mean that the experience of shame will "overwhelm" and "overpower" Edom (Ringgren 1984: 276). But more likely it expresses the metaphor of shame like a garment "clothing" Edom. Note Ps 89:46 [45]:

he'ĕṭîtā 'ālāyw bûšâ

You enwrapped him [the king] with shame.

(See also Jer 3:25; Mic 7:10; Pss 71:13; 109:29; 132:18.) A related expression is that of shame "covering" one's face, which apparently likens shame to a shawl or veil (Jer 51:51; Ezek 7:18; Pss 44:16 [15]; 69:8 [7]; cf. Gen 38:14–15). When a person is exposed and naked before others, the person experiences shame. Ironically the shame itself will "cover" and clothe Edom. Klopfenstein (1972: 71, 74) suggests that originally behind the metaphor lay a rite of covering the condemned with a type of garment. Such a hypothesis seems unnecessary; one need not assume that every metaphor derives from an institutional practice or custom.

The noun *bûšâ* (shame), a *qûlâ* formation from *bwš*, occurs only three other times (Ezek 7:18; Mic 7:10; Ps 89:46 [45]). Yet the vocabulary of shame is widely attested in Semitic and Biblical Hebrew (see Klopfenstein 1972). The statistics for the Hebrew Bible are as follows, including all verbal and nominal forms derived from each root: *bwš* (be ashamed) — 167 times; *klm* (be disgraced) — 69 times; *ḥpr* II (be abashed) — 17 times; *qlh* II (be of little account) — 24 times.

Anthropological study of traditional societies in the Mediterranean area sheds light on the significance of honor and shame in the ancient Near East. For an introductory discussion, see Muenchow (1989) and the literature cited there. In an agonistic society, where pervasive competitiveness yields social interactions that have a challenge-response quality, honor is a claim to precedence recognized by others. People are obliged to show deference to the honored person. Conversely, shame results from a public rejection of such a claim and often involves ridicule. In a society where it matters what others think, where individual autonomy is not an ideal, public shaming is virtually tantamount to a death sentence.

In Obad 10 *bûšâ* denotes not so much a subjective emotion as an objective status (Klopfenstein 1972: 74). "Shame," the loss of honor and prestige, can result from either the failure to achieve one's goals and expectations (Seebass 1975; cf. 1 Sam 20:30–31) or the experience of having one's trust betrayed (Odell 1991; cf. Isa 20:5). Both notions apply in the context. Instead of maintaining an honored status in the world, Edom experiences humiliation before the nations (v 2) and betrayal by its trusted allies (v 7).

Furthermore, the judgment of shame corresponds with the principle of *lex talionis* operative in the book of Obadiah (v 15). Because Edom shamed its brother Jacob by gloating (v 12) and doing violence (vv 13–14), and thereby betraying the fraternal bond, Edom itself will be put to shame. (For the association of "shame" with violence and gloating, see Gen 16:4–5; Pss 22:6–9 [5–8]; 44:14–17 [13–16].) The ideas involved are well illustrated by Mic 7:10, the closest parallel to our text:

> Then my enemy will see (my vindication),
> and *shame will cover her*,
> the one who keeps saying to me,
> "Where is he, Yahweh your God?"
> My eyes will gloat over her;
> now she will become something trodden down,
> like the mud of the streets.

wěnikrattā lě'ôlām.
and you will be cut off forever.

On the verb *krt*, see the Note under v 9. Here it denotes destruction and implies the lack of a remnant (cf. Jer 44:11; Ezek 25:7; Mic 5:8 [9]; Nah 2:1 [1:15]; Zeph 3:6). Thus Edom will cease to exist as a nation. The use of the passive indicates divine action. The phrase *lě'ôlām* (forever) stresses the unchangeable permanence of this future condition.

v 11.　*běyôm 'ămāděkā minneged*
　　　　běyôm šěbôt zārîm ḥêlô
　　　　wěnokrîm bā'û šě'ārāyw
　　　　wě'al yěrûšālayim yaddû gôrāl
　　　　gam 'attâ kě'aḥad mēhem.

A　　On the day when you stood opposite,
B　　on the day when strangers took captive his power,
C　　while foreigners entered his gates
D　　and cast lots for Jerusalem,
E　　also you were like one of them.

The addressee is still Edom, viewed as a collective and personified. The antecedent of the pronoun "his" in clauses B and C is "Jacob" mentioned in v 10. The syntax of the verse consists of four subordinate clauses (A–D) followed by the main clause (E): two temporal clauses beginning with *běyôm* + the infinitive construct (A–B); two disjunctive clauses beginning with *waw* + a nonverbal element (C–D); and a verbless clause (E). The disjunctive clauses are circumstantial; they elaborate on the situation mentioned in A and B.

The sequence of the actions depicted in the first four clauses seems at first to be disjointed. Did the enemies capture Jacob's property and people before they entered the gates (cf. Duhm 1911; Bewer 1911)? The key is to recognize what O'Connor (1980) calls the trope of "mixing." In this case clauses A and C belong together as do B and D (cf. Mic 1:4 for a similar example of *abab* mixing):

A   On the day when you stood opposite,

C   while foreigners entered his gates;

B   on the day when strangers took captive his power

D   and cast lots for Jerusalem.

The ACBD arrangement also reflects the chronological sequence of events: Edom stood and watched while strangers/foreigners entered Judah's gates, captured people and goods, and cast lots to determine who would get the prize, Jerusalem itself.

Verse 11 depicts a past event, as the context and the perfect verbs in C–D make clear. The historical event to which Obadiah refers is most likely the Babylonian crisis of the early sixth century (see the Introduction). It might have included both the 597 capture and the 587/6 destruction. One should note that the word "day" (*yôm*) can designate an entire period and not only a period of twenty-four hours.

you stood opposite. The complex preposition *min* + *neged* functions as an adverbial. It indicates a position "in front, opposite, within the field of vision": A faces B and can observe B (cf. Num 2:2; Deut 28:66; 32:52; Judg 20:34; 2 Kgs 2:15; 3:22; 4:25). Even when further qualified as "far-off," *minneged* still refers to a position within general eyesight of the other object (cf. Gen 21:16; 2 Kgs 2:7). When joined with a verb meaning "to stand," the clause can connote an attitude of indifference or hostility (cf. 2 Sam 18:13 — with *ysb*; Ps 38:12 [11] — with *'md*). Thus Obadiah condemns personified Edom for standing directly in front of Jacob as an indifferent or hostile observer instead of coming to the side of its brother Jacob when strangers and foreigners attacked.

strangers. The national identity of the attackers remains unspecified. In the prophets the term "strangers" often refers to foreign peoples and in Ezekiel specifically to the Babylonians (Ezek 7:21; 11:9; 28:7, 10; 30:12; 31:12; cf. Jer 51:51; Snijders 1954: 22–40). Here as well they were probably the Babylonians, but Obadiah nowhere explicitly states this. Note that in Lamentations and some of the exilic psalms (Pss 74, 79, 102) explicit mention of the "Babylonians" is also lacking, even though the Babylonian army is the referent of terms such as "enemy" or "foe." Obadiah prefers to stress their status as outsiders and non-natives in order to contrast them with Edom, Jacob's brother (v 10). This emphasis prepares for the charge in v 11e: "You, our very own brother, became like the hostile strangers and foreigners."

The word *zārîm* is a participle form of *zwr* (to turn away) used as a substantive (see Snijders 1954; 1980). It has the sense of "strangers, aliens," people who are outside of one's own circle of relationships, such as the family, the nation, the priesthood, or the devout, depending on the context. In Obad 11 it designates people who are completely different from and unrelated to "Jacob."

The prophets use the word with an unfavorable connotation, something like "barbarians" in English, those who lack respect for the accepted norms of their victims and who defile what their victims consider sacred. Their characteristic "is that they overthrow the established order, disturb the existant [*sic*] relationships and appear destructive in every way" (Snijders 1954: 55). Lam 5:1–2 expresses well the intensity of the Judahites' emotional repugnance toward witnessing strangers seize their property:

> Remember, O Yahweh, what has happened to us;
> behold, and see our disgrace!
> Our inheritance has been turned over to strangers,
> our homes to foreigners.

Ironically Obad 7 envisages a reversal in Edom's own fortunes when its land will become "a place for strangers" (*māzôr* from *zwr*).

took captive his power. The verb *šbh* typically occurs in a military context. Victorious armies "take into their possession" what belongs to the conquered side: men, women, and children (Gen 14:14; Num 31:9; 1 Sam 30:1–5; 1 Kgs 8:46–48; 2 Kgs 5:2; Ezek 6:9; 2 Chr 25:12; 28:8); livestock (1 Chr 5:21; 2 Chr 14:14 [15]); goods and property (2 Chr 21:17); and idols (Jer 43:12). Thus *šbh* usually but not always has a personal object.

The precise sense of the verb's object in Obad 11 is unclear, as the noun *ḥayil* is polysemous (see Eising 1980). It can mean "power, strength" (e.g., Ps 33:17), which Eising argues is its basic sense. Frequently it denotes "army" (e.g., 1 Sam 10:26; 2 Kgs 25:5) but also can have the more general sense of "company" or "band" of people without military overtones (e.g., 1 Kgs 10:2; Ezek 37:10). Finally, it often means "wealth," referring to money and household goods (e.g., Num 31:9; Zech 14:14; Ps 49:7, 11 [6, 10]). Compare the noun *hāmôn*, which has a semantic range overlapping with that of *ḥayil*, including "crowd," "army," and "riches."

For Obad 11, it is difficult to decide among the options. Since *šbh* normally takes a personal object, *ḥayil* might denote Jacob's "army" or more generally his "company." However, the object of *šbh* is property in 2 Chr 21:17 and therefore the noun might refer to Jacob's "wealth." A parallel to this usage appears in Gen 34:29 where *ḥayil* functions as an object of *šbh* and seems to denote property. Commentators and the ancient versions are split: for the former — Vulgate, Halévy (1907), Wolff (1977), Deissler (1984); for the latter — Targum, Caspari (1842), Keil (1888), Wellhausen (1963), Allen (1976). Watts (1969) translates with "fortifications," which is also a possibility for *ḥêl* but an unlikely object of *šbh*.

The choice between people and property seems a false alternative. The same noun occurs twice more in Obadiah where it denotes "wealth" (v 13) and a "company" of people (v 20). Historically the Babylonians took into captivity both people and treasures (2 Kgs 24–25), and furthermore, the charge that the Edomites acted like the Babylonians applies on both counts. They seized Jacob's "wealth" (v 13) and his "survivors" (v 14). The translation "his power" therefore leaves the specific referent ambiguous in keeping with the ambiguity of *ḥayil* itself (so also Keller 1965; Rudolph 1971). Note that the LXX translates with the noun *dynamis*, which in the Minor Prophets likewise denotes "power," "army," or "wealth" (Muraoka 1993: 58).

foreigners. The word *nokrîm*, an adjective used as a substantive, parallels *zārîm* (strangers) in the previous clause. The two roots, *zwr* and *nkr* in that order, form a common pair (Isa 28:21; 61:5; Ps 69:9 [8]; Job 19:15; Prov 2:16; 5:10, 20; 7:5; 20:16; 27:2, 13; Lam 5:2).

On *nokrî*, see Martin-Achard (1976) and Lang and Ringgren (1986). Occasionally it denotes a person outside of one's family circle (Gen 31:15; Ps 69:9 [8]; Job 19:15) or simply "another person" (Prov 5:10; 27:2). In the vast majority of cases, however, it denotes a "foreigner, non-native," a person from another people and country (e.g., Deut 17:15; 29:21 [22]; 2 Sam 15:19; 1 Kgs 8:41). Clearly both *zārîm* and *nokrîm* refer to the same group of people, probably the Babylonians. By using both terms Obadiah stresses the contrast in status between Edom as Jacob's "brother" and the unfamiliar outsiders who attacked Jacob.

entered his gates. Read the plural "gates" with the *Qere* rather than the singular with the *Kethib*. Pronominal suffixes occur only with the plural of this noun. For the construction *bw' + šaʿar* without the usual preposition *b*, see Gen 23:10, 18; Ps 100:4 (cf. Judg 18:18; Lam 1:10). Since the antecedent of "his" is "Jacob" (v 10) and since it is the next clause that mentions "Jerusalem," this clause refers to the gates of the cities of Judah as a whole. Thus v 11 progresses from Judah to its capital city.

Access to a city's gate was normally reserved for the local citizens, those with legitimate position in the community (cf. Gen 23:10, 18; Jer 17:20, 25). Usually foreigners would not enter a gate unless they were known and welcome (cf. Ezek 26:10; Lam 4:12).

and cast lots for Jerusalem. The practice of casting lots to reach a decision was common throughout the ancient Near East including Israel (Lindblom 1962; Hallo 1983). Although different kinds of small objects could serve as lots, such as stones, bones, arrow shafts, sticks, and cube-shaped chunks of clay, the Hebrew noun *gôrāl* probably refers to a small stone or pebble. Presumably the objects were marked in some way; for example, Hallo (1983) discusses a ninth-century-B.C. *pūru* (lot), a cube made of clay and inscribed on four sides in Akkadian (cf. Esther).

Different procedures are conceivable. In light of the verbs used with respect to lots (*hipʿil* of *npl*, "to drop"; *hipʿil* of *šlk*, "to throw"; *hipʿil* of *ṭwl*, "to throw"; *yrh*, "to throw"; *ydd*, "to throw"), we can infer that they were thrown from a container of some sort. Priorities and decisions could have been made by the order in which they came out of the jug or bowl or by the location in which they fell (Hallo 1983). According to Prov 16:33, they were dropped from the lap.

The Bible attributes to lot casting a variety of purposes (cf. Sasson 1990: 108–10):

1. selecting — individuals, such as warriors (Judg 20:9), persons to live in Jerusalem (Neh 11:1); or sacrificial animals (Lev 16:8–10);
2. assigning — duties (Neh 10:35 [34]), territory (Josh 15–19), or cities (Josh 21);
3. distributing — goods (Ps 22:19 [18]) or persons for slavery (Joel 4:3 [3:3]; Nah 3:10);
4. settling disputes (Prov 18:18);
5. identifying the guilty party (Jonah 1:7).

The construction that occurs in Obad 11, *ydd gôrāl* + *ʿal* + object, means "to cast lots for a desired object" (*gôrāl* is used as a collective). The same construction appears twice more in the Bible. According to Nah 3:10, conquerors distributed among themselves the nobility of Thebes apparently for the purpose of slavery:

"And for her nobles they cast lots,
and all her great ones were bound in chains."

The other text with this construction — except with the preposition *ʾel* instead of *ʿal* — appears in Joel 4:3 [3:3]. The verse makes it clear that the lot-casting distributed the people for slavery:

"And for my people they cast lots,
and they gave a boy for a harlot,
and a girl they sold for wine and drank it."

Obadiah uses the image of casting lots to depict the enemies' attitude toward Jerusalem. Unlike the rest of Judah's property and people, whom the foreign soldiers indiscriminately took into captivity, Jerusalem was considered the prize for which they vied with each other. They all wanted a piece of the action so to speak and therefore had to cast lots to determine who would get what. In light of the parallels in Nahum and Joel, one thinks primarily of Jerusalem's citizens and their capture for the purpose of slavery (cf. Job 6:27). In fact, Joel probably alludes to this passage in Obadiah just as he echoes Obadiah elsewhere. Yet Obadiah makes "Jerusalem" the desired object rather than its "people." This contributes shock value to the sentence. It serves to portray the hubris of the foreigners. For Obadiah, Jerusalem was Mount Zion, Yahweh's holy mountain (v 16) and the seat of Yahweh's eschatological rule (v 21), but for the attackers it was a commodity to be contested over.

also you were like one of them. The main clause of v 11 begins with the particle *gam*, what van der Merwe (1990) describes as a "focus inducing connector." It marks *'attâ* for focus and has additive force, "also you!" The word order pronoun + prepositional phrase gives additional prominence to the pronoun (cf. Muraoka 1991). The predicate *kĕ'aḥad mēhem*, "like one of them" (with partitive *min*), compares Edom with the "strangers/foreigners" who attacked Judah and Jerusalem. It designates resemblance in kind between the two groups while recognizing the distinctive identity of each (cf. Gen 3:22; Judg 17:11; 1 Sam 17:36; 2 Sam 9:11; 2 Chr 18:12). In other words, the preposition *k* is a marker of similarity but not a *kaph veritatis* (*pace* Joüon 1991 § 133g).

It is significant that the line is a verbless clause, which is neutral with respect to time (Joüon 1991 § 153). This temporal neutrality allows the clause both to refer to Edom's past actions (v 10) and to lead into the following prohibitions (vv 12–14), as if to say "you were like one of them and you still are." Allen (1976: 155) summarizes well the meaning and tone of the line:

> With all the force of *et tu, Brute*, the exclamation rings out with profound horror. So far from presenting a united front with Judah against the outsider, they made common cause with the enemy. Here is the acme of unbrotherliness, that he who should have regarded himself as "one of us" behaved *like one of them*.

v 12. *wĕ'al tēre' bĕyôm 'āḥîkā.*
But do not gaze upon the day of your brother.

Verses 12–14 consist of a series of eight bicola or line pairs that speak of Edom's anti-Judahite hostilities. Since vv 10–11 indicate that the prophet speaks from a historical time subsequent to these hostilities, one naturally understands vv 12–14 to refer to past events. Therefore some authorities translate the syntagm *'al* + second person jussive, which initiates each of the eight bicola, with past subjunctives in English. As an example, for the first colon of v 12 we read:

But you should not have gloated over the day of your brother (RSV);

But you should not have gloated over your brother (NRSV);

You should not have gloated over the misfortune of your brothers in Judah (TEV);

But thou shouldest not have looked on the day of thy brother (KJV);

How could you gaze with glee on your brother that day (NJPSV).

Also the Targumist interpreted the clauses as accusations of Edom's past activity:

wdhzyt' bywm' d'hwk

How you gazed on the day of your brother.

To be sure, the clauses of vv 12–14 refer to Edomite actions that took place in past time from Obadiah's position on the historical timeline. However, the grammatical form of the clauses should be taken seriously and given its full weight. To express a past subjunctive — "you should not have" — Hebrew uses *lmh* + perfect, "Why did you gloat?" (I owe this observation to C. R. Krahmalkov.) But the construction used in vv 12–14, *'al* + second person jussive, is the standard way to make a vetitive or negative command, as Hebrew does not negate the imperative form. Therefore it should be translated "Do not do so-and-so" (so LXX, Vulgate, Peshitta, NEB, NASB). The construction expresses the speaker's will and desire that the addressee not engage in the activity, often with the sense of urgency (Joüon 1991 § 114). By definition vetitives concern present or future time. One does not say "Do not gloat yesterday." They can be rendered "Do not begin an action" (e.g., Gen 22:12; 37:22) or "Stop doing an action" (e.g., Amos 5:5; Pss 35:19; 75:5–6 [4–5]). The context dictates.

So how should we understand the initial verbal clauses of vv 12–14? The most natural explanation is that the prophet imaginatively locates himself back to the time of Judah's fall, or he projects the past catastrophe into the present. From that vantage point he exhorts Edom not to engage in anti-Judahite behavior (cf. Rudolph 1971). By using negative commands Obadiah accomplishes several rhetorical effects. First, they serve to expand and clarify Obadiah's charges against Edom for its past treatment of Judah. Second, they express Obadiah's horror and anger at such treatment. Finally, by using negative commands, which by definition concern the present and future, Obadiah exhorts Edom to stop engaging in these kinds of hostilities. The motivation clause comes in v 15, "For the day of Yahweh is near . . ."

gaze upon the day of your brother. There are two possible ways to construe the clause: understand *běyôm 'āḥîkā* (upon the day of your brother) as a temporal phrase — "when your brother experienced ruin" — or as the object of the verb "gaze." It is best to take it as the object of the verb for two reasons. First, the following colon clearly functions as a temporal phrase ("on the day of his adversity"), and it is unlikely that the bicolon would have two temporal phrases. The other bicola in this section (vv 12–14) locate the temporal phrase only in the B-colon. Second, the same construction (*'al tēre'* + *b* + object) recurs in v 13 where the preposition *b* introduces the verbal object.

The idiom *r'h* + *b* + object appears frequently in the Hebrew Bible (115 times; Wehrle 1987: 122–23). It means "to look with interest" or "to gaze intently" upon the object. Depending on the choice of subject and object, it can connote looking with grief (Gen 21:16), with compassion (Gen 29:32; 1 Sam 1:11), with curiosity (1 Sam 6:19), with contempt (Isa 66:24; Pss 22:18 [17]; 69:9 [8]), or looking in triumph (Mic 7:10; Pss 54:9 [7]; 59:11 [10]; 112:8; 118:7). The last connotation is also attested in the Mesha stele, where Mesha, the king of Moab, says of the god Chemosh that "he allowed me to look (in triumph) upon all those who hate me" (line 4). In the context of Obadiah the construction clearly has a negative connotation, "to stare scornfully and triumphantly" and "to gloat" at the ruins and victims.

The verbal object, "the day of your brother," is a metonym for "your brother's ruin." The noun "day" is used to point back to v 11, which depicts the "day" of Judah's downfall. Compare "the day of Jerusalem" in Ps 137:7. The mention of "your brother" recalls the phrase "your brother Jacob" in v 10.

běyôm nokrô.
on the day of his adversity.
The phrase functions temporally to indicate when Edom should refrain from gloating. The antecedent of the pronoun "his" is "your brother" in the A-colon.

The noun **nōker* is a *hapax legomenon*. Based on its etymology from the root *nkr*, it must mean something like "foreignness, a foreign experience." At Mari the noun, *nukru*, denotes "something strange," such as a foreign object that can be brought from other lands (CAD 11, 2:328). Perhaps *nokrô* refers to the deportation into exile when Judah became a foreigner. Compare Vulgate: *in die peregrinationis eius*, "in the day of his peregrination"; Aquila: *apoxenōseōs autou*, "his banishment." The mention of Judah's captivity in v 11 lends support to this understanding. Since *nokrîm* occurs in v 11, "foreigners entered his gates," the phrase might designate "the day when foreigners attacked him." Compare LXX: *en hēmera allotriōn*, "in the day of foreigners." The related form *nēker*, also a *hapax*, occurs in Job 31:3 where it parallels *'êd*, "ordeal, calamity." In light of this parallel, **nōker* most likely designates any kind of experience that seems foreign or strange to someone, hence "adversity, misfortune." Compare Targum: *bywm tbryh*, "on the day of his breakdown." The use of *nokrô* points back to v 11: Jacob's "adversity" was brought about by the attack of "foreigners."

wĕʾal tiśmaḥ libnê yĕhûdâ.
And do not rejoice over the Judahites.

After exhorting Edom to stop gazing upon Judah's ruin, the prophet further urges Edom to stop gloating over the fall of the Judahites (lit., "the sons of Judah"). *Schadenfreude* is Edom's reaction to seeing their demise, a reaction condemned also by Ezekiel (35:15; cf. Lam 4:21). The sequence of "seeing" and "rejoicing" (*rʾh . . . śmḥ*) occurs frequently (Vanoni 1993: 812–13).

The syntagm *śmḥ* + *l* + object always designates the malicious glee that an enemy has over someone else's misfortune (Isa 14:8; Mic 7:8; Pss 30:2 [1]; 35:19, 24; 38:17 [16]; cf. Ezek 35:15; Amos 6:13; Prov 17:5). The only exception occurs in Job 21:12, which refers to the joy that the wicked have in their music. Israel's wisdom literature condemned such *Schadenfreude* (Prov 17:5; 24:17; cf. Job 31:29).

bĕyôm ʾobdām.
on the day of their ruin.

The phrase (lit., "on the day of their perishing") functions as a temporal clause. The pronominal suffix "their" refers back to "the Judahites."

wĕʾal tagdēl pîkā.
And do not open your mouth wide.

This colon further intensifies the series of prohibitions-accusations: "Do not gaze . . . rejoice . . . open your mouth wide." Although the construction *gdl* (*hipʿil*) + *peh* (lit., "make the mouth big") does not occur elsewhere, the meaning is clear. In this context it denotes uninhibited and scornful laughter over the fallen Judahites. The similar expression *rḥb* (*hipʿil*) + *peh* (to open the mouth wide) clarifies the sense. In Ps 35:19–21 the psalmist complains that his enemies mock and slander him in his distress:

> Let them not rejoice over me
> those who are my enemies without cause. . . .
> *They open their mouth wide against me;*
> they say, "Aha! Aha!
> our eyes have seen (it)!"

Note the use in the same context of "rejoice over" and "open the mouth wide" as in Obad 12. Isa 57:4 has the same expression where it parallels *htʿng*, "to make merry over," and *hʾryk lāšôn*, "to stick out the tongue" (cf. 1 Sam 2:1). Another phrase also relates, *pṣh* + *peh* + *ʿal*, "to open the mouth against":

They open their mouth against you [Zion],
all those who are your enemies;
they whistle and gnash their teeth;
they say, "We have consumed (them)!
Indeed, this is the day we have longed for;
we have attained (it); we have seen (it)!"
(Lam 2:16; cf. 3:46)

The above discussion reveals that *hgdyl* + *peh* refers to big talk, public mockery, and joyful satisfaction over the demise of others. According to Ezek 35:13, Edom in effect is guilty of boasting against Yahweh with its big talk against the ruins of Israel. The passage uses the same words as Obadiah although with a slightly different construction:

wattagdîlû ʿālay bĕpîkem
wĕhaʿtartem ʿālay dibrêkem
ʾănî šāmāʿtî

"You have boasted against me with your mouth;
and you have multiplied [?] your words against me;
I have heard (it)."

bĕyôm ṣārâ.
on the day of distress.
This temporal designation is a stereotyped expression, which with variations occurs twenty-three times:

bĕyôm ṣārâ	(Jer 16:19; Obad 12, 14; Nah 1:7; Pss 20:2 [1]; 50:15; Prov 24:10; 25:19)
bĕyôm ṣārâ + suffix	(Gen 35:3; Pss 77:3 [2]; 86:7)
lĕyôm ṣārâ	(Hab 3:16)
yôm ṣārâ	(2 Kgs 19:3 = Isa 37:3; Zeph 1:15)
bĕʿēt ṣārâ	(Isa 33:2; Jer 14:8; 15:11; Ps 37:39)
bĕʿēt ṣārâ + suffix	(Judg 10:14; Neh 9:27)
ʿēt ṣārâ	(Jer 30:7; Dan 12:1)

The common noun *ṣārâ*, from the verb *ṣrr* I (to be narrow, hard pressed), has the general sense of "distress, trouble, dire straits" (see Fabry 1989). The following collocations reveal its broad meaning: *rāʿâ*, "evil, misfortune" (Deut 31:17, 21; 1 Sam 10:19; Jer 15:11); *mĕṣûqâ*, "hardship" (Ps 25:17; Zeph 1:15); *ṣûqâ*, "oppression" (Prov 1:27); *ʿŏnî*, "affliction" (Ps 31:8 [7]). The noun *ṣārâ* can refer to internal anguish (Gen 42:21; Pss 25:17; 31:8 [7]) as well as external troubles

(Jonah 2:3 [2]; Job 5:19). It is likened to the pain of a woman giving birth (Jer 4:31; 49:24). Events that cause "distress" include: oppression by foreign armies (Judg 10:14); foreign rulers (Neh 9:37); deceit and slander (Ps 120:1); war, plague, and famine (Job 5:19; 2 Chr 20:9). In the context of Obad 12–14 the "distress" was caused by the attack of foreign armies (v 11). Instead of acting like a brother when Jacob was in dire straits (cf. Prov 17:17), Edom gloated and boasted.

v 13. *'al tābô' bĕša'ar 'ammî.*
Do not enter through the gate of my people.

The omission of the initial *waw* (and) both here and the next bicolon is difficult to explain. Perhaps it signals the start of the next sequence of actions or it may simply reflect stylistic variation.

Edom is prohibited from (and condemned for) acting like the "foreigners" who entered Jacob's gates (v 11). The construction *bw' + b + ša'ar* does not mean "to conquer or possess the gate" (*pace* Luciani 1983). It simply means "to go through the gate," in this case, into the city (cf. 2 Kgs 9:31; Jer 7:2; 17:20, 25, 27; 22:2, 4; Ezek 26:10; Ps 118:19–20; Lam 4:12; Neh 2:15). Here the clause begins a sequence that refers to Edom's actively aggressive behavior: they enter, gloat, and then loot.

Normally only the local citizens and members of the community were permitted to enter through the gate (Jer 17:20, 25, 27; Lam 4:12). Perhaps a "brother" could be so permitted, but Jacob was not merely Edom's "brother" (see below).

Unlike the plural "gates" in v 11 (see Note), here the singular is used. The phrase, "the gate of my people," might refer to Jerusalem (cf. Mic 1:9, 12) or to Judah's cities in general (cf. Ruth 3:11). In the latter case *ša'ar* would be a collective (cf. Gen 22:17; 24:60).

For the noun *'ammî* (my people), the suffix "my" refers to Yahweh, the speaker. Note the use of the first person "I" in v 8 and "my holy mountain" in v 16. The term *'am* as distinct from *gôy* (nation; cf. vv 1–2) frequently designates Israel as the covenant people of Yahweh. It evokes the well-known covenant formula, "I will be your God and you will be my people" (see Smend 1963).

bĕyôm 'êdām.
on the day of their ordeal.

The pronominal suffix "their" refers back to the collective noun "my people." As many commentators note, *'êdām* (their ordeal) produces a sound play that evokes *'ĕdôm* (Edom). The temporal phrase *bĕyôm 'êdām* with variations, like the parallel phrase "on the day of distress" in v 12 and v 14 (see Note), occurs fairly often in the Hebrew Bible (eleven times):

bĕyôm 'êd + suffix   (2 Sam 22:19 = Ps 18:19 [18]; Jer 18:17; Obad 13 three times; Prov 27:10)

lĕyôm ʾêd	(Job 21:30)
yôm ʾêd + suffix	(Deut 32:35; Jer 46:21)
bĕʿēt ʾêdām	(Ezek 35:5)

Traditionally the noun *ʾêd* is considered a derivative of *ʾwd*, "to be curved, bent," which denotes something under which one bends, "distress, calamity" (BDB). However, McCarter (1973) persuasively argues for seeing it as a loan word from Sumerian *id* (pronounced *id* in Akkadian), "the cosmic River." In Mesopotamian texts the divine River *id* functions as judge in certain legal cases, whereby innocence is declared if the accused, having been plunged into the river, withstands the rushing waters. McCarter contends that in some biblical texts *ʾêd* alludes to this Mesopotamian mythology of trial by river ordeal (Deut 32:35; 2 Sam 22:19 = Ps 18:19 [18]; Job 21:17, 30; 31:23).

From its original association with the river ordeal the sense extends to the more general meaning of "ordeal, distress." The latter is the case for Obad 13, where it parallels **nōker*, "adversity" (cf. Job 31:3), *ʾbd*, "ruin," and *ṣārâ*, "distress" in v 12. Elsewhere it is collocated with nouns that have a similarly general sense: *rāʿâ*, "misfortune, evil" (Jer 48:16); *ʾāwen*, "trouble" (Job 18:12); *paḥad*, "terror" (Prov 1:26); *pîd*, "ruin" (Prov 24:22).

The noun occurs twenty-four times in the Hebrew Bible, twelve times in Job and Proverbs, and five times in Jeremiah. In the old poem of Deut 32 it designates the ordeal that will confront disobedient Israel (v 35). Elsewhere it usually refers to personal distress or in Jeremiah's oracles against the nations to the ordeals prepared for other nations: Egypt (46:21); Moab (48:16); Kedar and Hazor (49:32); and significantly Esau/Edom (49:8). The closest parallel to our text comes from Ezek 35:5 where the prophet condemns Edom for anti-Israel attitudes and actions:

> "Because you possessed an ancient enmity and gave over the Israelites to the power of the sword *at the time of their ordeal*, at the time of their final punishment . . ."

By using *ʾêdām* (their ordeal) Ezekiel like Obadiah evokes the name "Edom."

ʾal tēreʾ gam ʾattâ bĕrāʿātô.
Do not gaze, also you, upon its misfortune.

This colon employs the same construction as v 12a, *rʾh* + *b* + object. It means "to gaze scornfully and triumphantly upon the object" (see Note for v 12). Yet the two verses use this construction in notably different ways. Whereas in v 12 Edom gloats from a distance, in v 13 Edom enters Judah's cities and gloats over the ruins at close quarters. Moreover, in v 12 the "gaze" leads to words of mockery but here to the action of seizing Judah's wealth (so Wolff 1977).

Two words of v 11, "also you," recur, again with additive force (see Note). The prophet continues to condemn (and warn) Edom for acting like the "strangers/ foreigners" mentioned in v 11.

The suffix of the noun "misfortune" *(běrā'ātô)* has switched to the singular from the plural in the previous colon. The antecedent might be "your brother" in v 12, but more likely it is "my people" in the first colon of v 13. The collective noun *'am* (people) can be construed both as a plural (*"their* ordeal") and as a singular (*"its* misfortune"), sometimes both ways in the same context (cf. Exod 1:20; Judg 9:36–37; 1 Kgs 18:39; Isa 9:8 [9]; Joüon 1991 § 150e).

The object *rā'â* (misfortune), a sound play with verbal root *r'h* (gaze), is a common noun derived from *r''*, "to be bad" (see Dohmen and Rick 1993). It denotes a negative experience in the widest sense, hence "evil, misfortune, trouble." Here it refers to Judah's misery and ruin brought about by the invading armies.

běyôm 'êdô.
on the day of its ordeal.
On this temporal phrase, see Note above. The antecedent of the singular suffix might be "your brother" in 12 (so Wehrle 1987: 54–55), but one naturally assumes that the suffixes of the thrice repeated *'êd* in v 13 have the same antecedent, namely "my people" (see previous Note).

wě'al tišlaḥnâ běḥêlô.
And do not reach out (your hands) for its wealth.
The form of the verb is difficult. The Masoretes vocalized it as a second (or third) feminine plural *(tišlaḥnâ)* in contrast to the second masculine singular form of the other verbs in vv 12–14. The Wadi Murabbaʿat manuscript reveals the antiquity of the MT form. However, the ancient versions translate with second singular verbs. Different proposals have been suggested (for surveys of views, see Caspari 1842; Wehrle 1987: 54).

1. Emend to *tišlaḥ yād*, "do not stretch out the hand."
2. Read the particle of entreaty, *tišlaḥ-nā'*.
3. Consider the feminine plural form to be incorrectly used for the masculine singular (GKC § 47k).
4. Assume an implied vocative *yādôt*, "do not stretch out (O hands)."

None of these suggestions is very satisfying. More likely the verb should be considered a second masculine singular energic form; read *tišlaḥanna / tišlaḥannâ* (Robertson 1972: 117–18). The use of the form in Arabic and Ugaritic makes the suggestion probable. Corroborating evidence exists in Judg 5:26 where the same verb *šlḥ* apparently uses the *-anna* termination (Freedman 1960: 102):

yādāh layyātēd tišlaḥnâ (read *tišlaḥanna*)

"Her hand to the tent peg she stretched out."

The sequence *šlḥ yād* + *b* + object (to stretch out the hand for the object, to seize the object) occurs frequently. In Obad 13 there is an ellipsis of the word "hands," as happens elsewhere (2 Sam 6:6; 22:17 = Ps 18:17 [16]). Objects that are seized include: someone else's goods (Exod 22:7 [8], 10 [11]); plunder (Esth 9:10, 15–16); lands (Dan 11:42); working tools (Job 28:9; Prov 31:19); persons (Gen 37:22; 1 Sam 24:7 [6], 11 [10]; 26:9, 11, 23; Ps 55:21 [20]; Esth 2:21; 3:6; 6:2; 8:7; 9:2). When the object is personal, the expression entails harming or killing the individual. In Obad 13 the object is *ḥayil*, which, as noted in v 11, can refer to people or wealth. In v 11 the noun refers to both, but here the referent seems to be wealth, namely, the goods located in the cities of Judah or in Jerusalem. The next verse then states how the Edomites captured people.

Verse 13 clarifies why Obadiah likened Edom to the invading "strangers/foreigners" in v 11; both groups seized the people's *ḥayil* (cf. Ezek 36:4–5; Lam 1:10; 1 Esdras 4:50). It also recalls v 5 where the prophet compares Edom with common thieves and plunderers.

on the day of its ordeal. For this phrase, see Notes above.

v 14. *wĕ'al ta'ămōd 'al happereq.*
   And do not stand at the fork in the road.

The preposition *'al* together with the verb *'md* has a locative sense, "to stand at/on" a certain place (Wehrle 1987: 124). One expects the prepositional object to refer to a place of some sort. Unfortunately the precise sense of the noun *pereq* is unclear. In Nah 3:1, the only other occurrence, it is paired with "prey" (*ṭereṗ*) and denotes "plunder, that which is snatched away." On the basis of the Hebrew verb *prq*, "to tear away, split," one can infer several possible meanings:

1. "Breach" in a city wall. LXX (*diekbolas*, "ways through") and Vulgate (*exitibus*, "ways out") perhaps had this sense in mind. Against it is the fact that the usual word for "breach" is *pereṣ*. Since *pereq* designates the place where the "escapees" are caught, one assumes a place outside the city walls.
2. "Narrow pass" into the Edomite mountains (Rudolph 1971). Yet one expects the places where the Edomites "stand" to be located in Judah, since the previous verse speaks of the Edomites entering "the gate of my people."
3. "Escape route," referring to a breach in the wall or a fork in the road (Wolff 1977). Compare Symmachus, *phygadeias*, "ways of escape."
4. "Fork in the road," the place where the road splits (BDB, KB; cf. Ezek 21:26 [21]).

Although the precise sense of *pereq* remains unknown — "escape route" or "fork in the road" appears most likely — the basic idea is clear enough. The Edomites station themselves at the places where they can most easily capture the fugitives of Judah/Jerusalem before they get away and scatter in different directions (cf. Jer 48:19). In the case of a fork in the road, it would be easier to watch there than to cover two roads.

lěhakrît 'et pělîṭāyw.
in order to eliminate its escapees.
The infinitive construct preceded by the preposition *l* indicates a purpose clause. The verb, a *hip'il* of *krt*, has been understood in two ways:

1. "To intercept" Judah's fugitives (Allen 1976; Clark and Mundhenk 1982: 24). While this interpretation makes sense, nowhere else does the *hip'il* of *krt* denote "to intercept, catch, set up road blocks."
2. "To kill" Judah's fugitives (Keil 1888; Rudolph 1971; Wolff 1977). Although one assumes murder for some contexts with the verb, the verb per se does not denote this. A reference to murder here would render the next bicolon anticlimactic, since it speaks of Edom handing captives over to others. Furthermore, one wonders why the prophet would prohibit Edom from standing at the fork in the road with intent to kill rather than simply and directly prohibit the killing of the fugitives.

The *hip'il* of *krt* occurs frequently in the Hebrew Bible (seventy-eight times). While the verbal root can have the literal meaning, "to cut, cut off," in the *hip'il* it has an extended sense, "to eliminate, eradicate" (Hasel 1984). Yet it does not specify the manner in which the elimination process takes place. Here the manner is clarified by the next bicolon; Edom intends "to eliminate" Judah's fugitives by delivering them up to others.

In this line the reader expects a verb such as "to capture." Yet Obadiah uses a stronger term to indicate Edom's vengeful desire. He interprets Edom's goal as that of seeking the complete eradication of Judah by eliminating the escapees and survivors.

The singular suffix of the plural noun *pělîṭāyw* (its escapees) again refers to the collective "my people" in v 13. The noun derives from the root *plṭ*, "to escape"; the same root recurs in v 17. It denotes "escapees, fugitives" (frequently used in exilic texts) and refers to the Judahites who fled from the attacking "strangers/foreigners" mentioned in v 11.

wě'al tasgēr śěrîdāyw.
And do not hand over its survivors.
Usually the construction *sgr* (*hip'il*) + object (to hand over the object) includes a prepositional phrase to designate the receiving third party. Obadiah omits any prepositional phrase (cf. Deut 32:30; Amos 6:8) in order to focus all attention on the deed of Edom. According to Obadiah, the Edomites are culpable on two counts: for betraying and surrendering fugitives and survivors, and for doing this to people who are not only their brothers but even more signifi-

cantly Yahweh's own covenant people. However, Obadiah's indictment apparently did not apply to all Edomites, since their Transjordanian homeland allowed Judahite refugees to remain there (Jer 40:11–12).

The Hebrew Bible documents Edom's involvement in this kind of activity at different times. The eighth-century prophet Amos in 1:6 and 9 connected Edom with the practice of slave trade (cf. Joel 4:4–8 [3:4–8]). Both Philistia and Tyre are indicted for "handing over" (*sgr-hipʿil*) an entire population to Edom. Edom's role in this relationship remains unclear. Perhaps they acted as middlemen in selling slaves to buyers from southern Arabia and elsewhere, or they employed the captives as slave labor in their copper and smelting operations. (On Amos's oracles against Philistia and Tyre, see Andersen and Freedman [1989] and Paul [1991] who defend the authenticity of the Tyre oracle. Haran [1968] argues for reading "Aram" instead of "Edom" in Amos 1:6, 9, but this is unlikely.) Later in the eighth century at the time of Ahaz, Edomites invaded Judah and took captives according to 2 Chr 28:17 (see Bartlett 1989: 127–28, 140). In the early exilic period Ezekiel in 35:5 charged Edom with "giving over" (*ngr*) Israelites to the power of the sword (cf. 25:12). We also have extrabiblical evidence of an Edomite slave seller, named Qôsnahar, attested in Samaria in 352 or 351 B.C. (Cross 1988). On slavery in the ancient Near East, see Mendelsohn (1949), Dandamayev (1984, 1992).

Obadiah does not specify all the details of Edom's deed, but one can plausibly reconstruct its nature and purpose. The Edomites seize Judahite escapees and survivors and then hand them over to a third party. Within the book of Obadiah the reader naturally takes the receiving third party to be the invading "strangers/foreigners" who took captives (v 11), and one assumes the extratextual referent to be the Babylonians. The Babylonians could then include the captured refugees in their deportations, or the officials and soldiers who were to remain in Judah could employ them as their own slaves (cf. 2 Kgs 5:2). Note that the reference in v 11 to "casting lots for Jerusalem" implies the allocation and sale of Jerusalemites into slavery (cf. Joel 4:3 [3:3]). Therefore in this respect as well, Obadiah could say that Edom was "like one of them" (v 11).

During the period of Obadiah's prophecy that is proposed (see Introduction), between the fall of Jerusalem (587/6 B.C.) and the campaign of Nabonidus (553 B.C.), the Edomites probably had a formal or informal alliance with Babylon (v 7). By capturing and surrendering Judahites — perhaps a stipulation of the agreement — the Edomites could further ingratiate themselves with Babylon and thereby preserve their Transjordanian state and their port of Elath. They could also secure permission to enlarge their landholdings in the Negeb, which would enable them to gain an interest in the trade route passing through the Negeb to Philistia and the port of Gaza (see Lindsay 1976: 30–31).

hand over. The *hipʿil* of *sgr* has two distinct meanings in the Hebrew Bible (cf. Haran 1968: 205):

1. In priestly texts it means "to isolate, close off" an impure person or object from contact with others (Lev 13:4, 5, 11, 21, 26, 31, 33, 50, 54; 14:38, 46).
2. Elsewhere it denotes "to hand over, deliver up" persons to stronger opponents — to their enemies (Deut 32:30; Amos 6:8; Pss 31:9 [8]; 78:62; cf. Lam 2:7); to those desiring to do them evil (Amos 1:6, 9; Job 16:11); fugitives to their pursuers (Josh 20:5; 1 Sam 23:11–12, 20); slaves to their masters (Deut 23:16 [15]; 1 Sam 30:15). Needless to say, this is the sense that applies to Obad 14.

The verb, with the second meaning, is attested also in Phoenician and Aramaic texts (see Paul 1991: 60). The fifth-century Phoenician inscription of Ešmunʿazōr pronounces a curse upon those who would disturb his sarcophagus (*KAI* 14, lines 9–10; cf. lines 21–22 and Isa 19:4). Note that, just as in Obad 14, the action of "handing over" serves the ultimate purpose of extermination: "May the holy gods *hand them over* to a mighty ruler who will exercise dominion over them, in order to exterminate [*qṣy*] them." The Aramaic Genesis Apocryphon (22:16–17) uses *sgr* for the Hebrew verb *mgn* of Gen 14:20 (Fitzmyer 1971: 72–73): "Blessed be the Most High God who *has handed over* your enemies into your hand." The alloform *skr* (cf. Isa 19:4) occurs in the eighth-century Aramaic treaty texts of Sefire (*KAI* 224, lines 2–3). In the hypothetical case of fugitives fleeing from their suzerain and seeking political asylum with the king of Arpad, the latter should *hand them over* into the suzerain's hand.

its survivors. The singular pronominal suffix "its" refers to "my people" in v 13. The noun *śĕrîdāyw* is related to the root *śrd*, "to remain, escape" (Josh 10:20); the noun recurs in v 18. It appears frequently in military contexts, especially those depicting Israel's early wars, to denote the "survivors" of a defeat (Num 21:35; Deut 3:3; Josh 8:22; 10:28, 30, 33, 37, 39, 40; 11:8; Jer 31:2).

The nouns *śĕrîdāyw* (its survivors) and *pĕlîṭāyw* (its escapees) of the previous colon form a morphological, semantic, and phonological word pair. Both words refer to the people who continue to live after a military defeat or other disaster, but they are not totally synonymous in meaning. The term "escapees" implies the act of fleeing from a catastrophe, while the other term emphasizes simply the fact of being survivors (see Kedar-Kopfstein 1993). When both occur together, they count as two items of a merismus that expresses the totality of those who remain (Josh 8:22; Jer 42:17; 44:14; Lam 2:22; cf. Alonso Schökel 1988: 83–84).

Obadiah accuses the Edomites of betraying and surrendering all of the remaining Judahites; those who flee they capture at the forks in the roads and the others they seize as well. To be sure, this is hyperbolic. Yet by using both terms, which evoke the important prophetic theme of the remnant (see Hasel 1974), the prophet portrays Edom as a threat to any future existence of Yahweh's people through its remnant (cf. Lam 2:22).

běyôm ṣārâ.
on the day of distress.
See Note under v 12.

v 15. *kî qārôb yôm yahweh*
    'al kol haggôyīm
    ka'ăšer 'āśîtā yē'āśeh lāk
    gĕmūlĕkā yāšûb bĕrō'šekā.

A   For the day of Yahweh is near
B   against all the nations.
C   Just as you have done, it will be done to you;
D   your deeds will return upon your own head.

Many scholars follow Wellhausen in transposing v 15a–b and v 15c–d (Duhm 1911; Bewer 1911; Rudolph 1971; Allen 1976; Wolff 1977; Deissler 1984; Wehrle 1987):

C Just as you have done, it will be done to you;
D your deeds will return upon your own head.
A For the day of Yahweh is near
B against all the nations.

Two considerations might lend support to this move:

1. It allows the book to be neatly divided into two separate halves without any overlap. The first half pronounces a historical judgment against Edom to be executed by the nations, while the second half pronounces an eschatological judgment against all the nations.

2. Verse 15c–d uses second person singular verbs and pronouns in keeping with vv 1–14 and provides a fitting conclusion to the first half of the book, whereas v 15a–b introduces the theme of universal judgment that continues in v 16.

With respect to the text critical question, one might hypothesize that the copyist's eye accidentally skipped over the initial *kî* (for) in v 15a to the initial *kî* in v 16 (homoioarkton). The omitted bicolon (v 15a–b) was then added in the margin and later misplaced before v 15c–d so as to locate the two "just as" clauses side by side (vv 15c, 16a).

However, two key arguments support the MT:

1. The Wadi Murabba'at manuscript and the ancient versions agree with the MT. A text critical transposition of lines simply on the basis of thematic content is unwarranted.

2. The clause "For the day of Yahweh is near" and similar clauses occur else-where, and in every case the conjunction *kî* (for) connects the clause with the preceding material. In several instances the *kî*-clause grounds the pre-ceding commands:

Wail, *for* the day of Yahweh is near . . . (Isa 13:6)

Hush before the Lord Yahweh!
For the day of Yahweh is near . . . (Zeph 1:7)

Blow the trumpet in Zion;
sound the alarm on my holy mountain!
Let all the inhabitants of the land tremble!
For the day of Yahweh is coming; *for* it is near. (Joel 2:1)

Wail, "Alas for the day!"
For a day is near,
a day of Yahweh is near . . . (Ezek 30:2–3)

In the other instances the *kî*-clause functions more generally to explain why the preceding assertions were made:

Alas for the day! *For* the day of Yahweh is near . . . (Joel 1:15)

Multitudes, multitudes, in the valley of decision!
For the day of Yahweh is near in the valley of decision (Joel 4:14 [3:14])

The earth quakes before them;
the heavens tremble . . .
For the day of Yahweh is great and very terrible . . . (Joel 2:10–11)

The haughty looks of people will be brought low,
and the pride of humans will be humbled;
and Yahweh alone will be exalted in that day.
For Yahweh of hosts has a day
against all that is proud and lofty . . . (Isa 2:11–12)

Do not insist upon comforting me
over the destruction of the daughter of my people.
For the Lord Yahweh of hosts has a day
of tumult and trampling and confusion . . . (Isa 22:4b–5)

The text states that Yahweh will destroy Edom followed by a *kî*-clause:
For Yahweh has a day of vengeance . . . (Isa 34:5–8)

It is best to follow the MT arrangement (so Laetsch 1956; Thompson 1956; Keller 1965; Weiser 1967; Watts 1969; Stuart 1987; R. B. Robinson 1988; Padilla

1989). In fact, the suggestion to transpose the two bicola of v 15 arises from a serious misunderstanding of the function of the verse in its literary context.

As noted under v 12, the prophet imagines himself standing in the midst of the crisis when Judah and Jerusalem fell to Babylon. From this perspective he employs eight vetitives in vv 12–14 in order to perform a twofold role: to specify Edom's past crimes and thus indict Edom and to warn Edom to stop this kind of anti-Judahite behavior. Verse 15 then functions as the motivation clause that grounds the vetitives in their warning role (cf. the above citations). Edom should stop its hostile activity *because* (*kî*) the day of Yahweh is near when he will judge all the nations, including Edom. Edom (and presumably the other nations) will be judged on the basis of the standard of the *lex talionis*, "Just as you have done, it will be done to you."

The conjunction *kî* commonly introduces motivation clauses after imperatives and vetitives throughout the Hebrew Bible, including legal materials (cf. Sonsino 1980), the Psalms (cf. Aejmelaeus 1986b), wisdom literature (cf. Richter 1966) and the Latter Prophets (cf. Tångberg 1987). In the Latter Prophets, note the following texts with the syntactic sequence of *vetitives* + *kî*-clause: Isa 28:22; 54:4; 56:3–4; Jer 11:14; 13:15; 29:8–9; 41:8; Amos 5:5; Zech 8:17; Mal 2:15–16. Some authorities understand *kî* in Obad 15 as an asseverative, "indeed" (Rudolph 1971; Allen 1976; Wolff 1977; Dick 1984: 7; NJPSV), but that cannot be sustained. Here it introduces a causal clause (on *kî*, see Aejmelaeus 1986a).

While v 15 brings the address to Edom to an end, the theme of the day of universal judgment in v 15a–b is picked up and further expanded in v 16. Thus v 15 acts as a Janus-like hinge between two contiguous blocks of material in that it concludes the preceding section and anticipates the following section (cf. Parunak 1983).

Admittedly, vv 12–15 present a perspective different from that of vv 1–10. Whereas vv 1–10 assert that God will definitely destroy Edom and will employ the nations as his agent, vv 12–15 warn Edom of the impending universal judgment and thereby offer Edom at least an implicit chance to avoid annihilation. Verse 18 sets forth still a third perspective, a certain and total eradication of Edom carried out by Israel. We should not seek to harmonize or artificially separate these varying perspectives. Rather, we should let them stand side by side as they merge one into the other.

the day of Yahweh. By the time of Obadiah *yôm yahweh* had become a stereotypical expression. It occurs in fifteen other texts, all prophets from Judah (Isa 13:6, 9; Ezek 13:5; Joel 1:15; 2:1, 11; 3:4 [2:31]; 4:14 [3:14]; Amos 5:18a, b, 20; Zeph 1:7, 14a, b; Mal 3:23 [4:5]). Because of its stereotypical nature, the third-person reference to "Yahweh" need not imply a non-divine speech. On the contrary, v 15 remains part of the divine speech begun in v 8 (cf. Ezek 30:3; Joel 3:4 [2:31]).

In this phrase the sense of the noun "day" is not to be restricted to a 24-hour period. Note Isa 34:8, which pairs Yahweh's "day of vengeance" with "the *year* of recompense" (cf. Isa 61:2), and Ezek 30:3, which qualifies Yahweh's "day" as "a *time* of (doom for) nations." The stress lies more on its character and the event that gives it significance than on its chronological duration. The phrase refers to the time when Yahweh manifests himself and intervenes in the world in a definitive and public way. Yahweh "has a time to act, a time to intervene in 'history'; what will take place then, he alone determines" (von Soden, Bergman, Saebø 1990: 30).

Amos provides the oldest witness to this phrase that we have, and perhaps he coined it. Yet the way Amos used it implies that some Israelites already had an idea about a future day. The origin of the idea is much debated. Proposals include: a cultic enthronement festival; holy war traditions; descriptions of theophany; covenant curses (for convenient summaries, see Prinsloo 1985: 35–36; Paul 1991: 182–84; Cathcart 1992). Although the idea's origin remains obscure, we can infer from Amos 5:18–20 that people expected a future time of divine intervention that would result in their welfare and salvation. Amos labels their idea "the day of Yahweh," but he reverses their expectation by portraying it as a day of darkness and disaster from which they cannot escape (cf. Hoffmann 1981). Possibly Isa 13 (vv 6, 9; cf. 2:12; 22:5) has the next occurrence of the phrase, although many scholars date the chapter to exilic times or later (cf. Erlandsson 1970). Its appearance in Zephaniah precedes that of Obadiah, and there the phrase along with other similar expressions plays a dominant role in the book. After Obadiah we find it in Joel, which also systematically develops the theme, and in Malachi.

Scholars debate to what extent "the day of Yahweh" should be considered an "eschatological" term (see Everson 1974; Hoffmann 1981). Part of the issue revolves around which texts are examined and the definition of "eschatological." Nevertheless, a few observations hold true for all sixteen texts with *yôm yahweh*.

1. All the texts locate the day in the future. However, none of them speak of the day as far off in the distant future, and many of them emphasize its nearness. Even the passage in Joel 4:14 [3:14], which is usually taken to be eschatological, states that "the day of Yahweh is near."

2. While the texts use a variety of motifs and images (see Černý 1948: Appendix I), they all depict the day as bringing destruction and disaster. The day manifests Yahweh's wrath, from which people cannot escape by their own efforts and devices.

3. All the texts portray the targeted recipients of the coming destruction as the deserving wicked, although the specific identification of these people varies (see Note below).

Closely related to our phrase are other expressions with "day" and "Yahweh" in the same phrase, all of which — with one exception (Lam 2:22) — appear in prophets from Judah (cf. von Soden, Bergman, Saebø 1990: 29). Apart from Lam 2:22, which refers to a past "day," the above observations apply to these texts as well:

Yahweh of hosts has a day (Isa 2:12);

the Lord Yahweh of hosts has a day of tumult and trampling and confusion (Isa 22:5);

Yahweh has a day of vengeance (Isa 34:8);

a day of Yahweh is near (Ezek 30:3);

a day of Yahweh is coming (Zech 14:1);

tnat day is (a day) of the Lord Yahweh of hosts (Jer 46:10);

the day of Yahweh's sacrifice (Zeph 1:8);

the day of Yahweh's anger (Ezek 7:19; Zeph 1:18);

the day of Yahweh's wrath (Zeph 2:2, 3; Lam 2:22).

is near. In the verbless clause *qārôb yôm yahweh* the subject is classified as "near" (cf. Andersen 1970). The adjective denotes "near, at hand" with respect to time (Klein 1968: 521–22). Terms paired with *qārôb* reveal this sense of temporal imminence:

"is coming" (Isa 13:6, 9; Joel 2:1; cf. Ezek 7:7; Zech 14:1; Mal 3:19 [4:1]);

"is hastening fast" (Zeph 1:14; cf. Deut 32:35; Jer 48:16).

The day is "near" as opposed to "far off" (cf. Ezek 12:27) or "delayed" (cf. Isa 13:22; Ezek 12:22, 25).

Prophetic texts frequently speak of the nearness of the day of Yahweh (Isa 13:6; Ezek 30:3; Joel 1:15; 2:1; 4:14 [3:14]; Zeph 1:7, 14). With this expression Obadiah stresses the urgency of the situation, the need for Edom to change its ways now before it is too late. A parallel to the way Obadiah uses the "day-of-Yahweh" theme occurs in Zeph 2:1–3, where the prophet calls Judah to repent before the terrible day of Yahweh's wrath. The note of urgency, which Zephaniah applied to Judah, Obadiah now applies to Jacob's "brother."

against all the nations. The preposition *'al* is to be construed with *yôm yahweh*, "the day of Yahweh," rather than with *qārôb*, "near" (*pace* Wehrle 1987: 124–25). Compare Isa 2:12, "For Yahweh of hosts has a day *against* [*'al*] all that is proud and lofty," and Zeph 1:16, "a day of trumpet blast and battle cry *against* [*'al*] the fortified cities."

The sixteen texts with "the day of Yahweh" and the twelve texts with related expressions depict the recipients of the coming destruction as the deserving wicked. The recipients fall into three general categories:

1. Israel (Amos 5:18–20) or Judah and Jerusalem (Isa 22:5; Ezek 7:19; 13:5; Joel 1:15; 2:1, 11; Zeph 1:7, 8; Lam 2:22). Zeph 2:1–3 and Mal 3:19–24 [4:1–6] distinguish between the righteous and the wicked within Judah.
2. All the nations *including* Judah (Isa 2:12; Zeph 1:14, 18), Babylon (Isa 13:6, 9), Egypt (Ezek 30:3; Jer 46:10), or Edom (Isa 34:8).
3. All the nations *excluding* Judah and Jerusalem or at least the faithful therein (Joel 3:4 [2:31]; 4:14 [3:14]; Zech 14:1).

Obadiah joins the last group in excluding Judah and Jerusalem. The reason is that they have already drunk the cup of wrath while the other nations have yet to drink it (v 16).

Just as you have done, it will be done to you. The particle *ka'ăšer* (just as, in the same way as) commonly introduces a comparative clause (Joüon 1991 § 174a). The clause sets up a correspondence between the protasis and the apodosis, in this case between the crime and the punishment. By repeating the same verbal root and the second person singular the line displays internal parallelism that further strengthens this correspondence:

> *ka'ăšer 'āśîtā*   Just as you have done
> *yē'āśeh lāk*   it will be done to you

Edom remains the addressee, as is the case throughout vv 1–15. The second verb, a passive *nip'al*, takes an impersonal subject in order to focus all attention on Edom as both actor and receiver. Therefore the line does not mention who will execute the punishment — although the use of the passive generally implies divine action — or how it will happen. Rather, it highlights that Edom will experience the same fate that it inflicted upon Judah.

Elsewhere we find the same type of sentence, with "just as" and the sin stated in the protasis and the punishment stated in the apodosis:

"Just as I have done, so God has requited me." (Judg 1:7)

"Just as your sword made women childless,
so your mother will be childless among women." (1 Sam 15:33)

"Just as you have forsaken me and served foreign gods in your land,
so you will serve strangers in a land not your own." (Jer 5:19)

"Just as she has done, do to her." (Jer 50:15; cf. v 29)

"I will do to you, just as you have done." (Ezek 16:59)

"Just as I called and they did not hear, so they will call and I will not hear."
(Zech 7:13)

This type of sentence has roots in the *lex talionis* of Israel's legal collections. Note that both Lev 24 and Deut 19 use the "just as . . . so" formulation:

"If there is bodily harm, you will give life for life,
eye for eye, tooth for tooth, hand for hand,
foot for foot, burn for burn, wound for wound,
stripe for stripe." (Exod 21:23–25)

"If a person inflicts a wound upon his neighbor,
just as he has done, so it will be done to him,
fracture for fracture, eye for eye, tooth for tooth;
just as he inflicted a wound upon someone,
so it will be inflicted upon him." (Lev 24:19–20)

". . . if the witness is a false witness and has accused his brother falsely,
then *you will do to him just as he intended to do to his brother.* . . .
Your eye will not pity; it will be life for life, eye for eye,
tooth for tooth, hand for hand, foot for foot." (Deut 19:18–21)

There is some question regarding the intended administration of the *lex talionis*. Was the talionic statement in its entirety to be applied literally, an actual eye for an eye? Judg 1:6–7 records one such application; Judah captured Adoni-bezek and cut off his thumbs and big toes just as Adoni-bezek had done to other kings. More likely the *lex talionis*, apart from "life for life," was intended as a formulaic expression that articulated the principle of equal retribution. Exod 21:26–27 treats the preceding talionic statement as a principle; if a master destroys a slave's eye or tooth, the slave goes free but the master does not lose an eye or a tooth. The same interpretation holds true for the case of the false witness in Deut 19:15–21, since, apart from the special case of Deut 25:11–12, Israel had no system of mutilation as punishment. (On *lex talionis*, see Frymer-Kensky 1980; Otto 1991; Huffmon 1992.)

The principle of equal retribution appears also in older Near Eastern law. It becomes a standard operating principle in the Old Babylonian period, perhaps under West Semitic influence (so Frymer-Kensky 1980). Before then cuneiform law assigned monetary fines for false accusation and physical injury.

In addition to Obadiah, Ezekiel in his oracles dealing with Edom applies the talionic standard to Edom for its hostility toward Judah. Note the repetition of key words in both the sin and the punishment lines:

"Because Edom has acted in *vengeance* against the house of Judah
and has become exceedingly guilty in taking *vengeance* upon them,
therefore thus spoke the Lord Yahweh . . .
I will lay my *vengeance* upon Edom by the hand of my people Israel . . ."
(25:12–14)

". . . since you [Edom] have not hated *blood*,
blood will pursue you." (35:6)

"I will do *according* to your [Edom's] wrath and your envy,
which you have done because of your hatred against them . . ." (35:11)

"*According* to your rejoicing over the inheritance of the house of Israel
because it was *desolate, so* I will do to you;
you will become *desolate*, Mount Seir and all Edom, all of it. . . ." (35:15)

your deeds will return upon your own head. The singular noun *gĕmūlĕkā*
(your deeds) is probably a collective; the plural form appears only once in the
noun's nineteen occurrences. It denotes deliberate acts done toward another person or group, acts that ought to be repaid. Although the lexicons often attribute
to it the sense of recompense, that idea derives more from the context than from
the word itself (Seybold 1978). The clause semantically parallels the preceding
clause:

your deeds	you have done
will return upon your own head	it will be done to you

The parallelism shows that the clause expresses in another way the correspondence between the crime and its punishment (see Miller 1982: 130–31; cf. Ps
28:4; Lam 3:64).

Lest Edom think that it can benefit from its actions against Judah, Obadiah
stresses that in the day of Yahweh Edom's deed will rebound upon Edom itself
(cf. Joel 4 [3], especially vv 4, 7). Thus v 15 portrays Edom's fate from two complementary perspectives; from a theocentric point of view it will be requital from
Yahweh, and from an anthropocentric point of view it will be self-inflicted.

The two other texts with the construction N + *šwb* + *bĕrō'š* (N returns upon
the head) clarify the clause's meaning. 1 Kgs 2:28–35 presents the narrative of
Joab's death. In fulfillment of David's wishes (2:5–6) Solomon commands Be-
naiah to kill Joab who had earlier murdered Abner and Amasa:

"Yahweh will return [*hip'il* of *šwb*] his bloodshed upon ['*al*] his own
head . . ." (v 32)

"Their blood will return [*qal* of *šwb*] upon [*b*] the head of Joab
and upon the head of his seed forever . . ." (v 33)

That the crime returns upon the culprit's head prevents the possibility of "getting away with it," as David says in v 6, "do not let his gray head go down to Sheol in peace." The parallelism of v 32 and v 33 reveals that the idea does not preclude the notion of divine retribution, as if it were a quasi-immanental process of one's fate flowing out of one's deed (*pace* Koch 1955). Rather, v 32 speaks of Yahweh bringing the crime back upon the guilty party and thus of divine retribution. The two ideas are complementary and not mutually exclusive.

The other text with the same construction appears in Ps 7, an individual lament. The psalmist is concerned with the establishment of divine righteousness for himself and for others lest the wicked successfully "get away with" oppressing the righteous:

Let the evil of the wicked come to an end,
and may you establish the righteous. (v 10 [9])

The psalmist has confidence in God's justice:

God is a righteous judge,
and a God who executes indignation every day. (v 12 [11])

Because of this confidence the psalmist knows that the wicked will not succeed:

His mischief will return upon his own head,
and on his own pate his violence will descend. (v 17 [16])

Again we see that the notion of God as judge and the notion of sin recoiling upon the perpetrator are not mutually exclusive.

Furthermore, note Prov 12:14, which has a slightly different construction:

From the fruit of one's lips one will be satisfied with good,
and the deeds [*gĕmûl*] of a person's hands will return [*yšwb*-Kethib] to
him [*lô*].

An extrabiblical parallel comes from the time of Pharaoh Ramesses IV, the twelfth century, in a text dealing with a conspiracy against Ramesses III (Yaron 1958):

"Let all that they have done fall upon their (own) heads;
while I am protected and defended forever, while I am
among the just kings, who are before Amon-Re, king of
gods, and before Osiris, ruler of eternity."

Finally, another set of texts makes the theocentric perspective explicit: Yahweh "returns" (*hipᶜil* of *šwb*) the deeds "upon the head" of the culprit (Judg 9:57;

1 Sam 25:39; 1 Kgs 2:44; Joel 4:4, 7 [3:4, 7]; cf. 1 Kgs 8:32; Ezek 7:3–4; 9:10; 11:21; 16:43; 22:31; Hos 4:9; 12:15 [14]; Neh 3:36 [4:4]).

COMMENT

The book's third divine speech has two sections: vv 8–15 addressed to Edom and vv 16–18 addressed to Judah. Verse 8 ties the speech to the previous one of vv 5–7. Its use of an interrogative creates a link with the interrogatives of v 5; it repeats the name "Esau" first mentioned in v 6; and its motif that Yahweh will destroy Edom's "understanding" further develops the thought expressed in the last clause of v 7.

The speech begins by continuing to evoke Jeremiah's Edom oracle in Jer 49:7–22: v 8 echoes Jer 49:7, and v 9 uses a motif that resembles the one in Jer 49:22. Thus the first two verses recall the opening and closing of Jeremiah's oracle. Beginning in v 10, however, Obadiah moves away from reliance on Jeremiah's oracle and goes his own way. While vv 8–9 continue to announce Edom's impending doom, v 10 introduces a new theme. For the first time in the book we read of "Jacob"; in fact, vv 10–14 refer to him fifteen times. Furthermore, although it was already anticipated in v 5, v 10 emphasizes that Edom's coming destruction is based on and merited by its acts of violence against its brother Jacob. Accordingly, v 10 serves as a transition between vv 8–9 and vv 11–15. Within the stated context, vv 12–14 play a twofold role. On the one hand, they look back to vv 10–11 and specify Edom's crimes committed during the fall of Judah and Jerusalem. Thus they function as accusations and indictments. On the other hand, they are in the form of a series of prohibitions and are linked with v 15, which serves as a motivation clause. Therefore they also function as warnings and exhortations for Edom to stop its anti-Judahite hostilities before the day of Yahweh's universal judgment.

Verses 9–14 focus the reader's attention on the human plane, on Edom's future destiny and its past conduct toward its brother Jacob. Yet both aspects of Edom are to be seen within the context of Yahweh's judgment, since v 8 uses a first person verb — "I will destroy" — and v 15 speaks of "the day of Yahweh." That is to say, v 8 and v 15 form a thematic bracket or inclusio around the rest of the material and thereby provide a theological perspective concerning Edom, that its destiny lies in the hands of Yahweh, and that its actions have made it guilty before Yahweh, the God of Israel who has authority over all the nations. Also the phrase "in that day" anticipates the phrase "the day of Yahweh" and thereby joins v 8 with v 15. While these two verses refer to the *future* "day" of judgment, between the brackets the phrase "on the day" occurs ten times — twice in v 11 and eight times in vv 12–14 — where it refers to the *past* "day" of Judah's ruin and

Edom's enmity. Thus the book situates the prophet between the two "days." The repetition of the word "day" helps to cement the whole section together.

Verses 8–9 bring to a conclusion the overall thematic concern of vv 1–9, that none of Edom's resources that provide safety will be able to forestall its coming doom. Essential to any country's national security are its wisdom — political acumen and/or technological skill — and its military. Upon the destruction of the former and the failure of the latter, the citizens will be left defenseless. The consequence is expressed by the concluding result clause of v 9: "with the result that everyone will be cut off from Mount Esau by slaughter."

Verse 10 functions to interlock the preceding with the following material:

Because of the violence you did to your brother Jacob
shame will cover you,
and you will be cut off forever.

The first line connects the verse with v 11 by supplying the pronoun "his" of v 11 with its antecedent, "your brother Jacob," and by introducing the theme of Edom's "violence" that will receive further specification in vv 11–14. The last line's use of the verb "will be cut off" ties the verse with v 9. By fronting the verse with a prepositional phrase, which breaks the verbal sequence of vv 8–9, Obadiah highlights his indictment of Edom. With the next two lines then he not only continues to announce Edom's destruction but also reveals its punitive character as a deserved sentence.

Moreover, for the first time he makes explicit the connection between Edom/Esau and Judah. The guilt of Edom does not simply resemble that of other nations; Edom was guilty not only of violence but of violence against its own "brother Jacob" (cf. v 12). The fraternal bond between the two peoples is based on that of the patriarchs Jacob and Esau. Andersen and Freedman (1989: 265) note that uterine siblings and especially twins were felt to be closer than half-siblings with the same father (e.g., Gen 43:30). Obadiah alludes to the Jacob-Esau stories: just as Esau pursued his uterine brother, so Edom acted with violence toward its brother. That Edom betrayed the fraternal relationship and broke the norms of what was considered appropriate behavior toward a brother gave rise to Obadiah's expression of surprise and shock.

Verse 11 begins to clarify the nature of Edom's perfidy by leveling two charges against Edom. Edom "stood opposite" while enemies plundered, and it acted "like one of them." The two charges receive expansion and clarification in vv 12–14. Edom stood by and gloated over Judah's downfall (v 12), and it acted like the enemies by entering the gates, looting, and seizing fugitives (vv 13–14). Although seemingly inconsistent, the two charges need not be considered mutually exclusive. One can conceive of the Edomites first passively allowing others to lead in the attack and then actively taking advantage of the situation. Furthermore, one sees an intensification in emotion, as if to say: "Instead of actively assisting your brother Jacob in defense against our enemies, you just stood there and watched. Why, you even became actively hostile just like these strangers and foreigners!"

While vv 10–11 and v 12 place the action on the level of siblings, v 13 heightens the import of Edom's conduct even further. There Jacob is identified as Yahweh's own "people." Edom displayed hostility not only against a brother, which was considered bad enough, but against the very covenant people of Yahweh and therefore implicitly against Yahweh himself (cf. Jer 13:11; Ezek 35:12–13).

Verses 12–14 form an impressive literary unit that exhibits several interlocking patterns.

12 But do not gaze upon the day of your brother,
          on the day of his adversity.
    And do not rejoice over the Judahites,
          on the day of their ruin.
    And do not open your mouth wide,
          on the day of distress.
13 Do not enter through the gate of my people,
          on the day of their ordeal.
    Do not gaze, also you, upon its misfortune,
          on the day of its ordeal.
    And do not reach out (your hands) for its wealth,
          on the day of its ordeal.
14 And do not stand at the fork in the road
          in order to eliminate its escapees.
    And do not hand over its survivors,
          on the day of distress.

The unit consists of a series of eight bicola that make extensive use of anaphora. All of the A-cola begin with a vetitive, that is, the negative particle *'al* followed by a second person jussive verb form ("do not" do so-and-so). Almost all of the B-cola begin with the prepositional phrase *běyôm* (on the day of) followed by a genitive. However, each pattern is broken once: for the former pattern, the sixth bicolon begins with an energic form of the verb unlike the other verb forms; and for the latter pattern, the seventh bicolon substitutes an infinitive plus direct object for the usual prepositional phrase. To make up for this last omission the prepositional phrase appears again in the unit's initial A-colon; thus "on the day of" occurs eight times to correspond with the eight bicola. Moreover, the fourth and fifth bicola break a pattern by omitting the initial *waw* (and). In terms of syntax, the first two A-cola have a vetitive + prepositional phrase, followed by an A-colon with a vetitive + direct object. The pattern then repeats itself: four

A-cola with the former sequence, followed by an A-colon with the latter sequence.

The unit refers to Judah twelve times: seven times with the third masculine singular pronoun "his/its"; twice with the third masculine plural pronoun "their"; once with the possessive genitive, "the Judahites," literally, "the sons of Judah"; and with the additional phrases "your brother" and "my people." Perhaps by this repetition Obadiah evokes the twelve tribes:

v 12	your brother	his adversity
	the Judahites	their ruin
	∅	∅
v 13	my people	their ordeal
	its misfortune	its ordeal
	its wealth	its ordeal
v 14	∅	its escapees
	its survivors	∅

Each verse accuses Edom of essentially one offense: gloating from a distance (v 12), looting (v 13), and capturing fugitives (v 14). The bicola of each verse are closely knit together: the three bicola of v 12 by the verbal sequence of gazing, rejoicing, and opening the mouth wide; the three bicola of v 13 by the verbal sequence of entering Judah's cities, gloating over the ruins at close quarters, and seizing the wealth, and by the threefold repetition of "ordeal"; and the two bicola of v 14 by the verbal sequence of standing at the crossroads and handing over captives, and by the word pair of "escapees" and "survivors." In addition, the unit can be seen as having two parts, v 12 and vv 13–14. Verses 13–14 are linked by third person pronouns that take the noun "my people" in the initial line of v 13 as their antecedent. Also each part concludes with the same syntax (vetitive + direct object) and the phrase "on the day of distress." While the first part depicts passive *Schadenfreude*, the second part describes active and aggressive hostilities. Yet the second part has a significant link with the first in that it repeats the vetitive used at the beginning, "Do not gaze, also you, upon . . ." Note too the repetition of the phrase "also you," which occurs at the conclusion of v 11.

Verse 15 brings the section of vv 8–15 and, in fact, the entire address to Edom of vv 1–15 to a strong thematic conclusion. Accordingly, it corresponds well with the concluding line of the whole book, "and the kingship will belong to Yahweh." Verse 15 reads:

For the day of Yahweh is near
 against all the nations.
Just as you have done, it will be done to you;
 your deeds will return upon your own head.

The verse functions as the motivation clause for the preceding vetitives in their warning role. Edom should immediately discontinue its anti-Judahite enmity, "for" the time will soon arrive when Yahweh will judge all the nations. With this verse Obadiah makes two thematic shifts. First, the nations no longer have the role of serving as Yahweh's weapon against Edom as they did in v 1 and v 7, but now they themselves are placed under Yahweh's impending judgment. Second, whereas previous verses distinguished between Edom and the other nations (vv 1, 2, 7), here Obadiah includes Edom among the nations that must face the judgment. What promoted this inclusion is the statement made in v 11, "also you were like one of them." Because Edom acted like the enemy nations, it will experience "the day of Yahweh" like the nations.

The standard of judgment for Edom and presumably for the other nations will be the *lex talionis*. It serves as incentive in a way similar to the Golden Rule, as if to ask, "Are you willing to have the same things done to you that you have done to Judah?"

Obadiah succinctly and elegantly summarizes the kind of poetic justice one frequently sees displayed in the prophetic judgment speeches: destroyers will be destroyed (Isa 33:1); devourers, devoured (Jer 30:16); reproachers, reproached (Ezek 36:6); slave sellers, sold into slavery (Joel 4:4–8 [3:4–8]); plunderers, plundered (Hab 2:8); and so on (see Miller 1982). In a variety of ways the prophets stress that the sin and its punishment correspond, which with roots in the *lex talionis* reveals the juridical character of Yahweh's judgment. The correspondence pattern serves to depict the just nature of the punishment, not some strange fate coming "out of the blue" but a rational and appropriate punishment, one that fits the particular crime committed by the guilty party. According to Ezek 18:25–30 and 33:17–20, Yahweh's judgment is "fair" because he judges people "according to their ways." Furthermore, the prophets announce the retribution ahead of time so that it will not come unexpectedly.

The last sentence of v 15 also expresses the judgment standard of correspondence between sin and punishment but from a different although complementary perspective. Whereas the first two sentences view the punishment from a theocentric perspective as requital from Yahweh, the final statement regards it from an anthropocentric point of view as self-inflicted.

B. PROMISE OF RESTORATION AND VICTORY ADDRESSED TO JUDAH (vv 16–18)

◆

16 For just as you have drunk on my holy mountain,
  (so) all the nations will drink continually;
      they will drink and slurp,
        and they will be as if they had never been.
17 But on Mount Zion will be escape,
  and (on Mount Zion) will be a holy place.
    The house of Jacob will possess their own possessions.
18   The house of Jacob will become fire,
  and the house of Joseph, flame,
  and the house of Esau, stubble;
      and they will set them on fire and consume them,
      and there will be no survivor for the house of Esau.
        For Yahweh has spoken.

NOTES

v 16. *kî kaʾăšer šĕtîtem ʿal har qodšî*
    yištû kol haggôyīm tāmîd
    For just as you have drunk on my holy mountain,
    (so) all the nations will drink continually.

For. The conjunction *kî* connects v 16 with v 15. It introduces a causal clause that explains *why* the previous verse stated that the day of Yahweh will be "against all the nations": "For . . . all the nations will drink" the cup of Yahweh's wrath (cf. Aejmelaeus 1986a: 202–3).

just as. The particle *kaʾăšer* (just as) signals a comparative clause that creates a correspondence between the protasis and the apodosis. What is being compared?

There are basically two possibilities. (On the history of the interpretation of v 16, see Elowsky 1992.)

1. Some older authorities (e.g., LXX; Targum; Rashi; Jerome; Calvin) and some modern ones (e.g., Hitzig 1838; Caspari 1842; Keil 1888; Isopescul 1914; Laetsch 1956; Watts 1969; Stuart 1987) take the subject of the A-line to be the Edomites. Two key arguments are given in support: first, the second person in the rest of Obadiah always refers to Edom (except for v 1 where the nations are addressed); and second, the comparative clause of v 16 supposedly sets up a correspondence between crime and punishment as it does in v 15. Hence the A-line means: "Just as you Edomites figuratively or literally drank wine in celebration of Zion's fall" (cf. 1 Sam 30:16; Joel 4:3 [3:3]). Because of this sacrilege, the punishment expressed in the B-line will happen. In keeping with this understanding of the A-line, various interpretations have been suggested for the B-line. Among them two are noteworthy: (1) all the nations will drink wine in celebration over Edom's fall (LXX [?]; Jerome; Isopescul) or will consume Edom (Calvin); (2) all the nations including Edom will drink the cup of wrath (Targum; Rashi; Hitzig; Caspari; Keil, Laetsch; Stuart).

    There are several difficulties with this general approach. First, it obscures the significance of the distinction between the two subjects, "just as you . . . (so) all the nations." In vv 2–15 Obadiah does not so markedly distinguish between Edom and the nations. Second, the view that sees the nations celebrating the fall of Edom reads too much into the B-line, whereas the other view attributes two different meanings to the verb "drink" — drink wine in celebration and drink the cup of wrath. Third, the parallel with other cup-of-wrath texts confirms the next interpretation.

2. Some older authorities (e.g., Ibn Ezra; Rupert of Deutz) and most modern commentators rightly understand the subject of the A-line to be the Judahites/Jerusalemites. In both lines the verb has the same significance, that of drinking the cup of wrath. Thus the comparative clause correlates not the crime and the punishment of the same group (unlike v 15) but the experience of two different groups: "Just as you Judahites/Jerusalemites have drunk the cup of wrath, so all the nations will drink it."

    Unlike the second person singular address to Edom in vv 2–15, the verb in v 16a is a second person plural. The shift indicates a change in addressee. To be sure, one expects a vocative to signal the shift but that is not absolutely necessary. For example, Nah 1:12 illustrates such a shift without an explicit vocative, where "they" refers to the Ninevites and "you" to Judah:

    Thus spoke Yahweh:
    Even though with allies and so numerous,

they are cut off and pass away.
Though I afflicted you,
I will afflict you no more.

One can easily infer from Obad 16 the identity of the plural addressee.
Since the addressees have drunk the cup of wrath "on my holy mountain,"
they must have lived there. Accordingly, they are "the Judahites" (v 12) and
"my people" (v 13).

on my holy mountain. The speaker is still Yahweh. Weingreen (1954) demonstrates that the construct + genitive, *har qodšî*, should be translated "my holy
mountain" rather than "the mountain of my holiness." The genitive functions
adjectivally and its pronominal suffix applies to the first noun ("mountain").

The phrase designates Mount Zion, as v 17 makes clear: "But on Mount Zion
will be escape" (cf. Isa 27:13; 56:7; 66:20; Ezek 20:40; Joel 2:1; 4:17 [3:17]; Zeph
3:11; Zech 8:3; Pss 2:6; 48:2; 99:9; Dan 9:16, 20). Here Yahweh's "holy mountain" or "Mount Zion" refers primarily to Jerusalem and the Temple Mount. Yet
one should not think of it in contrast to the rest of Judah but as the center of
Judah. Obadiah links Judah and Jerusalem (v 11).

According to the standard biblical view, Zion was "holy" or "set apart" to Yahweh not because of any natural or inherent holiness but by virtue of its election
within history. Yahweh had chosen it as the place where he located his presence
in the temple. (On Zion, see Levenson 1985; 1992; Otto 1989; Mare 1992.)

continually. Many Hebrew manuscripts read *sābîb*, "all the nations *around*,"
but the ancient versions and the Murabba'at manuscript support the Leningrad
Codex (*tāmîd*). The LXX took the word as *temed*, "wine" (Ziegler 1971: 248).

Although the experiences of Jerusalem and the nations correspond in that both
groups drink the cup of Yahweh's wrath, Obadiah with the adverb *tāmîd* stresses
a difference. In contrast to Jerusalem's temporary drinking of the cup, the nations
will drink it "continually." The note of nonstop drinking leads into the next bicolon, which further expands and clarifies the idea. In Prov 15:15 the image of a
continual feast functions positively:

All the days of the afflicted are evil,
but a happy heart has a perpetual feast [*mišteh tāmîd*].

Obadiah subverts the image's positive associations, as if to say, "The nations will
have a feast too! They will drink God's cup perpetually until they become as if
they had never been."

The adverb intensifies the judgment of the nations beyond that received by
Zion. If Yahweh's "holy mountain" had to experience divine wrath, the non-elect
gôyīm must experience it to a greater degree. This idea of intensification remains

in keeping with some of the other cup-of-wrath texts: All the wicked of the earth will drain the cup down to the dregs (Ps 75:9 [8]); the Babylonians will drink it until they sleep a perpetual sleep (Jer 51:39, 57).

wĕšātû wĕlāʿû
they will drink and slurp.

The sense of the second verb is uncertain. It derives from the root *lʿ* or *lwʿ*. In Job 6:3 and Prov 20:25 the root has the sense, "to stammer, talk rashly." Compare Arabic *laǵā*, *laǵiya*, "to chatter, talk carelessly." In this case the verb would refer to the effect of drinking; the nations continually drink the cup of wrath and incoherently babble like drunkards. However, the lexicons propose a homonym for *lʿ* or *lwʿ* in Obad 16, "to swallow, swallow down" (BDB), "to slurp" (KB, HALAT). Perhaps related is the noun *lōaʿ*, "throat" (Prov 23:2). Compare Syriac *lʿ* / *lwʿ* and Arabic *walaǵa*, "to lick, slurp," and Hebrew *lqq*, "to lap up." If we read with many commentaries a *pilpel*, *yĕlaʿlĕʿû* (to lick up eagerly) for MT *yĕʿalʿû* in Job 39:30, then the homonym occurs outside of Obad 16, but admittedly the emendation is uncertain.

Both meanings for the verb are plausible so that Obad 16 may be a case of word play with a double meaning. Nevertheless, the reader expects in this context a verb that refers to the drinking process rather than its resultant effect. Therefore a sense such as "slurp" or "gulp down" seems preferable:

> all the nations will drink *continually*,
>> they will drink and *slurp*.

By repeating the verb *šth* and heightening it with *lʿ* / *lwʿ*, Obadiah conveys the sense of vigorous and continuous drinking that he introduced with the preceding adverb *tāmîd*. Compare the reference to draining the cup to its dregs in other cup-of-wrath texts (Ps 75:9 [8]; Isa 51:17–23; Ezek 23:31–34).

wĕhāyû kĕlôʾ hāyû.
and they will be as if they had never been.

The preposition *k* has the force of a conjunction, "as if" (Joüon 1991 § 174d). Obadiah leaves behind the image of drinking and focuses on the subject of the metaphor. The nations will experience divine wrath to such an extent that they will cease to exist as nations. The authorities and rulers of the present age will become insignificant and of no more consequence. They will no longer be remembered (cf. Job 10:19; Sir 44:9).

The motif occurs fairly often in the prophetic oracles against the nations, which the following citations illustrate. Isa 17:14 speaks of the lot of Israel's enemies: "In the evening, behold, terror! Before the morning, they are no more." In Jer 46:28 (and 30:11) the divine speech says to Jacob: "I will make an end of all the nations to which I have driven you." Ezekiel's Tyre oracles announce that

Tyre and its king will be "no more" (26:21; 27:36; 28:19). According to Nahum, God "will make an end" of Nineveh (1:8). And Zephaniah speaks of Yahweh making a sudden end of all the earth's inhabitants (1:18; cf. 1:2–3; 3:8). Related motifs include: God will "wipe out all remembrance" of the foreign rulers (Isa 26:13–14); the enemy nations will be "like a dream" (Isa 29:7–8); they will not be found and will be "as nothing" (Isa 41:11–12).

EXCURSUS: DRINKING THE CUP OF YAHWEH'S WRATH

One of the more powerful metaphors used by the biblical writers is that of "drinking the cup of wrath." One finds it developed in different ways and to a lesser or greater extent depending on the context. Since Obad 16 utilizes this metaphor, it might be helpful to examine the other texts where it occurs in order to provide an interpretive framework for the Obadiah passage and to gain a better understanding of the biblical portrayal of Yahweh's wrath.

Recent years have witnessed a renaissance of interest and research into the nature of metaphor. Helpful surveys of research can be found in Ricoeur (1977), Johnson (1981), Soskice (1985), Brettler (1989), and Macky (1990).

This is not the place for an extended discussion of the nature of metaphor, but perhaps a few remarks will prove helpful. It is difficult to define precisely "metaphor." I. A. Richards in his influential work *The Philosophy of Rhetoric* contended that "when we use a metaphor we have two thoughts of different things active together and supported by a single word, or phrase, whose meaning is a resultant of their interaction" (1936: 93). He distinguished between the "tenor" or underlying subject of the metaphor and the "vehicle" or image that presents it. His emphasis on thoughts corrected the older more-limited understanding of metaphor as word substitution.

More recent definitions remain in continuity with Richards. Soskice (1985: 15) defines metaphor as "that figure of speech whereby we speak about one thing in terms which are seen to be suggestive of another." Bourguet (1987: 10) defines it as "the fact of intentionally describing, in a mediate or immediate manner, one thing in the terms of another that resembles it and that belongs to another isotopy," i.e., set of associated vocabulary. Macky (1990: 49) proposes that metaphor is "that figurative way of speaking (and meaning) in which one reality, the Subject, is depicted in terms that are more commonly associated with a different reality, the Symbol, which is related to it by Analogy."

Several considerations follow from these definitions. First, not all metaphors conform with one particular syntactic structure. They do not all correspond with the "*x* is *y*" form as in "Time is a thief." Sometimes the underlying subject or tenor is not explicitly stated. In the biblical texts to follow, the term "wrath" does not always appear, yet experiencing divine wrath is the subject being depicted.

Second, not all metaphors have the same length or the same degree of development. A metaphor can encompass as little as a phrase or as much as several verses. One should distinguish between establishing a metaphor and extending it. It "is established as soon as it is clear that one thing is being spoken of in terms that are suggestive of another and can be extended until this is no longer the case," that is, until its length causes one to forget the tenor (Soskice 1985: 23).

Third, a metaphorical statement can be recognized in the first place when a metaphorical reading is preferable to a literal one. "The decisive reason for choice of interpretation may be, as it often is, the patent falsity or incoherence of the literal reading but it might equally be the banality of that reading's truth, its pointlessness, or its lack of congruence with the surrounding text and nonverbal setting" (Black 1979: 34–35).

Fourth, since a metaphorical statement depicts a subject in terms more commonly associated with a different reality (symbol) yet one that is related to the subject by analogy, the competent reader must have some acquaintance with both the subject and symbol. In order to recognize the analogy, the reader must uncover the "associated commonplaces" or "associated implications" between tenor and vehicle (Black 1979: 27). For example, in order to understand the statement "God is king" one must know the features or entailments that belong to a king and to ruling (Brettler 1989). And since we are examining a metaphor used in the Hebrew Bible, we should seek to discover the commonplaces that would have been evoked in the mind of an ancient Israelite. To the extent possible, we need to hear a metaphor with its various denotations and connotations as the original audience heard it.

Finally, unlike some metaphors that are more superficial and ornamental, the metaphor of drinking the cup of wrath is a profound, insight-provoking example. It intends to give insight into the more intangible mystery of divine wrath through the window of the more concrete and better-known symbol of drinking wine. Such a profound metaphor cannot adequately be treated from an impartial and objective distance. Nor can it be paraphrased without losing much of its impact and power. Only by entering into the symbol, only be seeing, imagining, and feeling the physical experience evoked by the symbol can one gain insight into the subject.

In the metaphor of "drinking the cup of Yahweh's wrath" the tenor or subject is one's experience of divine wrath, and the vehicle or symbol is drinking a cup of wine. Thus experiencing Yahweh's wrath is like drinking a wine cup. Readers are invited to see what it is like to receive divine wrath in light of and against the background of drinking wine.

In keeping with the above considerations, the method adopted here is similar to that used by Brettler (1989). First, I will outline the terminology and characteristics associated with drinking wine in the Hebrew Bible. Then I will examine every text in its context that employs this metaphor. One should note not only the similarities between the features of normal wine drinking and these texts but also the differences. As with any lively metaphor these texts often go beyond the normal associations of the vehicle. For example, unlike the normal experience of drunkenness in which a person becomes sober again and awakens in the morning, some texts state that those who drink of God's wrath will sleep an eternal sleep. Finally, I will present some general observations and a brief discussion of its origin.

FEATURES OF WINE DRINKING

The features associated with wine drinking can be grouped under four headings: cup, wine, drinking, and drunkenness. These four categories encompass the semantic field or the commonplaces associated with drinking that serve as background for the metaphor of the cup of wrath. I will concentrate on texts other than the ones using this metaphor although some overlap is inevitable.

I. Cup. The term used most frequently for a "cup" is *kôs*, a feminine noun. It designates a vessel from which one drinks wine rather than a vessel used for pouring or storage. The same term applies to the cup of Pharaoh, which was perhaps made of gold (Gen 40:11, 13, 21; cf. Jer 51:7; 2 Chr 9:20), and to a (probably) ceramic cup of a poor man (2 Sam 12:3). 1 Kings 7:26 (= 2 Chr 4:5) refers to its distinctive "lip" and Ezek 23:32 mentions a "deep and broad" cup. Invariably *kôs* designates an individual cup that one holds in the hand, but it can be passed from one person to another. For example, Pharaoh's "butler" or "cupbearer" (*mašqeh* — literally, "one who gives to drink") puts a cup into Pharaoh's hand (Gen 40:11, 13, 21). Kelso (1948: 19–20) notes that *kôs* covers both the cup and the broad shallow bowl that frequently are found in archaeological sites.

Occasionally one finds *kôs* used metaphorically for a person's allotted portion and fate in life. This may consist of either disaster or blessing. Psalm 11:6 says that for the wicked "a scorching wind will be the portion of their cup." On the positive side is Ps 16:5 where the psalmist says, "Yahweh, you are my apportioned share and my cup; you hold my lot." Finally, note Ps 116:12–14:

v 12 What shall I return to Yahweh
      for all his benefits to me?
v 13 I will lift up the cup of salvation
      and will call on the name of Yahweh.
v 14 I will pay my vows to Yahweh
      in the presence of all his people.

In v 13 the psalmist promises to extol before others the gift of salvation that Yahweh has allotted to him.

II. Wine. The two most common terms for wine are *yayin* and *tîrôš*; the latter designates "wine made from the first drippings of the juice before the winepress was trodden" and not unfermented wine as sometimes suggested (Fitzsimmonds 1982: 1254). Also to be included in this semantic field are: *'āsîs*, "sweet wine" (cf. Isa 49:26; Joel 1:5); *šēkār*, "strong drink" (probably beer); *ḥōmeṣ*, "vinegar" (usually made from wine); **sōbe'*, "wine" or "beer"; *ḥemer*, "fermenting wine"; and *šĕmārîm*, "dregs" (of wine). Several texts speak of "mixing" wine (*māsak*; Prov 9:2, 5; cf. Isa 5:22), "mixed wine" (*mezeg*; Cant 7:3 [2]), and a "mixing vessel" (*mimsāk*; Isa 65:11; Prov 23:30). The only mixture that was added to wine, of which we know, was powdered "spice" (*reqaḥ*; Cant 8:2). Wine could also be diluted with water (Isa 1:22) or poisoned (Hos 7:5; cf. Deut 32:32–33).

Wine was used as part of the regular diet (Gen 27:25; Lam 2:12) and on special occasions such as a feast (Isa 5:12; Esth 5:6) or a cultic ceremony (Lev 23:13; Num 15:5, 10). Often the Bible portrays wine in a positive way. It is given by God to gladden the human heart (Ps 104:14–15); it comforts those who mourn (Jer 16:7) and sustains those who faint (2 Sam 16:2). It is featured as a prominent blessing of the promised eschatological age (Isa 25:6; Joel 4:18 [3:18]; Amos 9:13–14), whereas the lack of it results from God's judgment (Isa 24:11; Jer 48:33; Joel 1:5). However, the negative features of wine are what serve as the background for the metaphor of drinking the cup of wrath, and these will be discussed under the category of "drunkenness."

III. Drinking. The two verbs appropriate to this discussion are *šth*, "to drink," and the *hip'il* of *šqh*, "to cause to drink, give to drink." Both verbs can take "wine" or "cup" as their object, but what is particularly noteworthy in this context are those texts that employ these verbs in a metaphorical sentence. When these verbs have an object other than the normal objects of water, wine, or cup, one can usually recognize a figure of speech, which can be organized into three types.

A. Figure for Slaughter. In Num 23:24 Israel is compared with a lioness/lion that "devours" (*'kl*) prey and "drinks" (*šth*) the blood of the slain. The figure of speech signifies Israel's victory over its foes. Israel is assured of victory over its enemies also in Isa 49:26, but here the figure changes. Not Israel but its oppressors will "eat" (*'kl*) there own flesh and "be drunk" (*škr*) with their own blood as with wine. The image signifies that the enemies will slaughter themselves and have only their own flesh and blood with which to sustain themselves. Finally, note Deut 32:42 where Yahweh's personified arrows become "drunk" (*škr*) with the blood of his adversaries and his personified sword "devours" (*'kl*) their flesh.

B. Figure for Wickedness. Several texts employ the verb "to drink" (*šth*) to convey the sustenance and enjoyment the wicked receive from their wickedness. In Job 15:15–16 Eliphaz argues that every mortal is wicked in God's sight and is one "who drinks wrongdoing like water." It is as natural for those "born of woman" (v 14) to sin as to drink water. Elihu in Job 34:7 applies Eliphaz's indictment to Job, "What man is like Job? He drinks derision like water." Proverbs 4:17 exhorts the readers to avoid the way of the wicked "for they eat the bread of wickedness, and the wine of violence they drink." Again the emphasis is on how natural and common sin is for the wicked. They cannot even sleep peacefully unless they have done wrong (v 16). Violence is their "meat and drink." With the phrase "the wine of violence" one might add that they enjoy violence as one enjoys wine.

C. FIGURE FOR SUFFERING. Sometimes the drinking image is used to signify suffering and pain. Proverbs 26:6 says that "the one who sends a message by the hand of a fool cuts off his own feet (and) drinks violence." The point of the phrase "drinks violence" is not that the sender does evil naturally but that he experiences and receives a bitter result by sending a fool as a messenger (cf. Prov 10:26; 13:17; 25:13).

In other texts the suffering comes from God. In Ps 80:5–6 [4–5] the psalmist laments to God:

O Yahweh, God of hosts,
how long will you smoke against the prayer of your people?
You made them eat the bread of tears.
You made them drink tears in full measure.

Eating and drinking tears represent sorrow and grief as their normal daily experience.

In Job 6:4 Job explains that God is the source of his anguish:

For the arrows of Shaddai are in me,
whose poison/wrath my spirit drinks.
The terrors of God are arrayed against me.

Job pictures God as an archer, possibly Reshef (Habel 1985: 145), whose poison-tipped arrows penetrate the hunter's prey. Not only Job's body but also his inner "spirit" is affected. It "drinks" the arrows' ḥēmâ. Occasionally ḥēmâ denotes "poison, venom" which certainly fits the image here (Deut 32:24, 33; Pss 58:5 [4]; 140:4 [3]). But usually poisoned arrows do not affect one's inner spirit. Consequently, ḥēmâ might also bear its more common denotation of divine "wrath" and be deliberately ambiguous. In that case Job's spirit regularly "drinks," experiences, and lives on God's wrath rather than grace (cf. Job 21:20; 20:23).

Three times Jeremiah speaks of Yahweh making people drink "poisoned water," mê rō'š (Jer 8:14; 9:14 [15]; 23:15). In the latter two verses the parallel says that Yahweh makes them eat "wormwood" (la'ănâ). Instead of giving them the sustenance of life-enhancing food and water, Yahweh's judgment gives them bitterness, pain, and death (cf. Lam 3:15–19).

In contrast to this negative employment of such metaphorical drinking it is also used positively. For example, Ps 36:9–10 [8–9] extols Yahweh's "steadfast love" located at the temple:

They feast on the abundance of your house,
and from the river of your delights you give them drink.
For with you is the fountain of life.
In your light we see light.

However, it is the negative usage of this image that brings us close to the metaphor of drinking the cup of wrath.

IV. Drunkenness. As much as the Hebrew Bible values wine as a blessing from God, it also consistently condemns drunkenness. Wine is attractive and inviting "when it is red, when it sparkles in the cup; it goes down smoothly" (Prov 23:31). Because of its charm, a drinker often cannot stop. When one succumbs to its allurement, it soon overcomes a person and the drinker becomes the drunkard. "In the end it bites like a snake and poisons like a viper" (Prov 23:32). The negative and deleterious effects of drunkenness form an important part of the background to the metaphor of drinking the cup of wrath. Here I will summarize the effects of heavy drinking under several headings, effects evident today, of course, as much as in ancient Israel.

A. STUPOR. The stupefying effects of excessive amounts of wine include staggering, confusion, insensibility, and sleep. Isaiah 19:14 says that Egypt is confused and staggers "as a drunkard staggers in his vomit." In Isa 24:20 the same image applies to the earth, which "sways like a drunkard." According to Isa 28:7, even the priest and prophet "reel" and "stagger" from wine (cf. Isa 29:9). Psalm 107:27 compares the experience of sailors caught in a sea storm with the "leaping" and "swaying" of a drunkard. Finally, Job argues that God builds nations up and brings them down, removes understanding from their leaders, and makes them "stagger like a drunkard" (Job 12:24–25).

In addition to staggering, too much wine produces confusion in the mind and lack of clear judgment. A good narrative example appears in Gen 19:30–38. Lot's daughters make Lot drunk so as to lie with him and bear children. Each time the text states, "he did not know when she lay down and when she arose" (vv 33, 35). Another narrative example is that of Nabal who was too drunk to comprehend Abigail's report. Only after Nabal regained sobriety did his wife inform him (1 Sam 25:36–37). Isaiah 28:7 condemns priest and prophet who "are confused," "err in vision," and "stumble in giving judgment" because of wine. Proverbs 31:4–5 warns a king not to drink wine "lest he drink and forget what is prescribed, and pervert the right of all the children of affliction." In the next two verses, on the other hand, wine is recommended for the perishing and distressed since it allows them to forget their poverty and trouble. According to Prov 23:33, excessive drinking makes one virtually mad: "Your eyes will see strange things, and your heart will speak perverse things." Such madness is well illustrated by the story of Hannah (1 Sam 1:12–16). Hannah prays from her heart, moving her lips but without making an audible utterance, and Eli mistakenly considers her to be drunk. All of these texts illustrate one effect of wine, that it diminishes one's clear-headedness and decision-making reason and instead creates confusion of mind.

Drunkenness not only dulls the mind; it also dulls the body and makes it insensate so that one cannot feel pain and consequently avoid harm. Thus Prov 26:9 compares "a proverb in the mouth of fools" with "a thorn that goes up into the hand of a drunkard." Neither the proverb nor the thorn affects the recipient. According to Prov 23:35, drunkards are so impervious to pain that even a beating does not hinder them from foolishly seeking another drink. Rather they think to themselves:

They struck me, I was not hurt!
They beat me, I did not perceive it!
When will I awake
so that I can continue to seek it [wine] again?

Heavy drinking eventually makes one drowsy and brings on deep sleep. A well-known example is the story of drunken Noah who lay uncovered in his tent. "When Noah awoke from his wine and knew what his youngest son had done to him," he uttered a curse (Gen 9:24). Because wine makes one drowsy and lazy, and therefore eventually leads to poverty, Proverbs warns against excessive drinking: "The one who loves wine and oil will not be rich" (Prov 21:17). One should not consort with winebibbers, "for the drunkard and the glutton will become poor, and drowsiness will clothe one with rags" (Prov 23:20–21). Drunkenness brings on sleep but usually the drunkard later regains sobriety and awakens (Gen 9:24; 1 Sam 25:37; Prov 23:35).

B. HELPLESSNESS. Because of wine-induced stupor with its attendant staggering, confusion, insensibility, and sleep, a drunkard becomes helpless and defenseless before enemies. There are two striking narratives that illustrate such helplessness. In 2 Sam 13:28–29 Absalom's servants strike and kill Amnon for the rape of Tamar when Amnon's heart is "merry with wine." According to 1 Kgs 16:9–10, Zimri, the servant of Israel's king Elah, struck and killed Elah when Elah was "drinking himself drunk." In both cases wine made the victims defenseless before their assassins.

C. DISGRACE. The final characteristic of drunkenness to be noted here is the disgrace that accompanies it. Often those who are inebriated disgrace themselves with their degrading actions. Regarding Egypt Isa 19:14 says:

Yahweh has mixed [*msk*, "to prepare wine"] in her midst
a spirit of distortion/perversion ['*iw'îm*, BDB].

And it [the perversion] makes Egypt stagger in all its deeds
as a drunkard staggers in his vomit.

According to Isa 28:7–8, the priest and the prophet are drunk, reeling, and confused, "for all tables are full of vomit, (full of) excrement without a (clean) place left." The degradation involved could not be more vividly expressed.

Another aspect of intoxication's accompanying disgrace is the display of one's nakedness. When Noah became drunk with wine, "he lay exposed in the midst of his tent" (Gen 9:21). Such exposure of one's nakedness is considered shameful in the Hebrew Bible (cf. Gen 3:7, 10; Exod 20:26; 2 Sam 6:20; Isa 20:4; 47:3; Ezek 16; 23; Nah 3:5; Lam 1:8).

Conclusions. In the texts that utilize the metaphor of drinking the cup of Yahweh's wrath the features associated with cup, wine, drinking, and drunkenness form the background necessary for understanding the metaphor. They are the features that are developed in the metaphor's symbol in order to speak of the experience of divine wrath. The components that are the most pertinent include the following: a drinking cup that can be passed from hand to hand, much of the wine terminology, drinking as a figure for suffering, and the effects of drunkenness such as staggering, confusion, sleep, helplessness, and disgrace. Some of the metaphorical texts do not fully develop the image whereas others develop its individual features quite extensively. To those texts we now turn.

THE METAPHORICAL TEXTS

Fourteen texts employ the metaphor of drinking the cup of divine wrath, four in the Writings (Pss 60:5 [3]; 75:9 [8]; Job 21:19–20; Lam 4:21) and the rest in the Latter Prophets (Isa 51:17–23; 63:6; Jer 25:15–29; 48:26–27; 49:12; 51:7–8; 51:39, 57; Ezek 23:31–34; Obad 16; Hab 2:15–16). Two other texts are sometimes included, but they do not belong to this metaphor (Jer 13:12–14; Zech 12:2). On the former, see Bourguet (1987: 258–70), and on the latter, see Honeyman (1936). I will examine the non-prophetic texts first.

1. Psalm 60:5 [3].

You made your people see a harsh thing.
You made us drink [*šqh*] wine (that causes) staggering.

Psalm 60 begins with a communal lament addressed to God for executing his wrath on Israel: "O God, you have rejected us; you have burst out upon us; you have been angry [*'np*]." Verse 5 [3] begins with a literal statement: God made Israel "see" or experience a harsh thing. Then it moves to a metaphorical statement in which this harsh reality imposed on Israel by God's wrath (the tenor) is depicted in terms of being forced to drink wine (the vehicle). The feature of wine drinking brought to the fore is the "staggering" or "reeling" (*tar'ēlâ*) associated with drunkenness. Possibly this feature was chosen to continue the motif of tottering mentioned in the previous verse. Just as the land is "quaking" (r'š) and "tottering" (mwṭ) as if in an earthquake (v 4 [2]), so also the Israelites are reeling. Possibly implied in the image is that the people "are so overwhelmed with dismay and panic by this unexpected situation that they are dazed" (Briggs 1907: 61). The text presents the metaphor very briefly in only one line without subsequent development. It is very similar to the "figure for suffering" that one occasionally finds with the verb šqh (see above). However, because it associates such drinking with divine wrath, wine, and wine's attendant staggering, it belongs more to the sphere of our metaphor. Perhaps one might see this verse as a transition from "drinking" as a figure for suffering to the full-blown metaphor of drinking the cup of wrath. At any rate, this verse continues the emphasis of the previous verses, that it is Israel's God who has executed his wrath and imposed suffering on Israel. The verse functions as perplexed Israel's lament and complaint addressed to its God. The hoped-for response is that God stop his anger and instead restore his people.

2. Psalm 75:9 [8].

For a cup is in the hand of Yahweh,
and the wine foams, full of mixture.
He poured out some of it.
But its dregs they will drain dry.
All the wicked of the earth will drink.

The verse exhibits some textual problems. In the B-line the masculine singular noun yayin is the subject of the two verbs ḥāmar and mālē'. The verb ḥāmar probably means "to foam, ferment," related to ḥemer (fermenting wine), although it does not occur with wine elsewhere. The noun mesek designates the "admixture of spices" that makes the wine more seductive and intoxicating.

The C-line is an exceedingly difficult crux for which various solutions have been proposed (Wiesenberg 1954). The verb wayyaggēr, a waw consecutive hip'il of ngr, means "he poured out" with Yahweh as the subject. The hip'il of ngr in its other four occurrences takes a direct object (Jer 18:21; Ezek 35:5; Mic 1:6; Ps 63:11 [10]), which leads one to expect an object here.

The problem comes with the next word mizzeh, the preposition min + the masculine singular demonstrative pronoun zeh. Most commentators take the pronoun's antecedent to be kôs so that "Yahweh pours from the cup." However, this understanding not only leaves the verb without an object but also posits a grammatical incongruity, since zeh is masculine but kôs is always feminine. In fact, in the next line kôs is treated as feminine — šĕmāreyhā, "the dregs of it," i.e., of the cup. The LXX renders ek toutou eis touto (from this into that), apparently thinking that Yahweh pours from one cup into another (Briggs 1907: 164). This rendering appears to be an attempt to interpret MT's *mizzeh* rather than a reflection of a different Hebrew *Vorlage*. At any rate, the verse pictures only one cup.

The simplest solution is to take *zeh* as referring back to the masculine noun *yayin* (wine) and the preposition *min* as partitive, "Yahweh poured out some of the wine." A parallel construction occurs in Lev 8:12 and 14:26 in which a person "pours out [*ysq*] some of the oil" (*min* + *šemen*). This would provide the verb *wygr* with an object and would preserve grammatical congruity. One can construe the clause in one of two ways. (1) Yahweh poured out some of the cup's wine (i.e., his wrath) on the earth in the past, but now the wicked will drink it down to the dregs. (2) Yahweh tilts the cup to the lips of the wicked and begins to pour some of the wine. But the wicked, unable to stop, continue to drain it to the dregs (cf. Leupold 1959: 546).

It is difficult to decide between them since both understandings are possible. With the first option one thinks of the common idiom that Yahweh "pours out [although usually *špk*] his wrath." The second option adds a unique twist to the image. A *kôs* is a drinking cup, not a pouring vessel, and the drinker usually holds the cup to drink, but in this case Yahweh forces the wine down the drinker's throat. In either case there seems to be a contrast between line C and line D; Yahweh pours out from the cup some of the wine *but* (*'ak*) the wicked drink the cup down to its dregs.

The verse expresses an inner logic and a progression from line to line in keeping with the dynamics of biblical parallelism (cf. Kugel 1981; Alter 1985). It begins by stating that Yahweh's hand holds a cup whose contents are then described as desirable and potent wine. Then Yahweh pours out some of the wine, but the wicked end up drinking the cup to the bottom.

Although the verse does not explicitly mention divine wrath, it forces the reader to understand it metaphorically. A straightforward literal interpretation would be incoherent and pointless, as if the wicked simply get drunk on wine. The psalmist assumes the reader is acquainted with and can recognize the figure of the cup of Yahweh's wrath. The fact that the cup is in Yahweh's hand and that all the wicked of the earth drink it promotes such an understanding. Also the previous verses prepare for a metaphorical reading, since they emphasize God as a just judge who brings down the boastful. In light of the context, the verse points to the condemning wrath that the judge of the earth will execute against the wicked. It forms a basis — the third in a series, all of which begin with a causal *kî* (for) — for the warnings of vv 5–6 [4–5]. The sequence is as follows:

The proud should not boast (vv 5–6 [4–5]);

For exaltation does not come from the world (v 7 [6]);

For God is the judge who debases and exults (v 8 [7]);

For God will make the wicked drink the cup of wrath (v 9 [8]).

That Yahweh as judge will execute just punishment and condemnation against the wicked is the metaphor's subject, which is depicted with the symbol of drinking a cup of wine. The features of the symbol that are brought to the fore include the cup, seductive and potent wine, and drinking to the dregs. The metaphor emphasizes two complementary activities. First, Yahweh imposes his judgment on the wicked. The cup is in Yahweh's hand and he pours out some of the wine. Second, the wicked helplessly and irresistibly receive divine wrath to the full. The wine is so attractive and potent that they continue to drink until — unlike more normal drinkers — they have drained even the dregs or lees settled at the bottom of the cup. The verse functions as a threat by grounding the previous exhortations for the proud and wicked to repent.

3. Job 21:19–20.

v 19 (You may say), "God stores up his punishment for his [the sinner's] children."
    Let him [God] requite him so that he himself knows!
v 20 Let his own eyes see his ruin;
    and of the wrath [hēmâ] of Shaddai let him drink!

In this text Job rejects as unjust the idea that God reserves punishment for the children of the wicked while the wicked themselves prosper. Justice demands that the wicked themselves suffer and receive requital for their own crimes. The wicked should "know" and "see" ruin for themselves.

The first three lines read in a fairly straightforward and literal way, except possibly the verb "store up" [ṣpn]. But a literal reading of line D would be patently false and incoherent, since one does not actually drink wrath. The verb "drink" is paralleled by the verbs "know" and "see" so that the emphasis lies on the person's senses. Job wishes that the wicked would experience for themselves, both externally and internally, divine judgment.

Because the image of "drinking" is not developed beyond this one line, the reader remains uncertain whether wine is implied. One might just as well understand the image in light of drinking water (cf. Job 34:7). In fact, the statement could have been included in the previous discussion concerning drinking as a "figure for suffering." Yet the mention of divine wrath as the object of the drinking makes it unusual and leads the reader to relate it more to our metaphor. It states explicitly what was only hinted at in Job 6:4. There Job's "spirit drinks the hēmâ" of God's arrows, which plays on the multivalence of hēmâ as "poison" or "wrath." Here hēmâ denotes only "wrath."

The line invites the reader to think of the human experience of divine wrath and punishment (the tenor) in light of drinking water or wine (the vehicle). The main point is that the wicked should receive, experience, and feel personally the divine wrath. It functions as Job's complaint against the injustice of God withholding judgment from the wicked.

4. Lamentations 4:21.

Rejoice and be glad, O daughter Edom,
you who dwell in the land of Uz!
Also to you the cup will pass.
You will get drunk and expose your nakedness.

The poet announces judgment against the Edomites who assisted Babylon in attacking Judah and Jerusalem. This is in keeping with statements found elsewhere in Lamentations that divine wrath will be executed against Jerusalem's enemies (1:21–22; 3:60–66). Just as Zion suffered divine punishment for her iniquity, so Edom will receive the same for her iniquity (4:22; cf. 1:21–22; 3:64). According to v 22, Edom's judgment constitutes the reverse side of Jerusalem's restoration.

The opening line operates on several levels. The poet exhorts Edom to "rejoice and be glad." Why should Edom rejoice? On the level of the image the answer lies in the fact that Edom will soon drink a cup of wine, and wine gladdens the heart. But the last line subverts this positive expectation into the negative one of drunkenness. Edom will drink the cup, keep on drinking until drunk, and shamefully expose her nakedness. (The *hitpaʿel* of *ʿrh* means "to make oneself naked"; so BDB.) With the last two lines the reader recognizes the metaphor of the cup of wrath, since a literal interpretation would be nonsensical. The poet hardly wants Edom, personified as a "daughter," simply to become drunk and naked. Once the metaphorical nature of the verse is perceived, the reader now understands the first line differently. One might take it at face value, that Edom should be glad now while she still prospers because soon she will be punished. She should "eat, drink, and be merry, for tomorrow she dies." Or one might understand it as sarcasm. Instead of weeping, which is the proper response to impending doom, she should foolishly be happy. It is as if to say, "Go on Edom, continue to rejoice over the fall of Jerusalem! But look what's coming."

The verse presupposes the reader's familiarity with the metaphor of the cup of wrath, since it does not explicitly mention Yahweh's wrath. Certainly the next verse makes its metaphorical character evident: "He [Yahweh] will punish your iniquity, O daughter Edom. He will uncover your sins." In addition to rejoicing, the aspects of the symbol that the poet picks up are cup, drunkenness, and nakedness. Accordingly, we are invited to see divine punishment (the subject) through the lens of inebriety and its attendant disgrace (the symbol).

The metaphor posits three aspects of the divine punishment. First, Yahweh will impose his wrath and punishment on Edom, since "the cup will pass over to you." Presumably the cup is in Yahweh's hand and he gives it to Edom. The LXX makes this explicit with the words *to potērion kuriou* (the Lord's cup).

Second, the divine punishment moves from Jerusalem to Edom. Whereas Jerusalem has already experienced Yahweh's wrath — which is the concern of the whole book—while Edom has not, now Edom will be punished. This aspect is indicated by the phrase "*also* to you" and is confirmed by the next verse.

Third, the content of the divine punishment consists of shame and disgrace for Edom. Just as "all who honored her [Jerusalem] despise her, for they have seen her nakedness" (1:8), so drunken Edom will expose her own nakedness. Perhaps the use of the *hitpaʿel titʿārî* is significant. Yahweh's judgment causes Edom to disgrace and debase her own self in the sight of others. One might also conclude from her drunken state that Edom will experience a full measure of punishment, since one normally needs to drink a larger quantity of wine to reach inebriety. The idea is: the greater the drunkenness, the greater the punishment.

The verse serves as an indictment and announcement of impending doom against Edom. Its connection with v 22 indicates that it expresses the reverse side to the promise of the reversal of Zion's fortunes.

5. Isaiah 51:17–23.

v 17A Rouse yourself, rouse yourself,
 B stand up, O Jerusalem,
 C   you who drank from the hand of Yahweh
 D   the cup of his wrath,
 E   the goblet cup of staggering,
 F   which you drank, you drained.
v 18A There is no one to guide her
 B   of all the children she has borne;
 C and there is no one to take her by the hand
 D   of all the children she has reared.
v 19A These two things have happened to you—
 B   who will condole with you?
 C —devastation and ruin, hunger and sword—
 D   how will I comfort you?
v 20A Your children have fainted,
 B they lie at the head of every street
 C   like an antelope in a net;
 D they are full of the wrath of Yahweh,
 E   of the rebuke of your God.
v 21A Therefore hear this, you who are afflicted,
 B   you who are drunk but not with wine:
v 22A Thus spoke your Lord Yahweh,
 B   and your God who contends for his people:
 C "Look! I take from your hand
 D   the cup of staggering,
 E   the goblet cup of my wrath,
 F   which you will no longer continue to drink;

v 23A and I will put it into the hand of your tormentors and your oppressors,
  B   who said to you,
  C   'Bow down that we may pass over';
  D and you had to make your back like the ground
  E   and like the street for them to pass over."

There are a few textual problems. (1) The phrase *qubba'at kôs*, translated "goblet cup," is a construct chain, literally "the goblet of the cup" (vv 17E, 22E). The word *kôs* seems to be explanatory (possibly a gloss) for *qb't*, which occurs only here in biblical Hebrew but is found in Ugaritic, Phoenician, Akkadian, and Arabic. (2) Qumran and some versions read a third person verb in v 19D — *my ynḥmk*, "who will comfort you?" — instead of the first person of the MT. Since the variant parallels v 19B more smoothly and exactly ("who will condole with you?"), the more difficult MT is preferable (so Barthélemy 1986: 376). The MT *mî 'ănahāmēk* may mean "who am I that I can comfort you / How will I comfort you?" or "By whom will I comfort you?" (cf. Nah 3:7). (3) In v 23A, Qumran with the agreement of the LXX adds *wm'nyk* after *byd mwgyk* of the MT, "into the hand of your tormentors *and your oppressors*." Qumran's *wm'nyk* probably dropped out by homoioteleuton with *mwgyk* (Barthélemy 1986: 377).

The text begins by addressing Jerusalem, personified as a drunken woman. The second person address continues throughout except in v 18. The two initial imperatives in v 17 echo and anticipate the double imperatives in v 9 and 52:1, all based on the same root *'wr*. They call Lady Jerusalem, who is apparently sleeping in drunken stupor, to rouse herself and stand up. The reader identifies early in the reading process the text's metaphorical nature from the third and fourth lines of v 17, which state that Jerusalem drank "from the hand of Yahweh the cup of his wrath."

The next two lines intensify but also slightly alter the picture. She not only drank but also "drained" the cup, yet it is a cup that sent her "staggering" and groping in distinction from the earlier implication of her sleeping. Verse 18 picks up on this image of a staggering drunk and adds that she is a mother. Her children are not present to guide, lead, and support their tottering mother. The reader naturally wonders why not and the answer comes later in v 20.

But first v 19 intervenes with a nonmetaphorical, historical description of the calamity in line C. Line A mentions "two things," apparently referring to the two pairs of nouns in line C. The first pair, "devastation and ruin," happens to a city, whereas the second pair, "hunger and sword," affects its inhabitants. Except for line C, however, the verse keeps the personification of Jerusalem as a woman. The purpose of the two rhetorical questions in B and D is to heighten and magnify the tragedy that befell her. Her disaster is so profound and shocking that no one can or will console her, not even the prophet. (Presumably the prophet speaks in vv 17–21, since Yahweh is consistently treated in the third person.)

Verse 20 reverts back to the image and answers the reader's question addressed to v 18. Her children are unable to help her because they have "fainted" and helplessly lie on the street corners. The mention of "streets," however, causes the reader to continue to recognize the literal level of the referent, the geopolitical city of Jerusalem. On that level the verse implies that Jerusalem's inhabitants are unable to rebuild and restore the ruined city. On the image level the verse is more complicated. Why have her children "fainted"? Because they too are drunk? Elsewhere the verb '*lp* denotes fainting caused by exposure to the sun (Jonah 4:8) or by thirst (Amos 8:13). If the latter is involved here, then perhaps the verb continues the reference to "hunger" mentioned in v 19C. Her children are famished and consequently faint; they are weary to the point of lying down in the streets. Not death but utter helplessness is the point, as indicated by the simile "like an antelope in a net." Just as an antelope in a hunter's net "lies there exhausted, after having almost strangled itself by ineffectual attempts to release itself" (Delitzsch 1877, II: 293), so her children lie unable to assist her. The next line clarifies the situation. Her children "are full of the wrath of Yahweh"; they have drunk deeply of the divine wrath like their mother (v 17) and therefore faint and lie down.

Verses 19–20 seemed to move away from the drinking image a bit or at least to bring into the picture other images, but v 21 focuses our attention solely on the original picture. While the reader assumed earlier that the woman was drunk, now it is explicitly stated. Yet her inebriety is not due to ordinary wine but — the reader infers — to the previously mentioned "cup of wrath." The initial clause, "Therefore hear this," signals a switch from the depiction of her sufferings to a promise, and it introduces the basis for the initial imperatives to rouse herself and stand up (v 17).

Verse 22 begins with the messenger formula and affirms that the God who punished her is the same one now speaking. While no one else could help or comfort her, not even her children, she now has an advocate and defender (*yārîb* — v 22B), Yahweh her Lord and her God. The mention of God's "people" in the phrase "who contends for his people" again directs the reader's attention away from the image to the referent, the Jerusalemites. Yahweh will take out of her hand the cup of his wrath so that she no longer has to drink it.

The time has arrived for her tormentors to drink the cup, which Yahweh will put into their hands (v 23). These are the enemies who debased her, who walked all over her as if her back were the ground or a street. Verse 23 presumably fills in the blanks left open in v 19. Jerusalem's "tormentors" and "oppressors" were the ones who brought about the "devastation and ruin, hunger and sword" mentioned in v 19.

The unit has a bipartite structure: the prophetic speech of vv 17–21 depicts Jerusalem's present sufferings, while the divine speech of vv 22–23 announces Jerusalem's future, namely, the cessation of her suffering and the reversal of fortunes in that her enemies now must suffer. Verse 21 serves as a transition. The first part exhibits a symmetrical arrangement of motifs:

A   v 17   Jerusalem drank the cup of wrath and staggers;
B   v 18   Her children cannot help her;
C   v 19   The devastation of the city and its inhabitants; no one to comfort her;
B   v 20   Her children faint, lie in the streets, are full of Yahweh's wrath;
A   v 21   Jerusalem is drunk but not with wine.

The second part then announces that Yahweh will remove the cup from Jerusalem's hand and put it into the hand of her enemies. Note that v 22 connects the two parts by repeating much of the same vocabulary of v 17.

These seven verses develop quite extensively the symbol of drinking wine. The features of drinking that are employed include: the cup, passing the cup from hand to hand, drinking and draining the cup, drunkenness, sleep, and staggering. The metaphor depicts Jerusalem's experience of Yahweh's wrath (the subject) in terms associated with drinking wine (the symbol).

The unit draws one's attention to several aspects of the subject through its use of the symbol. First, Yahweh imposes his wrath on people. "The cup of his wrath" comes from "Yahweh's hand" (v 17), and he takes it from Jerusalem's hand and puts it in the hand of others (vv 22–23). The picture of Yahweh giving and removing the cup from one and then giving it to another presents divine judgment not as some impersonal sin-consequence mechanism at work. Rather, Yahweh personally inflicts and controls the suffering; he determines who experiences punishment and for how long.

Second, the perspective from which the text views the subject of divine punishment is from below. It focuses on the human experience of divine wrath, on what it is like when a city and its people suffer and undergo divine wrath, rather than on Yahweh becoming angry and what that entails. Verse 19 states the historical reality of this experience; the city becomes devastated and its inhabitants die.

Third, the primary characteristic of the experience that is developed in the image is the total helplessness of those being punished. Jerusalem cannot improve her lot by her own powers, since she staggers and reels like a drunken woman. Nor can anyone else restore her or assist her, not even her own children as they too lie helpless. Jerusalem has experienced a full measure of divine wrath and punishment. She "drained" the cup, and together with her children she is "drunk" and "full" of Yahweh's wrath. The tragedy is so shockingly profound that no one can even comfort her. Only her God can alter the situation.

Finally, the divine punishment moves from Jerusalem to her enemies. Her suffering has ended but that of her foes now begins, just as Yahweh takes the cup from her hand and gives it to others.

By portraying the gravity and magnitude of Jerusalem's suffering along with her utter helplessness the metaphor seeks to magnify her deliverance and the surpassing mercy of Yahweh (McKenzie 1968: 127). Accordingly, the text functions as a promise designed to give comfort and hope to Yahweh's people.

6. Isaiah 63:6.

I trample the peoples in my anger,
and I make them drunk in my wrath,
and I make their blood run down to the ground.

In the second line some manuscripts read *w'šbrm*, "and I break them," but the LXX and most ancient versions accord with the MT *w'škrm*, "and I make them drunk," which is to be preferred. Qumran has the *hipʿil* of *škr* instead of the *piʿel* of the MT.

Verse 6 completes the divine speech begun in v 3. The speech constitutes Yahweh's answer to the question asked him in v 2, "Why is your apparel red?" His garments are stained red from the blood of the peoples whom he, the divine warrior, trampled in his wrath. The verse lists three actions of Yahweh by using a first person verb to begin each line: "I trample . . . I make drunk . . . I make [to] run down." The verse and the context focus the reader's attention on Yahweh who alone in wrath destroys the peoples.

The first verb *bws* means "to trample over corpses," "to tread them into the ground" (cf. Isa 14:19; Ps 108:14 [13]), and the third verb (*hipʿil* of *yrd*) refers to spilling blood, literally "to make it flow down." In light of this context the reader understands the second verb metaphorically, since a literal interpretation would be nonsensical. Because the line mentions "wrath" one should relate it to the cup-of-wrath metaphor; it presupposes the reader's knowledge of the metaphor.

The text does not explicitly state what the peoples drink. The prepositional phrase "in my wrath" should not be construed grammatically as the object of the verb, as if to say, "I make them drunk with my wrath." Such an object would have the preposition *min* (Deut 32:42). Rather, the prepositional phrase like its parallel in the first line and in v 3 modifies the verbal subject, "I in my wrath make them drunk." Nevertheless, the implied object is divine wrath as in Isa 51.

This metaphorical statement is brief and undeveloped, only one line. Consequently, it carries little weight. But it does stress two points. First, Yahweh imposes his wrath on the peoples. They do not freely and voluntarily "drink" but are forcibly made to experience divine wrath. Second, Yahweh makes them experience his wrath to the full; they become "drunk" with it.

The whole unit, which v 6 completes (vv 1–6), functions as a promise for Israel. It depicts the climactic day of "vengeance" (v 4) when the divine warrior comes in wrath and destroys all the peoples who fought against his kingdom and people. This means "vindication," "salvation," and "redemption" for helpless Zion (vv 1, 4, 5).

7. Jeremiah 25:15–29.

v 15 For thus Yahweh the God of Israel said to me:
"Take this cup of wine, which is wrath, from my hand
and give it to all the nations to whom I send you to drink.

v 16 They will drink and convulse and act crazed
from before the sword which I send among them."

v 17 And I took the cup from the hand of Yahweh
and I gave (it) to all the nations to whom Yahweh sent me to drink:

v 18 Jerusalem and the cities of Judah and its kings, its princes,
to make them a ruin, a desolation, a hissing, and a curse, as at this
day. . . .

v 26 and all the kings of the north, near and far, one after the other,
and all the kingdoms of the earth that are on the face of the ground;
and the king of Babylon will drink after them.

v 27 "And you will say to them:
'Thus spoke Yahweh of hosts, the God of Israel:
Drink and get drunk and vomit and fall, and you will not arise
from before the sword which I send among you.'

v 28 And if they refuse to take the cup from your hand to drink,
then you will say to them:
'Thus spoke Yahweh of hosts:
You certainly must drink.

v 29 For look! In the city upon which my name has been pronounced
I am beginning to do harm, and will you yourselves indeed be exempt?
No, you will not be exempt!
For I am summoning a sword against all the inhabitants of the earth'" —
utterance of Yahweh of hosts.

Jeremiah 25 presents the most extensive treatment of the cup-of-wrath metaphor
in the Hebrew Bible. Before we discuss it, a few textual problems should be
noted. The difference between the MT and the LXX is a well known and complicated question. The MT collects the various oracles against the nations at the
end of the book (chapters 46–51), whereas the LXX inserts them before the cup-
of-wrath passage. Thus the LXX has the following sequence according to the
chapter and verse numbering of the MT:

	LXX Order
	25:13
omits	25:14
chaps	46–51
	25:15–38
chaps	26–45.

It is unnecessary to attempt to resolve this textual discrepancy here. (For a recent treatment, see Holladay 1989.) All commentators agree that the cup-of-wrath text and the oracles against the nations are related regardless of which sequence is preferred.

The phrase *kôs hayyayin haḥēmâ* in v 15 is sometimes emended, following some ancient versions. But the MT is to be preferred (Barthélemy 1986: 655). Jeremiah occasionally signals a metaphor by placing a literal word in apposition to a figure of speech (Bourguet 1987: 37–40). For example, Jer 17:13 reads "the fountain of living water, Yahweh," and Jer 23:19 (= 30:23) has "the storm of Yahweh, wrath, goes forth" (cf. 6:28; 9:2 [3]; 11:4). Consequently, *haḥēmâ* is in apposition to *hayyayin*, "this cup of *wine*, which is *wrath*." The demonstrative *hazzō't* modifies *kôs* (this cup) and the accusative pronoun *'ōtô* refers to *hayyayin* (and make to drink it [the wine]).

The reader recognizes the metaphorical nature of this text from the opening words "Take this cup of wine, which is wrath" (v 15). This clause explicitly states the metaphor's subject, divine "wrath," and its symbol, "wine." The features of the symbol that the text brings out include a cup that is passed from hand to hand, drinking wine, drunkenness, convulsion, madness, and falling down. The word translated "convulse" in v 16 is the *hitpoʿel* of *gʿš*. The root is used to refer to the convulsion and quaking of the earth (Ps 18:8 [7] = 2 Sam 22:8) and the surging of water (Jer 5:22; 46:7–8). Here it could refer to the staggering movement of a drunkard or to the surging of his stomach, hence vomiting. In light of the parallel in v 27, perhaps vomiting is the reference (Holladay 1986: 674).

The text goes beyond the features normally associated with wine drinking in two significant ways. Normally one may refuse a cup but here the nations must drink (v 28). And in contrast to the usual experience in which a drunkard later regains sobriety and awakens, the nations will "fall," never again to "arise" and stand up (v 27).

The passage progresses logically from the divine command given to Jeremiah to his compliance, and then to the divine commands given to the nations through Jeremiah. The scene pictures the prophet as acting like a cupbearer at a banquet. First, Yahweh orders Jeremiah to take the cup and give it to the nations so that they drink (vv 15–16). After Jeremiah executes the order (vv 17–26), Yahweh orders him to command the nations to drink (v 27). Yahweh further says to him that if they refuse, he should tell them they must drink (v 28) and give the reason why (v 29). The text contains three divine speeches with each one introduced by the messenger formula. In the first one Jeremiah reports what Yahweh commanded him to do (vv 15–16). The second divine speech is to be proclaimed to the nations through the prophet (v 27). Finally, Jeremiah is to proclaim the third divine speech if and when the nations refuse the cup (vv 28–29).

This metaphorical passage with its richly developed image makes several theological points. First, Yahweh forcibly imposes his wrath and judgment on the nations. The cup of wrath originates in Yahweh's hand (vv 15, 17). The nations are not permitted to refuse it; they must drink because they are not exempt from God's punishment (vv 28–29). Yahweh is the one who "begins to do harm" in Jerusalem and who "summons a sword against all the inhabitants of the earth" (v 29). Thus Yahweh controls the action, and the nations cannot resist his wrath.

Second, Jeremiah acts as Yahweh's agent. Just as Yahweh "sends" the sword among the nations (vv 16, 27), so he "sends" the prophet to them (vv 15, 17). Jeremiah stands as one who both executes Yahweh's judgment and proclaims Yahweh's speech; he delivers the cup and declares the divine sentence. In other words, the prophet functions as both the hands and mouth of Yahweh. One should not imagine some cultic ritual in which Jeremiah actually passed a cup around. This is, after all, a metaphor. But it does present a picture of the prophet executing divine wrath by announcing divine judgment (cf. Jer 1:10; 5:14; 6:11; 23:29).

Third, Yahweh executes his wrath upon all nations. Yahweh is "the God of Israel" (vv 15, 27), and therefore he begins judgment with Jerusalem and Judah (vv 18, 29); but the judgment does not stop there. The God of Israel has claims on all nations so that the cup of wrath passes to them also. The nations mentioned in vv 18–26 include those of chapters 46–51 — except Damascus (49:23–27) — and a few others, such as Tyre and Sidon. Finally, Babylon drinks the cup after the nations. The order of the nations in vv 19–25 does not appear to be significant, but the text does stress that judgment begins with Jerusalem and ends with Babylon. This is in keeping with the context of 25:8–14. In fact, by beginning with *kî* (for) v 15 ties the cup-of-wrath passage to the preceding verses in the MT, which makes vv 15–29 an explication of vv 8–14.

Verses 15–26 stress the unity of all nations; they are all grouped together. This implies that Jerusalem/Judah is only one among many included in Jeremiah's commission to "all the nations" (vv 15–17). That changes, however, in v 29.

Verse 29 provides the reason why the nations must drink the cup. Yahweh calls Jerusalem "the city upon which my name has been pronounced." The idiom *niqrāʾ šēm ʿal* indicates ownership (cf. 2 Sam 12:28; Isa 4:1). Because Yahweh has placed his name on the city (cf. Dan 9:18–19) and its temple (cf. Jer 7:10–11, 14, 30; 32:34; 34:15), he has committed himself to it. If Yahweh "begins to do harm" in the city that has this special elect status, certainly the non-elect nations must experience judgment. They hardly "will be let off scot-free" (Bright 1965: 159). The argument proceeds from the greater to the lesser.

Finally, the text depicts the human experience under divine wrath by using the symbol of drinking wine. The metaphor focuses on two features of this experience. First, the nations receive divine wrath to the full, since they "get drunk" (v 27). Second, the nations become helpless and defenseless before opposing armies. The cup has the effect of stupefying the nations so that they convulse, vomit, act crazed, and fall "from before the sword" (vv 16, 27). They lose their faculties and their ability to defend themselves, unable to fight back. Yahweh's destructive work consists of both this confused helplessness and "the sword," synecdoche for war. The end result is that the nations never again "arise" (v 27), because they drank no ordinary wine cup but the cup of wrath.

8. Jeremiah 48:26–27.

v 26 Make him drunk — for against Yahweh he made himself great
  — so that Moab claps in his own vomit
  and becomes a laughingstock, also he.
v 27 Surely Israel has been a laughingstock to you, has he not?
  Surely he has not been found among thieves, has he?
  For as often as your words are of him, you wag (your head).

The reader can detect the metaphorical nature of v 26 not only because a literal understanding of the opening command to make Moab drunk would be nonsensical, but also because the text focuses on the derision of Moab as the image's application. The features associated with the symbol of drinking mentioned by the text are drunkenness and vomiting with its attendant derision. Since this text is part of Jeremiah's oracles against the nations — here in the section concerning Moab — the reader naturally relates it to Jer 25, which includes Moab in its list of nations (25:21). Therefore the metaphor is that of the cup of wrath.

The addressee changes between v 26 and v 27. Verse 26 opens with a plural imperative, "make [Moab] drunk." The identity of the addressee is left unspecified; the metaphor concentrates on what happens to Moab rather than on the agent who performs the action. In light of other verses in the chapter, the reader identifies the addressee with the surrounding nations which will destroy and mock Moab (vv 8–10, 12, 15, 17, 39). Whereas v 26 speaks of Moab in third person, v 27 addresses Moab directly. Yet the two verses are held together by the catchword "laughingstock," by the phrase "also he" that receives clarification in v 27, and by the logic of the passage. (On the syntax of v 27a, see Holladay 1989: 360–61; on v 27b, see BDB under *day.)

The metaphor in v 26 depicts Moab's experience of divine wrath (the tenor) in terms of drunkenness (the vehicle). The image pictures personified Moab as being made drunk "so that Moab claps in his own vomit and becomes a laughingstock."

The verb *spq* is difficult. Driver (1957: 61–62), followed by Holladay (1989: 360), suggests that it means "to overflow" on the basis of Aramaic and Syriac evidence. With this one may compare biblical Hebrew *śpq* II (Ringgren 1986b). In that case the phrase would be translated, "Moab will abound/overflow with his vomit." This is certainly possible and fits the context (cf. Isa 28:8).

However, the verb *spq* in the Hebrew Bible consistently denotes either "to slap" one's thighs (Jer 31:19; Ezek 21:17 [12]) or "to clap" one's hands (Num 24:10; Lam 2:15). This meaning fits here as well. One might take it in the sense of "slapping" one's thighs in helpless rage and disgust (Bright 1965: 321), but "clapping" one's hands seems more appropriate. To "clap" one's hands can connote arrogant mockery and derision (Lam 2:15; cf. Job 27:23; 34:37). In Lam 2:15 "to clap" parallels "to wag one's head" (*nwʿ*) in scoffing, which is similar to our text. The idea is that Moab "claps" his hands and "wags" (*nwd*) his head scornfully at Israel, but now Moab too will be derided. Moab will be made drunk so that as he continues to "clap" his hands he will do so in the midst of his own vomit. The statement has an ironic intent. While thinking to mock Israel, Moab ends up degrading itself and thus evoking scorn from others.

The text emphasizes three points. First, Moab is forcibly made to experience divine wrath and to experience it to the full. He is "made drunk" from the cup of Yahweh's wrath.

Second, Moab's experience of divine wrath consists of derision. As depicted by the image of disgustingly clapping hands in the midst of his own vomit, Moab degrades himself and becomes a laughingstock to others.

Third, based on the principle of *lex talionis*, the punishment corresponds with the crime. Verse 26 presents the punishment and v 27 the crime: Just as "Israel became a laughingstock" to Moab, so also Moab "will become a laughingstock" to others. The metaphor gives a powerful picture of poetic justice. Drunken Moab continues to deride Israel by clapping his hands but in his own disgusting vomit. In the very process of ridiculing Israel Moab evokes ridicule from others. By scornfully laughing at Israel, Moab "has made himself great against Yahweh," Israel's God. Therefore Moab will receive Yahweh's wrath.

9. Jeremiah 49:12.

For thus spoke Yahweh:
Look! Those whose right it was not to drink the cup
will certainly drink, and are you one to be exempt?
No, you will not be exempt, for you will certainly drink!

This verse, part of the section concerning Edom (49:7–22) and addressed to Edom, recalls the cup-of-wrath passage in 25:15–29. There the same terms and message are addressed to all the nations, including Edom (v 21). Since the verse presupposes acquaintance with Jer 25, the reader understands it metaphorically as referring to "the cup of wrath."

The text does not develop the image of drinking except to make the point that, unlike a normal cup that one is free to refuse, Edom must drink the cup. The emphasis lies on the necessity and inescapability of punishment for Edom.

The verse also states the reason why Edom is not exempt. The Jerusalemites must experience Yahweh's wrath, even though it is not "right" (*mišpāṭ*) that they need do so. The point is not that Jerusalem is undeserving of divine judgment or that Yahweh is unfair in executing his wrath. After all, the whole book of Jeremiah takes great pains to emphasize just the opposite. Rather, the verse makes the same point as 25:29: if Jerusalem, which should not have to undergo judgment because of its special status as Yahweh's own city and its covenant relationship with him, must receive divine wrath, certainly Edom with no such status must experience divine condemnation (cf. McConville 1993: 140–41). Thus the argument moves from the greater to the lesser.

10. Jeremiah 51:7–8.

v 7 Babylon was a gold cup in Yahweh's hand,
  making all the earth drunk.
  Of her wine the nations drank.
  Therefore the nations act crazed.
v 8 Suddenly Babylon fell and was broken.
  Wail over her!
  Take balm for her pain.
  Perhaps she will be healed.

The reader recognizes the metaphorical character of the text from the first line by its equation of Babylon with a gold cup. Since that cup is filled with wine and makes the nations drunk and mad, the reader naturally relates this text with chapter 25 and the cup-of-wrath metaphor. Much of the vocabulary matches the terms used in chapter 25 and confirms the connection: "cup" (25:15, 17, 28); "Yahweh's hand" (25:15, 17); "drunk" (25:27); "all the earth" (25:26, 29); "wine" (25:15); "drink" (25:16, 26–28); "nations" (25:15, 17); "act crazed" (25:16); and "fall" (25:27).

However, chapter 51 diverges from chapter 25 in significant respects. That Babylon is the cup, that the cup is gold, that it falls and breaks, and that the nations wail over it are differences which develop the metaphor in a unique way.

The image progresses in the following manner. A gold cup of wine makes all the nations drunk and mad. Suddenly the cup falls and breaks. Then the drunken nations wail and lament, because their source of wine and joy is gone. This image or vehicle of the metaphor leads the reader to gain insight into the metaphor's subject or tenor: Yahweh's wrathful judgment against the nations and against Babylon.

The text presents several features of the divine judgment. First, Yahweh inflicts a full measure of his wrath on the nations. The cup remains in Yahweh's hand so that he is the source of the punishment. And the cup makes all the earth drunk, indicating the compulsory imposition and the full extent of the divine wrath that the nations experience.

Second, Babylon is the instrument by which Yahweh executes his wrath upon the nations. Babylon's role was implied in chapter 25 (cf. 25:8–14), but here it is explicitly stated.

Third, after serving as Yahweh's instrument, Babylon itself is condemned by Yahweh (cf. 50:17–18; 51:49). In chapter 25 Babylon *drinks* the cup of wrath after the other nations (v 26; cf. 51:39, 57). Here the text develops the image differently. In contrast to 25:27 where the nations including Babylon "fall" because they are drunk, here Babylon *as the cup* "falls" and "breaks." Note the wordplay: the cup makes others "drunk" (*škr*) and then "breaks" (*šbr*; Bourguet 1987: 470). Not only does judgment happen to Babylon after the nations, but it happens "suddenly." Babylon does not expect it and cannot prepare for it. To push the image, it is as if Yahweh quickly dropped the cup after he had finished using it. With the verb "to break" the image also emphasizes the definitive and irreparable nature of Babylon's downfall. She "was broken" never to be restored. This aspect of her judgment is expanded in the second half of v 8 and in v 9, although with a different picture. The nations are encouraged to heal her deadly affliction but they are unable.

Finally, the nations find Babylon desirable. She is depicted as a "gold cup," a valuable and precious treasure that is highly esteemed by all (cf. 51:13, 41, 44). Even though the nations have been made subservient to Babylon by Yahweh's wrath, they still find life under her rule attractive.

Verse 8 expresses this idea vividly. The nations are exhorted, "Wail over her!" According to the image, the drunken nations weep because their source of wine is broken. But the metaphor goes farther. The cup/Babylon has made the conquered nations so drunk and delirious that they lament over fallen Babylon. They love their cruel master and cherish their prison of gold (Bourguet 1987: 471). The text uses a nice wordplay to reinforce the irony: The nations are so "crazed" (*ythll*) that they "wail" (*yll*) instead of "praise" (*hll*) Babylon's end (Bourguet 1987: 471). Unlike Jer 25:16 where the drunken nations "act crazed" (*hthll*) and thus lack the skill and wisdom necessary to defend themselves before enemy armies, in 51:7–8 the drunken nations express their insanity by lamenting cruel Babylon's downfall and attempting to heal her.

Located in the middle of a judgment oracle against Babylon (51:6–10), the passage serves two purposes. First, it supports the imperatives of v 6 and v 9. Because Babylon will suddenly fall, those exiled in her midst should flee lest they perish along with her (v 6). Even those exiles who insanely love Babylon and desire to rebuild her must leave her (v 9). Second, Babylon's definitive downfall means vindication and hope for conquered Israel (v 10).

11. Jeremiah 51:39 and 57.

v 39 While they are hot I will set out a feast for them,
 and I will make them drunk so that they exult;
 and they will sleep a perpetual sleep
 and not wake up — utterance of Yahweh.

v 57 I will make drunk her princes and her wise men,
 her governors and her prefects and her warriors;

and they will sleep a perpetual sleep
and not wake up — utterance of the King, whose name is Yahweh of
hosts.

Because of their similarities I will treat both verses together. One textual problem
should be noted. On the basis of the versions, some read *yĕʿullāpû* (they faint)
for MT *yaʿălōzû* (they exult) in v 39. Although the former reading is possible and
can be compared with Isa 51:20, the latter seems more probable (Barthélemy
1986: 849–50).

The metaphorical nature of these verses becomes evident from the reference
to Yahweh making the Babylonians drunk so that they sleep perpetually. The
reader recognizes the metaphor of the cup of wrath here in light of its other
occurrences in Jeremiah. Both verses depict the experience of divine wrath (the
subject) in terms of inebriety and its accompanying drowsiness (the symbol).

The first line of v 39 seems to relate to v 38. According to v 38, the Babylonians
"like lions roar," presumably over their prey (cf. Amos 3:4). Verse 39 then continues: While they are hot in rage and greed (*ḥmm*), ready to devour their prey, God
sets out a feast for them.

The picture clearly changes, however, since this is a feast for humans and not
animals. Yahweh makes them drunk so that they joyfully "exult" (*ʿlz*). Much like
Lam 4:21, the reference to joy is used as sarcasm and irony. Instead of weeping,
which is the expected response to impending judgment, they foolishly rejoice in
ignorance of what awaits them.

What awaits them is a sleep, but a unique kind of sleep. Unlike the normal
sleep of drunkards, from which they awaken after regaining sobriety, both texts
emphasize that this is a "perpetual sleep" from which they will never awaken.
The image indicates that Yahweh gives the Babylonians a full measure of his
wrath with the result that they perish forever. It functions as a judgment oracle
against Babylon, which is intended to give hope to Zion (vv 35–37).

12. Ezekiel 23:31–34.

v 31 In the path of your sister you walked,
     so I will put her cup into your hand.
v 32 Thus spoke the Lord Yahweh:
     Your sister's cup you will drink,
     a deep and wide one.
     It will become an object of laughter and derision,
     containing much.
v 33 With drunkenness and sorrow you will be filled.
     A cup of horror and devastation
     is the cup of your sister Samaria.
v 34 And you will drink it and drain (it),
     and its sherds you will gnaw,

and your breasts you will lacerate.
For I have spoken — utterance of the Lord Yahweh.

Although the *BHS* apparatus suggests a number of text-critical options for this unit, the MT appears to be in good shape (cf. Barthélemy 1992: 195–97). However, one compelling variant occurs in v 32. Following the LXX and Symmachus one should probably read a feminine *hip'il* participle *marbâ* for the MT's *hapax* noun *mirbâ*, but the meaning remains the same in either case.

Verse 31 connects the following "song of the cup" with the previous divine speech of vv 28–30. Consequently, vv 32–34 continue the personification of Jerusalem as a woman addressed by Yahweh, and they further depict the disgrace she will experience for her harlotry.

The reference to Yahweh putting a cup into her hand in v 31 causes the reader to relate the passage to the cup-of-wrath metaphor. That she drinks and drains the cup (v 34) and becomes drunk (v 33) confirms the connection. It also distinguishes this metaphor from the figurative use of "cup" as one's allotted destiny.

The metaphor describes the punishment Jerusalem will receive in terms of drinking a wine cup. The passage includes several commonplaces associated with this image: a cup that is passed from hand to hand, drinking and draining the cup, and intoxication. However, the passage also exaggerates some of the image's associated commonplaces. According to v 32, the cup is so huge, so abnormally "deep and wide," and it contains so much wine that others laugh at its enormity. (The verb *tihyeh* in v 32 should be taken as a third person feminine construed with *kôs*, "cup," rather than as an inexplicable switch to a second person masculine addressed to Jerusalem. The text consistently employs the feminine gender for Jerusalem.) Furthermore, her gnawing the cup's sherds and lacerating her breasts push the image of a drunken woman to the extreme.

The text progresses in a fairly logical manner. First, Yahweh takes the cup from Jerusalem's sister Samaria and puts it into Jerusalem's hand (v 31). Then v 32 describes the enormous size of the cup.

In v 33 symbol and literal reality are mixed together. In keeping with the symbol v 33 says that she "will be filled with drunkenness" (cf. Jer 13:13), due to the cup's immensity. Yet the next word subverts the image. Instead of the joy and gladness that normally result from drinking much wine, she will be filled with "sorrow." The noun *yāgôn* together with its cognates denotes inner anguish and emotional grief, the opposite of joy (cf. Isa 35:10; 51:11; Jer 31:13; Prov 10:1; 17:21; Esth 9:22). Although the next sentence continues the image by mentioning the cup, it focuses attention on the literal level; this is "a cup of *horror and devastation*." In view here is not Jerusalem as a woman but Jerusalem as a city, parallel to Samaria. (The words *šammâ* and *šĕmāmâ* usually refer to cities, buildings, and lands that are laid waste.) Now the reader knows why Jerusalem the woman will lament in "sorrow"; it is because, like Samaria, Jerusalem the city will be devastated. By using a genitive construction the phrase "a cup of horror and devastation" brings together as tightly as possible the symbol and the reality. It is very similar to the expression "cup of wrath."

The final verse reverts back to the image: Lady Jerusalem will drink the cup and drain it to the dregs. The last two lines form a startling and shocking conclusion to the passage. The verb *grm* (*pi'el*) is a denominative of *gerem*, "bone," and apparently means "to gnaw bones" (cf. Num 24:8; Zeph 3:3; Ball [1988: 155–59] argues that in Zephaniah it denotes "to have strength"). Drunken Jerusalem is so intent on draining the cup to the last drop that she even "gnaws" on the sherds after the cup is broken, or she is in such torment and pain that she "bites" the sherds. Furthermore, she uses the cup's sherds to "lacerate" (*ntq*) her breasts. This last line takes the image to the extreme. It pictures her as so drunk and in such pain that she cuts and tears her breasts. One is reminded of suffering Job who scrapes his sores with a potsherd (Job 2:7–8). Recall also that making cuts and gashes was a sign of lamentation and mourning (Jer 16:6). Thus the line expresses her stupor and deep grief.

Nevertheless, it expresses more by echoing and responding to the picture developed earlier in Ezek 23. Jerusalem and Samaria are portrayed as two women who, although they belonged to Yahweh, played the harlot in Egypt and allowed their breasts to be handled (vv 2–4, 21). They lewdly flaunted their nakedness as they went after their lovers, the Assyrians and Babylonians. Now in response to her harlotry Yahweh's cup of wrath causes Jerusalem to "lacerate" her breasts. In fact, the verb *těnattěqî* carries a stronger sense: with the cup's sherds she "tears out" her breasts (cf. Ezek 17:9). Thereby her lovers will no longer be able to fondle her nor will they want to. Instead they will abhor her.

By means of the symbol of a cup of wine, Ezekiel's "song of the cup" presents several perspectives on the nature of Jerusalem's future punishment. First, Yahweh punishes Jerusalem as he punished Samaria. He puts Samaria's cup into Jerusalem's hand because Jerusalem emulated Samaria. Divine speech formulas bracket the text in order to emphasize that Yahweh is the one who condemns. Second, Jerusalem experiences divine wrath to the full. Her cup is "deep and wide," so huge that others laugh at it, a cup that contains much. Lady Jerusalem drains this large cup to the last drop so that she is filled with drunkenness. Third, divine wrath gives Jerusalem deep anguish and grief. Instead of the joy that usually comes from wine, she is filled with "sorrow." Implied here is the unexpected and surprising nature of what awaits her. Finally, Jerusalem becomes an object of derision and abhorrence, which is already implied in v 32. Although grammatically the cup is what becomes "an object of laughter and derision" because of its size, the reader naturally thinks also of Jerusalem. Verse 34 drives the point home; not only does Lady Jerusalem disgrace herself by baring her breasts, she also makes herself repugnant and repulsive by lacerating her breasts. The idea is that she brings upon herself her own punishment (cf. vv 29–30, 35).

Ezekiel's portrayal of Jerusalem is quite offensive and intentionally so. It undoubtedly shocked the original hearers/readers as much as it shocks us today. The repulsiveness of Jerusalem's fate matches that of her degenerate harlotry as depicted by the rest of the chapter. The radical imagery served to elicit contempt for Jerusalem's behavior and agreement with the justice of the sentence. As Hals (1989: 169) notes:

> To reach the end of this account and hear the fate of this degenerate tramp is to be moved to say, "How else could it end!" This is indeed the well-deserved fate of a psycho-social misfit whose behavior was as deliberate as it was disgusting. That is the perspective of a doxology of judgment, but carried to an extreme never before known.

13. Obadiah 16.

For just as you have drunk on my holy mountain,
(so) all the nations will drink continually;
they will drink and slurp,
and they will be as if they had never been.

The last line makes the metaphorical character of the "drinking" evident, that of drinking the cup of wrath. (For details, see the Notes and Comment.)

The verse employs the image of drinking to stress three points. First, there is a correspondence between the fates of Judah/Jerusalem ("you" plural) and of all the nations. Both parties "drink" the cup; the same divine wrath is experienced by both groups. Second, the experience of divine punishment moves from Zion in the past to all the nations in the future on "the day of Yahweh" (v 15). Third, although there is a correspondence, there is also a difference. Unlike Zion's temporary experience of judgment, the nations will undergo it "continually" until they cease to exist as nations, until their power is of no more consequence. In contrast, Zion becomes the place of "escape" from divine wrath on the day of Yahweh's universal judgment (v 17).

14. Habakkuk 2:15–16.

v 15 Woe to the one giving his neighbors to drink,
    mixing in your wrath,
    and even making (them) drunk
    in order to gaze on their nakedness.
v 16 You are satiated with shame rather than glory.
    Drink, also you, and expose your uncircumcision!
    The cup of Yahweh's right hand will come around upon you,
    and putrid shame upon your glory.

There are two text-critical problems worth noting here. (For a thorough discussion, see Barthélemy 1992: 849–55.) Various alternatives have been proposed for the MT *mĕsappēaḥ* (mixing in) in the second line of v 15, a *pi'el* participle of *sph*, "to associate, join together." The ancient versions attest to the consonants *msph* but differ in their interpretation of the *mem*. Some take it as the prefix of a noun and others as the preposition *min* (from). Acceptable sense can be made of the MT's *pi'el* participle, with which Symmachus, the Vulgate, and the Targum agree. The oscillation between third person pronouns ("his neighbors") and second person pronouns ("your wrath") is fairly common in woe oracles (Hillers 1983).

In v 16 instead of MT *hē'ārēl*, a *nip'al* imperative of *'rl* (expose your uncircumcision or be uncircumcised), Qumran's Habakkuk commentary in conformity with some ancient versions reads *hērā'ēl*, a *nip'al* imperative of *r'l* (stagger). However, in the commentary itself it refers to the wicked priest who "did not circumcise the foreskin of his heart" (Brownlee 1979: 190), and this seems to support the MT. Other cup-of-wrath texts can be adduced as parallels for each reading: for "expose your uncircumcision," similar ideas occur in Ezek 23:34 and Lam 4:21; for "stagger," see Isa 51:17, 22 and Ps 60:5 [3]. The difference between the two readings is simply a metathesis of ' and *r* and both readings fit, making a decision difficult. However, the MT gives stronger support to the talionic standard of judgment expressed in the passage and elsewhere in the woes (cf. 2:7–8, 17). Perhaps the passage uses *'rl* instead of *'rh* (*hitpa'el* — "to show oneself naked") in order to evoke *r'l* (to stagger).

Verse 15 begins the fourth woe in a series of five (Hab 2:6–20). The woes constitute the taunts spoken by the oppressed to their arrogant and wicked oppressor, whose identity is left unspecified (vv 5–6). On the basis of vv 5b, 8, 10, 13, and 17, most commentators consider the antagonist to be Nebuchadnezzar or the Babylonians in general, although Haak (1992) argues for Jehoiakim and his Egyptian and Assyrian supporters (at least until Assyria's demise). In any case, this woe condemns the oppressor for maliciously disgracing others.

Verse 15 progresses line by line with an intensification of assertion. It begins by addressing the one who gives his neighbors (*rē'ēhû* is collective) to drink. But the next line indicates that this is no innocent token of friendship and hospitality. He "mixes in" (*sph*) and joins to the drink his own wrath; his hateful anger lies hidden in this seemingly innocent gesture (cf. Isa 14:6).

The third line advances the action. Not only does he give his neighbors a drink but he even "makes (them) drunk" (*šakkēr* — *pi'el* infinitive absolute). The initial word *wĕ'ap* is ambiguous and maybe deliberately so. The woes are introduced as being "proverbs, taunts, and riddles" (v 6) so that the reader expects to find puns, wordplays, and elusive enigmas. The reader at first understands *'ap* as simply the intensifying particle, "he gives his neighbors to drink . . . *and even* makes (them) drunk." However, since it immediately follows *hēmâ* (wrath), *'ap* might be the noun "anger." This would yield the sense "mixing in your wrath and *in anger* making drunk." Perhaps it is a case of deliberate lexical ambiguity (cf. Raabe 1991: 214–17).

The fourth line gives the purpose for the intoxicating. He angrily inebriates his neighbors "in order to gaze on their nakedness." Not only does he expose their nakedness but he haughtily gloats over it and thereby shames and humiliates them (cf. Gen 9:20–23; Lev 20:17; Nah 3:5).

For the proud and cruel antagonist who attempts to exalt himself by degrading others, the punishment fits the crime. The first line of v 16 reveals the irony of the judgment: "You are satiated with shame rather than glory." The one who made others drunk is himself "satiated," and the one who sought to proudly magnify himself is instead saturated "with shame rather than glory." With two imperatives the next line intensifies the ironic reversal. The oppressor is commanded to "drink" just as his neighbors were forced to do. And just as he desired to gloat over their nakedness in their inebriated condition, so also he, himself inebriated, must reveal his own nakedness (cf. Lam 4:21). In fact, his disgrace is twofold: he must expose himself and his uncircumcision.

So far the reader does not have to understand the passage metaphorically. But that changes with the next line. Its reference to "the cup of Yahweh's right hand" causes the reader to relate v 16 to the cup of wrath. Again, the emphasis lies on the correspondence between sin and punishment. Just as the oppressor makes others drink the cup of his own wrath, so he must drink the cup of Yahweh's wrath. If the Babylonians are the primary referent here, the line might imply more (cf. Roberts 1991: 124–25). Yahweh uses the Babylonians as his instrument in bringing his wrath cup to Judah (1:5–11; cf. Jer 51:7). But because they mix in their own wrath, Yahweh's wrath cup will "come around" upon them. For a similar idea, see Isa 10:5–19.

With this cup comes a disgrace that goes beyond that which the proud inflicts on others: "and putrid shame (will come around) upon your glory." The noun *qîqālôn* is a *hapax*. Apparently it was coined to intensify the idea of shame. As noted earlier, one expects to find paronomasia in this section of woes, and *qyqlwn* might be one such example. The first syllable *qî* evokes the noun *qî'*, "vomit." Therefore *qîqālôn* can be taken as an intensifying formation of *qālôn* (used in v 16a), which also evokes the combination *qî' qālôn*, "vomit of shame" (cf. *'abṭîṭ*, "pledges/cloud of mud," in v 6). The line would then mean "deep shame and shameful vomit will come around upon your glory" (cf. Jer 48:26).

Through the vehicle of an intoxicating cup, the passage sets forth two features associated with the biblical portrayal of divine punishment. First, the judgment comes from Yahweh. It is not some mechanical and impersonal sin-consequence operation. Yahweh controls the judgment; he targets the recipients; the cup is in his right hand. Second, although there is no autonomously working sin-consequence mechanism, there is a correspondence between sin and punishment. The punishment is appropriate to the crime and illustrates the talionic standard of justice. Here the metaphor of the cup of wrath is particularly appropriate for conveying the poetic justice involved. The intoxicaters become intoxicated; those motivated by their own wrath receive divine wrath; and those arrogantly humiliating others become humiliated. The aspect of the drinking image emphasized the most is the disgrace that comes with drunkenness. What this image can convey perhaps better than others is self-degradation. It is not as if the proud passively receive disgrace. Rather, divine judgment forces them to disgrace themselves just as drunkards vomit and expose their own nakedness.

The passage occurs in a series of woes that function as mocking taunts addressed to the oppressor by the victims. The intention is to give hope to the Judahites who currently or soon will suffer unjustly (2:3–4) and to call the wicked oppressors to bow in silence before Yahweh (2:20).

GENERAL OBSERVATIONS

The fourteen texts we have discussed comprise the "cup-of-wrath" group. Although the genitive construction "cup of wrath" occurs only in Isa 51:17–23, the phrase provides a convenient label to designate the group (cf. "this cup of wine, which is wrath" in Jer 25:15). These texts present the reader with a truly profound and rich metaphor.

A metaphor by definition brings together into one view two different realities. It depicts one thing, the subject or tenor, in terms more commonly associated with a different thing, the symbol or vehicle, which is analogous to the subject in some respects. In this group the subject is Yahweh's "wrath" (ḥēmâ), to which every text refers either explicitly or implicitly. More precisely, the metaphor's subject is the human experience of suffering under divine wrath. The symbol or vehicle used to depict this subject is that of drinking wine from a cup. It is not so much the cup per se as it is the wine with its deleterious effects that is analogous to the experience of wrath.

The reader marvels at the multifaceted richness of the image, one that provides the biblical authors with an ample source for developing the metaphor. Each text works the symbol in its own way. Some texts focus on the large amount of wine to be drunk, others on the state of drunken stupor, and still others on the sleep or disgrace that accompanies inebriation.

When studied together this group of texts gives the reader an insight into the Hebrew Bible's understanding of the workings of divine wrath. To be sure, one should include other texts if one wants to gain a total panoramic view of the biblical portrayal of Yahweh's wrath. Our metaphor does not tell the whole story regarding the indignation of Yahweh. (For discussions, see Baloian 1992; Herion 1992; Peels 1995.) For example, some texts speak of Yahweh "pouring out his wrath," which carries an entirely different set of associations and connotations. But the metaphor of "drinking the cup of wrath" makes its own — albeit limited — contribution that is worthy of study.

The metaphor offers a "from below" depiction of divine judgment. It shows how the experience of divine wrath is a human experience that affects the whole person, one's thoughts, emotions, and behavior. It answers questions such as:

What is it like to experience Yahweh's wrath? How does it feel to suffer under divine displeasure? The wrath of Yahweh is a rather intangible concept that cannot easily be described in a straightforward and literal manner. Therefore the symbol of becoming drunk from wine offers the hearer or reader a tangible and concrete reality that can be seen, felt, and tasted. Therein lies the power and impact of the metaphor.

How do these texts depict divine punishment and the way it affects people? The following discussion will summarize the key points.

1. The wrath these texts speak of is the wrath of Yahweh. It belongs to him; he executes it and he controls it. It is not some irrational and impersonal force that works independently of him or a mechanical and immanent sin-consequence process. The cup of wrath always comes from Yahweh's hand. And he remains personally involved by targeting the recipients and determining how long they experience it.

   A few texts reveal that Yahweh employs agents such as prophets and nations to execute his wrath. According to Jer 25, the prophet passes the cup from nation to nation, which signifies that the prophetic word not only announces judgment but itself executes it. According to Jer 48:26, other nations administer the judgment; they make Moab drunk. And Jer 51:7 equates Babylon with the cup that makes all the earth drunk. But Yahweh still oversees and governs the whole process by commanding Jeremiah and the nations to do his bidding.

2. Except for the faithful Israelites who lament in Psalm 60:5 [3], the recipients of the divine punishment are always considered to be the deserving. Their sins are either explicitly stated in the passage or indicated by the context. Those targeted to receive judgment include: all the wicked (Ps 75:9 [8]; Job 21:19–20); all the nations (Isa 63:6; Jer 25:15–29; 51:7; Obad 16); Moab (Jer 48:26); Edom (Lam 4:21; Jer 49:12); Babylon (Isa 51:23; Jer 51:8, 39, 57); Samaria (Ezek 23:31, 33); and Jerusalem (Isa 51:17–22; Ezek 23:32–34; Obad 16). In every text except two the recipient is a collective, a group of peoples/nations or a single nation or city. Job 21:20 and Hab 2:15–16 alone target an individual: for Job, any wicked person, and for Hab 2, the oppressor.

3. Significantly, many texts indicate that Yahweh's wrath cup begins with Jerusalem, referring to the fall of the city. From Jerusalem the cup passes to all the nations (Jer 25:15–29; Obad 16) including Moab (Jer 48:26–27), Edom (Jer 49:12; Lam 4:21–22), and finally Babylon (Isa 51:17–23; Jer 25:26; 51:7–8; Hab 2:15–16?). The nations are condemned either because of their non-elect status as *gôyīm* — unlike Jerusalem that bears Yahweh's name — or their hostility to Jerusalem. Yet the image of a cup being passed

around is particularly appropriate for conveying the idea that the nations suffer under the same wrath of Yahweh as does Jerusalem.

4. The image of drinking the cup points to the full amount of divine wrath that the recipients experience. They do not receive just a little bit of punishment; they receive it to the full extent. Almost every text emphasizes this point. The recipients drain the cup filled with Yahweh's wrath down to the dregs and become drunk. Ezekiel 23 pictures the cup as deep and wide, so huge and containing so much that others laugh at it.

5. When Yahweh's wrath comes, it is irresistible and unstoppable. Yahweh forcibly imposes his judgment on the recipients from which there is no escape. He puts the cup in their hand and makes them drink. Unlike a normal cup that one is free to refuse, this cup they may not and cannot refuse; they must drink it. Once they start drinking they cannot stop. The wine is full of enticing spices (Ps 75:9 [8]). Practically all the texts state that they drain it to the bottom or become drunk from it. Only Yahweh can stop the experience and remove the cup (Isa 51:22).

6. When the recipients experience divine wrath, they become totally help-less and defenseless. According to Isa 51, drunken Jerusalem staggers in confusion. She cannot restore herself nor can her children support and help her. In fact, no one can even comfort her. Jeremiah 25 emphasizes that the nations become drunk and confused from before the sword that Yahweh sends; they become incapable of defending themselves before hostile armies. Here divine judgment seems to be a two-step process: Yah-weh's wrath first makes them helpless and then he smites them with a sword. According to Jer 51:7–8, divine wrath, administered by Babylon, stupefied the nations to such an extent that they insanely cherish subjuga-tion to Babylon.

7. Divine wrath puts a permanent end to the nations. The drunken nations fall, never to rise again (Jer 25:27), and inebriated Babylon sleeps a perpet-ual sleep from which it will never wake up (Jer 51:39, 57). These texts carry the image beyond its normal associations. Unlike ordinary inebriety in which a drunkard later regains sobriety and awakens, this drunkenness causes a perpetual sleep. Obadiah 16 extends the idea even further: ". . . they will be as if they had never been."

8. Yahweh's judgment brings open and public disgrace to its recipients. Drunken Moab, who gloats over Israel by clapping his hands, ends up clapping in the midst of his own vomit, and thereby becomes a laughing-stock (Jer 48:26–27). Instead of boasting and rejoicing over fallen Jerusa-lem, proud Edom gets drunk and exposes her nakedness, which means that her sins are exposed (Lam 4:21–22). So also Judah's oppressor be-

comes debased; he exposes his own uncircumcision and his glory is covered by shameful vomit (Hab 2:15–16). The most radical statement occurs in Ezek 23:34, where drunken Jerusalem, portrayed in chapter 23 as a prostitute, lacerates her breasts and becomes repugnant to her lovers. All of these passages indicate a reversal of fortunes. Instead of their joyful arrogance and honored position, they receive degradation and abasement. This leads to the next point.

9. Often a passage reveals a correspondence between the crime and the punishment (cf. Miller 1982). It is not as if the judgment is totally alien and foreign to the sin. Divine judgment operates on the basis of *lex talionis*; as you have done, it will be done to you. The mockers become mocked; the tormentors become tormented; the proud become humiliated; and those who make others drink the cup with their own wrath mixed in drink it themselves. In this regard Jer 51:7–8 is unique. Babylon, the cup in Yahweh's hand that makes the earth drunk, does not drink but, being the cup itself, falls and breaks. Divine justice is depicted as poetic justice.

10. Finally, the texts express a paradox in the workings of divine wrath. On the one hand, as mentioned above, it is Yahweh's wrath that is involved. He executes his wrath, targets its recipients, and determines its duration. Yahweh puts the cup into the recipients' hands; they do not freely take it from him. On the other hand, the wicked bring it down upon themselves and cause their own demise. They themselves drink and drain the cup; they become drunk, expose their own nakedness, and clap in their own vomit. Jerusalem lacerates her own breasts. The image of a cup of wine that intoxicates is especially apt for expressing this paradox.

The above points summarize the key insights into the biblical view of the workings of divine wrath that one gains from the metaphor of the cup of wrath. One marvels at the wide variety of ways that it is developed and applied. It is also used in a number of different genres: laments and complaints (Ps 60; Job 21); warnings (Ps 75); woes (Hab 2); judgment oracles against the nations (Isa 63; Jer 25; 48; 49; 51; Obad 16; Lam 4); a judgment oracle against Jerusalem (Ezek 23); and a promise for Zion (Isa 51).

However, the number of ways the metaphor rhetorically functions are relatively few. Usually it forms part of an announcement of impending doom against Jerusalem or the nations. When so used it calls the recipients of judgment to humbly bow in submission before Yahweh's justice and to acknowledge the appropriateness of their punishment. It does not seem to function as a call to repentance so as to avoid judgment, although occasionally that might be implied (e.g., Ps 75:9 [8]). Of course, for the biblical writers, Yahweh always has the freedom to "repent" and change his course of action. (On divine repentance, see the discussions in Andersen and Freedman 1989: 638–79; Fretheim 1988). According to the emphasis repeatedly made in our texts, however, the addressees should not delude themselves into thinking that some action or strength on their part, such as military defenses and political alliances, can exempt them from the impending doom. Rather, by using this metaphor the writers attempt to convince them that the judgment coming upon them is certain, necessary, unavoidable, and just. Furthermore, when judgment is proclaimed against the nations, the metaphor also intends to give suffering Zion hope of vindication. In Ps 60 and Job 21 it functions differently. Psalm 60:5 [3] includes the metaphor in a lament and a complaint that seeks to persuade Yahweh to stop his wrath and restore suffering Israel. In Job 21:19–20 it forms part of Job's complaint against God's injustice, which is designed to convince his friends of the justness of his complaint.

THE ORIGIN OF THE CUP OF WRATH

Numerous attempts have been made to identify an origin for the cup-of-wrath metaphor. For discussions of some of the views, see Brongers (1969) and McKane (1980). Generally they fall into four categories.

1. *An Ordeal Procedure.* Many posit the source to be a drinking ordeal such as described in Num 5:11–31 (cf. Exod 32:20). Van der Toorn (1988) isolates a group of Psalms that in his view have their *Sitz im Leben* in a nocturnal drinking ordeal (cf. also Schmidt 1934: 144). However, apart from Num 5, there are at best scant allusions to such a drinking trial in the Hebrew Bible. A problem with the Num 5 connection is that the ordeal prescribes treated water and not wine. Also Num 5 describes a trial whose primary purpose is to establish guilt or innocence and not to execute the penalty on the guilty, although that ensues.

2. *A Cultic Ritual.* Ringgren (1953), whose view is discussed by Brongers and McKane, attempts to relate the cup of wrath to the hypothesis of a drunk god-king during a New Year's Festival. However, the existence of such a ritual is quite dubious.

3. *A Cup of the Gods.* Dahood (1965: 89) points to a painted pitcher found at Ras Shamra that shows a seated god with a cup in his right hand. The identity of the god is El, the banquet giver, according to the texts found nearby. A. T. Hanson (1957: 28–29) cites other Ugaritic texts that speak of a cup of the gods, and Brongers (1969) refers to Mesopotamian parallels. However, nowhere is mention made of a "cup of wrath."

4. *A Cup of Poison.* According to Gruber (1980: 513–50), "poison, venom" is the primary sense of *ḥēmâ*, and "wrath" is only its secondary, derivative sense. Therefore he suggests that *kôs haḥēmâ* means "cup of poison" and that behind the image lies the practice of "capital punishment by means of a draught of poison" (p. 521). Two considerations call the hypothesis into

question. First, although *ḥēmâ* occasionally denotes "poison, venom" in the Hebrew Bible, it is doubtful that the noun has this sense in as many texts as Gruber cites (cf. Schunck 1980; *HALAT*). Second, *ḥēmâ* designates the subject of the metaphor and not its symbol or image. The latter is clearly "wine" (Pss 60:5 [3]; 75:9 [8]; Isa 51:21; Jer 25:15; 51:7). For example, Jer 25:15 juxtaposes the image and the subject, "this cup of wine, which is *haḥēmâ*" (cf. Jer 23:19). If *ḥēmâ* denotes "poison" here, then the phrase would juxtapose two different symbols (wine and poison) but what would be the metaphor's subject? More likely, *ḥēmâ* in Isa 51:17, 22 and Jer 25:15 denotes "wrath." Note the parallelism in Isa 51:20, "they are full of the *wrath* [*ḥēmâ*] of Yahweh, of the *rebuke* of your God," and the words construed with "cup" in Ezek 23:33, "A cup of *horror* and *devastation*."

None of these suggested sources gives a perfect or even close parallel to the way the Hebrew Bible speaks of the cup of wrath. There is a methodological problem with all such attempts to find an origin to "the cup of wrath" and it is a fundamental one. They all assume there is one single source behind this idiom, be it institutional or cultic or ideological. Ringgren (1966: 78) illustrates the assumption when he says, "Obviously some concrete reality must lie behind such a metaphorical expression; but unfortunately we are ignorant of any practice, secular or cultic, that could explain this mode of expression, either in Israel or in the neighboring religions."

My contention is that "drinking the cup of wrath" is a literary metaphor and should be treated as such (cf. Hillers 1972: 93). A metaphor by definition brings into one view two distinctly different realities. One can discover a single institutional origin no more for "the cup of wrath" than for "the broom of destruction" (Isa 14:23). Therefore to seek the source and background of a metaphor would entail seeking the source and background of the metaphor's subject and of its symbol. That might be difficult to do when it comes to its subject of Yahweh's wrath, but for its symbol or vehicle the background is clear, that of drinking wine from a cup and becoming drunk.

Finally, the reader might wonder who created this metaphor. Most scholars rank Hab 2 and Jer 25 as the earliest texts to use it, but a good case can be made for Ps 60 and Ps 75. Yet perhaps the question wrongly assumes that there must be one creative genius behind it all. A given metaphor often forms part of the speech patterns and working idioms of a society. It "happens" when a person (or persons) sees a similarity between two different realities (cf. Ricoeur 1977), and usually it is impossible to identify the one person who first saw the similarity. "Drinking the cup of wrath" might be such a case. In any case, it certainly became a popular metaphor, especially around the time of Jerusalem's fall to Babylon. It also appears in the New Testament (cf. Travis 1992), notably in the Garden of Gethsemane scene — although there is some debate whether the passages refer to the cup of wrath — (Matt 26:39, 42; Mark 14:36; Luke 22:42; John 18:11) and in the Revelation to John (14:10; 16:19; 18:6).

NOTES

v. 17. *ûběhar ṣiyyôn tihyeh pělêṭâ.*
But on Mount Zion will be escape.

A disjunctive *waw* introduces the clause so as to set up a contrast with the preceding verse. While the nations will drink the cup of wrath on the future day of Yahweh, Mount Zion will not have to drink it again. Rather it will be the place of "escape" from the coming wrath.

The subject of the verb *tihyeh* is the feminine noun *pělêṭâ*. The noun, from the root *plṭ*, "to escape" (cf. v 14), occurs 28 times in Biblical Hebrew and has two distinct senses. When it is definite or refers to people, it has a concrete denotation, "what has escaped, remnant" (Judg 21:17; 2 Kgs 19:30–31 = Isa 37:31–32; Isa 4:2; 10:20; 15:9; Ezek 14:22; Ezra 9:8, 13–15; Neh 1:2; 1 Chr 4:43; 2 Chr 30:6). But when it is indefinite and otherwise unqualified, as is the case in Obad 17, it has an abstract denotation, "escape, deliverance" (Gen 45:7; 2 Sam 15:14; Jer 25:35; 50:29; Joel 2:3; 3:5 [2:32]; 2 Chr 12:7; 20:24; cf. KB; *HALAT*).

Significantly Joel 3:5 [2:32] cites Obad 17:

kî běhar ṣiyyôn ûbîrûšālayim tihyeh pělêṭâ
ka'ăšer 'āmar yahweh

"For on Mount Zion and in Jerusalem will be escape,
as Yahweh has said."

Like Obadiah, Joel sets the deliverance in Zion within the context of the terrible "day of Yahweh."

wěhāyâ qōdeš
and (on Mount Zion) will be a holy place.

The syntax is difficult. Most translations and commentaries assume that *har ṣiyyôn* (Mount Zion) is the subject: "and *it* will be holy." Also the LXX and the Vulgate translate the clause this way. The Targum renders it with more of a paraphrase: "and they [the survivors on Mount Zion] will be holy." The parallel in Joel 4:17 [3:17] at first appears to support the usual translation:

wěhāyětâ yěrûšālayim qōdeš

"and Jerusalem will be a holy place."

However, the syntax of the Joel passage is notably different from that of Obad 17. In Joel "Jerusalem" is explicitly made the subject of the verb, but in Obadiah "Mount Zion" is embedded in a prepositional phrase (*běhar ṣiyyôn*) and therefore an unlikely candidate for the subject. It is more natural to take *qōdeš* as the subject of *wĕhāyâ*, just as *pĕlêṭâ* is the subject of *tihyeh*. Then both cola follow the standard Hebrew word order, verb + subject. (Note that also in v 18 the subject follows the verb *wĕhāyâ*.) The prepositional phrase applies to both cola, creating syntactic parallelism:

> But on Mount Zion will be escape,
> and (on Mount Zion) will be a holy place [*qōdeš*].

Thus v 17 asserts that two realities will exist on Mount Zion, "escape" and *qōdeš*.

What does the noun *qōdeš* mean here? It belongs to the *quṭl* noun class, which usually indicates an abstract. When it is the genitive of a construct chain it functions adjectivally, as in v 16: *har qodšî*, "my holy mountain." When it stands independently it is often rendered "holiness." However, Levine (1987) persuasively argues that only in the context of oaths taken by God does it bear an abstract sense (e.g., Amos 4:2). Elsewhere it denotes something identifiable and concrete, such as "holy place" or "holy thing." The same concrete meaning applies also to the related Ugaritic noun *qdš*. Therefore in both Joel 4:17 [3:17] and Obad 17 *qōdeš* should be translated "holy place."

In light of Obadiah's historical context following the Babylonian destruction of the temple, Obad 17 probably implies its future rebuilding. Note that *qōdeš* without the definite article can occasionally designate the temple (Ps 134:2; Dan 8:13–14). What will give Mount Zion its sanctity then is the presence of the Holy One of Israel in the temple.

By pointing to Zion's future sanctity Obadiah provides a prophetic response to exilic prayers that lament Zion's desecration:

> We are put to shame, for we have heard reproach;
> dishonor has covered our face.
> For strangers have come
> against the holy places of Yahweh's house. (Jer 51:51)

> Your foes have roared in the midst of your meeting place . . .
> They have set your sanctuary on fire;
> to the ground they have profaned the dwelling place of your name. (Ps 74:4, 7)

> O God, the nations have entered your inheritance;
> they have defiled your holy temple;
> they have turned Jerusalem into ruins. (Ps 79:1)

> The foe has stretched out his hand
> for all her [Jerusalem's] precious things.
> For she has seen the nations
> enter her sanctuary,
> concerning whom you had commanded:
> "They should not enter your assembly." (Lam 1:10; cf. 1:17; 2:15–16, 20)

wĕyārĕšû bêt yaʿăqōb ʾēt môrāšêhem.
The house of Jacob will possess their own possessions.
The *waw* consecutive verb continues the sequence begun with *tihyeh*. The phrase "the house of Jacob," a collective that takes a plural verb, designates the descendants of the patriarch Jacob. "House" is often used to denote a body of descendants (BDB). The mention of "Jacob" recalls its use in v 10. The phrase has an inclusive intention, denoting the whole nation and not only Judah. Most of its twenty-one occurrences in their contexts clearly indicate this inclusive intention and none of them necessitates limiting it to either the south or the north (cf. Andersen and Freedman 1989: 103–4, 124–25, 130). In Gen 46:27 "the house of Jacob" includes both Jacob's direct descendants and those of Joseph, all seventy who went down to Egypt. In Exod 19:3 the phrase designates the whole people gathered at Sinai. Elsewhere it appears only in the Latter Prophets and once in the Psalter (Isa 2:5, 6; 8:17; 10:20; 14:1; 29:22; 46:3; 48:1; 58:1; Jer 2:4; 5:20; Ezek 20:5; Amos 3:13; 9:8; Obad 17, 18; Mic 2:7; 3:9; Ps 114:1).

Obad 18 pairs "the house of Jacob" with "the house of Joseph":

The house of Jacob will become fire,
and the house of Joseph, flame,
and the house of Esau, stubble . . .

Most commentators assume that the pair provides a case of merismus, which parallels the south with the north and thus joins together two different groups. In this instance "the house of Jacob" would refer to Judah. It is better, however, to understand the parallelism in a different way. "The house of Jacob" is an inclusive term for all of Jacob's descendants. But since at the time of Obadiah in the sixth century the hearers/readers might have assumed that only the Judahites left in the land deserved the title, Obadiah made a special point of including the northern tribes (the house of Joseph). Thus the parallelism moves from the general and comprehensive to one noteworthy part. The relationship is one of inclusivity and not of addition. The metaphor supports this understanding. It is not as if "fire" and "flame" represent two different elements that together create a larger blaze. On the contrary, "the house of Jacob" as fire includes "the house of Joseph" as part of the fire, i.e., as "flame." Note that in Gen 46:27 Joseph's line comprises part of "the house of Jacob."

The verb *yrš* in the *qal* (160 occurrences) has three major uses (see Lohfink 1990; BDB).

1. When the verb occurs in familial contexts, it denotes "to become a legal successor, inherit" (cf. Gen 15:3–4; 21:10; Num 27:11; 2 Sam 14:7; Prov 30:23).

2. When the object is people, especially in Deuteronomistic usage, the verb is usually translated "to dispossess." "Here by right of conquest one people or nation succeeds another in ruling over a territory" (Lohfink 1990: 371; cf. Deut 2:12, 21–22; 11:23; 12:29; 19:1; 31:3; Judg 11:23–24).
3. With inanimate objects such as territory, the verb denotes "to take possession of" the object. This usage frequently has military overtones (cf. Num 13:30; Josh 19:47; Judg 3:13) but not always (cf. Deut 30:5; 2 Kgs 17:24; Isa 61:7; Jer 30:3; Ezek 36:12).

According to the MT of Obad 17, the verb takes an inanimate object, the cognate accusative *môrāšêhem*, "their own possessions." Therefore the verb denotes "to possess," here without any hint of a military conquest (so Lohfink 1990: 373). The antecedent of "their" is clearly "the house of Jacob"—which takes a plural verb here—and not "all the nations" of v 16 (*pace* Keil 1888). The masculine noun *môrāš*, from *yrš*, occurs only one other time in the Hebrew Bible, Isa 14:23. (The word *môrāš* in Job 17:11 probably derives from a different root ['*rš*] and means "desire.") In the Isaiah text it denotes "possession" and refers to territory: "I will make her [Babylon] into a possession of the hedgehog[?]."

The related feminine noun *môrāšâ* (9 occurrences) also designates a territory as someone's "possession." Usually it refers to the land of Israel (Exod 6:8; Ezek 11:15; 33:24; 36:2, 3, 5), once to the land of Ammon (Ezek 25:4) and once to the land of Moab (Ezek 25:10). The only exception is its use in Deut 33:4, where it refers to the law as Israel's legacy.

Given the normal usage of *môrāš* and *môrāšâ*, the meaning of Obad 17 in the MT is clear: The house of Jacob will possess *their own land*. With the cognate accusative Obadiah emphasizes that the land is their possession by divine right and promise. Verses 19–20 expand and clarify the statement by announcing that Judah and the returning exiles will regain Israel's entire land within its traditional boundaries as originally promised by Yahweh (including a new addition, "Mount Esau").

Another interpretation is possible on the basis of a significant textual variant. The ancient versions (LXX, Vulgate, Peshiṭta) support the Murabbaʿat manuscript's reading: *mwryšyhm*, a *hipʿil* participle of *yrš*. In this case read *môrîšêhem*, spelled defectively (cf. the defective spelling of *môšîʿîm* in v 21). The variant alters the sense of the clause: "The house of Jacob will dispossess *those who dispossessed them*," that is, those who dispossessed the house of Jacob. The Targum witnesses to both readings by conflating them: "Those of the house of Jacob will possess the property of the peoples who were dispossessing them."

The variant's plural participle, "those who dispossessed," probably refers to the Edomites and intends to lead into v 18, which speaks of Edom being consumed by Israel. It also anticipates the initial clause of v 19: "The Negeb will possess Mount Esau." Thus it continues the talionic theme of v 15, "Just as you have done, it will be done to you." Although the textual evidence for the variant is strong, several arguments support the priority of the MT.

1. The switch from a *qal* verb as the main verb to a *hip'il* participle as the direct object is inexplicable and unattested. The closest parallel occurs in Jer 49:2:

   wĕyāraš yiśrā'ēl 'et yōrĕšāyw

   Israel will dispossess those who dispossessed it.

   However, Jeremiah uses a *qal* verb throughout the sentence.
2. The variant was probably influenced by the talionic theme. But the theme that drives the clarification of v 17 given in vv 19–20 is the standard prophetic hope of Israel regaining all of the promised land; i.e., possessing "their own possessions."
3. According to v 19, the Negeb will not "dispossess" the Edomites but "will possess Mount Esau"; the object is territory and not people. The only personal objects mentioned in vv 19–20 are the Philistines and the Canaanites.

Therefore one should probably follow Lohfink (1981: 283–86) in preferring the MT as the older witness. The variant most likely arose under the influence of the talionic theme and the Jer 49 text. An alteration of *môrāšêhem* to *môrīšêhem*, which Murabba'at spells *plene*, would be easy enough to make, a difference of only one vowel. Yet given the antiquity of the variant, one cannot decide the issue with certainty. (Barthélemy [1992: 700–1] favors the variant.)

v 18. *wĕhāyâ bêt ya'ăqōb 'ēš*
   ûbêt yôsēp lehābâ
   ûbêt 'ēśāw lĕqaš.
   The house of Jacob will become fire,
   and the house of Joseph, flame,
   and the house of Esau, stubble.

Whereas v 17 treats "the house of Jacob" as a collective that consists of different parts (cf. vv 19–20) and therefore uses a plural verb, v 18 uses a singular verb to emphasize its unity. Collectives can take either a singular or a plural verb, sometimes both in the same context (Joüon 1991 § 150e).

The three lines form a tightly knit group. The initial verb *wĕhāyâ* is gapped in the second and third lines, an example of ellipsis that can easily be conveyed in English. What English cannot do so well but Hebrew can is backward gapping, that is, omitting an element in the first part and writing it in a later part (cf. O'Connor 1980: 122–29, 401–7). Such backward gapping is illustrated here. The preposition *l* is written with *qaš* (stubble) but it applies also to *'ēš* (fire) and *lehābâ* (flame). This creates a nice sound pair of *lehābâ* and *lĕqaš*. Thus the idiom *hāyâ* + *l* (to become) controls all three lines. In the close parallel of Isa 10:17, which perhaps was adapted in Obad 18 with the substitution of Israel for Yahweh (so Deissler 1984), the preposition is written with both *'ēš* and *lehābâ*:

> *wĕhāyâ 'ôr yiśrā'ēl lĕ'ēš*
> *ûqĕdôšô lĕlehābâ*

The Light of Israel will become fire,
and its Holy One, flame.

See Mic 3:12 (= Jer 26:18) for another example of *hāyâ* + *l* in which the preposition is gapped backward.

Regarding the phrase "the house of Joseph," technically Joseph's descendants were Ephraim and Manasseh (Gen 48). But since these two tribes held the dominant position among the ten northern tribes in terms of territory and population, "the house of Joseph" by synecdoche came to stand for the entire Northern Kingdom (cf. 2 Sam 19:21 [20]; Amos 5:6; Zech 10:6; Andersen and Freedman 1989: 109, 111).

As noted in v 17, "the house of Jacob" is an inclusive term referring to the totality of the descendants of the patriarch Jacob. But lest the hearers/readers think that only the Judahites left in the land deserve the title, Obadiah explicitly includes the Northern Kingdom. Thus the sequence moves from the whole to one significant part. Gen 46:27 reveals that Joseph's line could be considered part of "the house of Jacob" (cf. Gen 48:5). Since the prophets typically thought of Yahweh's people as comprising all twelve tribes, they made the future reunification of the North and the South a prominent feature of their restoration promises (cf. Isa 11:13; Jer 3:18; 23:6; 30:3; 31:27, 31; 33:7, 14; 51:5; Ezek 37:15–23; 47–48; Hos 2:2 [1:11]; Zech 8:13; 9:10, 13; 10:6).

The nouns "fire" and "flame" form a common word pair, in which "flame" is intended as synonym and substitute for "fire." Only one text (Dan 11:33) of the seventeen occurrences of "flame" lacks the pair. Both terms are either bound together in a genitive phrase (Isa 4:5; Hos 7:6; Pss 29:7; 105:32; Lam 2:3) or split up and distributed between two parallel lines (Num 21:28 = Jer 48:45; Isa 5:24; 10:17; 43:2; 47:14; Joel 1:19; 2:3; Pss 83:15 [14]; 106:18). When they are located in parallel lines, "fire" is always in the A-line.

Obadiah coined the phrase "the house of Esau" — which occurs nowhere else in the Hebrew Bible — in order to match "the house of Jacob" and "the house of Joseph." The metaphor equates it with "stubble," which is easily and thoroughly incinerated, especially in the dry heat of Palestine. Other texts also liken Yahweh's foes to stubble consumed by fire, either the nations (Exod 15:7; Isa 33:11; 47:14; Nah 1:10) or the wicked within Israel (Isa 5:24; Mal 3:19 [4:1]).

Verse 18 applies the *lex talionis* principle to the relationship between Israel and Edom. The future day of Yahweh will witness the reversal of the victor-victim roles. The closest parallel appears in the oracle against Edom in Ezek 25:14:

> I will lay my vengeance upon Edom by the hand of my people Israel,
> and they will do in Edom according to my wrath and according to my
> anger . . .

wĕdālĕqû bāhem wa'ăkālûm.
and they will set them on fire and consume them.

The object of both verbs refers to the collective, "the house of Esau," treated as a plural in order to prepare for the next line, "and there will be no survivor for the house of Esau." Although the first verb, *dlq* (*qal*), can denote "hotly pursue" (Gen 31:36; 1 Sam 17:53; Ps 10:2; Lam 4:19), in this context of fire and stubble it means "set on fire, burn" (*qal* — Ps 7:14 [13]; Prov 26:23; *hip'il* — Isa 5:11; Ezek 24:10; Sir 43:4; cf. *HALAT*); and it takes the prepositional object *bāhem* (Wehrle 1987: 126). Compare the verb *b'r* (to burn), which also can take the preposition *b* with its object (Isa 30:33; 42:25; 43:2; Ezek 39:9–10; Job 1:16). The second verb, *'kl*, often denotes "consuming" by fire (BDB). The two verbs together create a sequence, "set on fire" and then "consume" (cf. Isa 10:17).

wĕlō' yihyeh śārîd lĕbêt 'ēśāw.
and there will be no survivor for the house of Esau.

The construction *hāyâ* + N + *l* + N indicates possession; hence the negated clause means that "the house of Esau will have no survivor" (cf. Jer 42:17; 44:14). The translation attempts to show the Hebrew word order. The clause marks the climax of the verse's sequence and the point of the metaphor: Israel as fire will so thoroughly consume Edom as to leave behind no survivor.

The motif of a nation having no survivors and remnant occurs in holy war contexts (see Note under v 14). It also appears in other prophetic oracles against the nations: Babylon (Isa 14:22; Jer 50:26, 29); Philistia (Isa 14:30; Ezek 25:16); Nineveh (Nah 1:14). It answers the fear that a hostile nation might rebuild after its defeat and once again oppress (cf. Isa 14:20–21).

One noteworthy text with this lack-of-survivor motif is located in the archaic oracles of Balaam, specifically the fourth oracle (Num 24:15–19). A good possibility exists for seeing an influence of Num 24:19 upon Obad 18, especially given that Obad 19 echoes Num 24:18. However, the connection remains uncertain due to the corrupt state of the text. Num 24:18–19 reads as follows with two emendations of the MT:

wĕhāyâ 'ĕdôm yĕrēšâ
wĕhāyâ yĕrēšâ śē'îr 'ōyĕbāyw
wĕyiśrā'ēl 'ōśeh ḥāyil
wĕ[yirdēm] ya'ăqōb
wĕhe'ĕbîd śārîd m[iśśē]'îr

Edom will become (his) possession;
Seir, his enemies, will become (his) possession,
while Israel does valiantly.
Jacob will rule [over them]
and destroy the survivor from [Seir].

For the last two lines (v 19) the MT reads:

wĕyērd miyyaʿăqōb
wĕheʾĕbîd śārîd mēʿîr

Let him rule from Jacob
and destroy the survivor from the city.

I divide the first line after *m* (so Albright 1944: 221; O'Connor 1980: 193) and take *m* as an object suffix (so O'Connor); one could understand it as an enclitic *mem* (so Albright). The *BHS* footnote suggests reading *mśʿyr* (from Seir) in the second line for the difficult MT *mʿyr* (from the city). Because the letters *ś* and (a sloppy) *ʿ* resemble each other in the square script, perhaps *ś* was accidentally omitted by a type of haplography. If the second emendation is sound, then it is likely that Obad 18 drew upon Num 24:19.

kî yahweh dibbēr.
For Yahweh has spoken.
The clause, introduced by a causal *kî* (for), serves to verify the preceding speech as Yahweh's speech and to reinforce the certainty of the announced events. They will definitely happen, "for Yahweh has spoken." The formula occurs six times in addition to Obad 18 (1 Kgs 14:11; Isa 1:2; 22:25; 25:8; Jer 13:15; Joel 4:8 [3:8]; cf. Bretón 1987: 230–33). Related formulas include

For Yahweh, the God of Israel, has spoken (Isa 21:17);

For Yahweh has spoken this word (Isa 24:3);

For the mouth of Yahweh has spoken (Isa 1:20; 40:5; 58:14);

For the mouth of Yahweh of hosts has spoken (Mic 4:4).

Of the above twelve occurrences only two do not conclude a unit; both are joined with imperatives to introduce a speech (Isa 1:2; Jer 13:15). The formula clearly has a closure function in Obad 18.

COMMENT

Verses 16–18 constitute the second section of the divine utterance in vv 8–18. Yet the beginning of this section (v 16) is closely linked with the ending of the previous section (v 15). What was introduced in the first half of v 15, namely, the day of Yahweh's judgment "against all the nations," receives further development in v 16, "For . . . all the nations will drink" the cup of wrath. The addressee now shifts from Edom to the Judahites and Jerusalemites. The same shift occurs also in Ezek 35–36 and Lam 4:21–22.

The section contains thirteen lines that are linked by syntax. In normal discourse that concerns future events Hebrew uses the imperfect followed by *waw* consecutive perfects; when an element intervenes between the *waw* and the verb, the sequence must begin again with an imperfect. In this section the sequence occurs in v 16 and again in vv 17–18. Verse 17 restarts the sequence because of the fronting of the prepositional phrase ("But on Mount Zion . . ."), and v 18 concludes it with *waw* + negative particle + imperfect ("and there will be no . . .").

In contrast to v 15b, which created a correspondence between Edom's sin and its punishment ("Just as you have done, it will be done to you"), v 16 correlates the punishment experienced by two different groups: "For just as you [pl] have drunk on my holy mountain, (so) all the nations will drink . . ." The comparison begins by referring to the experience of Judah and Jerusalem, "you" plural. Whereas in vv 11–14 Obadiah portrayed the fall of Judah and Jerusalem from a human point of view, when strangers and foreigners attacked, now he interprets the same event as Zion's experience of Yahweh's wrath. He presupposes the hearers'/readers' familiarity with the cup-of-wrath metaphor found elsewhere (see Excursus). Given the metaphor's prominence in Jeremiah, who greatly influenced Obadiah (Jer 25:15–29; 48:26–27; 49:12; 51:7–8, 39, 57), it comes as no surprise to see its presence in Obadiah. In light of the many parallels between Jeremiah's Edom oracle and Obadiah, it is especially significant that the former uses the metaphor. Note that Jeremiah locates Jerusalem's cup drinking in the future while Obadiah places it in the past, a sure sign that Jeremiah's Edom oracle predates and Obadiah postdates the 587/6 crisis:

For thus spoke Yahweh:
Look! Those [Jerusalemites] whose right it was not to drink the cup
will certainly drink, and are you [Edom] one to be exempt?
No, you will not be exempt, for you will certainly drink! (Jer 49:12)

Zion has already experienced Yahweh's wrath but the nations have not. Therefore Obadiah announces that the nations will drink of the same cup as Jerusalem. He thereby answers exilic prayers that ask Yahweh to deal with the hostile nations as he dealt with sinful Israel (Pss 74; 79; Lam 1:21–22; 3:64–66; 4:21–22; cf. Jer 10:25). Other cup-of-wrath texts likewise portray the movement of the cup from Jerusalem to the nations (Isa 51:17–23; Jer 25:15–29; 48:26–27; 49:12; Lam 4:21–22; cf. Isa 63:6). Although the book of Obadiah does not explicitly state why all the nations must suffer under Yahweh's wrath, it suggests a threefold reason. First, the argument moves from the greater to the lesser (cf. 1 Pet 4:17). If Zion, Yahweh's "holy mountain," had to drink the cup of wrath, certainly the non-elect nations will have to drink it. Compare Jer 25:29 at the end of a lengthy cup-of-wrath text:

For look! In the city upon which my name has been pronounced
I am beginning to do harm, and will you [nations] indeed be exempt?
No, you will not be exempt! For I am summoning a sword
against all the inhabitants of the earth — utterance of Yahweh of hosts.

This type of argument differs from that of Amos 1–2. By concluding his oracles against the nations with oracles against Judah and Israel, Amos reduces Yahweh's covenant people to the level of the non-elect nations as being equally guilty and deserving of punishment (cf. Jer 9:24–25 [25–26]). Obadiah in contrast maintains a distinction with respect to status between Zion and the nations. Second, at least some of the nations participated in destroying Yahweh's people and therefore must be judged (v 11; cf. Isa 51:17–23). Third, because some of the nations currently occupy Israelite territory they are culpable (v 19).

In addition to a correspondence between the experiences of Zion and the nations, v 16 sets up a contrast: "all the nations will drink continually . . . and they will be as if they had never been." The intensification of the judgment is again based on the greater-to-lesser argument. It also needs to be understood in light of v 21, "the kingship will belong to Yahweh." The logic is that the authorities of the present age must be deprived of any future significance in order for Yahweh to manifest and exercise his sole authority as universal king.

Beginning with v 17 and throughout the remaining verses Obadiah develops the theme of the future reversal of Israel's fortunes. Verse 17a concentrates on Zion's future and sets it in contrast to Zion's past as depicted in v 11 and v 16. Thus the focus of the six lines of vv 16–17a moves from Zion's past to the nations' future to Zion's future.

The first clause in Obad 17 succinctly summarizes a major biblical theme, namely that salvation resides in Zion (see Hayes 1963). The theme occupies an important place in Zion theology, which Gowan (1986) argues lies at the center of Old Testament eschatology. One finds the theme frequently in the Psalter and the southern prophets, particularly in all parts of the book of Isaiah, the "Book of Consolation" within Jeremiah (chaps 30–33), Joel, Micah, Zephaniah, and Zechariah. While the psalmists tend to speak of Zion's security as a present reality, the prophets typically project it into the future after Zion's judgment. According to the Zion tradition, refuge and salvation are located in Zion because Yahweh's presence is located there. For Obadiah, Zion is Yahweh's "holy mountain" (v 16) and the center of Yahweh's future rule as king (v 21).

Obadiah does not identify who will enjoy the safety of Zion; he only states that deliverance from divine wrath is located there. The rest of the book indicates that he has in mind primarily Israel. However, he leaves open the possibility, at least, of non-Israelites being included. The fact that he warns the Edomites of the coming day of Yahweh (vv 12–15) perhaps shows that he held out some hope for them. One is reminded of another theme common in Zion theology, the prospect of non-Israelites coming to Zion. At any rate, Obadiah maintains that deliverance from the coming day of universal judgment resides only in Zion and in her God.

The next clause in v 17 states that on Mount Zion "will be a holy place." According to v 11, "strangers" and "foreigners" invaded Judah and "cast lots for Jerusalem." By treating the city as a common commodity they profaned it. In response Obadiah announces the future reversal of the situation. He repeats the noun *qōdeš* from v 16 in order to stress the sanctity of Zion. Yahweh's "holy mountain," which experienced his wrath (v 16) through the agency of foreign armies (v 11), will once again become a "holy place." Never again will it be violated and defiled by unclean outsiders. The meaning of the clause is clarified by the parallel in Joel 4:17 [3:17], which says that "strangers," those outside the covenant relationship with Yahweh, will never again be allowed to desecrate the holy city:

> You will know that I am Yahweh your God
> who dwells on Zion, my holy mountain.
> Jerusalem will be a holy place
> and strangers will not pass through it again.

Obadiah sums up an important theme in Zion theology: Holy Zion is for holy people (cf. Levenson 1985; Gammie 1989). According to the so-called entrance liturgies (Pss 15; 24), only the righteous can dwell on the holy mountain (cf. Isa 33:14–16; Jer 7). Prophetic texts speak of the future purification of Zion through the coming judgment (e.g., Isa 1:21–28; 4:3–4; Zeph 3:11–13). Zion will again be called "the holy mountain" (Zech 8:3), no longer to be overrun by oppressors (Zech 9:8) or to witness the presence of a "Canaanite" (Zech 14:21). The eschatological temple and the whole mountain portrayed in Ezekiel's vision will be most holy (43:12) so that no uncircumcised in heart and flesh may enter (44:7–9). Finally note the promise for exilic Zion in Isa 52:1:

> Awake, awake,
> put on your strength, O Zion;
> put on your beautiful garments,
> O Jerusalem, the holy city.
> For there will no more come into you
> the uncircumcised and the unclean.

While v 17a speaks of the destiny of Zion, vv 17b–18 focus on the future of Israel. This movement from Zion to Israel is then reversed in vv 19–21, thereby creating a thematic chiasm for the materials that promise restoration:

A the destiny of Zion (v 17a);

B Israel's repossession of the land (v 17b);

C Israel's victory over its enemy (v 18);

B Israel's repossession of the land (vv 19–20);

A the centrality of Zion (v 21).

With the statement that "the house of Jacob will possess their own possessions," Obadiah announces that Israel will regain the land that belongs to it by divine right and promise. The theme receives further attention in vv 19–20 because of its significance. Beginning with the patriarchal promises the Hebrew Bible repeatedly emphasizes the importance of the land as Israel's inheritance, the homeland given by Yahweh to Israel and the means by which Yahweh blesses Israel. In fact, Israel's life in the land functions as a sort of barometer of Israel's well-being and relationship with Yahweh. Therefore it is to be expected that promises of Israel's restoration would include references to its repossession of the land. E. W. Davies (1989: 354) expresses the point well:

> The land of Israel was Yahweh's land, and the people of Israel were Yahweh's people, and so close was the association between the people and the land that the destinies of both were inextricably connected. Thus Yahweh's judgement involved devastation of the land and exile of the people; by the same token, the restoration of the relationship between Yahweh and Israel could only be sealed conclusively by the restoration of the people to their land.

One concern of the Judahites during the exile was whether or not the people would regain their lost territories. Two other concerns were regarding the unity of Israel and the dominance of Edom. Therefore Obadiah addresses these issues in v 18. With respect to the former concern, he includes the northern tribes, "the house of Joseph," in the picture. Thus he remains in conformity with the other prophets who typically speak of the future reunification of all twelve tribes. With respect to the latter concern, he announces that this reunited Israel will extirpate Edom so that it will lack any remnant or survivor. The statement serves several purposes. First, it applies the talionic standard of justice: just as Edom sought to eliminate Israel's "survivors" (v 14), so Israel will do the same to Edom. Second, by promising total and unqualified victory it answers the fear that Israel's enemy might survive and continue to oppress Israel. Third, it returns to the motif expressed at the beginning of the third divine utterance: "everyone will be cut off from Mount Esau by slaughter" (v 9). However, the agent of Edom's destruction has changed from the nations (vv 1, 7) to Israel. Thus the victim brings about the judgment upon the oppressor (cf. Ezek 25:14; Joel 4:4–8 [3:4–8]; Hab 2:6–8; Miller 1982: 115). Finally, it brings the address to Judah to a conclusion in two ways: by providing a negative counterpart to the promise made in v 17a — there will be "escape" on Mount Zion, but Edom will have no "survivor" (cf. the use of the word pair "escapees/survivors" in v 14) — and by particularizing the announcement made at the beginning of the section in v 16, that all the nations "will be as if they had never been." Such oscillation between the universal and the particular is common in prophetic discourse.

IV. THE PROPHET'S EXPANSION: PROMISE OF ISRAEL'S RESTORATION AND YAHWEH'S KINGSHIP (vv 19–21)

◆

19 The Negeb will possess Mount Esau,
   and the Shephelah (will dispossess) the Philistines;
   they will possess the territory of Ephraim and the territory of Samaria,
   and Benjamin (will possess) Gilead.
20 The exiles of this company, those belonging to the Israelites, who are [in . . .
         will dispossess] the Canaanites up to Zarephath;
   and the exiles of Jerusalem who are in Sepharad
         will possess the cities of the Negeb.
21 Deliverers will go up onto Mount Zion to judge Mount Esau,
   and the kingship will belong to Yahweh.

NOTES

v 19. *wĕyārĕšû hannegeb 'et har 'ēśāw*
   wĕhaššĕpēlâ 'et pĕlištîm
   wĕyārĕšû 'et śĕdēh 'eprayim wĕ'ēt śĕdēh šōmĕrôn
   ûbinyāmīn 'et haggil'ād.
   The Negeb will possess Mount Esau,
   and the Shephelah (will dispossess) the Philistines;

they will possess the territory of Ephraim and the territory of Samaria, and Benjamin (will possess) Gilead.

Verses 19–21 follow the closure of the preceding divine speech and thus present Obadiah's own expansion. They function as clarification of the preceding speech, especially of v 17b. Although one expects an imperfect verb form to begin the new unit, the use of the initial *waw*-consecutive perfect (*wĕyārĕšû*) establishes the link with v 17b, which begins with the same verb form. It is not unprecedented to initiate a unit with a *waw*-consecutive perfect (e.g., Isa 11:1; 12:1).

Verse 19 has four pairs of place names in the following arrangement:

A verb + "the Negeb" + *'et* + "Mount Esau"
B *w* + "the Shephelah" + *'et* + "the Philistines"
C verb + *'et* + "the territory of Ephraim" + *'et* + "the territory of Samaria"
D *w* + "Benjamin" + *'et* + "Gilead"

The two verbs are identical. In the pairs of A, B, and D only the second name has *'et* while in C *'et* precedes both names.

The syntax of the verse is disputed. Wellhausen construed four of the names as direct objects — Negeb, Shephelah, Ephraim, and Gilead — and omitted the other names as secondary interpolations (so also Marti 1904). Many scholars adopt Wellhausen's basic approach by treating all the names as direct objects (Bewer 1911; T. H. Robinson 1938; Keller 1965; Weiser 1967; Allen 1976; Wolff 1977; Wehrle 1987; Dicou 1994). The implicit subject in this case would be the combined "house of Jacob" and "house of Joseph" of v 18 or simply the "house of Jacob" of v 17.

For the first two pairs (A–B), this approach takes "Mount Esau" and "the Philistines" as appositional to "the Negeb" and "the Shephelah" respectively. At the time of the author the Negeb was occupied by Edomites and presumably the Shephelah by Philistines, which necessitated an explanatory comment or gloss for "the Negeb" and "the Shephelah." The fourth pair (D) presents difficulties for this approach. Dicou (1994) treats "Gilead" as appositional to "Benjamin" but this makes no geographical or historical sense. Others consider "Benjamin" to be a marginal gloss that was misplaced before "Gilead" (Allen 1976; Wolff 1977). Duhm (1911) and Bewer (1911) read "the Ammonites" (*bny 'mn*) for "Benjamin" (*bnymn*). Dicou summarizes the arguments for the basic approach described above.

1. Because the verb in C lacks an explicit subject, the reader assumes the same for the verb in A.
2. Because the object of the verb "will possess" in v 20 is "the cities of the Negeb," "the Negeb" in v 19 must function as an object.

3. No other text uses "the Negeb" and "the Shephelah" as verbal subjects (cf. Wehrle 1987: 97, 294).

However, there are serious difficulties with this basic approach to v 19.

1. "Mount Esau" denotes a territory — the traditional homeland of Edom southeast of the Dead Sea — and not the Edomites as a people (cf. vv 8–9). Also in v 21 the phrase primarily refers to Edom's land although it certainly implies an occupied land.
2. Transjordan "Gilead" and Cisjordan "Benjamin" do not clarify each other. No textual basis exists for reading "the Ammonites."
3. The syntax proposed for A is very rare at best: a *qal* verb followed by two direct objects, both of which are definite nouns but with only the second noun preceded by *'et* ("They will possess the Negeb [i.e., Mount Esau]"). The syntactic parallels cited by Wehrle (1987: 97) do not apply (Isa 7:17; Jer 17:13; Ezek 4:1; 36:12; Mic 3:8). In each instance the first direct object is an *indefinite* noun unlike the syntactic structure of Obad 19; normally the object marker *'et* precedes only definite nouns. I can find only one example that has the proposed syntactic structure (Josh 8:13). In cases of apposition, *'et* is ordinarily repeated before definite nouns (Joüon 1991 § 131i; 132g).

Because of these difficulties it is far more likely that the reader should follow the syntactic understanding reflected in the ancient versions (so Keil 1888; Halévy 1907; Theis 1937; Laetsch 1956; Thompson 1956; Aalders 1958; Rudolph 1971; Dick 1984; Padilla 1989). For A, B, and D take the first noun as the subject and the second noun preceded by *'et* as the direct object. B and D gap the verb, while *'et* marks every direct object (cf. vv 20b, 21; *pace* Duhm [1911] who understands *'et* as the preposition "with"). Accordingly, the verse exhibits alternating parallelism in terms of syntax (except for the asymmetry of C, which has no explicit subject and a double object):

A verb + subject + *'et* + object
B subject + *'et* + object
C verb + *'et* + object + *'et* + object
D subject + *'et* + object

Two observations support this rendering.

1. The syntax of A conforms with that of its parallel line in v 17b:

wĕyārĕšû bêt yaʿăqōb 'ēt môrāšêhem

The house of Jacob will possess their own possessions

wĕyārĕšû hannegeb 'et har 'ēśāw

The Negeb will possess Mount Esau

The same verb-subject-object word order, normal in Biblical Hebrew, occurs also in v 21.

2. Wehrle's own research, despite his conclusion, provides evidence for the correctness of this view (1987: 94–95). Elsewhere one finds the syntax of *yrš* + subject + *'et* + object, but no text has the syntax of *yrš* + object + *'et* + object (cf. Gen 22:17; 24:60; Deut 3:20; Josh 1:15; Judg 11:21; Jer 49:2).

The explicitly named subjects — the Negeb, the Shephelah, and Benjamin — designate three areas of Judah. Because C lacks an explicit subject one must infer the identity of those who will possess Ephraim and Samaria. The restored "house of Joseph" of v 18 would make sense, but a more probable candidate is the main part of Judah located in the central highlands (so Keil 1888; Theis 1937; Aalders 1958). The second option has the advantage of maintaining the focus on the inhabitants of Judah in keeping with the rest of v 19. Thus all four areas of Judah are represented (cf. Jer 17:26; 32:44; 33:13).

Verse 19 concretizes and particularizes the general promise given in v 17b. The Judahites who were left in the land following the Babylonian deportations will fan out in all four directions running clockwise: S-W-N-E (cf. Gen 28:14; Isa 11:14; 54:3; Zech 10:10). The arrangement of subjects and objects makes good geographical sense: the inhabitants of the Negeb move south (and east); those of the Shephelah move west; those of the central and main part of Judah possess the northern territory; and those of Benjamin proceed east. Apart from the first clause, the verse promises the repossession of Israel's entire land within the traditional borders. Thus it expresses a theme that occupies a prominent place in the prophetic hope of Israel's restoration (cf. Jer 16:14–15; 23:7–8; 30:3; 31:5–6; 32:15, 37–41; Ezek 20:40–42; 34:13–14; 36:8–12, 24–36; 37:21–25; Hos 2:16–25 [14–23]; Amos 9:15; Mic 7:11, 14; Zeph 2:7–9; Gowan 1986: 21–32; Ricks 1988). The first clause, however, goes beyond these kinds of promises by announcing that Israel will possess the land of Edom (see below).

The Negeb will possess Mount Esau. The term "the Negeb" functions synecdochically for "the inhabitants of the Negeb" (cf. Josh 10:40; 1 Sam 27:10; 30:1, 14). Their geographical location made them the logical choice for occupying the land of Edom (cf. Josh 15:21). Therefore it presents no significant problem that "the Negeb" is never used elsewhere as a verbal subject (*pace* Wehrle 1987: 97, 294).

The name "Negeb" denotes "dryness," reflecting the arid climate of the region. The modern Negeb (or Negev) includes a triangular region bounded by the Arabah valley in the east, the Sinai Peninsula in the south and west, and the

Judean hills in the north. The points of the triangle are Gaza, Eilat, and the southern end of the Dead Sea. The biblical Negeb probably consisted of a smaller area that extended from the hills south of Hebron to Kadesh-barnea and that primarily centered in the Beersheba and Arad valleys (cf. Borowski 1989).

According to Deut 2:2–8, the land of Edom did not belong to Israel's inheritance. Moreover, the Israelites never "possessed" this land, although Israel ruled over Edom during the tenth and the first half of the ninth centuries. Whereas the rest of v 19 expresses the theme of Israel regaining the full extent of its land, the verse's initial statement has a different background. First, it applies the talionic principle of v 15: just as the Edomites seized Jacob's property (v 13), so Jacob will occupy Edom's land. Second, it repeats the motif announced in the restoration promise of Amos 9:12, "they [restored Israel] will possess [yrš] the remnant of Edom . . ." This connection was probably a major factor in the canonical placement of the book of Obadiah after the book of Amos (cf. Wolff 1977). Finally, it updates the promise given in the ancient oracle of Balaam (Num 24:18), which probably influenced the Amos passage as well:

Edom will become (Israel's) possession [yĕrēšâ];
Seir, its enemies, will become (its) possession [yĕrēšâ],
while Israel does valiantly.

and the Shephelah (will dispossess) the Philistines. The verb of the preceding clause is gapped. With a personal object it denotes "to dispossess." (On yrš, see Note for v 17.) The place name "the Shephelah" is used by synecdoche for "the inhabitants of the Shephelah" (cf. Josh 10:40). "The Shephelah," from the root špl, "to be low," refers to the strip of foothills west of the Judean highlands and east of the coastal plain of Philistia.

Although the reference to the Philistines evokes Israel's premonarchic period (see Comment), it is not anachronistic in the historical setting of Obadiah. In 604 B.C. Nebuchadnezzar destroyed Ashkelon (Esse 1992) and shortly thereafter Ekron (Gitin 1987). Archaeological evidence of destruction exists at both sites. Also Babylonian texts indicate the presence of Philistine exiles in Babylonia (Wiseman 1985: 77, 83). Nevertheless, the presence of Philistines as an identifiable social entity in the coastal plain did not come to an end (cf. Coelho Dias 1990). They receive attention in exilic and postexilic texts (Ezek 16:57; 25:15–17; Zech 9:5–7; Joel 4:4 [3:4]; Neh 13:23–24). A text from the reign of Nabonidus indicates that Gaza became a Babylonian garrison-town (Katzenstein 1992). Excavations at Ashdod and Ekron reveal postdestruction occupation in the sixth century (Dothan 1992; Gitin 1987). And many sites in the regions of Ashdod and Gaza were occupied in the Persian period (Stern 1982: 19–29, 243–44, 250–52).

According to the traditional land promises, the coastal plain formed part of Israel's inheritance (Gen 15:18–21; 28:13–14; Exod 23:31; Num 34:6; Deut

11:24; 34:2; Josh 1:4; 13:2–3). It is noteworthy that Josh 15:33–47 includes the coastal cities under "the Shephelah." Obadiah stands in continuity with these promises in envisaging the future dispossession of the Philistines (cf. Isa 11:14; Zeph 2:7; Zech 9:7).

the territory of Ephraim. Although Talmon (1978: 431) relates the noun *śādeh* (construct — *śĕdēh*) to Akkadian *šadû*, "mountain" (cf. LXX), here more likely it has the general sense of "territory, region" (*HALAT*). Compare related expressions: "the territory of Edom" (Gen 32:4 [3]; Judg 5:4); "the territory of Moab" (Gen 36:35; Num 21:20; 1 Chron 1:46; 8:8; Ruth 2:6; 4:3); "the territory of Aram" (Hos 12:13 [12]). "Ephraim," the name of the dominant northern tribe, often is used by synecdoche for the Northern Kingdom.

and the territory of Samaria. The phrase *śĕdēh šōmĕrôn* refers to the region immediately surrounding the city of Samaria, the capital of Ephraim. Compare Ps 78:12 and 43, "the territory of [the city] Zoan." Ephraim and Samaria form a word pair comparable to that of Judah and Jerusalem (cf. Isa 7:9; 9:8 [9]; Jer 31:5–6; Hos 7:1). The promise of possessing Ephraim and Samaria helps in locating the time of Obadiah as subsequent to the fall of the Northern Kingdom (722 B.C.).

and Benjamin (will possess) Gilead. The name "Benjamin" refers to the inhabitants of the tribal territory of Benjamin. Although the territory originally formed the southernmost of the northern tribes, throughout the period of the divided monarchy it was contested by Israel and Judah and by the sixth century considered part of Judah (cf. Jer 17:26; 32:44; 33:13; Schunck 1992). In general it extended from Bethel to just south of Jerusalem.

The land of Gilead in its widest extent reached from the Yarmuk River in the north to the Arnon River in the south (cf. Deut 3:12–13; 34:1; Josh 12:2–6; 22:9, 13, 15, 32; Judg 10:8; 2 Sam 2:9; 2 Kgs 10:33). It had been the residence of the Transjordanian tribes of Reuben and Gad south of the Jabbok River and of the half-tribe of Manasseh north of the Jabbok River. When Tiglath-pileser III captured Gilead and deported its people in 733 B.C., it became an Assyrian province. Although the subsequent history of Gilead remains unclear, Jer 49:1–6 states that the Ammonites possessed the territory of Gad (cf. Jer 41:10, 15). Archaeological evidence indicates that the Ammonites prospered and expanded while under Neo-Babylonian and then Persian rule (Sauer 1986: 16–18; Herr 1993).

Several episodes from the Former Prophets link the tribe of Benjamin with Gilead: the Benjaminites were given the women of Jabesh-gilead as wives (Judg 21); Saul of Benjamin delivered Jabesh-gilead from the Ammonites, for which he received the people's support (1 Sam 11); and Abner made Saul's son Ishbaal (Ishbosheth) king over Gilead (2 Sam 2). Perhaps some of this background influenced Obadiah (cf. Ottosson 1969: 240). At any rate, it makes good geographical sense that of the four areas of Judah (the Negeb, the Shephelah, the central highlands, and Benjamin) Obadiah would choose Benjamin to move east and possess Gilead.

In keeping with the overall thrust of v 19 in announcing the future possession of the full extent of Israel's land, the last clause envisages the reclamation of the Transjordanian territories of Reuben, Gad, and Manasseh. The same motif appears in other prophetic promises of Israel's restoration (Jer 49:1–2; 50:19; Mic 7:14; Zeph 2:9; Zech 10:10).

v 20. *wĕgālūt haḥēl hazzeh libnê yiśrā'ēl 'ăšer [b . . . yiršû 'et] kĕna'ănîm 'ad*
     ṣārĕpat
    wĕgālūt yĕrûšālayim 'ăšer bispārad yiršû 'ēt 'ārê hannegeb.
    The exiles of this company, those belonging to the Israelites, who are [in . . .
       will dispossess] the Canaanites up to Zarephath;
    and the exiles of Jerusalem who are in Sepharad
       will possess the cities of the Negeb.

Verse 20 is notoriously difficult. The Masoretes apparently understood its syntax to consist of two subjects, one verb, and one direct object:

    The exiles of this company, those belonging to the Israelites, who are
    [among?] the Canaanites up to Zarephath
    and the exiles of Jerusalem who are in Sepharad [*athnach!*]
    will possess the cities of the Negeb.

Accordingly, both groups of exiles will possess the Negeb's cities. Yet why would the author picture two groups occupying the Negeb's cities when in v 19 each group occupies a distinct territory? And what does it mean that "the Israelites" are Canaanites (i.e., Phoenicians)? Should we think of the northern tribes as having become assimilated to the Canaanites? Perhaps they dwelt "*among* the Canaanites," but there is no preposition *b* before *kĕna'ănîm* and such a possibility does not make much historical sense.

The text seems to have been corrupted by a scribal error of some sort. If so, however, the error must have occurred very early in the transmission process because the Murabba'at manuscript (ca. 135 A.D.) — although it is badly preserved here — and the ancient versions all reflect a *Vorlage* virtually identical with the MT. (See Barthélemy [1992: 701–4] for a thorough discussion of the text-critical problem.) One expects a verb in the first clause, in which case "the Canaanites up to Zarephath" would be an appropriate direct object. Perhaps the verb *yiršû* was gapped or assumed from v 19 — "(will dispossess) those who are Canaanites up to Zarephath" (cf. Barthélemy 1992: 704) — but one expects the direct object marker *'et* in light of its presence before all the other direct objects in vv 19–21. Or one could take *'ăšer* as a scribal corruption for an original *yiršû* — they "will dispossess the Canaanites up to Zarephath" — but again, where is the direct object marker *'et?* It seems likely that a phrase accidentally dropped out. Admittedly any restoration is guesswork, but Freedman (private communication) proposes a plausible restoration, one that recognizes the parallel structure of the two halves of the verse: the first subject, "The exiles of this company, those belonging to the Israelites," parallels the second subject, "and the exiles of Jerusalem"; the two relative pronouns (*'ăšer*) are paired; and the direct objects are the two phrases, "the Canaanites up to Zarephath" and "the cities of the Negeb." Therefore, the items that dropped out are the first relative clause, the first verb, and the first direct object marker: *'ăšer* [*b . . . yiršû 'et*], "who are [in Place Name will dispossess]." The omission could have occurred by virtue of homoioarkton — the scribe's eye accidentally skipped over *b . . . yiršû 'et* to *kĕna'ănîm* because of the similar shape of *b* and *k* in the square script. (See Tov [1992: 248] for examples of the *b/k* confusion.) Tentatively we offer this suggestion but we recognize the uncertainties involved. (For a similar proposal, see Barthélemy 1980: 300.)

The exiles. Verse 20 begins with a disjunctive *waw* instead of a *waw* consecutive verb in order to indicate that the actions depicted in v 20 are simultaneous with those depicted in v 19 (cf. Joüon 1991 § 118f).

The feminine singular noun *gālût* (written defectively, *gālūt*) derives from the root *glh*, "to depart, go into exile." It denotes either the abstract sense "exile, captivity" (2 Kgs 25:27 = Jer 52:31; Ezek 1:2; 33:21; 40:1) or the collective "(group of) exiles" (Amos 1:6, 9; Isa 20:4, 45:13; Jer 24:5; 28:4; 29:22; 40:1; cf. BDB). The Amos passages use the noun in reference to groups of people (Israelites?) taken captive by Philistia and Tyre and then handed over to Edom, apparently as part of a slave-trade network operating in the ninth or early eighth century. In Isa 20:4 it refers to the exiles of Cush who were deported by Assyria in the late eighth century. The other occurrences of the noun relate to the Babylonian deportations of Judahites in 597 B.C. (2 Kgs 25:27 = Jer 52:31; Jer 24:5; 28:4; 29:22; Ezek 1:2; 33:21; 40:1) or in 587/6 B.C. (Jer 40:1). In Obad 20 the noun has the concrete sense of "exiles," as the use of the plural verb in the second half makes clear: "the exiles [*gālūt*] of Jerusalem who are in Sepharad will possess [*yiršû*]." The reference is to the exiles of Ephraim and Samaria in the latter part of the eighth century B.C. and to the exiles of Judah in 597 and 587/6 B.C. (see below).

of this company, those belonging to the Israelites. The sense of the definite noun *hahēl*, which is a genitive with the preceding noun (*gālūt*), is uncertain. Among the various suggestions three are noteworthy.

1. For MT *hahēl hazzeh* read *hălah zeh* with the BHS footnote: "The exiles — that is Halah — of the Israelites." In this case, "that is Halah" would be a gloss that identifies where the exiles are located, either the northern exiles who were deported to Halah in Assyria by Sargon II (2 Kgs 17:6; 18:11) or

the Transjordanian tribes who were deported there by Tiglath-pileser III (1 Chron 5:26).

2. The noun *ḥēl*, spelled defectively, is the noun *ḥêl*, which denotes "outer wall, rampart" or more generally "fortress." In the other four texts with the defective spelling of *ḥēl*, the noun has this sense (2 Sam 20:15; 1 Kgs 21:23; Isa 26:1; Lam 2:8), which is preferred by the Committee of the Hebrew Old Testament Text Project, sponsored by the United Bible Societies (Barthélemy 1992). Accordingly, the phrase, "the exiles of this rampart belonging to the Israelites," refers to the exiles of Samaria and Ephraim. By using the term "rampart," "the prophet reduced Samaria or Ephraim to a defensive function in the progress toward Jerusalem" (Barthélemy 1992: 704). Ben Zvi (1993) suggests that *ḥēl* in 1 Kgs 21:23 denotes "territory" in light of the parallel in 2 Kgs 9:36, which uses *ḥēleq* (territory): "Dogs will devour Jezebel in the territory (*ḥēl* // *ḥēleq*) of Jezreel." However, it is more likely that *ḥēl* in 1 Kgs 21:23 refers specifically to the area between the city's inner and outer wall (cf. BDB), while the parallel text uses the more general designation of *ḥēleq* for the town-land of Jezreel.

3. While the previous option is plausible, the MT can be understood in a different way, following the lead of the ancient versions and taking *ḥēl* as a defective spelling of *ḥayil*, "company" (cf. 2 Kgs 18:17; Isa 36:2). Note that the previous noun *gālūt* is also spelled defectively. The noun *ḥayil* occurs in two other places in Obad, v 11 and v 13. Can *ḥayil* be spelled *ḥēl* without the *yodh*? In Ps 10:10 the *Kethib* reads *ḥlk'ym*, whose meaning is unclear, but the *Qere* reads *ḥêl kā'îm*, "hapless host"; (see Craigie 1983: 122). The *Kethib/Qere* variation indicates that the Masoretes were able to read *ḥl*—without the *yodh*—as *ḥēl*, from *ḥayil*. For other examples of nouns derived from middle-*yodh* roots that are written defectively (**ay > ê > ē*), see Andersen and Forbes (1986: 175–76). The difference between *ḥyl* and *ḥl* perhaps reflects the difference between the Judean dialect with the *yodh* and the Northern Israelite dialect without the *yodh*.

The ancient versions generally derived *ḥēl* of v 20 from *ḥayil*, "host, power, wealth":

Targum	*'m'*	"people"
Vulgate	*exercitus*	"army"
Aquila	*euporias*	"prosperity, wealth, property(?)"
Symmachus and Theodotion	*dynameōs*	"power"

The LXX also took *ḥēl* as *ḥayil*, although the Greek translators offered a unique rendition of the verse:

kai tēs metoikesias hē archē hautē tois huiois Israēl
gē tōn Chananaiōn heōs Sareptōn
kai metoikesia Ierousalēm heōs Sephratha [?]
kai klēronomēsousi tas poleis tou Nageb.

And this is the *domain* of the captives belonging to the Israelites,
the land of the Canaanites up to Zarephath;
and the captives of Jerusalem, up to Sephratha [Ephratha?];
and they will inherit the cities of the Negeb.

Many scholars assume that the Greek translators understood *hhl* as the *hip'il* infinitive of *hll*, "the beginning," a reference to the former exile of the Northern Kingdom: "And of the captivity—this is the first (one) for the Israelites." The Peshitta understood *hhl* this was (*qdmyt'*, "first, former"), perhaps under the influence of a misunderstanding of the Greek. However, the syntax of the Greek indicates that one should rather understand *archē* in the sense of "domain, realm over which one's sovereignty extends" (so Muraoka 1993; and *The Septuagint Version of the Old Testament with an English Translation*, London: Samuel Bagster and Sons; no date or author given). The Greek of Nah 3:8 also uses *archē* with the same sense to translate *hêl: hēs hē archē thalassa*, "whose dominion is sea." Apparently they took *hayil*, "power," in the extended sense of "authority" and "domain."

Frequently *hayil* denotes "army," but here it has the more general sense of "company" or "band" of people without military connotations (see Note for v 11). In 1 Kgs 10:2 (= 2 Chr 9:1) it designates the great "retinue" that accompanied the queen of Sheba to Solomon. In the dry bones vision of Ezek 37:10 it refers to a great "crowd" of people, the dry bones that had received flesh and were enlivened by God's breath/spirit. The phrase "the company of Samaria" (*hêl šōmĕrôn*) in Neh 3:34 [4:2] probably refers to the upper classes of the city (cf. Eising 1980: 352). Note also the places where *gibbôrê hayil* designates "able" men in general and especially the wealthy, such as priests (1 Chr 9:13; Neh 11:14) and gatekeepers (1 Chr 26:6; cf. Eising 1980: 350–51).

The demonstrative pronoun *hazzeh* is in attributive position modifying the definite noun *hahēl*, "this company." The pronoun's antecedent is all of the names mentioned in the previous verse. But lest the reader include in "this company" the Philistines mentioned in v 19, who also had exiles, the prophet adds a clarification, "those belonging to the Israelites" (*libnê yiśrā'ēl*). The preposition *l* indicates possession. The term "the Israelites" is not to be restricted to the northern tribes but includes the people of both Israel and Judah. In other words, those who will dispossess the Canaanites are the Israelite exiles of the Negeb, the Shephelah, the central hill country of Judah, Ephraim, Samaria, Benjamin, and Gilead. Whereas v 19 deals with the Judahites remaining in the land, v 20 brings the exiles into the picture. Thus Obadiah's overall depiction of the future restoration foresees a reunited Israel with both the local inhabitants and the returning exiles participating in the reclamation of the entire land. The rest of the verse goes on to include even the exiles of Jerusalem who dwell in distant regions.

the Canaanites. The word *kĕnaʿănîm* (Canaanites) lacks the definite article in agreement with *pĕlištîm* (Philistines) in v 19 (cf. Job 40:30 [41:6]). The reference to "Zarephath" indicates that the term "Canaanites" refers to the inhabitants along the coast north of Mount Carmel, that is, the Phoenicians. Although the Hebrew Bible normally uses the term "Sidonians" for the Phoenicians, Obadiah employs "Canaanites" in order to evoke Israel's settlement in the land during the premonarchic period. By using the verb *yrš* (to possess) and the names "Philistines" and "Canaanites," Obadiah portrays the future restoration of Israel as another conquest-settlement period (see Comment).

Elsewhere the Bible relates Phoenicia to Canaan or reckons its territory as part of Canaan. According to Gen 10, Canaan was the father of Sidon (v 15; cf. 1 Chr 1:13), and the territory of the Canaanites extended to Sidon (v 19). Judg 1:31–32 includes inhabitants of Phoenician sites among the Canaanites. Josh 13:4 and apparently 2 Sam 24:7 consider sites of the northern Levantine coast to be cities of the Canaanites. Note also Isaiah's Tyre oracle, which gives to Phoenicia the label "Canaan" (Isa 23:11). In extrabiblical texts as well, sites in the northern coastal region are included as part of "Canaan," such as the fifteenth-century Idrimi autobiographical text from Alalakh and the fourteenth-century Amarna correspondence. Some evidence suggests that the Phoenicians were able to designate themselves as Canaanites. Third-century-B.C. coins from the Beirut mint locate the city of Laodicea (modern Latakia) "in Canaan." The equation of Canaan with Phoenicia became common in later Greek sources. For a New Testament example, see Matt 15:22, which refers to a woman from the region of Tyre and Sidon as a "Canaanite." (On the name Canaan, see Schmitz 1992.)

up to Zarephath. The preposition *ʿad* has a terminative sense, "up to, as far as." The northern border of Obadiah's reconstituted Israel is the Phoenician city of Zarephath (Sarepta). The site is located on the coast of Lebanon, ca. 23 km north of Tyre and 13 km south of Sidon, next to the modern village of Sarafand. Archaeological excavations under James B. Pritchard have revealed a sizable city that was occupied throughout most of the first millennium B.C. Significant findings include an industrial quarter that revealed evidence of pottery making, the manufacture of purple dye, and metal working; inscriptions; and a shrine of the goddess Tanit-Ashtart in use from the eighth to the fourth centuries. Assyrian annals reveal that Zarephath was a satellite city of Sidon (cf. 1 Kgs 17:9) until the early seventh century when Esarhaddon transferred it to the hegemony of Tyre. A fourth-century reference by Pseudo-Scylax shows that the city still belonged to Tyre. (On Sarepta's history and archaeology, see Pritchard 1978.)

Apart from Obad 20 the Hebrew Bible mentions Zarephath only in 1 Kgs 17 as the city Elijah visited during a three-year famine, where he gave a widow a continuing supply of flour and oil and where he restored the life of her dead son. According to Ottosson (1984), the episode had the intention of demonstrating that Zarephath of Sidon rightfully belonged to Israel and Israel's God. The biblical promised-land texts typically include at least part of Lebanon within Israel's inheritance (Deut 1:7; 3:25; 11:24; Josh 1:4; 13:5–6; 1 Kgs 9:19), and some of them specifically mention Sidon (cf. Gen 49:13; Josh 19:28; Judg 1:31; 2 Sam 24:6). By placing Israel's future border at Zarephath, Obadiah evokes memory of the Elijah episode and remains in continuity with the promises about the land (cf. Ezek 47:15, 20; Zech 9:2–4; 10:10; Meyers and Meyers 1993: 162–69).

and the exiles of Jerusalem who are in Sepharad. The phrase "the exiles of Jerusalem" occurs also in Jer 40:1 in reference to the Babylonian deportation of 587/6 B.C. Whereas the previous line spoke of the exiles of all Israel, both north and south, this line focuses on those of the capital city. The relative clause serves to emphasize that even those dwelling in the farthest points will participate in the coming restoration of Israel; hence no one will be left out.

The identification of "Sepharad" (*sĕpārad*), which occurs only here in the Bible, is a well-known crux. The Septuagint translates it *heōs ephratha* (as far as Ephratha), which could be interpreted as the region around Bethlehem (cf. Mic 5:1 [2]) but more likely reflects a copyist's mistake — the initial *s* was accidentally omitted by haplography; read *heōs sephratha* (so Ziegler 1971: 113). The substitution of the letter *th* for *d* is strange. The Vulgate has *in bosforo*, "in Bosphorus" (i.e., the strait between Thrace and Asia Minor), which seems to have confused the Hebrew preposition *b* with part of the place name (*b sprd*) and to have ignored the final *d* (cf. Rudolph 1971). Of the various suggestions that have been made for "Sepharad" four are noteworthy.

1. Spain. The Targum and the Peshiṭta identified Sepharad as "Spain" (Targum — *spmy'* or *'spmy'*; Peshiṭta — *'spny'*), which became the traditional Jewish interpretation. Since the Middle Ages "Sepharad" has been the common Hebrew designation for Spain (cf. the term "Sephardi" as distinguished from "Ashkenazi"). Neiman (1963) argues that the Tyrrhenians, whose original home was the land of Lydia, took with them to Spain the name "Spard" (= Sardis, the capital of Lydia; see below). See also the discussion by Rabinovitz (1968).

2. Hesperides. Gray (1953; cf. Watts 1969) identifies Sepharad with Hesperides, later Berenice (Benghazi). He gives three arguments. First, "Hesperides" corresponds phonetically to *sprd*. Second, Israelite settlements in North Africa are attested from an early period. Third, the parallelism of the verse indicates that Sepharad should be located in the south. He takes the first line to refer to northern exiles (read: *ûgĕlût hattĕḥillâ*, "the former de-

portation") who will possess the northern territory. Therefore the second line should envision exiles from the south possessing the cities of the Negeb. This last argument is based on a doubtful interpretation of the verse's first line (see above).

3. Saparda. Some scholars identify Sepharad with a place in western Media, which Neo-Assyrian texts of Sargon II name *šaparda/šabarda* (Parpola 1970; cf. Astour 1976; Stuart 1987; LaSor 1988). Also an Esarhaddon text gives the name *sabarda* in conjunction with *ḫarḫār*, a city of Media (Parpola 1970). 2 Kgs 17:6 and 18:11 mention that exiles from the Northern Kingdom were relocated in Media. Can we assume that some of the Jerusalemites of the Babylonian deportation also made their way there? If so, the verse stresses that even those who were exiled beyond Babylon will participate in Israel's restoration.

4. Sardis. Perhaps the most popular view today identifies Sepharad with the city of Sardis in western Asia Minor. The Lydian name of Sardis was *śfar* or *śfard* and the gentilic form was *śfarda*. On the basis of *śfard* the name was rendered *sparda* in Old Persian, *sprd* in Aramaic (see below), *(i)sparta* in Elamite, and *sardeis* or *sardies* in Greek (Gusmani 1964: 201–3). The bilingual Lydian-Aramaic inscription found at Sardis in 1912 reveals that the city's name was spelled *sprd* in Aramaic (*KAI* 260; cf. Lipiński 1975: 153–61). The inscription is dated to the tenth year of Artaxerxes, which would be 455/394/348 B.C. depending on which Artaxerxes is meant; Lipiński favors Artaxerxes III Ochos and therefore 348. According to this view then, *sprd* in Obad 20 gives the Hebrew spelling of the Lydian name in agreement with the Aramaic spelling.

Sardis was the capital of the Lydian kingdom under the Mermnad dynasty (ca. 685–547 B.C.), whose last king was the legendary Croesus (see Hanfmann 1983; McLauchlin 1992; Pedley 1992). In 547 it was taken by Cyrus and became the seat of the Persian satrap for western Asia Minor until 334. (The name of the Persian province in the west was also *sparda*.) Recent excavations at Sardis have revealed the presence of a flourishing Jewish community, confirmed by the discovery of a large Jewish synagogue in use from the early third century A.D. until its destruction in 616 A.D. In the late third century B.C. many Jews were settled in the area and probably in Sardis as well. The Jewish name of the owner of a funerary monument (*'lnp br 'šyhw* — 'Elnap son of 'Eshyahu), given in an Aramaic inscription from Daskyleion in northwest Asia Minor, testifies to an even earlier Jewish presence in the region (Lipiński 1973). Cross (1966) dates the inscription to 450 B.C., plus or minus fifty years. It is possible then that Obad 20 refers to refugees from the Babylonian destruction of Jerusalem who dwelt in Sardis already in the sixth century (so Kraabel 1983).

It is unknown how Jerusalem's exiles might have made their way to Sardis. If Nebuchadnezzar's influence extended to Lydia (cf. Wiseman 1985: 41, 83–84), one can hypothesize that some of the exiles were moved from Babylonia to Sardis; a direct deportation from Jerusalem to Sardis seems less likely. Another possibility is suggested by Joel 4:4–6 [3:4–6]. Joel condemns the Phoenicians and the Philistines for selling Judahites and Jerusalemites to the Ionians. Ezek 27:13 also speaks of slave trade between Tyre and Ionia, and 27:10 refers to Lydian mercenaries serving Tyre. Since we know from Amos 1:6 and 9 that the Edomites were involved in slave trade with Philistia and Phoenicia, perhaps two centuries later something of this network continued. In that case Obad 14 might refer to a scenario in which Edomites "handed over" some of Jerusalem's survivors to Phoenicians — or Philistines, but that is less likely — who then sold them to Lydia. (On possible Phoenician-Edomite connections, see Homès-Fredericq 1987.) One assumes that the Edomites delivered the survivors to the Babylonians, but v 14 does not specify the recipients and therefore leaves open this other possibility (see Notes for v 14).

It is impossible to pin down with precision the historical situation to which Obad 20 refers, given the uncertainty regarding Sepharad and the lack of further information. Of the possible identifications for Sepharad mentioned above the third and fourth proposals appear the most plausible. Yet the basic gist of the verse remains clear: even the Jerusalemites who dwell in the farthest regions will participate in Israel's restoration.

will possess the cities of the Negeb. Why does Obadiah single out the cities of the Negeb? Two reasons suggest themselves. First, v 20 has a geographical logic in that it exhibits merismus of north to south: one group of exiles occupies the land to its northernmost boundary at Zarephath while the other group inherits the cities of the Negeb in the Cisjordan's southernmost boundary. Exiles from the city of Jerusalem are appropriately allotted cities. Second, recent archaeological work has revealed a growing Edomite presence in the Negeb during the seventh–early sixth centuries (see Introduction under "Date and Historical Setting"). Perhaps Obad 20 anticipates Israel's future retrieval of the Negeb's towns from Edomite dominance.

v 21. *wĕʿālû môšīʿîm bĕhar ṣiyyôn lišpōṭ ʾet har ʿēśāw*
wĕhāyĕtâ layahweh hammĕlûkâ
Deliverers will go up onto Mount Zion to judge Mount Esau,
and the kingship will belong to Yahweh.
Deliverers. The subject of the sentence is the *hipʿil* participle *môšīʿîm* which functions as a substantive. In the MT it has a defective spelling and a doubly defective spelling in the Wadi Murabbaʿat manuscript (*mšʿym*). The defective spelling apparently allowed some of the ancient translators to parse it as a

passive *hop'al* participle, "those having been delivered" (LXX, Aquila, Theodotion, Peshiṭta) — although the *hop'al* of *yš'* never occurs elsewhere in the Hebrew Bible — or as a *nip'al* participle. The Targum, Vulgate, and Symmachus take it as an active *hip'il*. The passive translation probably reflects an interpretive decision under the influence of v 17a (cf. Barthélemy 1992: 705–6).

In addition to Obad 21, the *hip'il* participle of *yš'* (to deliver, save) occurs thirty-two times in the Hebrew Bible. When the word refers to humans, it designates military heroes authorized and empowered by Yahweh to "deliver" Israelites from enemies or distress (cf. Judg 3:9, 15; 2 Kgs 13:5). Isa 19:20 is the only exception, according to which Yahweh promises to send a "deliverer" who will rescue the Egyptians from their oppressors. The plural *môšī'îm* occurs only one other time in the Bible. Neh 9:27 uses the word to refer to the judges of the premonarchic period:

> You gave them into the hand of their foes and they oppressed them; but in
> the time of their distress they cried out to you and you heard from heaven,
> and according to your great compassion you gave to them *deliverers*
> so that they would *deliver* them from the hand of their foes.

The Nehemiah parallel provides the key for understanding Obad 21 (cf. Aalders 1958: 55–56). Obadiah portrays Israel's future situation as in some respects a repetition of the period of the judges: just as Israel had mighty deliverers in the past, so it will have such heroes in the future. In light of v 18, one supposes that Obadiah envisioned these *môšī'îm* as those who would deliver the Israelites from the oppression of the Edomites. Afterwards, according to v 21, they will ascend Mount Zion to rule over Edom.

According to Sawyer (1965), *môšīa'* originally denoted the defender of the unjustly accused in a law court and applied to forensic contexts more than military ones. Regardless of the word's original meaning, however, the word's actual usage in the Hebrew Bible does not give any primacy to a forensic idea. The texts rather speak of a *môšīa'* as a deliverer "from" (*min*) enemies or distress (cf. Judg 12:2–3; 1 Sam 10:19; 2 Sam 22:3; Jer 30:10 = 46:27; Zech 8:7; Ps 17:7; Neh 9:27). Furthermore, the texts that refer to human "deliverers" usually have a military context (cf. Judg 3:9, 15; 12:2–3; 1 Sam 11:3; 2 Kgs 13:5; Isa 19:20; Neh 9:27).

will go up onto Mount Zion. The preposition *b* is to be construed with the verb. With the verb *'lh* (to go up) the prepositional phrase marks the direction and destination of the ascent (cf. Exod 19:12–13; Deut 5:5; 2 Sam 15:30; Ps 24:3). The initial sentence of v 21 implies a two-stage process: *môšī'îm* first deliver the Israelites from Edomite oppression, and then they ascend Mount Zion to rule over Edom. Obadiah gives Mount Zion centrality in his vision of the future kingdom of Yahweh. It will be the capital, the seat of government from which Yahweh's representatives will rule over Edom.

to judge Mount Esau. "Mount Esau," a term coined by Obadiah, refers to the territory of Edom (cf. vv 8–9, 19). The sentence clearly presupposes an inhabited territory, since it would be meaningless to speak of judging an unoccupied land. However, the term is appropriate here in that it matches "Mount Zion."

Along with *môšī'îm*, the verb *špṭ* evokes the premonarchic period of the judges. To maintain this connection I translate it "to judge." Yet the English translation is somewhat misleading, because the verb in the present context does not denote the juridical sense associated with a law court. The root *špṭ* in the Hebrew Bible has two primary senses: either the more restricted sense of rendering judicial decisions or the more general and encompassing sense of exercising authority and governing (cf. Soggin 1980). Both senses of the word also appear in the book of Judges, although the latter sense is more common: "to judge" — 4:4–5; 11:27; "to govern" — 2:16–18; 3:10; 15:20; 16:31. It has the latter sense in Obad 21. Although one assumes that, like the premonarchic judges, the "deliverers" of Obadiah will govern Israel, here the statement stresses that they will rule over Israel's enemy, Edom (cf. Num 24:18–19; Isa 11:14).

and the kingship will belong to Yahweh. The construction *hāyâ + l* indicates possession, "Yahweh will have the kingship" (cf. 1 Kgs 2:15). The feminine noun *mĕlûkâ* — a *qāṭûl* formation from *mlk* (to be king, rule) — always designates something having to do with royalty and most commonly denotes the office of king as distinct from the realm over which one rules (cf. Ringgren, Seybold, Fabry 1984: 940–41). Several pieces of evidence reveal the word's sense as "kingship." One sees this meaning of the word clearly in 1 Kgs 21:7, where Jezebel says to Ahab:

'attâ 'attâ ta'ăśeh mĕlûkâ 'al yiśrā'ēl

You, now, exercise kingship over Israel.

(KB compares the Akkadian expression *šarrūta epēšu*.) In 1 Kgs 2:15 Adonijah says to Bathsheba, Solomon's mother:

You know that the *kingship* had belonged to me,
and all Israel fully intended for me *to rule* [*mlk*].

The second line shows that *mĕlûkâ* denotes royal position and authority. Moreover, in 2 Sam 16:8 it is associated with the verb *mlk* (to rule) and in Ps 22:29 [28] with the verb *mšl* (to rule). Finally, note that 1 Sam 14:47 employs the prepositional phrase *'al yiśrā'ēl* (over Israel) with the noun, indicating that the office of king is meant rather than the domain. Yet the noun can also have an adjectival force, as in the phrase *zeraʿ hammĕlûkâ*, "royal family" (2 Kgs 25:25; Jer 41:1; Ezek 17:13; Dan 1:3).

With roots in the early monarchic period the word usually refers to kingship over Israel. The individuals who possess it include: Saul (1 Sam 10:16, 25; 11:14; 14:47; 18:8); David (1 Chr 10:14); potentially Absalom (2 Sam 16:8); Solomon (1 Kgs 1:46; 2:15, 22); Jeroboam (1 Kgs 11:35; 12:21); and Ahab (1 Kgs 21:7). There are two places that speak of a non-Israelite *mĕlûkâ*. 2 Sam 12:26 uses the phrase *ʿîr hammĕlûkâ*, "the royal citadel," in reference to Rabbah of the Ammonites. According to Isa 34:12, after the coming divine judgment Edom's nobles will proclaim in reference to Edom, "No kingship/government there."

The closest parallel to Obad 21 occurs in Ps 22:28–29 [27–28]:

All the ends of the earth will remember and turn to Yahweh,
and all the families of the nations will worship before you.
For to Yahweh belongs the kingship [*layahweh hammĕlûkâ*],
and he rules over the nations.

The parallel suggests that with his final statement Obadiah used liturgical language. The parallel furthermore indicates that Obadiah was referring to Yahweh's kingship over all the nations and not only Israel (cf. 1 Chr 29:11). Yet there is one notable difference between the two texts: the psalmist attributed Yahweh's universal rule to the present whereas Obadiah projected it into the future. In light of the rest of the book of Obadiah, it is clear that the prophet considered Yahweh to be ruling over the nations already in the present. But from an empirical perspective within the history of Israel, it appeared that Babylon and Edom held the kingship at the moment (cf. Ps 106:41; Lam 5:8). Therefore, Obadiah used the future tense in announcing a time when the nations will cease exercising their oppressive tyranny and instead "the kingship will belong to Yahweh," a kingship generally characterized by the biblical writers as one of righteousness and peace.

The statement provides an appropriate prophetic response to the exilic laments that appeal to the kingship of Yahweh (Pss 74:12–17; 102:13 [12]; Lam 5:19; cf. Klein 1979: 22). For Obadiah, Yahweh's ultimate objective is not simply the defeat of the enemies or the restoration of Israel but Yahweh's kingship over the whole world (cf. Lillie 1979). With the book's last clause Obadiah expresses what was an essential feature of ancient Israel's hope. The theme also occupied a central position in the ministry of Jesus. In the Christian tradition the second petition of the "Our Father" continues to evoke Obad 21: "Thy kingdom come." For surveys of the primary and secondary literature concerning the kingdom of God in the Hebrew Bible, the Apocrypha and Pseudepigrapha, Qumran literature, and the New Testament, see Willis (1987) and J. P. Meier (1994: 237–88).

COMMENT

The book's final section is written in prose, albeit a parallelistic style of prose. It contains a series of eight clauses connected by *waw*: four in v 19, two in v 20, and two in v 21. The employment of *waw* consecutive perfect verbs indicates three primary actions: Israel will possess the full extent of the land (vv 19–20); deliverers will ascend Mount Zion to judge Edom (v 21a); and Yahweh will rule as king (v 21b). Note how the sequence progresses from Israel in the land to leaders in Zion and finally to Yahweh. With these statements the section provides an extension and interpretation of the preceding discourse in vv 15–18. Verses 19–20 clarify the nature of what v 17b announced: "The house of Jacob will possess their own possessions." Verse 21a portrays Israel's dominance over Edom and thus parallels v 18. And the reference to Yahweh's "kingship" in v 21b relates to the depiction of "the day of Yahweh" given in vv 15–16.

The language used in these verses evokes the language of Joshua and Judges. Verses 19–20 are reminiscent of the tribal allotment depicted in Josh 13–21 in that specified groups within Israel are apportioned different parts of the land. Note the use of the words "possess," "Philistines," and "Canaanites." Furthermore, v 21 speaks of "deliverers" who "judge" and of Yahweh's "kingship," all of which brings to mind the time of the judges. In this way the prophet portrays Israel's future restoration as another premonarchic period when Israel possessed the land, deliverers/judges were raised up, and Yahweh alone ruled as king. Perhaps Obadiah employed prose in this section in order to confirm for the reader this association with the narratives regarding premonarchic Israel.

Nevertheless, the future will not simply repeat the past but will differ in two ways. First, Obadiah portrays the future in a way that remains congruent with the historical and geographical realities of his own time during the exilic period; he has not moved into the realm of apocalyptic. Thus he distributes the land to the Judahites living in the four areas of Judah: the Negeb, the Shephelah, the central highlands (by implication), and Benjamin (v 19). He also includes the exiles of Israel and of Jerusalem (cf. v 11) in the future restoration (v 20). Second, his depiction of future events diverges from the accounts of Joshua-Judges. Israel will possess the land apparently without warfare. Furthermore, he brings in the Zion theme so that the deliverers judge from Mount Zion. Note also that they judge Edom instead of Israel, although presumably they exercise authority over Israel as well.

Verses 19–20 are bracketed by the term "the Negeb," leaving v 21 to serve as the book's conclusion. And it is a most fitting conclusion viewed from a literary and a theological vantage point: "Deliverers will go up onto Mount Zion to judge Mount Esau, and the kingship will belong to Yahweh." First, it pits Mount Zion against Mount Esau and attributes to the former authority over the latter. With this statement Obadiah envisages a reversal of fortunes: the governed will govern, and therefore Israel will never again be threatened by oppression from Edom. Although Edom dwells seemingly secure in the heights (vv 3–4), for Obadiah, safety and refuge can be found only in Zion (v 17a), for Zion alone is the seat of Yahweh's rule. Second, the last clause sounds a climactic note by promising the public and definitive manifestation of the royal power and authority that "the Lord Yahweh" already exercises over the nations (v 1). Just as the reference to the impending "day of Yahweh" brought the address to Edom to closure (vv 1–15), so this statement provides a strong conclusion for the sections dealing with Israel's future (vv 16–21). In fact, the dual themes of Yahweh's day and Yahweh's kingship undergird every part of the book's message.

INDEXES

◆

INDEX OF SCRIPTURE REFERENCES

◆

INDEX OF AUTHORS

◆

INDEX OF SUBJECTS

◆